Z^{50}

D1739334

CITY OF INDUSTRY

CITY OF INDUSTRY

*Genealogies of Power
in Southern California*

VICTOR VALLE

RUTGERS UNIVERSITY PRESS
NEW BRUNSWICK, NEW JERSEY, AND LONDON

Library of Congress Cataloging-in-Publication Data

Valle, Victor M.
City of Industry : genealogies of power in Southern California / Victor Valle.
    p.   cm.
Includes bibliographical references and index.
ISBN 978–0–8135–4573–8 (hardcover : alk. paper)
   1. Police—California—City of Industry.   2. City of Industry (Calif.)—Social
   conditions.   3. Los Angeles (Calif.)—Social conditions.   I. Title.
HV8148.C58V35 2009
364.109794'94—dc22

2008051484

A British Cataloging-in-Publication record for this book is available from the British
Library.

Visit our Web site: http://rutgerspress.rutgers.edu

Manufactured in the United States of America

Typesetting: BookType

CONTENTS

ACKNOWLEDGMENTS

My deepest thanks to Carrie Mullen, wherever you are, for encouraging me to start; Francisco H. Vázquez for your patient early readings; Rudy Torres for rescuing me near the end; and, above all, to Mary, Lucena, and Alexandra for putting up with me all the way through. Because the list of colleagues and institutions who lent me their generous support is too long to recite here, I only acknowledge the indispensables: my parents, who taught me faith and patience in the pursuit of justice; Carl Gutiérrez-Jones, Michelle Habell-Pallan, Otto Santa Ana, and my former research fellows at UC Santa Barbara's Center for Chicano Studies; Harry Gamboa, Ignacio López-Calvo, and my colleagues at Cal State LA's American Communities Program; and all of my colleagues in the Ethnic Studies Department at Cal Poly, San Luis Obispo. Last but not least, I want to thank Martha Eowyn Williams for hunting down what no one else could in UCLA's archives; Carolyn Kozo Cole for your continued stewardship of LA's image memory; Mark Arax for your early property sleuthing; Roy Ulrich for your wise counsel; Claire Schlotterbeck for growing another citizen's archive and rescuing it from the flames; and Jean Bernstein for always encouraging me, whether you realized it or not, with your courageous example.

CITY OF INDUSTRY

INTRODUCTION

DECODING THE *CHINATOWN* TECHNOLOGIES

I think one day soon, when this country is more free, when all this is over and the stuff we go through now is just stories, and my daughter's going through the old files, and she says "what awful times you lived through, ..." When she asks me "and what were you doing?" My answer will be very simple and it will reflect these times: "I was writing detective novels."
　　　　　　　　　　　—Juan Hernandez Luna, *Tobacco for the Puma*

It is already a cliché to say that movies such as *Chinatown* take the place of memories that residents of Los Angeles have never bothered to save or even live. At least that's the dismissive judgment I've heard from those who prefer not to puzzle over the city's Byzantine enigmas. The journalists who see the film as a universal metaphor of the corrupting power of politics and money also gloss over its rooted specificities.

I saw a different film with a different gaze. I noticed the Mexican boy on the sad swaybacked horse appear to witness suspicious water flows in the riverbeds of my youth. I heard the LAPD chief of detective's last name, Escobar, suggest the broom (*escoba*) with which he did his job. The film's fleeting Macondo reference did not escape me either. Nor could I forget the unsettling questions the film's story still evoke. You see, I belong to that post-Watergate Chicano generation that found hope in the film precisely because it was so bleak. But hope of what? That I'd find the code with which to link my disconnected place intuitions to my memories of the city I loved; that the film's radical skepticism wasn't the answer but the means to an answer.

In any case, the theme that still troubles me centers around the incest that Noah Cross, the biblically named real estate tycoon, commits with his daughter, Evelyn. Viewers learn about this twist in the scene when Cross acknowledges the deed to private detective Jake Gittes. Screenwriter Robert Towne softens the blow of his revelation in the now famous slapping scene, when Evelyn admits to Gittes that Cross had raped her.

Previously, we have learned that Evelyn was the wife of Cross's business partner, Hollis Mulwray, head of the city's water department until Cross murdered him, and that Evelyn is hiding her daughter, the result of her liaison with Cross, at the El Macondo Apartments, a direct reference to Gabriel Garcia Marquez's fabled town in *One Hundred Years of Solitude*, a novel of incest foretold. We also learn that Cross has clashed with Hollis over control of the city's water supply. The crusty pioneer resents losing his water to the city and his daughter to Hollis and intends to get both of them back. Meanwhile, Cross and other members of the Albacore Club, a cabal of secret investors, have acquired huge tracts of land in the names of the doddering old folks they house in a convalescent home. Armed with inside knowledge of the city's next water project, club members are set to enjoy a real estate windfall. Their faceless minions have poisoned wells and faked a water shortage to force orange grove owners to sell their land cheap, which club members will sell dearly when the water arrives.

Although the film's action unfolds in the 1930s, filmgoers hip to the brackish end of Southern California water history know it fictionalizes a real estate swindle so massive it required the theft of a wild river in the eastern Sierras and sequestration of a city's water department to pull off. The richest men in the city, so the story goes, not only forced the city's water department to implement a complicated scheme to divert the Owens River via aqueduct to the 44,000-acre San Fernando Valley ranch they optioned at drought-level prices, but they also tricked the voters into paying for it. Their scheme required infiltrating a federal agency to secure Owens River water rights, while preventing the agency from developing the river for local ranchers. Then the connivers maneuvered the city of Los Angeles into acquiring the river's water rights and subsequently designing and building a 233-mile-long aqueduct. All the while, the conspirators ordered their operatives to infiltrate city agencies to extract details of the aqueduct's route before anyone else did. Some moviegoers may even recall that *Los Angeles Times* publisher general Harrison Gray Otis and his son-in-law, Harry Chandler, organized LA's richest men into two secret land-buying syndicates, and played up drought stories in their newspaper to gin up voter support for the city bonds that built the aqueduct. Thanks to the passage of these bonds and the aqueduct's completion in 1913, the syndicates netted the equivalent of billions of dollars in the real estate development that followed.

That, I believe, is the history the film mythologizes, a version that assumes that the real estate syndicates set out to control the city's water department and the minds of dim-witted voters so that they could ravish a river and corner the San Fernando Valley's real estate market. The advantages of hindsight, however, allow for a more nuanced understanding of what occurred and what it may mean today. My admittedly subjective reading of that episode dispenses with the biographies of the ringleaders to search for its underlying pattern. In my view, the wealthy real estate speculators were opportunists who aided and abetted a city's audacious plan to rob a river. They quietly witnessed, encouraged, and cashed in on the city's scheme to prevent the federal government from developing the river for local ranchers and acquire the water rights for itself. At different stages of the aqueduct's development, the city's water engineers and planners exhibited multiple conflicts of interest, simultaneously working for the bureau and city agencies or for the bureau and the Los Angeles Chamber of Commerce, which convened meetings of the real estate syndicate's wealthy investors. At least one city water planner tried to cash in on the scheme, and none of the planners prevented their colleagues from leaking the aqueduct plan to the developers.

So a crime did occur but one that baffled the aqueduct's early critics. The crime of learning a secret and then conspiring to keep and exploit it anticipated the sophisticated Wall Street insider trading of our time. Even today, however, crimes of knowledge seem too abstract to inspire much passion, which probably explains why the aqueduct's critics exaggerated to clearly draw the villains they needed. But no one really duped the Los Angeles city officials and engineers into taking the Owens water. Like most people in the city at that time, the aqueduct's designers assumed that LA could not grow without that water. Its top engineers also figured that plotting their scheme in secret would reduce opposition until after they had secured the water, even if they did underestimate the controversy their silences later generated.

The secrecy that initially surrounded the project, however, did have one undeniable benefit. The syndicates that were privy to it acquired a tremendous advantage over other real estate investors. The city's water engineers and planners also understood that they would soon enjoy the power of running the world's largest, most technically advanced municipal water system, not to mention receiving the endless gratitude of its citizens. We can also imagine the private conversations among the city's financial and governmental elite. Appreciation of the syndicates' discretion would have been quietly conveyed in the private, wood-paneled clubs where city and business leaders mixed. We know from the media coverage that both sides patronized the common folk, that both presumed to know what the little people needed. The private side of the partnership, moreover, had already crafted an ideology of growth, which its operatives reiterated each time they told the city's story. The *Times* and the Southern Pacific Railroad had been spreading the spores of that ideology years before the city began to devise its aqueduct. Their mastery of real estate marketing, among other cultural technologies, was therefore vital to cultivating the hubris of the city officials and engineers who led that ambitious undertaking.

Knowledge Becomes Technology

In conspiring to keep the aqueduct under wraps, however, both sides allowed something else to occur. Whether they realized it or not, the aqueduct's eventual success not only made the investors a fortune and rewarded smaller players who got in on the action, it also consolidated a set of practices that others could emulate. The aqueduct's effect on development reinforced the value of that knowledge by giving its earliest imitators the financial and political resources to implement an even bigger water development scheme.[1] The formation of the Metropolitan Water District (MWD) in 1928 expanded the scale of the Los Angeles Department of Water and Power to the size of a small nation, which some fittingly called the "Empire of the West." The MWD's first directors, nearly all of them men whose real estate developments had benefited from the agency's projects, enforced that agenda when it mattered most. They ran the MWD during its first five formative decades, a period in which they pushed their engineers to design a vast water transport system to guarantee the region's rapid development. By the time the system was completed in 1971, the agency's arteries were pulsing water from the Colorado River and the American River north of Sacramento to Southern California's 17 million residents.[2]

The wealth and power that the Owens Aqueduct had conferred to its first exploiters and administrators, and the example and resources it generated for its successors, thus marked an important transformation. Knowledge of the project went from an insider's hot commodity with a finite shelf life to a conceptual technology, a kind of formula that developers, engineers, and bureaucrats continually refined in Southern California's laboratory of government. *Chinatown*'s suspicions therefore express anxiety about the region's experiments in the technologies of power as well as their rewards, which almost always accrued to the Noah Crosses of the world. But the film portrays Cross, the founder, as the sole villain in Southern California's creation story, while the laboratory's lessons tell us that the developer class he embodied could not have reaped the rewards or inflicted so much damage without the active and willing collaboration of government, particularly its local varieties.

Incredibly, *Chinatown* suggests this second understanding of power when Cross modestly refuses to take all the credit for his success. "Hollis Mulwray," he tells Gittes, "made this city and he made me a fortune," a statement that connotes the engineering prowess that delivered the water but also the forethought needed to imagine a grand city. That conclusion may not seem very original, given the corporate sector's long record of buying politicians and laws. But the possibility of owning a city's most valuable public organs offered a novel alternative to the need for recurring investments in electoral politics.

For the first time, Southern California's technologies of privatization gave its developer class the power to design the government it needed. As in genetic experiments in which DNA from one species is inserted into a host of other species, the developers implanted the knowledge and technologies they wanted to reproduce in specific organs of the state. Despite their microscopic scale and apparent immateriality, the new conceptual technologies had profound effects. We can see now, for example, that the aqueduct did damage pristine mountain habitats, did raise choking dust clouds from parched Mojave lakebeds, did establish a precedent for water policies that spread suburban sprawl into fire-prone wilderness, and did fuel development practices that have worsened air pollution and global warming.

Although *Chinatown* suggests much and prophesizes a little, it also leaves many questions unanswered. The film does not tell us how Cross acquired his wealth and power, how he simulated the drought that Hollis Mulwray discovered, or how he plans to resume control of the city's water supply without actually owning it. Instead, the movie highlights a number of disturbing ambiguities, daring us to ask, as Gittes does, why Cross wants more money and power when he already has more than he can use in a lifetime. Cross answers Gittes with another enigma: "The future, Mr. Gittes, the future!" Then he hurriedly interjects, "Now where's the girl?" as if his real estate swindle depends on recapturing a daughter and a granddaughter. His answer thus establishes an implicit equivalency between incest and capitalist accumulation. As Vernon Shetley argues, that symbolic convertibility allows the filmmakers to link the plot strands represented by water, real estate, and daughters into micro- and macro-scaled metaphors of incest. In Cross's view, daughters and water, like land, are valuable commodities worth monopolizing because, according to Shetley, both embody the future "possibility of fertility, of the growth and renewal of life. Each is a means of projecting oneself into the future, either through bloodlines, or the creation of wealth, for what is capital but wealth that has outlived its creation, even its creator?"[3] Moreover, the film's fluid logic anticipates the postmodern rationality that will follow the machine-age city that Mulwray has built on Newtonian principles.

Equally important, the film's interwoven metaphors of incest dare us to imagine scenarios beyond the final scene in which Cross recaptures Evelyn's daughter. Will Cross initiate incest with Katherine, and how will that enhance his power? We know from his actions thus far that conventional morality does not inhibit him in the least, which is why the scene hits us with such crushing force. If he is powerful enough to survive the bullet that Evelyn fires into him to save her daughter, if he is powerful enough to order the police to erase his daughter's death, he is surely powerful enough to expect a male heir from his new prize. Securing such a gift might even allow Cross to mold a son in his image, to create the vessel through which his personality, or at least his legacy, can live on after his death. The film's plausible horrors thus offer us a counter-mythology with which to nurture our suspicions until we can conduct a proper critique of power and imagine the instruments Cross will need to execute his schemes.

Well, perhaps this book will do its part to hasten that day's arrival. To accomplish the task, however, I had to put the film's water swindle into perspective. *Chinatown* alludes to only one ensemble of governmental technology, or what Michel Foucault called a governmentality.[4] I argue that more than a half-dozen other such innovations contributed to the generation of Southern California's present landscape. Nonetheless, finding the archive that would allow me to see how these governmentalities operated together was a challenge. With so many technologies scattered across its vast landscape, no one place appeared to offer a way to see how most of these governmentalites interacted together in ensemble. Yet my focus on the formation of the City of Industry, a major industrial suburb situated in eastern Los Angeles County, did eventually allow me to study the fabric of these interwoven governmental technologies.

SEQUENCING THE TECHNOLOGIES OF POWER

The City of Industry—known to locals simply as Industry—embodies the best documented and most comprehensive sample of the region's formative governmentalities.[5] But there was nothing natural or inevitable about their invention, or how I assembled the archive to detect them. If not for a series of high-profile FBI investigations and convictions in the mid-1980s and the subsequent recovery of a trove of irreplaceable sealed court records, key elements of Industry's story would remain buried to this day. The FBI's investigations, led single-handedly by special agent John Keller, focused on James "Marty" Stafford, the wealthy grain dealer credited with founding the city in 1957. The federal indictments generated by Keller's investigation identified Stafford as the mastermind behind a conspiracy that had defrauded the city of millions of taxpayer dollars. According to the *Los Angeles Times*, federal prosecutors indicted six people for their involvement in the kickback scheme: "Stafford, one-time Bank of Industry chairman Robert K. King, Burbank contractor Frank C. Wood, two other contractors, and the project manager of the publicly financed Industry Hills Exhibit-Conference Center." Prosecutors also indicted another banker who conspired with Stafford in an unrelated loan fraud scheme. All seven men pleaded guilty, and Stafford received a ten-year sentence. The *Los Angeles Times* later called the convictions the "biggest" municipal corruption scandal in California history.[6]

The city would never have attracted the passing attention it did receive without these indictments and convictions. Even today, few people associate the city's industrial parks, 80,000-member daytime workforce, and more than seven hundred residents with the quintessentially Southern Californian lifestyle stereotyped in sun-drenched *O.C.* and *90210* reruns. Few people outside of Los Angeles County know where to find this city with a larger-than-life name and more factories and warehouses than residents. The city's blurry cartographic history surely didn't increase its visibility. Its elongated shape occupies what native old-timers used to call the La Puente Valley, a horseshoe basin formed by the La Puente Hills that drains northwest into the San Gabriel River. But most recent references to the city erase the valley's older name by locating it in that larger geographic entity known as the San Gabriel Valley, the often smog-filled suburban corridor with a population of 1.7 million that stretches southeast from downtown LA along the inner ribs of the San Gabriel Mountains. Nor do many non-Southern Californians stop to consider how the City of Industry's role in the global economy insinuates itself into the Chinese-made clothing they wear, the big-box-store appliances they buy, the processed Asian and Latino foods they crave, or they way they work. Yet the city has served as the laboratory for all of these experiments. Thirty years ago, Industry was known for its high-paid manufacturing jobs. But increasingly, the locals have seen those jobs replaced by lower-paid warehousing, food processing, and service industry tasks.[7]

Even for locals, grasping the full impact of Industry and neighboring clones can be daunting. Like the MWD's monumental water system, whose totality is visible only on maps or satellite photographs, the scale of Southern California's transportation, distribution, and warehousing infrastructure—otherwise known as the logistics industry—is too large for a pedestrian to comprehend. A casual observer would need to take to the air to grasp Industry's footprint, a fourteen-square-mile serpent of rectangular warehouse rooftops positioned between roughly parallel Union Pacific and Southern Pacific rail lines. And recent trade projections indicate that the city's logistics industry will grow apace with the Pacific Rim trade flows that are still surging through Southern California.

Currently, the ports of Los Angeles and Long Beach combine to form the world's second busiest port after Hong Kong. According to rail authorities, more than 3 billion dollars in public subsidies paid for the redesign and expansion of rail systems connecting these ports to Ontario International and Riverside airports, infrastructure investments which should double or even triple the cargo offloaded in the region. Two railroads—the Santa Fe and the recently merged Union and Southern Pacific—now haul these goods to distribution centers concentrated within a rail corridor that stretches in a southeasterly arc from the ports to the rail yards of East LA, the City of Commerce (an Industry clone), Vernon (Industry's governmental ancestor), Industry itself, and onto San Bernardino County, where the cargo is then flown out of the Ontario International Airport or trucked or trained from the Colton switching yards.

The logistics network's owners offer customers a choice of truck or rail access or both, a transformation that worries homeowners who have fled LA's congestion and air pollution. They have discovered that the threat of deadly train derailments and environmental pollution—ultra-fine particles of burnt diesel and crumbled tires that lodge in the lungs—and the twenty-four-hour rumble of trains and big rigs coming to and from the ports to the warehouses, has followed them to their new San Bernardino and Riverside County suburbs.[8] Penny Newman witnessed this onslaught from her own backyard in formerly rural Riverside County, where she has lived for forty-one years. Newman saw more than 120 warehouses push out "cow pastures and vineyards" in the span of a decade. "Our mountain views have been replaced by looming cement monoliths," she said. "The Union Pacific is now directly next to our high school. Hundreds of trucks park and idle 20 feet from the athletic fields where our children play." According to the World Health Organization, Newman's community of Glen Avon/Mira Loma now suffers from the world's fourth-highest level of diesel particulate pollution, preceded only by Jakarta, Calcutta, and Bangkok.[9]

I did not immediately link Newman's experiences and Industry's story. At first, I only saw Industry's uncanny resemblance to *Chinatown*'s fictions—for instance, the time in 1957 when the city's organizers blurred the line between fiction and reality by recruiting senile and mentally handicapped convalescent-home patients to vote for the city's incorporation. A few decades later, the city cited the Owens Aqueduct project as a legal precedent that justified its own ambitious water project. Interested in these behaviors, I began gleaning Industry's governmental patterns from the predecessors and members of what some call the Los Angeles school of urban studies—above all, from scholars such as Harvey Molotch and Mike Davis. But the city's governmental technologies came into even clearer focus after I embraced a few radical assumptions.

In my research, I tried to ignore Southern California's self-evident truths and approach the region as a literary critic might approach a library of volumes written in a strange language; I tried to see Industry's property records, state comptroller's reports, transcripts of FBI wiretaps, city resolutions and regulations, aerial photographs, canceled checks, financial databases, technical drawings, appointment calendars, newspaper articles, maps, and scores of other documents as texts rich in cultural meaning. The metaphor I'm striving for here is embedded in another noirish film, this time *The Matrix*, with its fabulously paranoid vision of the future. In the movie, the reality accepted as truth is actually a monumental, computer-generated simulation powered by the brains and bodies of its enslaved citizens. But Industry's reality cannot be traced back to one Orwellian centralized state under the control of a single, all-knowing entity, much less a single criminal mastermind. Regardless of its scale, the entity we call the modern nation-state remains a field of effects generated by its contributing mix of governmental technologies. Industry's founders and corporate benefactors simply generated their matrix from governmental technologies already available in their environment. More often than not, they learned how to use these technologies from others who had improvised their own experiments in neighboring suburbs. Still, the absence of a grand vision does not prevent us from sequencing the genealogies of Industry's power matrix. As with any text, we can try to discover the set of authors who slowly contributed to each volume in the archive; in other words, we can understand Industry's specific debts to earlier governmental technologies, textual qualities that permit us to reconstruct its discrete lineages of power.

Industry's genealogies of power, as it turns out, share a common stock with other cities derived from European models. That body of law, knowledge, and practice, originating in the medieval city charter, endowed twentieth-century California's cities such as Industry with the legal authority to, among other things, expropriate private property, draw jurisdictional boundaries, levy taxes, and regulate its population in the furtherance of a so-called "public good." The home-rule laws California enacted in the 1920s subsequently gave its cities the legal authority to increase their autonomy from state and federal authority. These laws were the first in a series of genetic ruptures that devolved greater fiscal and political authority to local government.

In its privatizing pedigree, Industry, like other California cities, also needed the ubiquitous and ancient disciplinary technologies it shares with other municipalities. Again, Southern California stepped forward, earning the dubious distinction of pushing these police technologies to more extreme thresholds. New instruments of criminal and civil law and new moral rationales and fiscal technology with which to monitor and discipline residents were devised to further privatize public spaces. Cities in the region achieved these ends by means of relatively undetectable disciplinary practices that inculcated citizen obedience or new punishments when citizens disobeyed.

As the county's police, court, and property archives demonstrate, the technologies of police discipline and its subgenres of public exposure played an especially crucial role in Stafford's rise and fall as a city leader in Industry. Because the verdicts and property seizures they recorded fed local journalists an inexhaustible supply of fodder, the courthouse and the police station functioned as media institutions when prosecutors, judges, or cops generated narratives and images for journalists to translate into moral judgments disguised as facts. The journalists who dominated the representation of crime in Stafford's day were, in essence, rewrite men for the state's judicial- and property-recording organs. The symbiotic relationship through which they derived their livelihood guaranteed them the police reports and court judgments that they then translated into fantasies of judgment and punishment. When journalists invited readers or viewers to stand in the prosecutor's unforgiving shoes, or to imagine the victim's pain or humiliation, their quasi-official roles protected their power to elicit empathy or pity.

Jim Stafford suffered these exposures at key moments in his life. At the tender age of thirteen he saw his father, Clifford Clayton Stafford, otherwise known as C. C., humiliated in a 1929 rape trial that sent him to jail a year later. I believe that this traumatic experience, and the financial disappointments his father's business suffered after the trial, made the younger Stafford vulnerable to the lure of power. That attraction, when combined with his business savvy and knowledge of local culture, later made him a valuable front man for corporate developers. Eventually, he watched the courts and the press invent an identity for him, one whose benefits he enjoyed and believed in until the courts and the press destroyed it in a scandal that outdid his father's.

I admit that I contributed to the final phase of Jim Stafford's character formation. My colleagues and I at the *Los Angeles Times* mined elements of earlier newspaper stories about his father to build the son's image as city founder. In other words, we re-created the father's story to explain how the son had acquired, abused, and lost his power. But we mistook the biography we wrote for him for a theory of political power. Our narratives assumed that Stafford, like *Chinatown*'s Cross, owned his power. We reinforced this motif when we equated power with the real estate he owned. "Stafford and his family," my colleague and I reported at his indictment, "own or have owned large tracts of land in the city." The naturalness with which we represented power as a commodity paved the way for our next conflation. When we soberly reported that "the City of Industry—and Stafford—have been the focus of controversy since the city was founded 27 years ago," we equated Industry's history with a man's life.[10] It is hard to know how many of us deliberately reduced a complex history to one man's life, but it's no mystery why it occurred. Modern journalism constantly demands that reporters paint personal portraits to tell larger stories. Finally, the manner in which we framed our stories in themes of "corruption" and governmental "abuse" reminded readers to inspect the character of the accused for those qualities that marked him as good or evil.

We didn't know it then, but a profound, orchestrated silence had encouraged our narrative habits. If one of police discipline's most penetrating and therefore most efficient effects stems from its power to expose, then the legal technologies that render knowledge invisible would seem to be its antithesis. But that equation is incomplete. The technologies of subtraction or erasure can just as easily reinforce the news media's unrelenting interpretation of police literatures, permitting a well-entrenched practice to continue by removing apparent contradictions. The city demonstrated that power when, in 1988, it asked the court to seal FBI agent John Keller's investigative reports in a civil suit it filed against Stafford and his co-conspirators. During the trial that the city launched to recover damages from the conspirators and restore its reputation, the city's attorneys prevailed upon the presiding judge to permanently seal Keller's seventeen-volume chronicle of reports otherwise known as FD 302s. No one stood before the judge to argue on behalf of the city's other unnamed victims, the surrounding communities that suffered Industry's legacy but had little to say about its affairs. No one spoke up for the students of political history or the journalists who might wish to learn about the workings of power from Keller's narrative. The judge permitted only the litigants to read the agent's logs, effectively suppressing a political debate about the kickback conspiracy's public and political consequences. The city was now free to represent itself as the ultimate victim, and so focus the power of the courts and press on individual wrongdoers, instead of revealing the technologies that produced the environment in which Stafford's conspiracy had flourished.

Whatever we would have made of the city's arguments at that time, its reasons for sealing these records have evaporated with time. All criminal investigations inspired by Keller's 302s were concluded twenty years ago, and the individuals whose privacy could arguably be unfairly damaged by their release have died. Even the FBI's own Freedom of Information analysts approved the release of his logs, as did the conspirators. I therefore believe that the benefit of releasing them far outweighs the inconvenience that may come from making them public. I also hope that my decision to use Keller's 302s will inspire the press to demand their release and so restart a debate about the city's legacy and the debt of explanation that Industry's economic and political heirs still owe to their neighbors. The logs' release would offer object lessons on the threats that technologies of secrecy pose to our political system and on the public's expectation that courts will pursue the "truth" wherever it may lead.

Deconstructing Biography

As I have already suggested, I believe that the suppression of Keller's logs also had an unintended literary effect: it encouraged our admiration of the biographer's art. We, the journalists, looked for stories of individual transcendence or a villain's descent into evil; we strove to universalize the protagonist's personality by abstracting from it qualities we believed would live on after death. That tendency remains especially pronounced today among members of the political right, whose ideologues swamp readers and viewers with secular hagiographies of a leader's exceptional virtues—moral qualities, if you listen carefully to the storyline, that will identify and express an essential soul.

Modern journalism has inherited its hagiography from eighteenth- and nineteenth-century memoir and biography, genres that narrated the lives of illustrious men. Whereas religious historians wrote the lives of the saints to inspire devotion, the humanist biographer employed novelistic techniques to extol the character of self-made businessmen or politicians, often using the "science" of social Darwinism to explain an exceptional leader's irresistible rise to power. At first, only the most illustrious members of the eighteenth-century nobility and bourgeoisie possessed the rare moral qualities that signified superior character. But late nineteenth- and early twentieth-century representations of the emerging middle classes soon followed the examples of the elite. Middle-class men saw upward mobility as evidence that they had attained high moral character through hard work, education, and earnest emulation. They enlisted religious didacticism to narrate their own secular biographies, today epitomized by the newspaper or magazine feature profile of the businessman who displays an exceptional, or at least admirable, individual character.[11]

These biographical narratives have dominated Southern California's modern history, even as some of their authors have tried to subvert them. For me, there has been no getting around them. Visionaries—whether taciturn yet wise or ruthlessly malevolent—thickly populate our popular versions of local history and function as substitutes for the industrial history that Southern California still needs. To extract their morsels of economic and governmental history, I therefore needed to crack the bones of these stories to show how power had made the "truths" it needed. Moreover, my skepticism (the kind we expect of our best fictional detectives) required me to interpret Stafford's personality as both an effect of and a response to his relationship to power. The sacrifices he made in his attempts to shape and possess the City of Industry reflected the myriad ways in which power rewarded, punished, and molded what we call personality. His mastery of the city required continual self-invention, subtle revisions of his identity to extend and consolidate his influence. That influence, in turn, depended upon the expertise of countless engineers, bureaucrats, and financial and legal specialists who were quite capable of executing their own schemes with or without his permission. Stafford, in short, responded to the technologies of power in the same way that other people would have, if they had enjoyed his influence and wealth and had sustained the scars that had marked him since youth.

Edward P. Roski, Jr., head of the nation's largest privately held industrial real estate development enterprise, an empire now worth more than 2.6 billion dollars, inherited Jim Stafford's place in the city's genealogy of power. Industry and its sister cities gave Roski the publicly subsidized resources to grow a more than 60-million-square-foot commercial real estate development empire clustered at the key gateway and distribution nodes of the global trade network. By the late 1990s, he had leveraged his bread-and-butter industrial development into Las Vegas hotels and casinos and a half-ownership interest in the Staples Arena in downtown Los Angeles, as well as in the NBA Lakers and NHL Kings sports teams that play there. By early 2004, a comprehensive search of property records revealed that several decades of playing the role of Industry's favorite developer had allowed him to own or control, via long-term leases, more than 1,400 acres, or nearly 19 percent of the city's approximately 7,600 acres. His plan to turn between 600- and 800-million-dollars' worth of city-owned real estate into a stadium that would return a long-absent NFL franchise to Los Angeles represent his latest demonstration of influence. The long-term lease the city granted him in 2005 for more than six hundred acres means that his controlling share of the city's real estate has surely increased.[12] The manner in which he acquired his wealth and influence in the city illustrates the way in which capital defies death by finding and molding a suitable host—that its drive to narrate our lives is powerful enough to perform those creative acts we commonly ascribe to genealogies of blood.

CHAPTER 1

HIS THEATER OF SHAME

And just as a person might pass from anonymity to celebrity without ever understanding why, it is equally common for that person, after preening himself in the warm public glow, to end up not even knowing his own name.
—Jose Saramago, *All the Names*

Miss Rae Schade is slender and wears a modest dress. She tilts her head down toward the taller, older man on her right, as if embarrassed. A veil of chiffon gauze hides her eyes. Her body seems to yield to the pressure of watching eyes as she steps from the shadows of the Hall of Justice onto a downtown sidewalk. That taller, older man on her right is her father, Fred. He wears a suit, a wide tie, and a fedora. He, too, averts his eyes as if avoiding the gaze that magnifies a shame made public during a week of police interviews and court hearings. He lets the outer part of his left shoulder touch the inner part of his daughter's smaller right shoulder. In that exposed moment on March 28, 1929, his closeness suggests protectiveness or a need to hide. The fear he expresses is understandable. His daughter, Rae, has just filed rape charges against her former employer, C. C. Stafford, and set off a media frenzy that will last for months.

Los Angeles readers got their first good look at Miss Schade and her father on March 29, when the *Los Angeles Times* printed the photo it had shot the day before, along with a brief news story.[1] Eventually, four local newspapers combined to publish eighty-four news stories (not counting wire stories) that tracked C. C. Stafford's case, from his arrest to his release from jail. At least fourteen of the stories made the front pages, with the balance appearing inside as local news. In the months preceding the stock market's infamous Black Tuesday, these stories became a long-running show in a theater of shame, one that featured tales of illicit sex for an audience of thousands of readers. Exposure of these violent intimacies certainly punished C. C.'s family, including his thirteen-year-old son, who was old enough to be embarrassed by the scandal, especially if he chanced to meet Miss Schade in the office of his father's grain mill.

Jim Stafford would always nurse a special hatred for the press—above all, the *Times*. That newspaper alone published fifty installments of the scandal, a proportion that reflected its power to create an image of him as "the wealthy grain merchant" and then destroy it. Under Harry Chandler's command, the *Times* ran the state's Republican party, selecting its candidates up and down the party roster, from Los Angeles to Sacramento. The paper also marketed Southern California as both a real estate opportunity and a tourist destination, targeting middle-class WASPs who could preserve Los Angeles as a "white spot of America" as well as an anti-union, open-shop city for industrial investors.[2]

The two-column story that the *Times* published on March 29 was short on news but long on details and characters that would lure readers to the photograph printed above the story, and to the next suspenseful episode narrated at a high emotional pitch, the signal features of journalistic melodrama. "Her face [was] masked in a white silk scarf," the lead paragraph began, whetting the reader's appetite for clues that would reveal the 21-year-old El Monte bookkeeper's "true" identity.

The mystery-woman motif reiterated the theme of the previous day's *Times* story, which had mentioned the existence of undisclosed evidence that promised to exonerate C. C. Stafford.[3] But the current story's second paragraph also denied Schade family members their privacy, noting their El Monte address, before returning to the mystery motif. "Her presence in the Hall of Justice with the heavy mask over her face caused a curious throng to follow her from place to place," presumably into the street, where the "beautiful" young woman cast her spell on onlookers. The article did not identify the people in the "throng." Doing so might have revealed that it mostly consisted of photographers chasing down this story, thus breaking the illusion of spontaneous civilian curiosity in which the reader could vicariously participate. No matter. The photograph and article, which introduced Miss Schade as if she were a Hollywood starlet on opening night, promised a look under the scarf in a future installment. The scarf that masked her face invited readers to imagine the eyes, the face, the soul, and even the body under the veil, absences they could fill in with images of the "feminine exotic" that the media was circulating at that time.

The ever-classy *Times* dressed up its innuendo in moralizing understatement. Although the indictment filed against Stafford simply accused him of "rape," the *Times* alluded to an unmentionable "statutory offense," language that implied a sordid "attack" on the bookkeeper's body without calling attention to the reader's appetite for sexual violence.[4] Newspaper editors knew how their readers, many of them recent immigrants from the midwest and New England, would decode these words. They flattered readers for having the moral aptitude to fill in the absence indicated by the word *"attack."* The *Times* and other newspapers ensured their popularity by giving readers a Puritan moral certitude in which the meaning of reported facts was as evident as God's demonstrations of love and punishment.[5]

The liberal *Los Angeles Record*'s coverage, which began a day after the March 23 attack, strove for a more visceral brand of melodrama:

> An El Monte merchant was being held in the county jail today as the result of a twenty-one-year-old girl's hysterical story of an attack in an isolated cabin at Puente.
>
> Crying, "He has ruined me, he has ruined me," Miss Rae Schade, twenty-one, of 641 Washington Street, El Monte, sent deputy sheriffs to the home of C. C. Stafford, forty-two, of 1894 Homewood Drive, Altadena, whom she accused as her attacker.

The victim's recollected protests suggest the dismaying pose of the Victorian stage heroine who presses the back of one delicate hand to her pale, uplifted forehead. Her quoted words invited readers to imagine the expression on Miss Schade's face, whereas the paragraphs that follow force the readers' attention downward, onto the landscape of the female body:

> An examination revealed that the girl had been criminally attacked. According to her story, her employer took her to his cabin near Puente "to check up on his books."
>
> After attempting to force her to drink from a bottle of liquor, the girl charged, Stafford dragged her from his car into his cabin and choked her into insensibility.
>
> The girl was badly bitten on the neck and body, according to Dr. Farrington of El Monte, Dr. Smith of Santa Monica and Dr. Chapman of Los Angeles, who examined her.

As the prominence of the medical testimony illustrates, scientific discourse is one way of sustaining the suspension of disbelief essential to modern journalism. The story also refers to police sources (members of the surveillance and control culture already accepted as its authoritative crime interpreters) as well as an unnamed reporter's observation of events inside and outside the courtroom. Both of these elements characterized the rough empiricism of the journalism at that time. Bundling the language and logic of science and police authority in the ideology of objectivity created the "truth" effect readers expected from their nonfiction narratives.

It's easy to see, therefore, how the expert testimony of doctors confirmed Miss Schade's version of events so convincingly; not even Stafford's defense attorneys contradicted the science upon which that testimony was based. Still, as long as reporters portrayed her testimony as hysterical, as long as they represented her body as appealingly feminine, then scientific discourse had not yet defeated all of her gender's liabilities. In accordance with the traditions of English law, the rape trial required that the virtues and vices of both accuser and accused be exposed to judgment. Feminist communications scholar Lisa M. Cuklanz stresses that a society that saw rape as the theft of female chastity owned by husbands or fathers considered it reasonable to question "the rape victim's general 'reputation for chastity.'" In such cases, the courts departed from normal procedures to determine whether the victim possessed "the narrowly defined characteristics of chastity and virtue that could establish her as a 'legitimate victim.'"[6] The widely held belief that the allegation was by itself exceptionally damaging to the male defendant's reputation justified such proceedings. After all, because the courts viewed rape as "an especially heinous crime, accused rapists could expect little sympathy or pity from juries or the public at large. Thus special protections were allowed in cases of rape" to shield the invariably male defendant from the spurious allegations of vengeful women. The jury would also consider if the victim's behavior, speech, style of dress, or innate gender weakness had provoked the attack.[7] The press thus invited its readers, as surrogate jurors, to determine the nature of Miss Schade's true character. Was she as morally blameless as her words, clothing, and her protective father seemed to proclaim? Was she an innocent deceived by power and wealth or a scheming flapper who was trying to use Hollywood stagecraft to send her boss to jail? Future installments of trial coverage promised to answer these questions for readers—and for C. C.'s family.

C. C.'s case was not the first time the local press had used suspense and melodrama to gin up reader interest. The Los Angeles press had scandalized readers in the decades leading up to his trial. Since the late nineteenth century, the region's newspapers had successfully mobilized readers to fear the "red" and "yellow" perils, water shortages, and crime waves. By the 1920s, the local press had added the culture of celebrity, fostered in the magazines and the new film and radio media, to its news agenda. As in previous decades, the papers exploited every opportunity to repeat ready-made stories in which scandal and novelty supplied pretexts for remembering well-known villains and discovering a fresh crop of victims.

In May 1929, the *Los Angeles Evening Express* reminded readers of the decade's biggest Hollywood scandal when it reported that police had netted four gangsters during a riot at Roscoe "Fatty" Arbuckle's Plantation Club in Culver City.[8] The article did not need to reprise the 1921 trial in which the comic stood accused of raping and crushing Virginia Rappe to death during a wild San Francisco hotel party. Although he was later acquitted, outraged religious crusaders, egged on by the press, branded Arbuckle a sexual pervert, ending his career and providing the pretext for the censorship policies of the Hayes office.[9]

That same month, the *Evening Express* gave newly appointed district attorney Buron Fitts a forum to announce what he would not do—reopen prosecution of Sister Aimee Semple McPherson, the hugely popular Charismatic Christian cult leader—unless he got fresh evidence.[10] Only two and a half years earlier, the local press had treated readers to a suspense thriller relating McPherson's mysterious abduction by a nefarious Mexican couple. District attorney Asa Keyes, later thrown out of office for taking bribes in the Julian Oil stock fraud, accused the theatrical preacher of filing a false police report to hide an affair with her married radio engineer. But Keyes dropped the charges against Sister Aimee, which only increased her popularity among her followers.[11] The radio preacher had attained her huge following thanks, in part, to the *Times*-owned KHJ radio station, which broadcast her nightly "circus-like" services from the stage of the Angelus Temple in Echo Park.[12]

The press rounded out that year in scandal when it reported in August that seventeen-year-old Eunice Pringle had accused Alexander Pantages, owner of a national chain of movie and vaudeville theaters, of raping her in his office. The court found Pantages guilty, a decision reversed on appeal after defense lawyers "established that Eunice Pringle, an aspiring actress, had tried to compromise Pantages in an effort to get work on the Pantages circuit."[13]

That same August, an Alhambra judge found C. C. Stafford guilty of punching Reverend Robert P. Shuler, otherwise known as "Fighting Bob" Shuler, in an El Monte drug store.[14] C. C. really knew how to pick his enemies. Shuler had built a huge following among recent midwestern immigrants. The aging midwesterners who had sold their farms and dry-goods stores to retire in Southern California's eternal spring typified his constituency. By 1930, the churchgoers and club joiners whom

H. L. Mencken loved to portray as narrow-minded religious bigots and hypocrites comprised 37 percent of California's population, a plurality including 160,000 Iowans who had arrived during the previous decade.[15] As their numbers grew, the transplants formed voluntary societies to promulgate their evangelical agenda throughout the city. Shuler cleverly used the new radio technology to rapidly build himself up as their spokesman. By 1929, the year C. C. stood trial, Shuler's congregation had grown to 3,654 members and 900 enrolled students, while thousands more were subscribing to his magazine and listening to his popular radio sermons, which substituted for the tent revivals they had enjoyed back home.[16]

The attack that blacked the popular radio preacher's eye occurred in July. Shuler said that C. C. struck him four times in the face without provocation as the reverend innocently prepared to order a fountain drink. He said he did not learn who had attacked him until after the assault. "I began to get mad when I found out who he was," Shuler said right after the attack, words calculated to restore his reputation as "the fighting pastor." C. C., however, claimed that the pastor not only recognized him but also provoked him when he said, "Good evening," "sneeringly."[17]

Although C. C.'s attorney, W. Joseph Ford, did not deny the assault, he pleaded extenuating circumstances, arguing that his client was "incensed over the bitter words the minister has used [against him] in his air addresses."[18] Shuler based his radio sermons, Ford alleged, upon secret grand-jury testimony against his client; and C.C. feared the broadcasts would ruin his chances of getting a fair trial from jurors swayed by Shuler's grandstanding. The attorney intimated that Shuler had poached the grand-jury transcript from the district attorney's office before the soda fountain scuffle, a charge that the pastor denied. He did admit, however, "that Dr. G. A. Briegleb, one of his close friends and a minister, had obtained the legal document."[19] Shuler insisted that he had read only a few excerpts from the purloined document, but his reluctant admission tempered the ruling against C. C., who settled the dispute by paying a 250-dollar fine.

The first image of C. C. to appear in the press reaffirmed Shuler's stature as the victim. The photo, titled "Pastor Signs Complaint Against Stafford," shows a tall C. C. in a slightly sloppy suit that suggests a wiry build underneath. Shuler, who is at least five inches shorter than C. C., stands to his right, dressed in a dapper three-piece suit and looking down at the complaint he has just signed in front of a seated Los Angeles police captain, who appears on his far left. C. C. stares left, up, and beyond the frame, with the facial expression of someone who is barely tolerating a humiliating display.[20]

The press did not offer a verbatim transcript of Shuler's offending broadcast, but other sources give us the flavor of his statements at that time. In December 1920, the *Times* published his sermon "Vernon Country Club vs Decency—Will Los Angeles Stand For It," in which he describes a party at the infamous nightclub to illustrate the flapper generation's degrading excesses. The revelers, Shuler charges, "engaged in a drunken carousel; defying the laws of the nation with officers of the law assisting; hugging, kissing in drunken fashion; women displaying their nakedness brazenly, openly, flagrantly and viciously, booze sold openly contrary to law, the most suggestive dancing engaged in."[21] That liquor freely flowed at the Vernon Country Club during Prohibition was not surprising. Vernon, the city from which the club took its name, had been designed more than twenty years earlier with one idea in mind: to house factories, not homes filled with voting workers. Its business-first philosophy therefore made it easy for its officials to turn Vernon into a mini-Tijuana, a few miles east of LA's city limits, specializing in the kind of entertainment—boxing, dog racing, drinking, gambling, among others—prohibited in staid Los Angeles.

Shuler also published and broadcast sermons that denounced the threat of Darwinian "monkey" theory, McPherson's false prophecies, the perils of race mixing, the Jewish-Catholic money men who ran City Hall, and, of course, Hollywood's Sodom and Gomorrah. He delighted in showing up adversaries such as the "putrid and filthy" district attorney Asa Keyes, whose office he described as "contemptible and nauseating . . . so full of perjury that it smells to heaven."[22] No doubt, Shuler's agents had infiltrated the county grand jury to collect damaging evidence against Keyes, whom the pastor portrayed as the corrupt leader of City Hall's Jewish-Catholic cabal. For a time, Shuler even acted as the spiritual leader of Southern California's resurgent Ku Klux Klan.[23] He also loved to portray himself as the defender of the little guy and gal in their struggle against ruthless power and greed. Fighting Bob's raw populism assigned C. C. to the ranks of his favorite villains while reserving a place for Miss Schade among his vulnerable, unprotected underdogs. She, after all, had stepped out of the protective shadow of domesticity to enter the male world of work, an unsettling social transformation that had reached a crescendo during the economic expansion of the 1920s.

Shuler's radio congregation and newspaper readers would have read Rae Schade's body and words for moral clues. What kind of "American working girl" was she? Was she the party girl, the flapper, the movie vamp? All three were late-1920s, media-generated icons that symbolized the consequences of taking the working girl's independent self-reliance too far. Both the party girl, often portrayed as a frivolous college graduate, and the flapper, a sexy working girl smart enough to prevent unwanted pregnancies, got into trouble during their seemingly lighthearted pursuit of fun.[24] Did Miss Schade resemble the gorgeous gold-digging movie vamp, or an innocent Mary Pickford waif, Hollywood's first and most popular movie star? Los Angeles moviegoers were well acquainted with Pickford's girlish beauty, down-to-earth humanity, and youthful energy. She was a perpetual ingénue, an all-American innocent whose need to work exposed her to the dangers of a world dominated by men. Her audiences thrived on the dramatic tension that arose from her screen persona's struggle to maintain her dignity in a man's world.[25]

Although her vulnerabilities endeared her to a female audience, Little Mary's virginal body also appealed to men. Biographer Eileen Whitfield reminds us that Pickford "was far from prudish, though her sexuality was not announced in the manner of a silent movie vamp."[26] As other popular icons would later demonstrate, she allowed herself to become the vessel of her public's desires, some of them innocently professed, others savored as secrets too perverse for polite conversation. Pickford suggested these possibilities each time her persona innocently discovered sex as a natural fact, as she did in film after film without taxing her audience's credulity.[27] Her male observers suspended disbelief as long as she gave them reasons to project their desires. Her graceful body, which fit the jazz dancer's ideal—a "very young girl's . . . straight and yielding" figure—could shimmy and thrust to the same syncopated African American rhythms that the working girls flirted to in urban dance halls.[28] To her male and female audiences, the magic of back lighting made her long brown hair shimmer in such a way as to suggest that it was actually golden and ringed in rich tresses. Both images—one recalled in movement, the other in stillness—imbued her angelic femininity with carnal overtones, a simultaneously "childlike and erotic" sensuality.[29]

So it's not hard to see why Miss Schade's predicament intrigued the male press of her day. They would have read the mystery of Miss Schade's veiled face against what was not explicitly marked yet still invoked by the image—the scoundrels and victims the press had helped created during that decade. Curious readers who wanted clues to her persona would have avidly read the next newspaper installment to find out what had befallen the "pretty girl shopkeeper," a characterization that stressed her wage-earning status and her unprotected sexuality.[30] Press descriptions also stressed her modest demeanor, her pained whisper, and her slender figure, all of which stressed her girlish naïveté and financial vulnerability.

On October 30, as C. C.'s trial approached, the *Los Angeles Evening Herald*, a typically yellow Hearst newspaper, printed a photo of Rae Schade under the title "Girl to Accuse Stafford in Court," referring to her as the "pretty stenographer." Her eyes look up and to the right, beyond the frame, as if looking to the future for merciful judgment. To remind readers of C. C.'s menacing presence, the *Evening Herald* printed a smaller photo of him beneath Miss Schade's. His image reclines in a handsomely filled-out suit, a pose that connotes the smug self-confidence of his gender, race, and class. To the left of the photo, an ominous caption states that Miss Schade "has been under guard since attempts by three men to take her from a train." The sentence suggests the existence of a violent plot to possess and silence her, a plan that the reader could link, via the logic of proximity, to the "rich grain merchant" who already stood accused of another aggression.[31]

On the following day, a *Times* article and its accompanying photo took a more discreet route to Miss Schade's body. She began her day on the witness stand in a neatly coifed bob and flapper's cloche and a faintly forlorn gaze. On the witness stand she testified in "a low clear voice" that Stafford had driven her up to a lonely cabin up in the La Puente Hills under the pretense of taking her to examine the books of his newly built grain mill in the nearby La Puente lowlands. "Miss Schade then told the jury Stafford became amorous toward her, addressed her in endearing terms and sought to kiss and caress her. She declared she protested but that her resistance only seemed to anger him. 'I told him to let me alone and to take his hands off of me; that such things were against my ideals,' she said."[32]

After dramatically "faltering a moment" in her testimony, Miss Schade said that Stafford "forced her into the lonely cabin, choked her until she could no longer resist him and then forced his attentions on her." In an eerie foreshadowing of his son's courtroom drama several decades later, C. C. interrupted his trial in September to undergo an operation to remove kidney stones "to save his life."[33] Two months later, the prosecution reintroduced the testimony of the three doctors who had examined Schade soon after the attack. They reported that, in one place on her body, her "flesh had been torn, apparently by physical violence."[34] Defense lawyer W. Joseph Ford, who had represented Alexander Pantages in his rape trial in the same courthouse, then introduced conflicting medical testimony from Dr. Arthur G. Houghton, who did not dispute Miss Schade's injuries but made the preposterous claim that she had inflicted the "flesh tear" on herself.[35]

Ford did begin the trial with at least one bit of testimony in his favor. Miss Schade had previously admitted to visiting the cabin with C. C. "a few days prior to the alleged attack," when she had strolled with him "on the hillside and look[ed] at some ferns growing there." She also acknowledged C. C.'s efforts to kiss her at that time; "but I told him I wasn't that sort of a girl," and she repeatedly denied having an "affair with her former employer."[36] The Brigham Young coed buttressed her claims with the recollection that, just before he threw himself on her, she had told him that she had "a sweetheart, and had promised him that no other man would lay hands upon her."[37]

Ford then attacked Miss Schade's motives, arguing that, before the alleged tryst, she had hinted about her need for money while suggesting to C. C. that his wife did not give her hardworking man the loving attention he deserved. Ford also claimed that the Schade family had "made remarks indicating they would seek a financial settlement from Stafford." To legally unsophisticated jurors, the 90,000-dollar civil suit that Miss Schade had filed against her boss suggested blackmail.[38] C. C. reinforced that possibility when he testified that the Schade family had asked him for 12,000 dollars in exchange for their daughter's silence, an allegation that positioned Miss Schade as a greedy vamp who had lured a good man to perdition.

Many aspects of the case, however, seemed to favor Rae Schade. A news story published a day before the trial's start reminded readers about C. C.'s conviction for the battery of Reverend Shuler.[39] Miss Schade's attorney also reminded the jury that the law did not prevent his client from pursuing civil remedies to rectify the harms she had suffered. In addition, the confusing and incriminating testimony of friendly witnesses weakened C. C.'s case. Some of the witnesses who had driven by the grain dealer's car on the afternoon of the alleged rape said they saw Miss Schade resist him; others said they saw her embrace him. Although the defense portrayed her inconsistent resistance as consent, the prosecution argued that witness testimony confirmed Miss Schade's claims that she had vigorously resisted the rape. Moreover, the jury interpreted the testimony of one of C. C.'s witnesses as evidence of defense-orchestrated lying. Leland Jordan, a motorist who had testified to seeing C. C. with his arm around the bookkeeper's shoulder, admitted under cross-examination that he had written a letter to Miss Schade in which he had quoted biblical passages "advocating forgiveness of sins." Although Jordan insisted that Stafford had nothing "to do with his action," the letter clearly presumed the grain dealer's guilt.[40] And C. C.'s attempt to deflect the rape charges by conceding that he had wanted to seduce the bookkeeper did not help his case either. Although he was not on trial for adultery, admitting these desires to the jury gave the scandalizing press one more excuse to insinuate his criminal motives.

Two weeks later, on November 10, 1929, after eleven hours of secret deliberations, the jury returned a guilty verdict against C. C. on one count of forcible rape. Presiding judge Emmet H. Wilson then set his sentencing hearing for the following week, on November 13, before handing C. C. over to police custody. The next day's newspapers reminded readers that one count of forcible rape could earn C. C. one to fifty years in San Quentin Penitentiary. But we will never know the length of the sentence C. C. actually got because the presiding judge did not spell it out in any of the court's records, a silence that suggests a few possibilities. Either the wily jurist had succeeded in keeping his lenient ruling out of the newspapers that day, or he half-expected his decision to be overturned on appeal.[41] One thing was clear, however. Defense attorneys meant to keep their client out of jail, no matter the length of his sentence. They quickly filed a motion arguing that the prosecution had unfairly labeled defense witnesses as liars without presenting evidence to support those allegations. The jurors also ignored court instructions requiring them to determine beyond a reasonable doubt that Miss Schade had exercised "every physical means or faculty or resistance within her power prior to and until the consummation of the offense." According to these lopsided instructions, the jury could not find the defendant guilty if she had given "any kind of consent, no matter how reluctantly."[42] Worse yet, the defense argued that the prosecution had bullied the jury into ignoring the testimony of witnesses who said they did not hear her call out, or use every ounce of her strength to resist her attacker. C. C.'s attorneys insisted that only a new trial and a new jury could properly weigh the truth of Miss Schade's rape allegation, but now under an early-nineteenth-century standard of truth that favored his client.

Judge Wilson answered the defense's motion for a new trial on November 22, 1929. Not only had C. C.'s attorneys failed to produce credible evidence of any improprieties during the trial, but Wilson said their efforts to put Miss Schade back on the stand were "merely filed for the purpose of degrading" her. Wilson next reminded C. C. of the severity of his crime before he shot down his request for probation: "So far as a crime of this kind is concerned, I am not prepared to right now say whether I think it is greater or lesser than murder itself. In any event, I shall never consider granting probation to any defendant convicted of a crime of this nature."[43] C. C.'s attorneys did not relent, however. They took their crusade for a new trial to the state court of appeals.

Meanwhile, C. C., who was now serving time in the county jail while he awaited the court of appeal's reply, tore a tendon in his left leg as the result

of a "friendly tussle" with his cellmate in March 1930.[44] In August, the state
court of appeal found sufficient merit in the allegations of prosecutorial
misconduct to order a new trial. In granting that trial, the three-judge
panel observed that the allegations of C. C.'s attorneys did not necessarily
invalidate the jury's earlier verdict. "Although [Miss Schade's] story is
unusual in that she did not call out to people near or make any attempt to
escape from him," the judges explained, "nevertheless the jury must have
found her evidence to be true."[45] In other words, without new evidence,
the next jury might reach the same verdict based on the same evidence
and what they already knew about wealthy men's abilities to coerce poor
female employees.

A new jury did not get that chance. In November 1930, the prosecution, citing Rae Schade's unwillingness to return from Utah to testify in a
new trial and re-publicize her shame, requested dismissal of the charges
against C. C. Stafford. The defense gambit worked: the effort to put Miss
Schade back on the stand had intimidated her into silence. Although the
presiding judge refused to dismiss the rape charge and referred the matter
back to the grand jury, the case against C. C. died there anticlimactically.
In September 1931, with no indictment forthcoming, the court voided the
rape charge and made C. C.'s conditional release permanent. The decision,
which a few newspapers reported as "exoneration," allowed him to stay out
of jail on a technicality after a year of time served.

As much as he may have welcomed it, that decision did not give C. C.
the right to say that a jury had affirmed his innocence. Instead, he had
to settle for something more ambiguous. To the press and his intimate
friends, he tried to portray himself as the victim of a frame-up, while
everyone outside that circle was free to remember him as a convicted
rapist.[46] Despite C. C.'s efforts to reclaim his reputation, only two newspapers briefly reported on the decision in their back pages; in other words,
the press refused to fully restore a public reputation damaged by a year of
scandal.

Jim Stafford was fourteen years old when the courts released the most
powerful man in his life from police custody. During C. C.'s trial and incarceration, the younger Stafford saw his father become someone else, not
the man his workers and neighbors respected. He had witnessed how his
father's need for admiration had exposed him to public humiliation and
vicious gossip, learned that his father had betrayed his mother for a pretty
girl, and heard about his fight with another prisoner. The son, in other
words, had watched the courts and the press turn his father into a man
he was tempted to hate because neither institution had clearly proclaimed

his innocence. I do not base my interpretation on what Jim said because he did not, as far as I have been able to determine, write down what he thought or felt about the trial. But we do have the text of his adult deeds, which is a lot. Rather than shun the courts, the branch of government that punished his father, Jim, I believe, thirsted to take possession of the power that had humiliated his father and his family. He could not do this without overcoming his own fears of shameful public exposure. And he could not do it alone. He would need allies to erect walls to shield him from the penetrating gaze of police and press surveillance—need people he could trust, people like himself, who had been scorned, ignored, or ridiculed for being too rural, too poor, too ignorant. The years he dedicated to his obsession suggest the depth of his passion and the private desires that made him vulnerable to those who could grant his wishes. Some might also say that the humiliations he suffered gave him that special quality we call a soul.

CHAPTER 2

A LEGACY OF DEBT, RAILS, AND NOOSES

Your title deeds may be in order. But
Did you buy your land from its true owner?
And he from its true owner? And the latter . . . ?
Though your title go back to the grant of a king
Was
The land ever the king's?
— Ernesto Cardenal, "Unrighteous Mammon"

The rape scandal that sent C. C. Stafford to jail and fixed his image as the "rich grain merchant" represents just one of his possible life stories. There are several other versions of that life, including the one he fashioned from his deeds and dreams and the one his son told out of love or pride. And like other infamous men, C. C. had other biographers, the ones who narrated the versions of his life he did not bother, or flat out refused, to acknowledge.

The autobiography that C. C. fashioned refused to recognize tragedy or failure, insisting instead on his epic quest and its destination. Like the immigrants of his day, he portrayed California as an Eden famous for offering second and third chances, a place where newcomers could invent new identities to hide their failures or modest pedigrees, where appearance became reality if you could persuade folks to believe the stories you told about yourself. The trick was to tell your story to the right crowd—to the small-town folks who gathered in churches, lodges, and private clubs to perform their own epics of social improvement, and where the local newspapers came to validate a person's ascent up the social ladder.

THE FATHER'S VERSION

C. C. left a respectable record of his climb. It appears in the dues he religiously paid to the Hay, Grain, and Feed Dealers Association; to the El Monte Chamber of Commerce; to the Los Angeles Elks Lodge; and to the Jonathan Club, cultural center of the region's pioneer capitalist class.[1] The club, which excluded Jews, blacks, and women (except maybe for the aspiring starlet who was willing to jump out of a party cake dimpled in whipped cream), showcased LA's old money and political elite, making it the perfect setting for C. C. to exhibit his character and charm to his Babbitt peers.

Elite club life must have been particularly attractive to a man who traded in unglamorous goods and hailed from the corn- and cotton-growing town of Bunkie, Louisiana. Inside the club's downtown headquarters, then owned by the Southern Pacific railroad, and at its exclusive Malibu Beach clubhouse, he could cavort with LA's rich, powerful, and beautiful people and maybe pick up a hot real estate tip from the likes of Harry Chandler, the up-and-coming *Los Angeles Times* publisher, who had already used the newspaper to build a vast real estate empire.[2]

Chandler's newspaper, Southern California's preeminent social register, also recorded C. C.'s club appearances and business dealings. The newspaper that eventually dramatized his fall first documented his rise, mentioning his cattle purchases; the warehouse he had built in El Monte and the post office he had opened inside it; the homes, mill, and warehouse he later built in La Puente; the feedlots he and his partners ran across the tracks on Valley Boulevard.[3] Meanwhile, the *Times* society pages duly noted the appearance of Mr. and Mrs. Stafford at a 1926 performance of *Charlot's Revue* in the then-new Hollywood Theater. C. C.'s wife, Louise, promoted her husband's social ambitions by hosting and attending bridge parties in El Monte's better homes.[4]

You can't fault C. C. for trying. Although his culture classified him as a white male, his southern Catholic rural origins made him an outsider in a town in which middle- and upper-class Midwesterners and easterners, most of them WASPs, typified the ideals of wealth, virtue, and social respectability. In that environment, his success was notable. In 1928, the *Times* went so far as to portray him as the "plutocrat of local Democrats" because he had used his support of presidential candidate Al Smith to garner "postmasterships" for his pals, having already secured one for his

El Monte warehouse.[5] Just as the orbit of a small planet is bent by a larger one's gravitational pull, C. C. adjusted himself to the expectations of his time and place. Even the way he initialized his name suggests an effort to convey an image of success via the modern efficiency of streamlined technology. The discovery that he shared his initials with wealthy oilmen C. C. Chapman and C. C. Julian might have reinforced the wisdom of adopting the abbreviation. And certainly he understood the booster-club rhetoric of reverse ostentation. In Middle America (which in his day included LA as its westernmost outpost), men of substance knew that understatement signified success. A tall, large, muscular man such as C. C. would have understood this idea better than most: as a vigorous man of business, he counted on his physical presence to speak for itself.

The double Cs he emblazoned on his trucks and, in huge letters, on top of the La Puente grain mill suggests another possibility.[6] The mill, erected in 1926, dominated the surrounding landscape, a rolling tapestry of oat and alfalfa fields, vineyards, and citrus and walnut orchards, with La Puente's Mexican barrio on its immediate southern flank. The towns-folk who approached the structure on foot or by car would have sensed the mill's dominating presence. Its economic shadow, and the elevated placement of C. C. Stafford's name, reinforced that paternalistic image. The jobs it provided to La Puente's Mexican community made C. C. a folk hero, while the feeds and feed credit it offered both sustained and indebted local ranchers, dairy farmers, and sheepherders.[7] The loud whistle the mill blew, which the Puente locals mistook for a fire alarm or the signal that the walnut growers used to summon picking crews, symbolized another way in which he forced them to recognize his heroic achievement.[8]

C. C. also narrated the grandeur of his possessions in photographs. In one, visibly older than his rape-trial likeness, he leans his left elbow on his truck's right front fender. Millworker Pete La Maison stands shyly to his right dressed in ordinary work clothes, while C. C. wears a suit, a tie, and a broad smile. He squints into the sun, a facial expression that connotes the masculine outdoor environment in which he has made his money, and casually holds a cigar, the businessman's talisman, between his left index and middle fingers. His physical contact with his shiny new Autocar-Diesel, a powerful symbol of industrial progress, and the "C. C." painted on the front bumper convey his pride of ownership. Someone has decorated the truck with a patriotic tricolor sunburst over the driver's cab and a matching sash wrapped around its loaded hay trailer. The photo is dated July 4, 1941, the day of La Puente's centennial parade, which took place in the early months of World War II and less than a year before his death.[9]

THE SON'S VERSION

Another version of C. C.'s biography surfaced nearly a half-century later. In 1975, a special edition of the *City of Industry News*, published by the city's chamber of commerce—an organization controlled by Jim Stafford—announced that the city had renamed a road in its new civic center "Stafford Street"—after C. C. Stafford, of course. The special edition included two stories and a photo spread that said only good things about Stafford's father.

One story began by looking back to 1906, when, "at the age of eighteen, Mr. Stafford decided that greater opportunity existed in California and so he came west." This opener conveyed the epic grandeur often found in the literature of American westerns but with darker undertones. C. C.'s quest for "greater opportunity" acknowledged that the realities of southern poverty had motivated his long trek to paradise.[10] The tribute repeated a predictable maneuver: it prepared readers for the story of a self-made man who disciplined his mind and body to husband his modest resources and ennoble his humble origins:

> His first job after arrival was with the Nichols-Loomis Company in El Monte. Being a prudent, frugal and determined man, Mr. Stafford saved his money and planned for the day he could start his own business of marketing hay, ground feed and grains for all kinds of livestock.
> In 1916, at the age of twenty-eight, Stafford's cattle and poultry feeds store was opened in El Monte and grew rapidly. It was soon evident that the El Monte Store would not be able to meet the needs of his customers and so the search for a new and larger facility began.[11]

The preceding passage glosses over C. C.'s 1911 move to El Monte, where he and his wife took up residence.[12] But the sentences that follow the extract hint at the structuring influence railroads exerted on his life. Still in a biblical register, the tribute tells us that "Stafford looked east" from El Monte "to find a suitable building site which offered growth potential, railroad access, and a central location with easy access to the farmers and ranchers in the area."[13] The article does not explain that suburbanization and rising land prices had pushed C. C.'s customers deeper into the eastern San Gabriel Valley, but it does acknowledge the presence of an unnamed railroad—the Southern Pacific (affectionately and derisively known as "the SP")—which hauled grain to his mill on a spur it had built, and which leased him, via one of its subsidiaries, the 5,000-square foot El Monte warehouse in which he started his business.[14]

In 1920, C. C. acquired his first property in La Puente: 4.3 acres bought from Clara Baldwin Stocker, daughter of notorious developer and horse-racing enthusiast Elias Jackson "Lucky" Baldwin, for an undisclosed amount.[15] The property that C. C. acquired abutted the SP's main line from the northwest, giving him plenty of room to expand his milling business.[16]

On April 2, 1926, C. C. announced that he would spend 50,000 dollars to erect a feed processing plant on his La Puente property. He also made plans for new "hay sheds with spur tracks and large buildings to house barley rollers, bean and grain cleaners, scouring machines, attrition mills, mixers and concrete bins to handle grain." The track extension onto the property reinforced his contractual relationship with the SP.[17]

On January 24, 1929, two months before his rape scandal erupted, C. C. moved his offices from El Monte to La Puente. Then, after the scandal, in 1932, he erected "an auxiliary mill west of the Southern Pacific railroad track, just south of the station and adjoining the cattle yards of the railroad company."[18] Clearly, C. C. built his life and his business in, on, and near the SP's warehouses, stockyards, and rail lines. Yet the story only briefly acknowledges the presence of the railroad beneath and around these constructions, which is odd. As in many other late-nineteenth- and early-twentieth-century histories of the west, the railroad is the silent player that connects C. C.'s character-building story with a nation-building narrative. The story's silence fails to acknowledge the obvious: namely, that the railroads opened up virgin land for industrial development.

Why did the tribute's authors choose to gloss over the SP's crucial role in C. C.'s success story? Perhaps giving the railroad a more important part would have reduced the scale of C. C. accomplishments, or perhaps it had, by this time, more or less melted into the scenery. Whatever the reason, the narrative that Jim Stafford commissioned stressed the mill, that "familiar landmark" that his father had built, before it characterized him as a tireless, honest, and conscientious man whose "business dealings established an enviable reputation."[19] The commemorative issue asked its readers, primarily city insiders and local business owners, to weigh C. C.'s business reputation against his accomplishments and their nostalgic (or so his son hoped) memories of the mill and the man. The articles could pull off this maneuver as long as they focused on the heyday of his business years, as long as Jim Stafford retained control of the mill's business ledgers, as long as the SP remained C. C.'s silent partner, as long as readers could forget his other indiscretions.

C. C.'s Other Theater of Shame

Anyone who had known C. C. Stafford and who did not choose to indulge his son's selective forgetting would have recognized his phantoms: the handful of neighbors who had passed along their recollections of a flawed man, the rare family member who had betrayed family secrets. These phantoms could have told of a man who had mercilessly pursued his creditors and had sacrificed himself to deceive his debtors and inspire the devotion of his intimates.

Archives of C. C.'s possessions confirm the existence of these alternate stories; the Los Angeles County General Index of Grantors and Grantees, an omnivorous collection of real estate records, offers an especially rich source for reconstructing them. The annually updated index currently identifies 111 records that chronicle C. C.'s business affairs between 1920 and 1943. It also offers us a way to imagine the scars those transactions might have left on the man himself. For the loss of property, and the loss of prestige that it threatens, conveys its own special negative inheritance, one that tortures the body from within with debilitating shame and nights of insomnia.[20]

C. C.'s Depression-era affairs offer a rich tale of financial trauma; and the index supplies more than a compelling record of that violence because it was one of the instruments of that violence. The index functioned omnisciently, identifying and mapping a vast library of transactions that recorded changes in property relations, cross-referencing time coordinates and alphabetizing all grantor and grantee names within the county's territorial jurisdiction.[21] It recorded quitclaim deeds, property liens, notices of default, and second mortgages; it confirmed all actions upon the subjects and objects of property. It included everything a banker or a judge would need to inspect a property owner's real estate holdings and debts on those holdings.

Each record reinforced a network of business practices codified in law and capitalist culture. As a whole, the index was a method for governing the meanings of property relations, for fixing the identities and rights of buying, selling, and lending parties as well as heirs and tenants. Its power to generate and fix meaning endowed it with police functions, enhancing the state's authority over citizens by allowing the state to identify and locate all property owners. Such a penetrating system of surveillance also archived an inexhaustible supply of details that narrators could use to fashion stories about property owners. In C. C.'s case, the index amplified his exposure to the technology of public censure.

For the language of real estate transactions was always positive in its effects and could be revoked or altered only by other duly recorded entries. But the index did not create the language of property or its meanings. Several other technologies and discourses supplied the codes for translating its contents into business stories or court decisions. Double-entry bookkeeping headed that list. It was the preferred method for assigning value, and therefore credit risk, within the system of finance capital. A banker judged the creditworthiness of a business on how well it had repaid its debts and multiplied the value of its business.[22] The technology, when fused with well-entrenched discourses of family governance and Calvinist and Puritan notions of divine Providence, gave the banker the means to make social judgments about creditors. In the banker's eyes, the man of business held a role equivalent to the head of a household. In this vision, the good government of nations rested upon the good government of businesses, which rested on the good government of families, which ultimately rested upon a father's fiscal mastery of his household. The good father could not expect to govern his family well if he could not master his own demons of profligacy. The technology of double-entry bookkeeping therefore equipped these fathers of business with a convincing way to demonstrate their self-mastery. Each transaction was entered twice:—once on the debit side, once on the credit side. In essence, the method was a truth-testing promise to the ledger's readers.

And because it opened all fiscal transactions to moral interpretation, the technology of double-entry bookkeeping invited its readers to conflate business and ethical codes. Its irresistible logic promised wealth to those who could keep the seductions of credit in check and shame to those who could not. Its technology promised to penetrate the most elaborate financial frauds as well as the sinister perpetrators of those frauds. The businessman who opened his books thus cloaked his business in a richly suggestive religious aura. By confessing his debts and liabilities, he demonstrated the countless ways in which he had resisted financial temptation.[23]

In the vigorous capitalist economy of early-twentieth-century Southern California, where so much of its business life depended on real estate development, C. C. could count on business rivals, family members, attorneys, bankers, and journalists to read the text of his business story for signs of credit mastery or failure. So as the Depression deepened, C. C. must certainly have feared a dangerous double exposure: a financial scandal joined to a sex scandal. He knew that both friends and enemies would read his financial failures as further evidence of moral depravity, knowledge that would have been particularly painful because he believed in their code of judgment.

The records in the General Index of Grantors and Grantees confirm the external outlines of Jim Stafford's biography of his father, but not its drama. C. C.'s business did undergo rapid expansion in its early years. Between 1926 and 1938, however, his mill appears to have received no repayment for nearly 57,000 dollars' worth of feed and seed credits advanced to dairy owners, cattle ranchers, and alfalfa farmers. The loans he made took the form of chattel mortgages, an agrarian lending instrument dating back to feudal times, when animals on the hoof counted as currency. In other words, C. C. had secured his loans with livestock, which made collection difficult when farmers could not make payments on feed credits. Again and again, he was forced to go to court to obtain rulings that would allow him to liquidate his customers' real estate assets.

Without access to the mill's financial ledgers, we cannot know for sure how many of C. C.'s customers repaid their loans. Still, at least two factors make the index records reliable enough for general inferences. First, given the risks of offering livestock as security, borrowers were strongly motivated to officially record their release from loan obligations because failure to show repayment of debt marred a rancher's future credit prospects. And according to the index, at least fourteen persons or businesses that received feed credits from C. C.'s mill did officially record their repayment or renegotiation of a chattel mortgage. Second, other lending institutions used the index record, in conjunction with the civil courts, to encourage repayment of debt. On at least five different occasions, for instance, C. C. recorded his own repayment of chattel mortgages secured with his own cattle. Like the criminal archive, the index continually supplied the state with knowledge that enabled it to scrutinize, seize, hold, and punish the accused. But the index also allowed the state and finance capital to monitor a property holder's debts and possessions and thus encourage compliance with property law before it could be violated. So a lender who had already secured a favorable ruling in civil court could leverage that ruling to compel a debtor to sell off his or her assets.

Like other capitalists of his time, C. C. skillfully inflicted these techniques on dozens of debtors so that he could seize, repossess, and auction their livestock or land, actions that potentially exposed his debtors to moral judgment. But as the Depression's effects sank into Southern California, the court rulings he won failed to produce their desired result. The state could use criminal law to assert control over the body of the accused, but an economic catastrophe of the Depression's scale thwarted any efforts to fix property values and the financial morality that sustained property ownership.

Records in the general index repeatedly illustrate this paradox. For instance, on February 2, 1928, the courts ruled in C. C.'s favor, confirming the validity of the $10,342.70 owed to him by Charles C. and Glada Hill. More than two months later, the Los Angeles County sheriff certified that C. C. had satisfied repayment of the chattel mortgage on the Hills' property by purchasing it for the cost of the balance remaining on its 3,000-dollar mortgage. In other words, he assumed a 3,000-dollar debt, on top of the more than 10,000 dollars in feed credits he had already extended, in hopes of recouping these funds at a later date.[24] To do this, however, he would have to sell the purchased property for more than 13,342 dollars. Reaching that price might have seemed to be a good bet in the market conditions of 1928, but not after the crash, and would explain why no such sale was recorded while he lived. Moreover, his earnest efforts to recover ever-smaller sums from customers suggest a growing desperation. On July 7, 1932, for example, C. C. recorded a justice of the peace's judgment against a Louis Sing totaling $209.12, which gave him the right to the tenant farmer's crop of corn. Sing, most likely an East Asian immigrant who picked citrus for local growers, had mortgaged his labor to C. C., betting he could sell enough corn to pay his debts and have some left over to escape the drudgery of orange and lemon picking. Helen Walsh, one of C. C.'s oldest neighbors, claimed that even well-established farmers succumbed to his lending: "If the farmer did not give him hay at a bargain price, he would refuse to buy [it,] causing the farmer to go broke. Stafford bought the farmer's land" when this happened.[25]

C. C.'s failure to recover larger debts foreshadowed the moment at which his growing losses transformed him from creditor into debtor, from punisher into victim. On March 12, 1929, in the midst of his rape scandal, a Pomona-based law firm deeded three lots totaling forty-two acres, located in San Gabriel in the Wolfskill Orchard Tract, part of California's largest citrus orchard, to C. C. and his wife to hold as security on a loan of an undisclosed amount.[26] When the law firm defaulted on that loan,

C. C. and two other investors took possession of the acreage and assumed its $17,823.35 mortgage balance. But that repossession did not stop his creditors from hounding him in court to collect on a $1,039.30 debt he had failed to repay, or make it any easier for him to serve his jail time.

When C. C. walked out of jail in 1930, he found that home building in the San Gabriel Valley's new suburbs had continued to expand the market for dairy products, although at a slower pace due to the worsening Depression.[27] Eventually, the advent of World War II jumpstarted demand for dairy products—good news for dairy production in Southern California, which did not suffer winter slowdowns.[28] But C. C.'s mill could not help dairy farmers meet that demand if housing tracts continued to eat up alfalfa fields. By the early 1930s he was sending his trucks beyond the San Gabriel Valley into the Mojave Desert, all the way up to the Colorado River, to locate new hay supplies.

So it is not surprising that, in 1931, C. C. and his wife looked for a way to protect their elegant Altadena home, signifier of their hard-won social status, from being pulled under by their other troubled real estate investments. They settled on deeding their shares of the Wolfskill lots to the mill for ten dollars to free it from future debt liabilities.[29] Then, hoping to spin off a new revenue stream from the mill's feed production, C. C. and two partners filed incorporation papers for the Southwestern Feeding Yards the following June. The venture's incorporation papers and bookkeeping entries show that the partners took out a ninety-nine-year lease on SP-owned feedlots located across the tracks from the mill.[30] But the partners' failure to make payments on the Wolfskill lots forced the bank, on December 7, 1933, to start foreclosure proceedings. On July 31, 1935, the mill finally relinquished a portion of its Wolfskill lots to Citizens National Trust and Savings Bank of Los Angeles after the bank had failed to sell them at auction to recover their mortgages.[31] C. C.'s share of the loss on this deal came to at least $4,455.83.

C. C.'s private drama coincided with the wave of labor strife that swept through his part of the San Gabriel Valley. The El Monte Berry strike, one of the most widely reported agricultural work stoppages of 1933, pitted 1,500 Mexican workers living in El Monte's and La Puente's barrios against the Japanese American strawberry growers who rented fields from Anglo landowners.[32] C. C. may have also felt labor's gaze in 1936, when the International Longshoremen's and Warehousemen's Union launched its "march inland" to organize LA County's warehousing industry and unionize the choke points linking west coast docks to inland warehouses.[33] Warehouse owners like himself would have had a hard time ignoring the strike news spread by word of mouth and the *Times*, which waged a vicious campaign against the longshoremen.

The annual report that C. C. filed in 1937 with the state railroad commission provides another perspective on the mill's business seven years after the 1929 stock market crash. In that 1937 report, the business shows assets of $360,195, an amount that equaled its liabilities. Interestingly, nearly 45,000 dollars of those liabilities consisted of a 25,000-dollar bank loan and 15,000 dollars in "trade acceptances"—most likely feed credits extended to customers—which the mill took on in late 1937 and that were due in early 1938. Moreover, the report shows that the mill's revenues of $148,348 barely managed an 897-dollar gain over expenses.[34]

Clearly, C. C. was feeling the pressure. The *Times*, which had covered his rape trial, reported on March 7, 1938, that he had "struck [deputy tax collector William B.] Osmond when the latter started to take inventory of his stock because of delinquent taxes assertedly [*sic*] due the county." Although the news item does not state the amount of C. C.'s tax bill, the county had assessed the mill's tax burden at $1,826.69 a year earlier, a great deal of money when a person was having trouble paying the bills.[35] The pressure increased in October, when the Western Feeding Yards failed to make payments on the $8,529.76 chattel mortgage it had accepted from the mill. C. C. began foreclosure in March 1939, recording a sheriff's certificate of sale in May that authorized him to auction the property. But the auction failed to produce a viable buyer, thus forcing the mill to assume the mortgage on the property and increase its debt load.[36]

In 1938, C. C. had had the foresight to deed his share in his Altadena home to his wife, Louise.[37] The house was a prize worth protecting from creditors. It was located in a new suburb on Pasadena's northern boundary, an area that allowed the wealthy to escape from lowland Los Angeles, which each year was attracting more unsavory newcomers. The state had built new auto roads in the 1920s; and now that the SP had completed an electric commuter rail line between Los Angeles and Monrovia, a rising middle class found itself able to display its social position from these elevated lots on the San Gabriel foothills.[38]

Less than a decade after his trial, however, C. C.'s world had changed. His wife no longer recorded the family's affairs in the social pages. For entertainment, C. C. preferred to run down to Tijuana's infamous Caliente Resort to drink and play cards with Clark Gable, Wallace Beery, and John Barrymore for three or four days at a stretch. There, according to family lore, he played "the big shot" who liked "driving luxury cars and hobnobbing with [Hollywood] celebrities."[39]

The index recorded another sign of C. C.'s financial distress in 1940. That year, the mill, in an apparent effort to reduce its debt exposure, deeded over its remaining Wolfskill lots to C. C.'s wife, daughter, and business partner, Lefty Horst.[40] But the mill's cash flow problems prevented Lefty from making mortgage payments on the Wolfskill property. On July 7, 1941, about eight months before C. C.'s death, a Los Angeles Superior Court judge let the Southern County Bank foreclose on the property.[41] When we tally the loss of the Wolfskill property and the unpaid chattel mortgages, we see that the mill had apparently failed to recover nearly 65,500 dollars' worth in bad loans. The sketchiness of some of the index entries makes exact calculation of those debts difficult. But given what we know about the cycle of business and bank failures triggered by a rapidly contracting money supply, we can easily imagine the emotional strains that the Depression placed on the mill's owners and their families. All of them had witnessed business failures that forced banks to call in loans secured with worthless stock or heavily mortgaged real estate, developments which, in turn, set off a new round of bank failures.

C. C. and Lefty Horst, the mill's president, deserve credit for staying solvent during those treacherous times, an achievement that their business partners and employees also appreciated. C. C.'s family "carried most of the people in the area during the depression," one neighbor later recalled. "The people the Staffords helped have not forgotten"—sentimental debts that his son would collect on years later.[42] But in the meantime C. C. and Lefty were forced to cut back on feed credits to customers and instead mortgaged their own cattle, even the alfalfa they baled in Arizona. The weight of debt and business responsibility they had shouldered at that moment must have felt immense.

And then, on February 24, 1942, C. C. drove his car through an SP railroad switch and into a parked hay truck, fatally injuring himself.[43] His death certificate represented the collision as a single event. The *Times*, however, reported the collision as two separate events: "Stafford's car became stuck on railroad tracks at his place of business, and in extricating it the driver lost control and crashed into the other vehicle."[44] A rapid acceleration after initial entrapment explained the collision's ferocity.

According to the Los Angeles County Coroner's Register, Louise Stafford told a county sheriff that her husband had crashed his car into a Southern Pacific derailment switch, whereupon the "injured driver continued [in the car he was driving] into [a] parked" truck. In her account, the car was moving fast enough to plow through the switch and slam into the stationary hay truck while not being slowed by the tracks. Neither the death certificate nor the coroner's report explains why C. C. was driving his car fast enough to suffer a fatal collision in an area that was often crowded with equipment.

His death was not instantaneous: he lingered until February 28, when he died at 11:30 A.M. in Saint Luke's Hospital in Pasadena. As is customary in all sudden, violent, or unusual deaths, the coroner conducted an inquest; the autopsy was performed at the Reynolds and Eberle Mortuary in Pasadena. The county-appointed coroner, Dr. Homer R. Keyes, noted that the cause of death was "cerebral hemorrhage into the lateral ventricles due to spontaneous hemorrhage into the left internal capsule" and "a right cerebral and cerebellar contusion contra-coup." In other words, C. C.'s head sustained injuries of such force that his brain's right and left ventricles, its largest inner cavities, were immediately filled with blood. The coroner's report does not explain how his head struck the interior of the car after impact or whether parts of the collapsing interior, such as a steering wheel, might have crushed his head. Whatever the exact sequence of events, his head had suffered a violent deceleration that slammed his brain against the inner cranium walls, rupturing arteries and veins within and outside his brain. The blows to his body also caused "traumatic pneumonia," the result of a "fractured rib and sternum" that had pierced his lungs.[45]

But the coroner listed the coup-contra-coup injury as the primary cause of death. Sufficiently strong cranial pressure, a contemporary physician explained to me, would have shut down the brain's breathing center when "forced down through the foramen magnum, the small opening at the bottom of the skull." An underlying condition of high blood pressure may have contributed to the coup-contra-coup's lethality, maybe even triggering the "heart attack" that Jim Stafford claimed his father suffered after the collision.[46] The inquest's six-member jury ruled C. C.'s death an accident due to his "incompetent handling" of the vehicle, a loss of control that collided with his image of self-mastery.[47]

Jane Stafford, Jim Stafford's estranged wife, did not attribute her father-in-law's death to incompetence but to intention. In an interview with the FBI in 1983, she said that her account had come from a reliable source—Jim's sister, Margaret. During a family gathering held several years after Jane's 1942 marriage, Margaret, to Jane's surprise, began telling her sister-in-law about her father's rape trial. According to Jane, Jim Stafford "had never mentioned that to her before," even though "Margaret [now] treated it as a family joke and told her it was quite a scandal at the time and was sensationalized in the newspapers." But Margaret also offered more disturbing information. She said that "C. C. Stafford committed suicide by starting up his car in front of the mill and driving it into one of his parked trucks at a high rate of speed. . . . The cause of his death was disputed by the family for insurance reasons and was eventually listed as accidental. [Jane] related it was not until after C. C. Stafford's death that the family learned that his business was $500,000 in debt. Everyone assumed he had money because he continued to live like a wealthy man to the end."[48]

If Jane's account of C. C.'s death is correct, New York Life, the firm from which he had purchased his insurance policy, should have records documenting her claim and the insurer's decision to accept the coroner's findings. But when I contacted the firm, the agent refused, as a matter of company policy, to discuss the case.[49] One thing is clear, however: at his father's death, Jim Stafford suddenly inherited C. C.'s crushing responsibilities and debts, which must have threatened his identity as the son of a wealthy man.

Between April 2, 1938, and August 3, 1943, a year before C. C.'s will could settle his estate, the mill borrowed $60,238.15 in chattel mortgages on livestock and alfalfa crops from the Citizens National Trust and Savings Bank of Los Angeles and the Valley National Bank of Phoenix. Those mortgages nearly equaled the 65,450 dollars' worth of loans that the mill had failed to recover since 1928 and that were apparently not repaid before C. C.'s death.[50] It is hard to know how much the property foreclosures and unpaid taxes added to the mill's debt burdens or whether they ever reached the 500,000-dollar mark that Jane claimed her husband had inherited. Still, persistent financial danger colors our overall picture of C. C.'s business and personal debts.

The full weight of the mill's financial difficulties, as well as his father's troubled legacy, fell on Jim's shoulders when he assumed his role as company secretary in 1942. Accepting control of his family's one-half ownership interest in the mill and its one-third interest in the feedlot also meant accepting the obligations of servicing debt, paying taxes, and meeting payrolls. From that moment forward, he also signed all official papers involving confiscation of the mill's properties and devised financing to save the business.

Jim incurred the last and largest of the mill's chattel mortgages in 1943 while he followed the final accounting of his father's estate. The auditors told the twenty-five-year-old married man that his father had bequeathed him a business worth less than its debts. The documents filed in C. C.'s legal will estimated the value of his feed and grain business at slightly more than 58,000 dollars, or about 2,000 dollars less than the mortgages on the mill's merchandise and property, not counting unpaid loans. The auditors concluded, not surprisingly, that "there was no money in the estate" and said that "none has been received" when they filed their final report in 1944.

The heirs needed to cash insurance policies to bury C. C. They then raised money to cover the mill's operating expenses by signing nearly 5,850 dollars in promissory notes to the Southwestern Feeding Yards. The arrangement protected the mill from default and rescued the feedlot from having to find someone to buy C. C.'s shares. On paper, at least, his one hundred shares of stock, originally appraised at 32,295 dollars, accounted for 66 percent of the appraised value of his estate.[51] Getting that price for the shares in the middle of a war, however, would have been another matter.

The Other Narrators

One clear irony endures. C. C.'s violent impact with the switch connecting his mill to the SP's vast network—that silent player in Jim Stafford's parental tribute—caused his death. In order to appreciate both this bitter twist and the SP's role as unacknowledged narrator of the Stafford family's business story, we must consider the railroad's part in developing the San Gabriel Valley.

The markers are plainly visible in Southern California's industrial landscape. The Southern Pacific leased C. C. his first warehouse, extended a rail spur onto the mill's property, bought his feed for its stockyards, and later leased its stockyards to C. C. and his partners. It even owned the building in which his Jonathan Club pals smoked cigars and sipped brandy.[52] The SP could accomplish these trifling tasks because it had written the early chapters of Southern California's industrial history and because its plans continued to structure the region's economy and society for decades afterward.

In preparing the ground for Southern California's multimillion-dollar citrus industry, the SP also reinforced the racialized division of agricultural labor that business owners such as C. C. would later exploit. To orchard and grain farmers, to packing-house and mill owners in the La Puente Valley, the appearance of an SP rail spur on their property confirmed Los Angeles County's emergence as the nation's leading agricultural producer. Moreover, the SP's rail monopoly shaped the migrations that made industrial and suburban growth possible.

This much of the Southern Pacific story has been told before. What the railroad's historians do not always appreciate is the degree to which the SP's achievements depended on its mastery of cultural technologies. No one could evade the armies of railroad agents who visited school halls, agricultural societies, and county fairs; who lectured from educational railcars; who stuffed handbills under wagon benches during circuses; who published magazines and newspapers, and secretly bankrolled newspapers and journalists.[53] A man might chance to turn the pages of *Sunset Magazine,* the SP's most influential publication, which offered its readers a colorful dream world of southwestern landscapes and exotic Indians. Perhaps the SP mail cars brought him letters stuffed with dollars or celebrity gossip from sons who had already left home for the promised land of Southern California. In these and other ways, the SP flooded the rural south with romantic images that represented the Golden State's bounty: golden citrus fruit, sun-drenched vistas, radiantly youthful Aryan women, and mysteriously seductive "Spanish" beauties. The Southern Pacific and other railroads supplied technical know-how, distributing literature about manufacturing and tourist enterprises, farming and ranching, even the citrus-growing methods most efficacious for each western locale. The mail car and telegraph lines that paralleled the rail lines distributed the national magazines and news stories that enhanced the SP's cultural penetration. No doubt, its rail network, which stretched from New Orleans to California, transmitted this dream of possibilities to a young C. C.[54]

Yet the Southern Pacific and the Union Pacific did not think of domestic immigrants as ticket-buying customers. Rather, they recruited them to colonize the farms, factories, mines, towns, and cities that would produce and consume what the railroads valued most: freight, particularly in value-added manufactured goods that permitted them to levy higher fees. The railroads, writes historian Roy Scott, "discovered that in some ways they were like manufacturers; they produced a commodity—a service—and good business judgment" required that they "'manufacture a demand' for that commodity."[55] The economic circularity of freight hauling—building railroads that resulted in economic growth that, in turn, produced freight-hauling customers—depended upon the execution of a railroad's strategic market plan. Like mineral prospectors, railroad planners started by identifying those stretches of country with the greatest economic potential and then set in motion a colonization process to realize it. "A new manufacturing plant or warehouse usually meant new business," writes Scott, "while the industrialization of a region generally could be counted upon to increase business, enhance economic conditions, and help stabilize traffic flow."[56] Regional industrialization also depended upon building the right kind of social and economic infrastructure. Before investing, client businesses needed to know that they could secure reliable access to raw materials, natural resources, labor, technology, and markets. Railroads therefore not only promoted the feasibility of business development but also secured the land and then colonized it to ensure its future industrial development.

Prosperous railroads such as the Southern Pacific and the Union Pacific were particularly adept at setting aside land for settler housing, industrial parks, and warehouses and orchestrating political support for the massive irrigation and energy projects needed to develop the west. Just as importantly, they knew to foster the right kinds of facts and thinking—that is, the knowledge to justify development. The railroads encouraged chambers of commerce to undertake their own studies "to determine the needs of their communities for new businesses and to discover those resources and other attractions that might be of interest to enterprisers."[57] Because marshaling resources on such a scale exceeded the capacity of even the largest railroads, the national railroads continually recruited government and private investors to support their projects. They undertook "educational" campaigns to mobilize political support for their projects and lobbied government for regulations and policies that made railroad subsidies appear to be natural, despite the bitter dissent such subsidies attracted in many quarters. Their campaigns to enlist government support, or to thwart what they perceived to be government interference, accumulated and refined their knowledge of the best techniques for managing government and shaping land planning policies.

That knowledge was several decades old when C. C. headed west. Policies that had granted the railroads as much as 131 million acres of federal public land and 49 million acres in state lands were the founding act that had ushered these private corporations into existence. Government subsidies followed land giveaways. The railroads effectively deployed nationalist rhetoric to persuade voters and policymakers of the need for these entitlements and their government-sponsored monopolies. They argued that, because the railroad contributed to economic growth and "speeded the settlement of the west by from ten to fifteen years," citizens and policymakers should look upon their monopolies as "natural" necessities of a healthy nation.[58] Between 1873 and 1885, for example, the Union Pacific simultaneously sold a commodity (real estate) and a discourse (the nation-building benefits of developing the 12 million acres it had obtained from federal and state authorities) by means of 9.1 million pieces of literature, a figure that does not include the railroad's periodicals, free western exploration tours, and exhibits at Philadelphia's Centennial Exposition.

Not to be outdone, the Southern Pacific used its vast rail network and administrative resources to circulate both promotional literature and people. It established three immigration houses in Texas that offered free board and temporary jobs to men like the young C. C. Stafford, even providing movable cars for transporting families at reduced rates.[59] In 1917, the SP claimed to operate a fifty-man railway development department, the largest in the United States, with an annual budget of 225,000 dollars.[60] But the Southern Pacific and the Union Pacific did not produce and circulate their knowledge without assistance. Despite intra-railroad competition, the saturating effects of pro-railroad propaganda meant that support for railroad development came to seem overwhelmingly rational to municipal, state, and federal legislatures, as well as to the courts. Earlier critics had been bent on exposing the railroad's monopolistic land avarice, but they had underestimated the industry's cultural influence on the development of the western states. In addition to helping manufacture California's image as the promised land, the Southern Pacific and the Union Pacific patiently constructed an elaborate knowledge-generating system that created the "truths" upon which the state's industrial planning and development were founded.

These narrative strategies, however, do not show the full range of signifying activities in which railroad agents engaged. Nor do they show how their publicity expenditures leveraged millions of dollars in government-subsidized railroad promotion, nor how railroad agents acted as both official and unofficial lobbyists, nor how they persuaded chamber of commerce groups and newspapers to underwrite railroad research. Neither can we estimate the value of railroad-friendly laws that were extracted by means of threats to deny service, free passes to legislators and journalists, unreported bribes and plum jobs, and freight discounts for friends. The same goes for the shadow partnerships that the railroads arranged with private citizens to dispense favors or secure land for their development agendas. Historian William Deverell writes that the railroads often "helped local investors accumulate land for industrial location by acting as a 'straw-party' to preserve the identity of their clients."[61] The Southern Pacific proved especially skilled at these off-the-books real estate development techniques.

When coupled with their power to bring real estate customers to their projects, the railroads' ability to plan, subdivide and sell land, and even build new cities, must have seemed godlike. They were among the first to map subdivisions, thus dictating how and where development would occur. The knowledge produced by and for the railroads, and the techniques they perfected to mobilize and apply that knowledge, thus seemed to guarantee a new life for young men such as C. C. Stafford.

That vision had already influenced a previous generation of eager entrepreneurs. In 1882, a group of Los Angeles businessmen, organized as the Society for the Promotion of Manufactures, decided that Wilmington, California, should be the future site of LA's deepwater port. Now that the SP had completed its southern route through Arizona, these businessmen sketched out their vision of the region's industrial destiny in *Los Angeles Times* articles laden with booster rhetoric. Although the SP's Henry Huntington favored a harbor in Santa Monica, *Times* owner General Harrison Gray Otis and the city's new business elite feared that that alternative would be detrimental to their Los Angeles interests. Eventually, the David in this fight—Otis's emerging local business powers—prevailed over the railroad Goliath. What interests me here, however, is not the battle itself but the business society's vision. Regardless of members' sympathies in that contest, the society as a whole looked toward a not-so-distant future when Southern Pacific trains would haul wares from ships hailing from Manila and Shanghai down its southern road to points in Arizona and Texas, all the way to the docks of New Orleans, and from there by ship again to Liverpool. The *Times* found the railroad's strategic vision irresistible, declaring:

> Connecting at Wilmington with Australia, New Zealand, China, and Japan, the position of Los Angeles will always be unrivaled, possessing as it does the shortest line across the continent within the United States, and through the most eligible pass, geographically, in the whole Sierras. . . . Los Angeles is admirably situated as a distributing point for manufactured goods, especially so, in view of the fact that within the territory subservient to it is a diversity and unlimited quantity of raw materials unsurpassed anywhere, many of which, now going to waste, would be an important source of revenue if utilized. The extent of the territory which can be rendered commercially subservient to Los Angeles depends upon her ability to furnish goods at lower rates than competing points, hence the importance of inaugurating extensive and diversified manufacturing industries.[62]

Heard with our ears today, the article's pronouncements transparently betray its backers' imperialist ambitions. But rendering the vast western territories "commercially subservient" makes sense if we remember that the region's military conquest had been consolidated only a few decades earlier. The description of a bounty of "raw materials" that were "going to waste" is a narrative of manifest destiny, which justified the conquest of less civilized peoples because they were such miserably poor stewards of evident riches. The authors also drew upon the California-as-Eden motif to boost their project's virtues in the eyes of would-be investors. But Los Angeles was not yet Eden: it was an arid city without enough water to support the population required to run this touted manufacturing sector. Moreover, despite the confident assurance with which the authors inventoried Wilmington's possibilities, the harbor fight was far from over. Yet their fevered imaginings anticipated the elements—manufacturing, distribution, and international trade—that eventually did transform Los Angeles into the nation's leading twentieth-century industrial city.

In 1913, with the selection of the port's locale all but settled, the Los Angeles Board of Harbor Commissioners soberly reaffirmed elite concerns for that decade: "Los Angeles is destined to be one of the really great ports of the world." It was the board's job to implement the material, technical, and political infrastructure to ensure that the harbor would "build up great commerce for this city and the territory tributary to it."[63] Their pronouncement did not take a side in the port battle either. Rather, it promised wealth for everyone involved: the railroads that would distribute a bounty of international goods to the nation; the local elite who would build the towns, warehouses, factories, and stores where goods would be made and sold; the residents who would consume these goods.

Nonetheless, Southern California was still decades away from becoming the industrial city-state that would compress a massive global trade network, the nation's largest manufacturing sector, and huge consumer markets into a few counties. Therefore, the region's continued focus on agricultural development represented, as the Society for the Promotion of Manufactures had foreseen, a necessary intermediary step toward that future. Thanks to its booming citrus industry, Los Angeles County had entered the twentieth century as the nation's fastest-growing and most lucrative agricultural and manufacturing sector.[64] Between 1913 and 1945, citrus orchards—most of them planted in fairly inexpensive lemons and Valencia oranges—accounted for only 16.3 percent of agricultural plantings in the La Puente area. Yet their production increases mirrored the valley's phenomenal growth pattern. Valencia production rose from slightly more than two hundred truckloads in 1929 to nearly eight hundred in 1945. Similar patterns were recorded for lemons, Washington navel oranges, and grapefruit.[65] (A single truckload contained 462 packed boxes of oranges or grapefruit and 406 packed boxes of lemons.)

The Southern Pacific, which had distributed literature promoting citrus farming and had laid track for the valley's citrus haulers, could take substantial credit for the citrus industry's success. So after having successfully exploited its freight-hauling formula, the railroad turned to the landscape's secondary opportunities. By 1907, the SP was offering a vacation tour through the valley, which it advertised in its magazine, the *Inside Track*, with a map showing the railroad track as "The Way through the Wonderful Fruit and Flower Garden of Southern California."[66]

In 1872, the Southern Pacific obtained its right-of-way through the La Puente Valley, the narrow basin that roughly parallels the larger San Gabriel Valley on its western side. By 1888, it had completed its connection to Los Angeles from the east. A forerunner of the Union Pacific had laid track on the southern flank of the creek in 1902.[67] Anyone riding the SP line through La Puente in 1906 would have discovered what must have seemed an immense and intricate garden tended by invisible hands.[68] The valley's Mediterranean latitude, its bounty of pure groundwater, and the topographic convolutions created by encircling mountains and hills created microclimates perfectly suited to citrus and avocado growing. Just below the point at which the west-facing San Gabriel Mountains shot upward, shiny bands of lime-green lemon trees and taller, almost black-leafed avocado groves girded the foothills at an elevation above the frost zone. Underneath this band of trees, a belt of bushy Washington navel and Valencia orange groves snaked in and out of view. Lower still, where the frost danger increased, farmers planted less profitable and therefore less prestigious walnut groves and vineyards as well as fields of alfalfa, wheat, oats, and barley.[69] Livestock grazing and a new dairy industry filled out the remaining lowland spaces.

The valley's settlement pattern reflected its topography. Wealthy citrus farmers lived in the warmer, frost-free foothills, where they cultivated valuable Washington navel oranges. C. C.'s mill served the lowland farmers who occupied the valley's economic middle rung—people whom California's famed chronicler, Carey McWilliams, has labeled the "in-between folks." Neither the in-between folks nor the citrus elite wanted the farm workers (primarily Mexican and Japanese laborers) as neighbors; but soil conditions, scattered microclimates, and the year-round demands of navel orange groves required a resident workforce. Labor camps, barrios, and affluent townships thus clustered around the valley's citrus groves.[70] The high prices that citrus fetched also ensured the profitability of relatively small farms. In 1929, the owner of a ten-acre citrus farm unburdened by debt could expect to net as much as 2,900 dollars, or four times more than the average American's per capita income. Not surprisingly, many of the valley's orchard owners found themselves able to live out the fantasy of the Jeffersonian gentleman farmer, blending the ideals of democratic self-reliance with scientific crop husbandry and genteel suburban living.

Citrus farmers used science-tinged rhetoric to express their sense of class entitlement and justify racial segregation. In 1916, for example, *California Citrograph* writer O. F. Cook argued for a natural eugenics based upon citrus farming, in which "the human individual attains a more normal acquaintance with the environment and a full endowment of the intellectual and social faculties of this [white] race." The tone is uplifting; yet as historian Matt Garcia writes, "Cook espoused the belief that nonwhite people would eventually become extinct through natural selection."[71]

C. C. Stafford did not need to read Cook's articles to recognize that El Monte and the La Puente townships condoned racial segregation or that La Puente ranked near the bottom of the San Gabriel Valley's social hierarchy. The valley's power relations had been written on the social landscape since conquest. The text was clearly legible when he arrived, and his son grew up reading it.

The Narrative of Race

La Puente, one local history claims, began as a bent bamboo foot crossing over San Jose Creek that grew into a small cluster of ranches and farms with a granary that sustained the San Gabriel Mission after 1771. Its population began to grow after 1824, when the Mexican government distributed land to encourage settlement in the La Puente Valley, which by then had earned a reputation for rich soil. The Secularization Proclamation of 1834 accelerated this process by redistributing 50,000 acres of mission lands. The Mexican government granted some of the acreage to John Rowland and William Workman, Anglo ranchers who arrived in 1841 from New Mexico. By July 1845, Rowland and Workman, now Catholic converts naturalized as Mexican citizens, were marrying into elite Mexican families, a tried and true strategy for joining the landed gentry.[72]

Basque herders with names such as Vejar also settled there. Later, near the end of that century, a wave of Swiss, Italian, French, Portuguese, and Spanish Basque immigrants arrived. These European immigrants, with names such as Ferrero, Pellisier, Didier, Iriarte, and Perez, carved out niches in ranching and dairy farming; and by the 1920s, they were hiring Mexican and Japanese workers for their orchards, ranches, and dairies.[73]

La Puente's multiethnic population was notably different from the San Gabriel Valley's first officially white-only city, El Monte. Yet La Puente's relatively greater diversity did not stop the town from segregating its housing after the 1920s or from concentrating its Mexican community into an area between Central Avenue and Valley Boulevard.

On arriving in California, C. C. settled in El Monte. Although the community lacked Louisiana's population of poor white and African American sharecroppers, its demography would have seemed familiar. El Monte took pride in segregating its schools and passing zoning ordinances and restrictive covenants to segregate its housing.[74] Residents made sure that Mexican workers employed on nearby orchards and farms slept out of sight in the work-camp barrios known as Hicks Camp, Las Flores, and Medina Court.[75]

Segregation in twentieth-century El Monte had grown out of the nineteenth-century Anglo conquest of Alta California, and the pro-slavery sympathies of its townspeople. As late as 2005, a visitor to the El Monte Historical Museum could find remnants of that history in the museum's giveaway pamphlet, the *Gazette*.[76] Its front-page article, "'Monte Boys' Were Feared Vigilantes of Pioneer Days," nostalgically recalled the exploits of the Monte Boys, a vigilante group known for its anti-Mexican violence. While not explicitly condoning racial hatred, the article does nonchalantly establish a bond of identity between the town's male residents and the gang's membership:

> El Monte men were called by surrounding neighbors, including those in the Pueblo de Los Angeles, "The Monte Boys." Mere mention of them brought instant respect and trepidation.
>
> There were many hangings and it was these, according to old stories, where the Monte Boys shone. A man did not have to be convicted by courts—the boys took it into their own hands more often than not.
>
> The story is told that when the Los Angeles boys had a job to do, of which they were a little doubtful, they would send a call to Monte for the boys. As they came riding over the river the cry would go up, "Here come the Monte boys" and excitement began![77]

As it strives to evoke a bygone era, this last sentence makes the boys seem more like harmless summer picnic guests than a lynching party. The *Gazette* article thus clearly ties itself to the Monte-Boys-as-saviors narratives that once appeared in the *El Monte Herald*, a defunct weekly now archived at the museum, as well as in other local histories. Fred Love, the museum's research librarian responsible for the *Gazette* article, had, until he left his post, served as one of the last living links to these narratives. Like his nineteenth-century predecessors, Love framed the gang's practices in the rhetoric of rough justice, the extralegal rationale that embraced suspension of the rule of law as a pragmatic method of civilizing the west. His wistful remembrances acknowledged that the Monte Boys "were considered a vigilante group, but whenever a law was broken and they started to riot, they caught the villain, and they hung him. They didn't bother with trials, like nowadays, where the criminal has more rights than the victim."[78] Love's reference to the unreasonably extravagant demands of due process expressed a nostalgic yearning for a less complicated time when a vote for mob violence was no cause for shame.

He did not invent that nostalgia, however. Love had lived long enough to hear stories about the Monte Boys and to witness El Monte's demographic transformation. His town, after all, had sent fourteen of its sons to fight for the Confederate cause, housed a Nazi party office into the 1970s, and once boasted a 90-percent "white" population which was now more than 78-percent Latino and increasingly subject to Mexican political leadership.[79] His remembrances also drew from early twentieth-century texts archived at the museum—local histories such as Harold D. Carew's, who wrote in 1930 that "bandits and killers are afforded every loophole of escape from punishment, with the assistance of lawyers miscalled 'officers of the court,' who compound the crimes by invoking 'technicalities.'"[80] The museum's archives paralleled Love's Monte Boy recollections in practically every detail, an echo he tried to downplay.

Standards of decorum in C. C.'s day did not require such modesty, however. His peers heard and matter-of-factly shared these stories. They listened to the radio sermons of Fighting Bob Shuler, who described Mexicans as "diseased of body, subnormal intellectually, and moral morons of the most hopeless type."[81] This knowledge of racial inferiority was also disseminated through the city's official policies and residents' front-porch conversations. C. C. encountered it in the newspapers and magazines he read, the people he hired, the contracts he signed. He saw it in the pastoral landscape he scanned from a train and the way in which white men used money and technological know-how to transform his valley into a leading agricultural and oil producer.

These racial narratives may have also waited for him in the rafters of the hay barn he had recently acquired on Main Street and Hoyt Avenue. Once, not so long ago, the Monte Boys had coiled hanging ropes around those rafters.[82] The *Times* acknowledged that legacy in 1925 when C.C. replaced the "landmark" barn with a "modern brick structure." The article quoted unidentified "old timers" who noted that "'lynching parties' are reported to have been held within its walls." It's hard to imagine that C. C. missed that newspaper story. He may even have passed along the tidbit to promote his business.[83]

When Jim Stafford took over his father's business, his ability to prosper in his new role required a mastery of ranching, property, and race. He needed to learn the local languages of racial and class exclusion if he hoped to maximize the privileges of his white male status. But he would need more than that legacy could teach him before he could acquire the wealth and power he had expected, but did not get, from his father. Therefore, until he learned what else he needed to know, Jim and Lefty would struggle to make the mill "financially sound again" but certainly not "rich from the hay and grain business." As Jane said, "her husband made his millions [afterward] with the incorporation of the City of Industry."[84]

CHAPTER 3

IN THE SCHOOL OF POWER

*If the cathedral was the Age, then a formidable explosion had indeed over-
thrown its most solid walls.*

—Alejo Carpentier, *Explosion in a Cathedral*

Jim Stafford's civics education continued under the tutelage of Los
Angeles County's infamous and visionary supervisor Herbert Legg. Legg
represented the first district, a huge political-economic jurisdiction that
stretched east from downtown Los Angeles, following the contours of the
San Gabriel Valley, to the San Bernardino County line. The LeRoy, New
York, native held that powerful position for nearly three terms—from
1934 to 1938 and again from 1950 to 1954—practically a political lifetime,
until a heart attack ended his career.

Jim's habits of secrecy obscure the early roots of his relationship with
Legg, but their first contact appears to have occurred in the early 1950s via
several lifelong friends who were Legg staffers.[1] The most likely matchmaker was Robert S. Rope, then an administrative assistant on Los Angeles
County's powerful regional planning commission. Jane Stafford credits
Rope with cultivating her former husband's interest in politics. Suddenly,
she said, Jim "began attending political functions and fundraisers that
had previously meant nothing to [him]. . . . [He] got involved in politics
because he saw it as a way to make money. Bob Rope showed him the way
and [Jim] took it from there."[2] Jane herself never understood what either
Legg or Rope saw in her husband, whom she deemed to be unqualified for
government service.[3] Yet clearly they sensed he had the necessary qualities
to help them drive Industry toward incorporation, and Legg appointed
him to the regional planning commission in early January 1954.[4]

Why was Legg interested in Jim Stafford? Surely real estate was a major reason. Along with his family and friends, Jim owned significant acreage in the La Puente Valley, which was located in the middle of Legg's district. Rope's job required knowledge of the biggest property owners in the supervisor's district, and he certainly would have passed on that information to his boss. Just as important, the Stafford family had a history in the corridor, and Jim would be likely to inspire the loyalty and respect of the smaller property owners that Legg would need to recruit to the cityhood campaign.

But another fact is also clear: the frantic land rush sweeping through the La Puente Valley was threatening to devalue Jim's property holdings if he didn't find some way of taking action. After 1945 the number of subdivision plans submitted for the valley's southeastern quadrant increased significantly, as did newspapers articles promoting the land boom. Even before the end of World War II, returning GIs were searching for ways to escape from congested metropolitan Los Angeles, with its increasing population of ethnic and racialized minorities, and to raise families in the new pastoral suburbs. To attract this clientele, postwar Los Angeles bankers, real estate developers, newspaper publishers, and politicians revived the previous decade's alluring sun-drenched narratives. Real estate retailers promised their customers the wholesome virtues of hobby farming, a small-town lifestyle defined by personal relationships, responsive local government, and the racial and class exclusivity needed for the invention of a respectable middle class. Federal housing policies condoning the creation of racially exclusive housing developments and restrictive housing covenants underlay these "vanilla suburbs."[5] It did not occur to policymakers that their exclusionary goals would some day clog freeways with traffic and carpet the valley with shoddy tract homes and poorly designed communities.[6]

Not all of the valley's large landowners saw the onslaught as a chance to fleece a new class of suburban suckers. Land adjacent to the Southern Pacific and Union Pacific lines was too valuable to clutter with houses. Some of the valley's other absentee landowners also worried about the trend. During World War II, they had been planning for industrial development in the valley. As part of a strategy to decentralize arms production, weapons factories had begun to relocate outside the Los Angeles city limits; and wartime publicity scares had convinced military planners of the region's susceptibility to aerial bombing and the need to scatter and duplicate these factories to make them less vulnerable. Planners reasoned that by breaking up assembly lines into smaller units, factories could continue to pump out weapons even if some plants were destroyed.

Pastures of Arsenals

Weapons manufacturers were on the lookout for new contracts, while local government was on the lookout for new growth; and both groups jumped at this new rationale to spread weapons production beyond the Los Angeles city limits.[7] W. A. Smith, the Los Angeles County supervisor representing the La Puente Valley at the war's end, made a pitch to manufacturers at a meeting with local newspaper editors. Smith, the same the supervisor who had failed in 1939 to persuade his colleagues to reintroduce the early-1930s deportation tactic of cutting Mexicans off from county relief, now proposed to reserve the valley as a future industrial district. He highlighted its strategic reserves of vacant land, its "two trunk lines of transcontinental railroads," its proximity to metropolitan Los Angeles, and a postwar population boom that would increase demand for industrial "jobs and goods." He also coyly mentioned that "railroad leaders and county capitalists were interested" in the plan—his way of hinting that he had their backing.[8] Given the Southern Pacific's interest in bypassing crowded downtown rail yards by creating a new line through the supervisor's district, these supportive "railroad leaders" may themselves have invented the plan. In any case, Smith's presentation promoted LA's growing role as a clearinghouse for goods hauled between the southwestern and southern states, northern Mexico, and the ports of Asia. Increased rail traffic through the valley's rail corridor, he reasoned, would make the proposed industrial district attractive to factory developers eager to hook up to a region they already recognized as the "control center for western resources and products."[9]

The Southern Pacific confirmed Smith's argument at the end of 1944, when it told stockholders that the explosion of arms-production industries during the war would create postwar prosperity in Southern California. Company president A. T. Mercier told stockholders that "the war has brought vast industrial development and accompaning influx of population to this territory, [which promises] a substantial increase over prewar years in industrial and other activity and consequently railroad traffic." Wartime resource rationing, labor shortages, and regulation were giving way to freight tonnage gains fueled by increased industrial and agricultural production in the southwestern and southern United States and northern Mexico.[10] The subsequent removal of warehouses and distribution centers from downtown Los Angeles to the suburbs meant that the SP would need to build switching yards in or near the new industrial suburbs where they expected cargo amounts to surge. In 1951, the railroad formally announced its plans for the Puente Bypass, which would run southeast from the line connecting San Pedro and Long Beach to downtown Los Angeles and then northwest to connect at a right angle with Southern Pacific's main Yuma line at sleepy La Puente's doorstep. The SP began to build a new switching yard immediately south of the bypass, with room for eight sidings and enough acreage to triple the yard's size if freight volume warranted it.[11]

Because it allowed shippers to shorten freight transit times from the ports by three days, the project proved to be a wise one. Six years after the bypass was built, traffic passing through the valley had risen to 40,000 railcars a month. Meanwhile, the recently completed San Bernardino Ten freeway, which paralleled the valley's eastern flank, and plans for the Pomona Sixty freeway, which would parallel the valley on its western flank, promised similar growth opportunities for Southern Pacific's trucking operation.[12] Not surprisingly, the SP instructed its agents to buy investment property in the corridor and to install spurs for factory and warehouse owners who wanted them.

But Southern Pacific now needed to protect its infrastructure investments from suburban encroachment. The railroad could not afford to let uncontrolled home building interfere with its operation of the Puente Bypass and its new switching yard or influence how it served its industrial customers. Records of the SP's rare words and numerous deeds strongly suggest that if the railroad had not previously decided to carve out a new city to protect the corridor, it was certainly ready to consider that option in 1954, when it completed the bypass.[13]

Implementing such a directive required the support of local property owners; and at some point, Jim Stafford volunteered to recruit them to support the idea of an exclusively industrial city. Given his fear of public exposure, he may have required some coaxing. But the Southern Pacific and the Union Pacific, both of which would later back the city's incorporation, were not novices at this game. When the time seemed right, they ratified Legg's decision and recognized Jim as a made-to-order leader with excellent grassroots credentials. He had inherited the gratitude of local ranchers and dairy owners who recalled the feed and hay his father had sold them on credit during the Depression. He had also inherited some helpful silences because the property owners that C. C. had foreclosed on were no longer around to run him down for his allegedly predatory lending. The surviving property owners knew that Jim shared their rural values, that he was an authentic good old boy who could keep his word and hold his liquor. Just as important, at least from the perspective of the valley's large property owners, Jim shared Supervisor Legg's fierce determination to cash in on the valley's development opportunities.

Although the details of his courtship remain unrecorded, Legg clearly realized that Jim could help him achieve his planning objectives in the San Gabriel Valley. But Jim wasn't the only student in Legg's class. By the early 1950s, growing demand for new housing, factories, and warehouses was bringing developers into areas they had passed over in earlier booms. Legg and his colleagues already knew that their planning policies could stoke that demand. They soon discovered that fostering suburban development in their district could also increase the county's planning authority and revenues, and therefore its power, because it made homeowners more dependent on county services.

With rare exceptions, historians and journalists have relied upon a handful of narratives to interpret Southern California's suburban development in the postwar period. The region's developer elite generated the most prevalent of these narratives, portraying the region as a dream factory, a sun-drenched Eden cultivated by heroically visionary men of business or science to fuel the demand for growth. County supervisors embraced that philosophy so thoroughly they made it their motto, which they engraved in gold like a biblical commandment in the Los Angeles County Board of Supervisors meeting hall: "This County Is Founded on Free Enterprise. Cherish and Preserve It."[14] Supervisors portrayed themselves as the champions of capitalism, a role that made their cozy relations with developers appear to be downright wholesome and undercut their occasional critics, whom they saw as un-American and Communist-inspired.[15] For at least five decades after World War II, free enterprise in the "vacant" suburbs equaled rampant real estate subdivision and land development. County officials eagerly encouraged and subsidized this business because it bolstered their authority to run their districts like private fiefs.

The supervisors had little to fear from voters. Their predecessors had engineered a jurisdictional system that limited electoral competition in the incumbent's favor. As long as they routinely harvested 90 percent or more of the campaign contributions, most of it from developers, the supervisors did not lose their seats. They knew their would-be challengers would have to surmount the difficult hurdle of drawing comparable sums from sources already committed to them. Not surprisingly, only eighteen officeholders shared five supervisors' seats from 1945 to 1990, with average tenures of fourteen years on the board. "Most [supervisors] either retired voluntarily or died in office," writes election historian J. Morgan Kousser.

"Their margin over their chief opponents has averaged a whopping thirty-six percent, and they have usually gathered a sufficiently large majority (not just a plurality) of the vote to avoid November runoffs."[16] Because supervisors spent only a fraction of their war chests to win reelection, they could easily afford to bankroll parties, candidates, and political causes. These officeholders, particularly those who were Republicans, thus operated as political bankers who funded the local, state, and national party apparatus, effectively selecting candidates and causes and underwriting the production of ideology for electoral dissemination.

The county's jurisdictional and budgetary system reinforced the supervisors' hold on power by giving them wide discretionary powers to control services provided in their districts. A supervisor could reward a neighborhood by granting it county-funded improvements such as streetlights, libraries, recreation facilities, sewers, sheriffs' substations, clinics, or hospitals, many of which might now bear officeholder names. In a county as large as Los Angeles, one supervisor could rule the fate of a district that often exceeded the population and area of a large city; and gerrymandering controlled the political balance of each district to perpetuate this system of political patronage.

A developer who planned a housing project knew that his district supervisor could decide whether or not the project would receive the expensive infrastructure investments necessary for success: adequate sewage services, street signs, water, electricity, county-maintained roads, flood control, zoning exemptions, and fire protection. Developers logically responded to such concentrated power with generous and repeated campaign donations, an arrangement that suited both parties because it left little room for citizen interference. The biggest contributors expected their money to buy them the opportunity to write zoning laws or design the infrastructure to support their suburban residential and industrial development projects. The supervisors knew that fragmented jurisdictional authority made it difficult for cities to check their decisions beyond municipal boundaries. The county's maze of bureaucratic departments and regulations, the board's obfuscating business practices, and the complications of traveling from an affected suburb to an early-morning board meeting downtown further shielded the supervisors from the critical eyes of ordinary residents.[17]

Legg's rise to power occurred during the heyday of this supervisor system. He was a lifelong Democrat who had made his money by subdividing orange groves, and his tendency to equate developer interests with the public interest was natural. His investment experiences, socially mirrored by his Jonathan Club membership, made it easy for him to understand his fellow developers, a sympathy that got him into trouble at least once before he died. According to Kenneth Hahn, his rival on the board during the early 1950s, Legg also deserves credit for reinforcing the legal foundation of Industry's single-use structure and the political technology for implementing its incorporation.[18]

The Devil's Bidder

Jim Stafford has mostly been viewed as the power behind Industry's throne, a perception that emerged after Legg, the railroads, and other large property owners made him their leader. But Supervisor Hahn, who saw Legg operate up close, never bought that story. He told a *Times* reporter in 1984 that the new city's "[incorporation] plan was conceived and executed by Herb Legg" and no one else. Given Legg's own accomplishments, Jim's behavior and comments on the commission seem instead to cast him in the role of a bright student who learned to use county planning policy to advance the interests of large property owners, himself included. As one observer wryly said, Legg did "the devil's work" of developing Industry's governmental technology, while Jim did "the devil's" bidding, using his face, voice, and hearty handshake to install that technology.[19]

No doubt, Jim's two-year stint on the commission also taught him the minutiae of bureaucratic procedure. He learned that such specialized knowledge, when carefully deployed, could leverage more influence than any single business could muster on its own. He owed these discoveries to good timing. Legg's new legal-political technology was rupturing the land-planning status quo that had dictated growth during the Depression and war years, and Jim was lucky enough to be at the supervisor's side when he and a handful of administrative technocrats were dismantling and reassembling the functions and purposes of local government in ways that made previous attempts seem timid by comparison.

Legg and his fellow real estate developers knew they could make fortunes by building homes for newcomers. In this they were no different from entrepreneurs during previous land booms. What made this boom unique is that developers were focusing on the county's last remaining quadrant of undeveloped land; and they calculated that whoever put in the last housing tracts, freeways, shopping malls, and factories would reap untold wealth from the county's rapidly growing population. Weapons manufacturers had already touched off a demographic explosion in Southern California, and local government and corporate developers were betting on population growth as the fuel that would power the home-building industry.[20] But capitalizing on growing land values required a clever maneuver: developers needed to form new cities with which to subsidize and facilitate their plans, yet they also needed to avoid excessive voter interference and prevent meddling older cities from spoiling their big chance.

Therefore, they moved to organize homeowners to demand the creation of new cities, usually in the name of local control, to block interference from revenue-jealous older cities. Originally, Legg and his fellow supervisors saw these land-owner revolts as a threat to the county's formidable bureaucracy, which had grown large and powerful in the course of administering to 5 million people within a twenty-five-mile area.[21] A crop of new cities might not only reduce the need for county services but also cut into the county's tax-collecting power just when property values were surging. The older cities, for their part, resented the county for levying property taxes from their resident homeowners to pay for infrastructure and services in the new suburbs mushrooming beyond their political boundaries.

Not surprisingly, these conflicting agendas and fears created a climate of mutual suspicion in which county government, cities, and developers jumped to defend their individual interests in the courts and the state legislature.[22] At first, the county responded to these challenges by trying to discourage new incorporations, but it soon realized that it needed to redirect the movement to its advantage. Then Legg and the developers stumbled onto a solution out in the bean fields north of the city of Long Beach.

Inventing Lakewood

In 1950, developers Ben Weingart, Mark Taper, and Louis Boyar had acquired (with partial financing from the Federal Housing Administration and the backing of Prudential Insurance) nearly 4,000 acres of farmland in an area known locally as Lakewood. Each partner was already a wealthy man. Weingart owned more than two hundred hotels and apartment buildings; Boyar owned Aetna Construction, which had built homes for defense workers during the war; and Taper's Biltmore Construction had earned a solid reputation as a quality homebuilder.

At some level, Legg must have also felt a certain emotional investment in the Lakewood project. After all, he had had the foresight to build the first housing development there in 1942 and name it the Lakewood City

Tract.[23] Now, eight years later, Weingart's team wanted to advance Legg's dream. In addition to proposing thousands of new tract homes, the men planned to build the largest shopping center in the United States. Borrowing the assembly-line methods of the nearby auto and aerospace industries, the partners built, within two years, more than 10,000 homes around an anchor shopping center, with more than 7,500 homes following soon afterward.[24]

But even before construction began, they demonstrated their genius: they got the county to hand over design authority for the project. In other words, the architects on the Weingart team assumed planning tasks that up to this point had been performed by cities. Like those nineteenth-century capitalists who built company housing for their workers, the Weingart team built a town, which, even without factories, was second in size to the nation's biggest suburban development, Levittown, Pennsylvania.

The city of Long Beach assumed that its greater size and wealth entitled it to annex the new development. In time Lakewood residents would surely see the wisdom of joining a city that had enough offshore oil revenues to build a 10-million-dollar park system.[25] But the Weingart team understood the thinking in Long Beach and knew how to counter its implied offer. The Lakewood proponents hired public relations operative John Todd to head a secret campaign to gather signatures to trigger a cityhood election. Todd also entered into discussions with a Legg appointee over how to finance the new city. He proposed that Lakewood, which lacked a manufacturing tax base with which to build its own administrative center, forgo that cost by contracting with the county for city services. Legg saw promise in the proposal, even though Todd could not show a precedent for a policy that would require the county to continue providing services to new cities.[26]

Making the Truth That Power Needs

Todd's wealthy backers worked quietly to make Lakewood seem irresistible to county bureaucrats and would-be homeowners. In 1953, they hired Boyle Engineering to conduct a feasibility study, which, not surprisingly, recommended that the new city contract with the county for road maintenance and repair services, health, sanitation and police, fire protection, land planning, and library services. As Todd and his backers later confided, the report was very useful. To anyone who would listen, they promoted it as the Bible of the incorporation movement since it supplied the economic rationales and accounting methods with which to represent incorporation campaigns as fiscally reasonable and thus anticipate the voters' biggest objection to new government initiatives.[27]

In January 1954, the county supervisors voted to hold an incorporation election. In the meeting at which the deciding votes were cast, Legg cried out, "Let's give [Lakewood residents] this chance to govern themselves and one of these days they'll be showing us a thing or two about government." But some county officials argued that advancing the new city a year's worth of revenues before it could set up a tax-collecting system constituted an illegal gift of funds. Weeks before the election, they insisted that only new state legislation would permit them to maintain a separate set of books to pay Lakewood's contract services from tax revenues already collected by the county. That objection forced the incorporators to rush to Sacramento to obtain the necessary legislation.[28]

On March 9, residents approved Lakewood's incorporation, reversing twenty years of anti-incorporation policy. After the vote, Legg pushed the county to use the new accounting law to reinforce its relationship with the city. The county created a bureau to offer accounting services to Lakewood, subtracting the costs of those services from the client city's revenues. Suddenly, an entrenched county bureaucracy had been energized.

Sensing an opportunity for expansion and a chance to smooth the path of future incorporations, Legg pressed the new accounting bureau to offer its services to other contract cities, a move that spurred further governmental innovation.[29] Contract cities defended the idea, pointing to the savings they would accrue by purchasing services outside of city hall. But Legg had even bigger plans. If the county could sell its accounting services to cities, why not also sell those services to corporations? Thus, the seeds of private contract law and market economics were sown in the public realm of municipal government. The practice appeared desirable as long as voters and bureaucrats agreed to narrow the definition of government to that of a "consumer service provider."

The success of the contract cities movement rested on California's municipal home-rule provisions of the 1920s, which had given cities the autonomy to build and finance their own water, power, harbor, and airport projects.[30] Aspects of home-rule technology were extended to county governments in the 1930s, giving individual property owners the voting leverage to oppose or support future incorporation efforts.[31] In their contract cities experiment, Legg and his board allies used that added autonomy to amplify the power and reach of county government. These innovations were an exception to the national rule. Whereas the sovereignty of aging eastern and midwestern cities was being checked by voters from below and state and federal authority from above, the city and county of Los Angeles, with their covey of new cities and mega-utilities such as the Metropolitan Water District, were developing techniques to circumvent that stalemate.

The Lakewood plan, with its roots in the medieval city charter, further skewed the definition of municipal autonomy in favor of developer interests. It now supplied developers with the legal tools to reorient an entire city government, not just a branch of it, along the lines of a business-investor and consumer relationship. They then sealed the deal by using their practical, and therefore seemingly superior, business experiences to set up comparisons that inevitably shed an unflattering light on previous New Deal definitions of government. The strategy proved especially effective during the honeymoon decade of the 1950s. In a cold war climate dominated by aggressive anti-Communist and pro-capitalist rhetoric, the modern, technologically efficient corporation embodied the organizational ideal. Corporate practices and values were vaunted as progressive and modern, while public practices and values were dismissed as outdated, inefficient, corrupt, and suspiciously pink.

More than any other innovation in governmental technology of the period, the Lakewood plan made corporate takeover of a city seem to be an entirely feasible idea. Just as the takeover of prisons and hospitals in previous centuries gave government sophisticated new methods for individualizing the surveillance and control of citizens, the Lakewood plan gave government and developers in the San Gabriel Valley new techniques for individualizing the control of an entire governmental apparatus. As one Industry official later said, "to correctly understand . . . the City of Industry, one must conceive of Industry's basic municipal purpose as one of becoming as much like a private industrial developer as possible while retaining full municipal powers to raise taxes, [and] use power available to all cities."[32]

It took several more decades, however, for middle-class voters to understand how the plan's legal technology and fiscal logic would fuel suburban sprawl and enable the first dismemberments of the body of the state. These voters did not see, or did not want to see, how the plan's hidden subsidies gave developers a lucrative homebuilding and -selling formula. To homebuilders, the plan was a one-time profit-making model that depended on a finite resource: the county's so-called vacant land. That short-term dynamic encouraged them to view the last surviving farms and orchards as transient business opportunities. To continue to earn profits, builders needed to rapidly organize new cities to subsidize the next wave

of suburban construction and turn the county's pastures and fields into a
new kind of factory floor.

Clearly, the older cities that resisted the Lakewood plan did not foresee
these dangers in 1954. Instead, non-contract cities argued for fiscal responsibility, an approach that conflated a city's budget with a family's checkbook. These cities complained that the county had tricked its residents
into paying for Lakewood-style cities by enticing them with new suburbs
that artificially subsidized cheap county services.[33] County government
did not deny that it was charging contract cities less than non-contract
cities for county services. Its accounting data showed that this differential
was possible because the county enjoyed economies of scale that gave it
a competitive advantage over smaller cities. Moreover, the sheriff of Los
Angeles County, already an authoritative figure among county's residents
and an aggressive supporter of the Lakewood plan, promised to maintain
the cost of policing contract cities at pre-incorporation levels, a bargain
by any measure. The county in essence promised Lakewood-style cities
a subsidy whose per capita value would increase as its population grew,
and keep their books for free. Yet this controlled release of accounting
data depended on fiscal misrepresentations that remained uncorrected for
almost two decades.[34]

The county's ability to control what people learned about the plan
was a major ingredient of the plan's success. That control started with
the Lakewood developers, who hired a team of professional public relations operatives and lawyers to organize a media campaign that simulated
a citizen's movement. These consultants precisely managed the release
of arguments, factual assertions, and strategic silences. They knew that
homeowners would not invest too much time in evaluating a proposal
if they believed that their sole vote would not decide the contest. Thus,
whenever Lakewood residents showed signs of resisting incorporation, the
team released more "free information," thus wearing away voters' ability
to make independent judgments.[35] As a clincher, the public relations team
secured free home delivery of the *Los Angeles Daily News* for all residents,
a pro-incorporation paper that helped homeowners reach the desired
conclusions.[36]

The developers' campaign success quickly established a formula. First,
publicity operatives persuaded would-be developers to give the public
relations team the authority to make certain tactical and strategic decisions. According to urban historian Gary Miller, the consultants used
that authority to handpick incorporation committees and a first slate of
city council candidates, "making sure all important community groups

were represented and no factions left out."[37] Second, the public relations firms lured homeowners with the promise of financial reward. A vote for incorporation, they claimed, would be repaid in higher land values and cheaper public services. That message encouraged homeowners to think of themselves as consumers and entrepreneurs first and citizens second and to ignore the social and environmental costs of incorporation. Third, the consultants convinced their principal audience, property holders, that incorporation meant a vote for local control.[38] By using the rhetoric of an embattled populous demanding democratic rights, they invited property owners to imagine themselves as players in a patriotic cause, a strategy that stirred up sufficient confusion to hide the motives of the developers who financed the campaign. Fourth, operatives imposed a militaristic chain of command among campaign functionaries, reasoning that petty rivalries between egotistical landowners and political neophytes could be quelled by authoritarian discipline. Finally, public relations consultants understood the dual benefits of recruiting "a few local figureheads in each community" to head their campaign. That leader's visibility did more than simply sustain the illusion of a grassroots mobilization; hunger for social recognition made the person easy to manage.[39] The election-winning formula even factored in ways to manage information flow to small suburban newspapers as they struggled to keep pace with a rash of new incorporations.

In Los Angeles County, more than a dozen incorporation campaigns quickly picked up on the Lakewood formula. And in the middle of this flurry, taking notes with his colleagues in Supervisor Legg's office, was Jim Stafford, who had joined the county's regional planning commission several months earlier. These incorporations were teaching Industry's advocates more than a methodology for winning cityhood. The Lakewood plan gave them a recipe for extracting the most useful technologies of city government, complete with readymade defenses against fiscal accountability critics as well as instructions for putting themselves, the representatives of corporate capital, into power. It must have been a heady moment.

Industry's advocates, however, did not conceive of city incorporation as a one-shot opportunity to build houses and walk away. Instead, they envisioned the ongoing profit opportunities that would flow from permanently controlling the city's formidable planning, financial, and legal apparatus. With the guidance of county government and the railroads, Jim and his circle considered the benefits of running a city populated with factories and of creating a captive market of warehouse and factory owners. By putting their friends in charge of this new city, they could monopolize plum city contracts, leverage their zoning authority into bribes, expropriate prime real estate for themselves, and, if they were lucky, be invited into partnership with the big boys, the corporate entrepreneurs.

And Jim had an important advantage over the Lakewood publicity team. He would launch his cityhood campaign from within county government, with the backing of an already influential supervisor. What he needed to do first was to finish his training in county government and to answer yes to one particular question.

CHAPTER 4

GRADUATION DAY

For work or war, the Anglo world needed him, but it refused to allow him to live among its citizens. Mexicans had to be pushed away and kept at the periphery.

—Alejandro Morales, *The Brick People*

Jim Stafford's first year on the planning commission involved organizing the formation of newly incorporated Lakewood, dealing with the accelerating pace of homebuilding in the San Gabriel Valley, and, most importantly, executing Herbert Legg's idea of reserving portions of the adjoining La Puente Valley for industrial use. At one point, however, in about 1954, when the Lakewood plan began to reveal its potential, Legg and perhaps the railroads decided that creating an industrial city offered the best vehicle for obtaining their desired results. According to Laurence Peck, Industry's first chamber of commerce director, the push for incorporation unquestionably came from the railroads, which needed to secure "a warehouse distribution center to compliment their extensive railroad switching operation in nearby Colton, California."[1] A savvy reader could have gleaned as much from a *Los Angeles Times* item published in May 1954, a few months after La Puente's residents had announced their intention to submit their own incorporation petition. "Both the Southern Pacific and Union Pacific Railroads are aiding in the development of the valley," the business story noted, adding that "Puente is the terminus of the Southern Pacific's $4,000,000 branch line, which will connect the company's main line with the Los Angeles and Long Beach Harbor areas."[2]

The speed at which competing plans for the La Puente Valley appeared suggests that Jim might have felt torn, if only briefly, between defending

his agrarian lifestyle and pouncing on the biggest money-making opportunity ever to come his way. Still, a few of his neighbors actually believed
that he was too much of a rancher to change his stripes. Helen Walsh, a
real estate broker who described herself as an early convert to Industry's
incorporation, recalled that Jim "was initially opposed to . . . incorporating
the area because he thought the rezoning would force his cattle feed yard
on Valley Boulevard out of the area."[3]

Grandfather Vernon

Apparently, Jim sought the advice of Leonis Malburg, mayor of nearby
Vernon, to help him make up his mind. Matthew Patritti, a property owner
whom Stafford recruited to his cause, has credited the mayor with selling
Jim on the benefits of a single-use city. Years later, Patritti recalled that Jim's
longstanding friendship with Malburg and his familiarity with Vernon made
him susceptible to the mayor's advice.[4] No doubt, Malburg reminded Jim,
perhaps during a tour of Vernon, how the SP's main line and spurs had
made his father's milling, warehousing, and feedlot operations possible in
the first place.

Jim would have understood Malburg's point of view. A descendant
of Basque ranchers, the mayor came from the small circle of late-
nineteenth- and early-twentieth-century European immigrants who had
been his father's oldest customers and friends.[5] Perhaps Malburg told Jim
the story of how Vernon got its start in 1905, when John Baptiste Leonis,
a French Basque hog rancher, persuaded the Union Pacific and Southern
Pacific railroads to extend tracks to his city to attract new factories, their
preferred freight-hauling customers.[6] As it had for C. C., rail access
encouraged Leonis to open the Vernon National Feedlot and Stockyards
and operate a feed mill for the cattle he was fattening for slaughter. These
Leonis ventures set the stage for the arrival of new meatpacking plants
and stockyards east of Vernon along new railway spurs and for the Santa
Fe Railroad's expansion of its switching yard in 1912.[7]

No doubt Malburg told Jim how he had improved Vernon's single-use
technology by making the city buy or condemn existing housing to reduce
its residential population, thus eliminating voters who could oppose his
program of unrestricted industrial development. His city had established
the authoritarian ideal of a city without citizens, not so much as a company
town but as a precursor of the corporate city-state. His "policy of negative
population growth" carefully spared the homes of political allies and loyal
employees; he carved out the city's boundaries by reducing a preexisting,

mostly working-class Mexican population of nearly 5,000 residents. By 1980, the city's population had dropped to about one hundred live-in city employees.[8] Not surprisingly, the handpicked employees who now formed Vernon's electorate ensured maintenance of the city's political status quo. These indentured voters depended on city hall for jobs, city-owned housing, and rent subsidies.[9]

Jim knew that he needed to make a decision, however, and he needed to make it soon. In the early 1950s, property owners with the largest holdings between the Southern Pacific and Union Pacific tracks had asked members of the county's regional planning commission to rezone the corridor for industrial development and block further housing construction there.[10] Anticipating a showdown between homeowners and factory owners, the commission had proposed the zoning change in 1953, a year before Jim's appointment. Its solution no doubt reflected the special consulting relationship the commission had cultivated with local industrial developers but not with local homeowners. The planning report noted that the East San Gabriel Valley Industrial Association was "organized to work with the Regional Planning Commission and the Board of Supervisors on this study," yet the commission did not identify either the association's members or who had invited their opinions.

Despite the vagueness of its methods, the commission's intent was clear. They planned to reserve the La Puente Valley's rail corridor for industrial development, a conclusion that the city's official history inadvertently supports. Regional planning commission director Milton Breivogel told corridor property owners at one of their monthly meetings that the commission was proposing "industrial expansion into the area" and that they should form their own city if they wanted "to determine how this industrial expansion would be planned and managed." No date or place is given for this meeting, but it did occur after Jim's January 1954 appointment to the planning commission. Breivogel's meaning was unmistakable. Whether or not property owners liked it, industrial development was coming to the valley, so they might as well take advantage of the opportunity. It appears that Jim was brought in at about this time to close the deal. According to City of Industry history, Jim "was the lead figure in the planning and execution of the city's incorporation," the one with the credibility "to convince the property owners of the viability of incorporation." The city's version does not mention whether he used his position and the resources available to him as a planning commission member to do his persuading since admitting that would implicate him in a serious conflict of interest.[11]

City history, however, doesn't address whether the planning commission had decided on its industrial agenda before Jim's appointment or discuss Supervisor Legg's or the railroads' motives for pushing Industry's incorporation. Certainly it ignores the contract-city technology and other technical advice that Jim received from county staff as well as Legg's original reasons for appointing him to the planning commission. Rather than revealing him as a visionary, then, his emergence as a spokesman for corridor property owners highlights his role as an "active entrepreneur," the term that economic historians John R. Logan and Harvey L. Molotch have assigned to smaller-scale property owners of the period who tried to cash in on investment opportunities created by larger-scale "structural speculators."[12] In this case, the structural speculators—the railroads and other corporate developers—combined capital and political influence to invent government policies that gave permanent advantages to one locale over another. As an active entrepreneur, Jim simply sought to exploit the new land-use values created by the structural speculators who had mobilized county government to rezone the corridor for industrial use and Industry's incorporation.

But to recruit popular support for their plans without alerting the lowly homeowners to their presence, the structural speculators still needed the credibility that Jim had earned among the corridor's middle-rung property owners. These landowners saw themselves at a great disadvantage because they lacked the clout to speculate structurally on their own. It is therefore hard to imagine that Jim and other middle-rung property owners would turn down an offer to play ball with the big boys when the game would give them a chance to profit from a dramatic increase in corridor property values.

But there was another group of players to consider. These La Puente residents didn't know they were crashing the party when they submitted their Lakewood-inspired incorporation petition to the Los Angeles County Board of Supervisors in early 1954. As "serendipitous entrepreneurs," to use Logan's and Molotch's term, the homeowners were "only very marginally entrepreneurs at all," and only because they were lucky enough to own homes near an area slated for development.[13] The professionals needed to step in before the amateurs went too far. So in 1955, while the board of supervisors used administrative procedures to reject La Puente's first petition, the planning commission prepared to rezone most of the agricultural land lying inside the rail corridor for heavy manufacturing and thus shut down further residential development within the corridor.[14]

The proponents of the corridor's industrial future suffered a setback in October 1955, when a county grand jury indicted Legg on felony perjury charges. The indictment alleged that he had lied to the grand jury about accepting a 10,000-dollar bribe from Andrew V. Hohn, a donor who had testified to paying the money to secure a lucrative garbage franchise. In his grand jury testimony, Legg denied ever knowing or meeting Hohn, even though the supervisor acknowledged that his political campaign had received a 2,000-dollar contribution from Hohn in 1950, the biggest gift the campaign had received that year.[15]

Meanwhile, in September, while Legg was dealing with his legal troubles, enthusiastic La Puente homeowners had launched their second incorporation drive, netting enough signatures to file their petition in December. If unaltered, the proposed city of La Puente would include at least 23,000 residents and encircle 17.75 square miles of property, including land that had been recently rezoned for industrial use. The suburb's blue-collar residents realized that locating a city between Los Angeles and the growing economies of the southwestern states would create trade opportunities for the industries popping up inside the rail corridor. Moreover, La Puente's incorporators believed that their plan had a major advantage over Lakewood's: a transportation infrastructure that would ensure long-term industrial development and thus a reliable stream of jobs and revenues generated by one of the county's highest property- and sales-tax bases.[16]

But unlike any of the other Lakewood-style incorporators, La Puente residents did not enjoy the backing of the railroads or other large developers. The industrialists had no intention of undertaking the social costs of running a city, nor did they have any interest in giving La Puente's working class a steady source of municipal revenue. They preferred to defend their own land-planning prerogatives, dismissing the homeowners as a fickle majority that would tire of perpetual factory sounds and smells and be likely to rescind industrial zoning.[17] The homeowners didn't know how to answer this rebuff. Those who had rushed to the suburbs had already embraced the industrialists' philosophy of growth. They failed to realize, however, that their democratic expectation of sharing in the valley's economic planning posed a threat.

Meanwhile, Jim and his fellow commissioners played for time, stalling La Puente's incorporation attempts with technical objections while Industry's proponents quietly organized themselves. To scuttle the first two resident petitions, the commission cited "boundary description errors and inadequately assessed property valuation." Clearly, the fate of the

La Puente incorporators hung upon their incomplete knowledge of incorporation law and Jim's use of his commission position to push quietly for Industry's incorporation. As Chester McIntosh, La Puente's first mayor, told a *Times* reporter in 1984, Legg, with the commission's recommendations in hand, "took our map and cut it down to about half the size. Legg showed hostility right from the start. He just took his finger and outlined what he thought we should do, [which] was all favorable" to the unborn City of Industry.[18]

In January 1956, the board of supervisors approved the La Puente homeowners' third petition but only after Legg had trimmed another 3.2 miles from the city's proposed boundaries. "They emasculated us in terms of people," McIntosh said. "We didn't get any industrial land. Everything along the railroad was zoned into Industry." The only dissenting vote came from Supervisor Kenneth Hahn. The others gave Legg what he wanted because they expected him to return the favor in their districts when they asked him for one. "I don't think there is any question but that there was collusion with some of the members," McIntosh said.

La Puente's supporters fought on, hoping to recoup "their lost tax base" after residents had voted for cityhood. But that chance never arrived.[19] Instead, Legg's success at redrawing La Puente as a lower-middle-class suburb allowed Industry's proponents to make their big play. They enjoyed another boost in February when a jury dramatically cleared their patron of perjury charges. On his deathbed, Legg's campaign treasurer had signed an affidavit in which he accepted all responsibility for taking the bribe. The jury "chose to believe the affidavit, rather than the man who paid the bribe and who testified that Legg himself had thanked him personally for the 'package' in the corridor of the county administration building."[20]

By April 1956, Jim and the regional planning commission, with supervisor and developer backing, had completed an area master plan. Titled "The East San Gabriel Valley: An Area Use Plan," the document laid down rules for future development in the La Puente Valley. In addition to stressing the advantages of the Lakewood subcontracting model, it gave Industry's incorporators a legal instrument for protecting the corridor's agricultural and industrial areas.

The plan's silences spoke even more forcefully than its statements. The commission could have implemented policies to slow homebuilding while still permitting industrial development. Doing so, however, would have required it to reject the half-century's worth of county land-planning practices that had turned Legg and his colleagues into wealthy men. Instead, the commission moved to return control of land planning to corporate developers. Like nineteenth-century treatises on manifest destiny that represented exploitation of the west's mineral wealth and destruction of its forests, streams, and indigenous populations as unavoidable, natural, and necessary, the commission's document took a fatalistic view of growth, claiming, with a hint of regret, that nothing could stop residential, commercial, and industrial development from "rapidly displacing the once omnipresent citrus and walnut groves" and creating "a general urbanization of the valley."[21] In other words, the commissioners had no intention of preventing themselves and the interests they represented from uprooting the valley's last remaining orange groves. They preferred to mourn those losses in advance, on everyone's behalf, as long as they got to drive the bulldozer of development and eradicate unwanted competition from upstart homeowners who thought they deserved a chance to cash in on the land boom.

The commission's control of zoning, its newly minted land-use plan, and its knowledge of the intricacies of incorporation gave Industry's proponents almost all the power they needed to make their dreams a reality. Now, on June 11, 1956, eight days before La Puente residents would vote for cityhood, they presented their own petition for incorporation (which they had quietly drafted while fighting La Puente's) to the county board of supervisors. Aire "Ike" Keuning, chairman of the board of Puente Ready Mix, a cement company inside the would-be City of Industry, recalled years later that Jim then asked "a group of businessmen . . . [to] draft a boundary for the proposed" city.[22] Other property owners later confirmed Jim's role in recruiting, staffing, and funding the campaign to qualify Industry's incorporation petition. He delegated the job of collecting petition signatures to Edward Lustgarten, new owner of the Suzy-Q Ranch, and to his friends Gene Brown and Kenneth Brown, local sanitarium owners who offered decisive aid in the city's formation.[23] Jim's behind-the-scenes orchestration of the petition drive clearly violated the civil servant's pledge he made to put the public before his need for personal gain. Although no record has turned up to confirm it, it is also likely that he found other ways to violate the law, such as lobbying his fellow commissioners or supervisors to delay La Puente's incorporation or whittle down its boundaries. And he would intervene again to advance his cityhood plan.

The railroads, the large landowners, and Supervisor Legg had groomed Jim Stafford to be the patriarch of their proposed city. Now they invented his patrimony. In a brilliant act of economic gerrymandering, they drew Industry's petition map so that the city would include most of the La

Puente Valley's industrially zoned property and transportation network and very few of its residential areas. Such creative mapping was a far-reaching innovation. During the nineteenth and early twentieth centuries, modern nation-states had refined mapmaking and census taking to define, monitor, and control the populations they governed. Industry proponents, by contrast, drew city boundaries to exclude as many small property owners, or voters, as possible while including numerous large properties, more than 50 percent of them owned by absentee landlords. "About 100 registered voters, among a population of 300," would reside within the city's boundaries; and 62 percent of the 577 parcel owners in the proposed eight-mile-long city were large property owners. The assessed value of the property owned by the petition signers totaled 1.3 million dollars; and with property assessed at 58,590 dollars, Stafford and his partners at the mill and feed yard were nowhere close to being the largest landowners. The largest owner, Southern Pacific, reported holdings valued at 265,120 dollars, while the Sunkist Shopping Center, the second-largest owner, reported holdings of 101,650 dollars. The property of the El Encanto Sanitarium owned by Gene H. Brown and his wife was valued at 27,930 dollars.[24]

Yet even though the board supported the concept of an exclusively industrial city, they admitted that Industry's boundary makers had gone too far. The proposed map marked out thin tentacles of included property, many of them drawn down the middle of city streets, whose only function was to attach delectable morsels of real estate to the city's body. The supervisors cut many, but not all, of these tentacles before approving the petition.[25]

Few noticed, or were willing to admit, that corporately owned property, through its voting proxies, had acquired the legal status and protections of citizenship without relinquishing the legal immunities enjoyed by anonymous investing societies. Industry's voters would consist of property owners, many of them ranchers, businessmen, and factory or warehouses owners. Its incorporation would therefore allow capital to completely swallow the functions of citizenship. Corporations would no longer need to buy elected officials to draft and enforce the laws they needed. Capital now had the means, for example, to induce a city to borrow from the financial markets and impose accounting practices and debt repayment terms that served its interests.[26]

The Southern Pacific, whose influence-buying practices early in the century had attracted a bitter voter backlash, had its own motives for welcoming Industry's innovations. Despite its reputation for political omnipotence, the railroad had never succeeded in buying the electorate itself. Ranchers, townspeople, labor radicals, muckraking writers, and rival corporations had strenuously opposed the Southern Pacific, even during the years of its greatest power; and eventually, this rowdy cast of adversaries succeeded in fixing the octopus image that led to Progressive-era reforms to reduce the railroad's influence.[27] Industry's incorporation, however, gave the SP and other corporate interests a technology they could use to redesign part of California without angering too many voters. By the 1950s, as truck transport over freeways and interstate highways quickly diminished the profitability of the rail cargo business, the railroads remembered that they did not need to control politics in Sacramento and the major industrial cities to get what they wanted. They merely needed to control affairs in particular strategic localities.

La Puente's disgruntled homeowners and their supporters did not yet comprehend the consequences of their new disenfranchisement when they vented their anger to the Los Angeles County Board of Supervisors. They made procedural objections claiming that the proposed City of Industry did not include the five hundred resident voters required by state law. Industry's incorporators responded by redrafting their petition to expand the city's boundaries to include the 169 patients and 31 employees of the El Encanto Sanitarium, thus raising the city's population to 629. Critics next argued that the sanitarium's senile or mentally challenged patients could not be counted as legal residents because their diminished capacity prevented them from voting or performing any of the obligations of permanent residency. Industry's friends countered that state law at that time did not specify that voters satisfy specific residency criteria.[28] The county's staff attorney agreed with the Industry backers, saying that the sanitarium's inmates "could be legally counted as inhabitants" regardless of their voting status.[29]

The opinion inflamed further protest before the board of supervisors. At one meeting, Supervisor Hahn argued that Industry's incorporation would "create a town which would employ thousands of citizens of the San Gabriel Valley, but would provide a voice to virtually none of them." Years later Hahn amplified his reasons for opposing Industry's incorpora-tion: "I said then it was a fraud against what our forefathers wanted for a city" because Industry would be a city with "no residents, no churches, no libraries, no hospitals, no jails." But at the same contentious meeting, Legg reminded Hahn that board tradition permitted him to run his district as he saw fit. His remarks were a veiled warning: if Hahn persisted in raising questions, he could not expect to receive Legg's vote when he needed funding for a project in his district. The threat did not deter Hahn from voting against Industry's incorporation, but it did influence the board's other three members, who meekly deferred to Legg.[30]

CHINATOWN PREFIGURED

On November 2, 1956, the property owners, led by Walter F. Pyne, petitioned the Los Angeles County Superior Court to halt Industry's incorporation election, which was scheduled for December. They argued that the sanitarium's inmates had been illegally counted as voting residents so as to "establish a population count of more than 600."[31] In the petitioners' view, the sanitarium's inmates could not be counted as legal residents because they did not own land or rent homes in the proposed city or possess the mental faculties to cast informed votes. But Judge Bayord Rhone agreed with county's interpretation of state law. As long as the patients had been counted in the census, they were qualified to vote in an incorporation election. On December 3, the residents of the proposed City of Industry voted to approve its formation, winning by a margin of 118 to 22.[32]

The El Encanto Sanitarium census eerily prefigures the scene in *Chinatown* in which Gittes discovers that a secret land syndicate has purchased hundreds of San Fernando Valley parcels in the names of unwitting Avalon Retirement Home residents. Industry's creative method of counting the patients of the sanitarium (whose Spanish name translates as "The Enchantment") allowed capital to define the image of the ideal citizen. In Industry, that person was either a wealthy property owner, an employee of a wealthy property owner, or a hospital patient kept in a numbing slumber. The city's legal interpretation of a citizen was so outrageous that it led to the passage of a new law to prevent its recurrence, but by that time Industry had already joined the class of 1957, the year when thirteen new cities were incorporated in Southern California.[33]

Before incorporation could take place, however, Pyne told the press that he intended to appeal the court's decision, which meant that Industry's backers could not rest on their victory. Their enemies could still undo the court decision that had permitted the election to go forward. Sure enough, a few days after the vote to incorporate, the California District Court of Appeals issued a stay ordering the county to halt the city's certification until the court had ruled on Pyne's appeal. The irascible Pyne, who was known for his ranting and bitter missives, now threatened new accusations against Industry's incorporators. His attorneys—Payne Ferguson, who later became a judge on the U.S. Ninth Circuit Court of Appeals, and James F. Judge, who later became an Orange County superior court judge—charged that Jim, in his role as a planning commissioner, had "wrongfully exercised complete and direct control over the report of the Regional Planning Commission on the number of inhabitants, [and] that the mere presence of Stafford on the Regional Planning Commission was per se an exercise of undue influence." The attorneys further accused Jim of knowingly abusing his position on the commission to make decisions that would have increased the value of his property in the proposed city. According to Pyne, Jim accomplished this goal by thwarting the La Puente proponents at every turn and by making decisions that favored the Industry proponents.[34] No doubt, Pyne's attorneys were prepared to argue that it was impossible for a businessman in Jim's position to avoid a conflict of interest when voting on matters that affected his property. In their opinion, his early decision to support Industry's incorporation as a defense against La Puente's designs showed that he had willfully engaged in a pattern of interference and favoritism when voting on boundary disputes concerning both cities.[35]

For Jim, who had already suffered through his father's humiliation in the courts and the press, the suspense of waiting to be subpoenaed must have been intense. It would likely take months, even years, for him to testify if the appeals court judge were to decide to assert his independence and ignore the boosterism that pervaded Southern California politics.[36] The conflict-of-interest allegations, if proven, could lead to a reversal of the lower court's decision and thus prevent Industry's incorporation. As it was, Pyne's appeal had already succeeded in stalling Industry's incorporation drive. "They knew it was going to be years before they could get [the incorporation] certified," attorney James Judge recalled.[37]

THE SOUTHERN PACIFIC'S BACKDOOR MAN

Given these circumstances, Jim and his backers may have been worried enough to ask for help. And help did indeed arrive, in the person of Wilfred W. Steiner, one of the SP's Southern California real estate buyers. His timely intervention consolidated a pact among the incorporators that would outlast their individual members, including both the Southern Pacific and the Union Pacific railroads.

Steiner explained years later, "I was sent down [from San Francisco headquarters] to buy industrial sites of not less than 300 acres. I did buy a lot for Southern Pacific." Attempting to diminish his role in the matter, he added, "I should be a rich man," a reference to the property deals he had passed up while buying for the railroad.[38] But he wasn't shy about helping others; and according to Steiner, he and the railroad were of one mind when it came to supporting Jim's efforts. The SP demonstrated that support by instructing Steiner and a fellow employee to play the parts of old-school straw buyers. In June 1957, the pair bought an option to purchase Pyne's parcel at the same moment that Jim countersued Pyne for libel. Jim's suit was calculated to raise the stakes for the beleaguered property owner and discourage his legal crusade. Attorney Judge recalled that his client, who had never been overly enthusiastic about the lawsuit, now wanted to drop it because he had received an offer from an unidentified buyer. That buyer was Steiner, who, when taking take Pyne's property off his hands, eliminated his participation in the appeal by causing him to forfeit his standing as a property owner.[39]

Robert G. Beverly was one of the attorneys representing the Industry proponents, and he later served as the city's attorney before being elected to the state senate in 1980. Beverly doubted that Pyne's suit could have prevented Industry's incorporation. "I judged the city's methods of incorporating to be valid," he told the *Times* in 1984. "They would have been a city regardless of the suit. [Pyne] was just harassing the city."[40]

But Pyne's attorneys, Ferguson and Judge, held a radically different view of the case. At the time, they saw Pyne as a natural ally. "There was a tremendous amount of politics going on at the time," Judge said. "It was very important for La Puente [to stop Industry]. They were hoping to expand. As it turned out, they [La Puente's leaders] were cut off from . . . any industrial development."[41]

Steiner and his partner immediately sold the option on the Pyne parcel at cost to the city's incorporators. County property records show that Steiner transferred the option to a firm called Canyon Rock Products. No public record listing the firm's principals has turned up, but we do know the name of the notary public who officially recorded the transaction: Glenn R. Watson, lead defense counsel representing Jim and his backers.[42] Steiner had orchestrated the transaction so stealthily that Industry's opponents were shocked when Pyne, "in a surprise move," "asked for a change of lawyers, who then moved for dismissal of the case."[43] Worse, the local press did not discover Steiner's role in the affair until decades later.

Industry's incorporation had survived its first serious challenge. On June 18, 1957, the board of supervisors certified its incorporation election and the formation of a city with 588 official residents. Two days later, Industry's new city council met inside the offices of the Utility Trailer Company, owned by one of the city's co-founders. The council hired Robert S. Rope, the regional planning commission's executive assistant during Jim's tenure, as Industry's first city manager, and Glenn R. Watson, that quick-witted notary public, as Industry's first city attorney.[44]

In 1958, Herbert Legg, the man to whom Jim Stafford and the new city owed so much, died at age seventy, nine months shy of completing his third term as district supervisor.[45] Not surprisingly, the Republican-owned *Times*, which had endorsed the Democrat Legg's pro-growth philosophy, said only good things about him, stressing his role, as both county supervisor and WPA administrator, in building the huge flood-control projects that had ensured wall-to-wall development of eastern Los Angeles County. Every article ignored the scandal that had almost sent him to jail.[46]

Legg's passing did nothing to disrupt the development boom he had presided over or the political infrastructure that was sustaining it. His successor, Frank Bonelli, who cultivated the image of himself as a law-abiding fiscal conservative who despised gambling and Communists, continued Legg's practice of banking tens of thousands of dollars' worth of developers' campaign contributions. Bonelli died with 95,000 dollars of untraceable contributions in his "dinner committee" account and a million-dollar estate he had assembled on a modest 35,000-dollar annual salary.[47] Industry also retained its link to the board of supervisors. Not only did Jim recruit city manager Rope from the county planning commission, but he also maintained his friendship with Hugh Dynes, Legg's former chief deputy, who stayed on under Bonelli.[48] And the city did not forget to reward Steiner for his loyalty. It hired him for a series of plum city jobs, including directorship of the city's chamber of commerce, after he retired from the Southern Pacific.

Nine years after securing Industry's incorporation, Jim admitted to funding and participating in the incorporation campaign and to attempts "to block La Puente's incorporation." The bitter deposition he gave in a 1969 lawsuit filed against the city revealed his personal reasons for wanting "to stay the hell out of a place called Puente." He construed the idea of being forced to pay taxes for schools and libraries that served a growing Latino community as an infringement on his personal liberties: "Doesn't a man have a choice in this country anymore?"[49] Like so many of the other property owners swept up in the Lakewood movement, Jim construed freedom of choice to mean the unfettered pursuit of real estate development to the exclusion of any other public good.[50]

In the decades that followed, La Puente stagnated in its role as a middling suburb with above-average crime and below-average public schools. A basic economic trend emerged to explain the city's underachievement. Like a Siamese twin that slowly starves its less vigorous sibling, Industry kept an increasing share of the wealth they both created. By the early 1970s, La Puente, with its diminished tax revenues, had to settle for whatever jobs its sibling could provide. According to a 1972 survey of Industry's industrial labor force, 4,705 of the workers employed in the City of Industry resided in La Puente, generating more than 52 percent of its wages.[51] As the years passed and La Puente's ability to generate its own revenue sources decreased, it became increasingly vulnerable to any drop in the number and quality of Industry's jobs.

Legg and his colleagues failed, or did not care, to grasp the impact of their innovations: privatized government, suburban sprawl, air and groundwater pollution, freeways crowded with loaded tractor-trailers spewing diesel fumes. In a preview of a rationality that would spread beyond Industry's borders, the injection of contract cities and single-use technologies had excluded an inconvenient and expensive citizenry from its boundaries in the name of preserving the "county's prime industrial land from residential encroachment."[52] That emptying act produced a radically different governmental matrix. Like those experiments in which a cell's DNA is removed and replaced with the genes of another species, incorporation injected knowledge that sparked the gestation of a new governmental creature.

CHAPTER 5

"WE DON'T LIKE THE DIRTY DEAL"

He would look just like a landowner, a feared species in this country due to its aggressiveness and the little consideration it showed for other peoples' lives, as might be gathered from reading the one thousand one hundred pages.
—Horacio Castellanos Moya, *Senselessness*

Jane Stafford did not know that her husband had served on Los Angeles County's regional planning commission until she saw it on a TV newscast that aired in 1967. As she recalled, George Putnam, the flashy KTLA Channel 5 reporter known for his rightwing populism, would "all but call him a 'crook'" during the evening news" for pushing the city to condemn an eighty-acre landfill located within a five-hundred-acre area known as the Little La Puente Hills. Putnam, who loved to defend the little guy against city hall, not surprisingly sided with the landfill owners against the city, which wanted to attach the whole cluster of hills to its narrow body via a threadlike easement it drew down the middle of Azusa Boulevard.

When Jane walked into the kitchen after the newscast to tell Jim what she had just heard, "[he] merely shrugged his shoulders and said something like they can say what they want and you can't do anything about it."[1] The incident, which she related years later to the FBI, reveals more than Jim's penchant for secrecy and the kind of relationship he had built with his wife. Putnam's allegation added a nefarious gloss to Jim's still developing media image, but Jim's resigned response seemed to arise from lessons he'd learned during his father's scandalous treatment in the press. He also knew from his own experience that the media's spotlight would eventually move on to something else. He and his pals would then return to sorting out their plans for their city on a hill: its golf courses and equestrian facilities, a hotel and a conference center, a golf museum, even a wild animal park built on a mountain of trash, an undertaking so big and expensive it would take decades to finish.

This grandiose scheme, which later became the focus of his criminal enterprises, marked a huge leap in both his and Industry's ambitions. Jim and his friends were dreaming big dreams, thanks to the municipal technologies they had begun to master as well as new ones the city was prepared to absorb. But new technologies called for new technicians, and Jim found himself having to defer to their legal, financial, and planning expertise. Decision by decision, each injection of knowledge would slowly complicate and diffuse his authority, a state of affairs that contrasted starkly with his first crude try at cashing in on the city. That controversy flared in 1961, when the Los Angeles County Sheriff's Department announced its intention to build a new sheriff's substation on a 3.3-acre parcel that Stafford owned. The ensuing scandal offers us a glimpse into Jim's idea of a city's purpose and provides our earliest evidence of how he was able to consolidate his influence in Industry.

The episode began when Supervisor Frank Bonelli, Herbert Legg's successor in the first district and Jim's current political patron, decided to persuade the other county supervisors to build the district's next sheriff's substation on Jim's property. Bonelli made his proposition with the knowledge that Industry's neighbor, La Puente, had already offered the county free land so that it could win the substation project.[2] Nevertheless, the county chose to ignore this opportunity to save money and instead offered Jim 80,950 dollars for his property. As a result, Jim was able to earn a tidy profit while stationing a band of property protectors in his city. All's well that ends well, right?

Not exactly. After Jim had expressed dissatisfaction with the county's offer, the Industry city council voted to offer him 134,420 dollars for the property—53,470 dollars more than the county had offered—although they intended to use the land for exactly the same purpose: to install a sheriff's substation inside the city limits. But in order to build such a facility on the property, the county would need to pay for constructing a road through adjacent properties, twenty-three acres of which also happened to belong to Jim. The county agreed to put in the road. Not surprisingly, Jim accepted both the city's price and the new county road, which would increase the value of his unsold property. Then Industry matched La Puente's unbeatable offer, deeding Jim's former property to the county free of charge.[3]

Meanwhile, as these events slowly unfolded, the local press had announced a January 9, 1962, luncheon to be held in honor of visiting Southern Pacific president Donald Russell. Industry billed the event as an opportunity to "foster a closer relationship with the head" of the railroad. "After all," said city manager Bob Rope, "the Southern Pacific tracks run the length of the city and therefore the railroad is a key factor in our future [industrial] development here."[4] The luncheon would be held at the country club, which, although technically open to the public, functioned as Industry's unofficial city hall and a favorite watering hole of the San Gabriel Valley's power elite.

At the luncheon, Russell played up the SP's construction of a million-dollar fruit processing plant. "We want to promote industry here. We are continually seeking ways to hold our operating costs down so we can pass on the savings to the industrialist," he said to the gathering of about 250 people, which included members of the local press, a state legislator, a congressman, and Los Angeles County sheriff Peter J. Pitchess.[5] The sheriff's attendance at that gathering was no surprise; after all, Industry was giving him free digs for his garrison. The department's subsequent participation "in a land swap involving [the Southern Pacific] and the West Hollywood sheriff's station" could have been another motive for his presence.[6]

A few weeks later, a group of Industry's smaller property owners, middle-rung entrepreneurs who wouldn't have been invited to Russell's luncheon, seized upon the substation deal as the basis for a civil lawsuit in which they charged the mayor and the city council with conspiracy to defraud taxpayers. The nine plaintiffs intended to use the suit as a bargaining chip in their efforts to overcome city opposition to a shopping center development they proposed. But for the moment, they took the high ground, arguing that city funds should not have been used to enrich a single property owner when La Puente had already offered free land for the substation.[7]

Notably, that "single property owner" wasn't just anyone. For the first time, Jim Stafford was appearing in the starring role: as Industry's criminal mastermind. The lawsuit alleged that he "was and now is the political boss of the City of Industry" and that he had "initiated" the scheme to defraud the city in furtherance of a price-fixing conspiracy.[8] Although the *San Gabriel Valley Tribune* echoed the lawsuit's "political boss" accusation in a series of news stories beginning on January 25, not everyone in the media wholeheartedly endorsed the mastermind motif. In contrast to the *Tribune*'s approach, for instance, the half-dozen related stories in the *Times* portrayed Jim as one of several conspirators.[9] And in a rare yet typically truculent response to *Tribune* reporters' questions, Jim retorted, "The charges are so ridiculous I don't even want to talk about them."[10]

The trouble between Jim and the plaintiffs had a history, which began in the fall of 1961, when James O. Hamilton, a would-be developer who represented eight other investors, visited City of Industry manager Bob Rope to obtain a permit to build a shopping center on 260 acres zoned for commercial use. Hamilton later discovered, however, that the parcel had been promised to one of Jim Stafford's best friends. Decades later, Hamilton recounted his visit to Rope in a letter he wrote to the judge who eventually sent Jim to jail:

> I was told by Bob Rope . . . that [neither] I nor [any] other citizen in our neighborhood would be allowed to build on our commercial property. I objected strenuously. Mr. Rope looked out the sliding glass door and said, "Here comes Jim Stafford, ask him."
>
> Jim Stafford entered the room and I asked him what Bob meant. I could not have a permit to build my shopping center. His statement was simple and straightforward: "You paid $35,000 for that property. We will give you $60,000, and you get the hell out."[11]

To Hamilton, the incident proved that Jim, a private citizen with no official government position, called the shots in the city. It also motivated Hamilton and his partners to prove their suspicion. In January 1962, the following year, the developers filed a lawsuit against the city in which they accused Jim of exercising "dominion and control over" Industry's elected and appointed officials. Jim responded with a countersuit accusing Hamilton and the other plaintiffs of slander.[12] Hamilton meanwhile pressured a Los Angeles County grand jury to investigate Jim's sweet deal. The April 1962 city council elections, which returned three incumbents to office by predictably wide margins, supplied the plaintiffs with fresh ammunition to amend their lawsuit to include voter fraud allegations and press the grand jury to investigate the election.

Later that month, Industry's city attorney Glenn Watson bent to the pressure and released the results of his own investigation into the voter fraud allegations. That report Watson handed over to the grand jury acknowledged that three residents had voted illegally in the April election. For a time, it seemed that the court might sustain the voter fraud allegations and replace the roster of incumbents Jim had selected with a slate of pro-Hamilton candidates. City manufacturers and property owners in the city reportedly took that threat seriously enough to hire Graham A. Ritchie, a young attorney who was beginning to build a reputation in municipal law, to defend the incumbents.[13]

The drama shifted from the grand jury to the press when the *Times* reported on March 24, 1962, that city manager Rope had received a death threat from an unidentified group of World War II veterans. The anonymous letter "referred to 'bossism and dictatorship in our community,'" a not-so-subtle echo of the allegations made in the Hamilton lawsuit. The writer boasted that he and his buddies had "a machine gun and we know how to use it" but hit an unintentionally comic note when referring to the city's decision to pay Jim a higher price for his property at the expense of other property owners and taxpayers: "we don't like the dirty deal handed them." Finally, in language reminiscent of a bad detective movie, the letter writer warned, "Get out now or die—one or all of you. The boss comes first."[14]

By December 1962, however, Hamilton's crusade had faltered. The grand jury did not find enough evidence of price fixing or voter fraud, notwithstanding the evidence of illegal votes, to invalidate the election or continue its investigation: "There appears to be no evidence of any malfeasance in office of any officials or of any felony having been committed." But Hamilton's shopping-center gambit had worked. Less than a month later, in January 1963, the city agreed to de-annex 260 acres owned by the Hamilton group and allow those investors to develop their strip mall. About a year later, as the *Times* reported, both sides agreed to "bury the hatchet."[15]

Jim had by then realized that the civic association had not obtained enough evidence to sustain a credible legal challenge against either him or the city, which allowed his defense to remove all language from the lawsuit that asserted his control over the city and its officials.[16] These deletions effectively removed Hamilton's allegations from public view for two decades. Before signing off on the case, however, the presiding judge could not help but comment on the way in which Jim's influence over the city was blurring the boundary meant to separate public from private interests: "It would appear that Glenn R. Watson, city attorney, was personal attorney for the Stafford interests."

A week later, in February 1964, sheriffs' department and Industry officials dedicated the 625,000-dollar, county-funded substation.[17] And apparently, Jim got even in another, more personal, way. Later in the year, the city directed its staff to draw up plans for extending Railroad Street to Hatcher Avenue, right through the middle of a three-acre chicken ranch owned by Paul E. Stevens, one of Hamilton's backers. Instead of following a straight route along the parcel's northern boundary, the proposed road cut a sharp S-curve though the ranch. According to Stevens, the city was using its roadway design as a pretext for condemning his property and demolishing his home. Whatever the facts of the matter, the city did decide to abandon the road project once it had acquired the Stevens property.[18]

The way in which Jim had prevailed against Hamilton and his associates was an object lesson for anyone who owned property in the city. Business, for Jim, was personal. He treated the city and its officials like kin, a leadership style that was attractive to his friends and closest business associates. The paternalistic family-government hybrid that emerged during Industry's first decade enabled Jim and city officials to approve plans, ordinances, and expenditures that advanced their personal interests without arousing significant opposition from their charges, who accepted Jim's style of leadership as natural, moral, and charismatic. The rural insularity that had once made the La Puente Valley seem like a backwater now proved to be a crucial asset for Jim, not just for the railroads and other large property owners.

An Inventory of His Powers

Not enough evidence exists for us to re-create a precise history of Jim's early experiments in governmental technology, but we do know how his enemies, former friends, and business associates remembered him during the period. Their record allows us to construct a rough inventory of his powers. First, no one could work in any city job, serve on any city commission, or build anything in Industry without Jim's permission. Not even the most trivial appointments or development projects escaped his attention. He relished the power to give and take jobs and favors as a means of reinforcing loyalties or circulating fear among city staffers and elected officials who might defy him. And he regularly meted out punishment to those who opposed him. He could force the city to block an enemy's development project and threaten rivals with financial ruin in order to make them sell their property to the city.

Second, Jim played matchmaker in his role as advocate of railroad development. The railroads did not challenge his authority to run the city as long he continued to deliver what one Union Pacific executive coolly described as development that "served the needs of the railroad": in other words, new freight-hauling customers. It was Jim's job to make sure that the city secured development subsidies and promptly delivered building permits and zoning changes when the railroads asked for them. Donald E. Clark, director of real estate operations for Upland Industries Corporation, a Union Pacific subsidiary, confirmed this role years later when he jokingly described Jim as Industry's "godfather" and as the "man to 'contact to get things done' there." Clark recalled that if Upland had problems "getting a subdivision map or a utilities plan approved, he would take the problem up with STAFFORD and STAFFORD would tell him that he would see what he could do about it. After that, the problem would invariably be resolved."[19]

Third, Jim took punitive actions to protect railroad interests. Laurence Peck, director of Industry's first chamber of commerce, said that Jim "quickly and decisively" quashed his idea of inviting car dealerships into the city, informing Peck that the city "would continue to promote warehouse facilities in conjunction with the needs of the railroads." Jim's decisiveness convinced Peck that Stafford had entered into "an informal partnership arrangement with both the Southern Pacific and the Union Pacific that [was] beneficial to all of them."[20] The railroads also had a big say in these matters. John Kinnick, general manager of Trammel Crow Distribution Corporation, then a warehouse developer, said that the "railroads are very particular as to who buys their land at preferred prices because it can mean future business to the railroad if it is able to service the facility that is subsequently built on the land it sells."[21]

Fourth, Jim's mastery of the local culture as well as the city's Lilliputian scale meant that he could keep Industry's governmental apparatus under perpetual surveillance. The ways in which he employed his sister, Phyllis Tucker, perfectly illustrate the methods of his vigilance: not only was she personal secretary for several of Jim's businesses, but she also doubled as Industry's treasurer. At times, Jim retained Industry's city attorney as his private counsel; Frazer and Torbet, the Los Angeles accounting firm that audited the city's books, also kept track of Jim's personal and business accounts.[22] According to his critics, Jim signed off on every penny the city spent and every ordinance it passed, thus securing unfettered access to the city's knowledge network without needing to serve in elected office.[23]

Jim also made his vigilance visible. He paid unannounced visits to city officials, pulled city directors out of meetings for private consultations, and supervised city council meetings from a seat at the back of the room, nodding his head to signal approval or disapproval. When Industry's business became more complex, and outsiders complained of Jim's backseat driving, city staffers gave detailed voting instructions to elected and appointed municipal officials. Sometimes, however, no amount of coaching could prevent those officials from making mistakes. After all, the people that Jim had put onto the city's governing panels were farmers and ordinary working folks. The running joke was that they had so little grasp of government, law, and high finance that they could not explain what they had voted for. Their ignorance could therefore produce comic results, as when an inattentive council member lost his place in the agenda and voted no when he should have voted yes.[24]

At some point, Stafford's corporate supporters must have suspected that they had created a monster. But the influence wielded by the railroads, Jim's habit of self-dealing, his childhood traumas, his cultural milieu, and his incomplete mastery of the city's financial and legal technologies still constrained the ways in which he exercised his power. Moreover, his schemes exploited but did not create the Union Pacific's and the Southern Pacific's long-term vision for his city. The railroads had designed and invested for the long haul, favoring industrial development that would deliver sustained revenue flows from warehousing rents, rail-access fees, and freight-hauling charges. Above all, the railroads wanted to manage their rail facilities without interference. Jim, however, preferred quick profits made from single real estate transactions.

His methods did not vary much from New York State's nineteenth-century Hudson County alderman William Bumstead, who was convicted of lending a realtor money to buy "land to be purchased for a Jersey City reservoir" and then "resell it to the city for a profit."[25] Jim appreciated Industry's administrative and executive technology, which allowed him to make quick money and enhance his personal influence among his peers. But his schemes showed that he still thought a like grain dealer and a land speculator who was busy exploring the Lakewood plan's investment angles. He was also exploiting the city's power to preserve pastures and fields in a valley that developers were quickly carpeting with tract homes.

Jim's relationship to Mayor John Ferrero illustrates his idea of agrarian government at that time. Despite an apparently glaring conflict of interest, the city found ways to permit Ferrero, one of Jim's longtime grain-mill customers, to farm or ranch on hundreds of acres of city and railroad land either free of charge or at bargain lease rates without giving other ranchers the chance to bid on these opportunities. Sometimes the city functioned as Ferrero's land procurer, giving him first pick of land the city had acquired through eminent domain, including parcels expropriated from other farmers and ranchers. The railroads gave Ferrero the same consideration when they acquired property in the city.

In the annual statements of economic interest he was required to file, the mayor disclosed some but not all of the land that he farmed and ranched. State political law did not require elected officials to list the use of free or discounted farmland as a gift of public funds, nor did Ferrero report the oat hay he grew on city and railroad lands and later sold to Jim's mill. The mayor's land costs were minimal, and he paid nothing for water because he depended on winter rains to sow his crops. Jim, however, like any good businessman, carefully recorded the weight and price he had paid for the mayor's hay, which he then milled into pellets and sold back to Ferrero and local dairies.[26]

The city argued that the mayor's farming and ranching operations kept down weeds on vacant land that was awaiting development, and state law did not require Ferrero to report the profits he made from the use of such land as long as the city had defined his activities as weed abatement.[27] Not even complaints from other farmers made Ferrero's fellow city council members curious enough to press the mayor to produce records of his cattle and grain sales so that they could see if his weed abatement service was a ruse to get illegal campaign contributions.

No doubt, keeping the mayor in business ensured a cheap supply of oat hay for Jim's mill and an opportunity to ingratiate himself with the railroads by tidying their lands. But the profits Jim could realize from the mayor's ranching and farming operation paled in comparison to what could be had from long-term industrial development. His motives for using the city's powers to help a friend continue to maintain a rural lifestyle therefore suggest a deeper cultural rationale. A defiance of suburbanization reaffirmed his conservative rural values, both among his peers and to himself. He held onto this identity even though corporate types saw him as an anachronism, a quaint "Mr. Old West in modern times," as one railroad executive later described him.[28] Jim and his supporters implicitly shared the goal of preserving their community, but their folksy nostalgia for communal wholeness radically diverged from the expectations of Industry's largest developers.[29] Whereas corporations such as the railroads saw the city as an unsentimental means to a wealth-producing end, Jim and his supporters wanted to cash in on Industry while preserving their rural identities and culture. Whether they realized it or not, Jim and his supporters were trying to reconcile two opposing notions: capital's drive to maximize profit via investments in global trade versus the deep human need to root one's cultural identity in a homeland. But the city's technocrats and its corporate clientele quickly figured out Jim's cultural code. They learned to advance their own interests by letting Jim play the role of a city father who cares for his flock.

New Lessons in Power

But Jim could not take advantage of new business opportunities without acquiring greater mastery of the city's governmental technology and access to major-league investment capital. In 1964, city manager Bob Rope paved the way for that knowledge infusion by commissioning the Stanford Research Institute to conduct a series of studies on the City of Industry's economic significance.[30] Rope, a college-educated technocrat who understood how to craft necessary truths, knew he needed to demonstrate the city's viability to potential investors and identify the financial technology the city would require to realize its industrial goals.

Although it was never completed, the Stanford study did offer convincing evidence of Industry's growth potential. It noted that Industry, since its inception in 1957, had sustained California's fastest spurt of industrial growth, averaging 28-percent annual increases in manufacturing payroll and shipments during a five-year span. The number of manufacturing firms in the city had increased from 53 in 1958 to 203 in 1963, with 690 projected by 1970. Likewise, its number of non-manufacturing industrial firms (all of them warehouses) had jumped from 12 in 1958 to 57 in 1963, with 213 predicted by 1970. The study predicted that, by 1970, the city's overall annual industrial payroll would reach 204,725 dollars and that manufacturing shipments would soar to 725,838 dollars.

Although the study reported that the number of industrial jobs in Industry had climbed from 3,286 in 1958 to 8,603 in 1963, with more than 30,000 projected by 1970, it became clear by 1966 that those projections had been too modest. The arrival of corporate satellites such as Allied Carrier, Burroughs, Celotex, Crown Zellerbach, Masonite, and Kern Foods had boosted the city's daytime industrial workforce to 25,000 and had increased assessed property values to more than 56 million dollars, the highest of any San Gabriel Valley city and the eleventh-highest in the county.[31] While clearly reflecting the major capital investments in the city, the study had overlooked Industry's growing disparities with its neighbors.

The extent of that disparity can be deduced from assessed property values. In 1961, La Puente registered a per capita property-tax assessment of 849 dollars, well below the county's 1,600-dollar median, which itself was much lower than Industry's, which had reached 41,865 dollars per resident, or 32.5 million dollars in assessed property value divided by 778 residents. La Puente's low property values underscored its position as a lower-middle- and working-class suburb that depended on its neighbor for jobs. If La Puente's original incorporation petition had been approved, its per capita assessed valuation would have climbed to at least 1,918 dollars, about three hundred dollars above the county median, providing a handsome tax base with which to fund its schools, recreation, and health services.[32] But as La Puente's valuation declined, Industry's accumulation of wealth, as measured in property values, continued to skyrocket. By 1963, its assessed property value had surpassed 53 million dollars.[33]

The authors of the Stanford study saw Industry's pattern of increasing wealth as a temporary revenue windfall for county-funded schools, libraries, and hospitals in the suburbs.[34] They said, however, that the county's short-term gain would be the city's long-term headache if it did not find a way to recoup the revenues necessary to fund its municipal government. Keeping Jim's incorporation campaign promise to run the city with sales-tax revenues and other fees rather than municipal taxes would not help matters either. Ironically, because the sales of many factory-made goods were recorded in corporate headquarters outside of California, the city found itself relying instead on sales-tax revenue collected from small commercial retail businesses that had sprung up at the city's edges. If Industry did not take steps, the study warned, these small businesses would draw resources away from the city's preferred industrial clientele.

The Stanford study therefore recommended that the city should reverse this imbalance by availing itself of redevelopment laws that entitled cities to keep a greater share of the tax revenues that were usually levied by state and county agencies.[35] More importantly, the study gave Rope what he needed most: the recommendation to assemble a staff of experts to write the city's first general plan. The team he assembled conducted a detailed inventory of Industry's "socioeconomic deficiencies and potentials." Released in 1971, the resulting document—"[a] formulation of definitive programs of implementation, including financing through legally available methods such as the City, quasi-public non-profit corporations, urban renewal, joint powers authorities, and state and other governmental assistance"—was loaded with California's latest governmental technologies and written in a strange new privatized language.[36] Jim could never have used such vocabulary, but Rope certainly had ideas about what city officials could do with these governmental tools to prepare for Industry's next phase of transformation.

CITY ON A HILL

That transformation began when Industry attempted its first redevelopment project. Jim had been eying his target, the Little La Puente Hills, since Industry's incorporation, when he had persuaded property owners in the area to sign his petition. But the process of planning and executing that redevelopment project was anything but simple. According to available evidence, it was a confused process during which short-term schemes clashed with changeable and often unrealistic long-term plans.

Jim's earliest plan for the hills glimmered in 1965, when he, along with Vicente Perez and three other partners, formed the Industry Salvage Company to compete against more than a dozen firms that were also hauling trash in the city.[37] Their outfit envisioned a trash-hauling business with an exclusive contract for the city's valuable industrial refuse. The outfit's formation clearly anticipated the subsequent ordinance that authorized it to monopolize the city's garbage business.

Compared to the plot to create a trash-hauling monopoly, Industry's official plan for the hills seems rather whimsical if not contradictory. In August, the city sent city councilman Darius Johnson to England to purchase the British Railways coach that had carried the body of Sir Winston Churchill from London's Waterloo Station to Hansborough, near his burial site at Bladon. Just a month earlier, Johnson had learned in a *Times* article that the coach would be sold for scrap. "A number of us here in the City of Industry admired Mr. Churchill and thought we would like to have the coach here," he explained to the *Times*. Johnson said the coach would be restored and put on permanent display with other Churchill memorabilia, including a collection of his papers, inside a dedicated museum to be built on a Little La Puente "hillside" parcel the city had yet to purchase.[38]

That Jim and his colleagues saw the dead prime minister as the epitome of noblesse oblige is understandable. For men of their generation, many of them World War II veterans, the mythical image of Churchill courageously facing down the Nazis blended paternalistic nobility with irreproachable patriotism. So despite protests from one member of Parliament and a few British citizens, Johnson, with logistical help from a deputy speaker of the House of Commons, spent 980 city dollars to buy the maroon and gold coach, which was shipped in September to Los Angeles Harbor and then towed it to a rail siding in the City of Industry.[39]

A year later, in 1966, the city disclosed a few more details about the five-hundred-acre "wilderness" park where the Churchill Museum would be built. Industry planned to float an 8.5-million-dollar general obligation bond (an older governmental technology) to finance the project, which would be structured as a joint powers agreement (a newer governmental technology) between the city and the La Puente school district. Industry promised to set aside a million dollars of that bond money to develop an "industrial exhibition center," a two-story structure for showcasing the city's commercial and manufacturing wares. The building would also be used for "community meetings, youth programs and possibly for La Puente high school basketball games." The city would allocate as much as 3.5 million dollars for a park with "picnic facilities, recreation equipment, hiking and riding trails" to be made available to area residents. Churchill's coach as well as his "letters, books and paintings" would be housed in a separate facility. But there was a sticking point: construction of park and exhibition facilities, which the city expected to complete in 1970, could not begin until Industry was able to acquire the site through its powers of condemnation. Apparently, however, Industry voters were unconcerned about that problem. In January they passed the bond by a margin of ninety-five to twenty-six.[40]

At first blush, the project's recreational component looked to be an altruistic offering to the school district. But neighboring communities soon began to suspect that Industry did not intend to open the grounds of the park to just anyone, particularly not to local Latino youth. Rather, the plan was a way to keep the area, which was not suited for industry, out of the hands of residential developers.[41] Industry's neighbors also realized that they lacked the means to interfere with the city's growing economic might. In 1965, Industry businesses had generated 933,966 dollars in sales-tax revenues for a city of 739 residents. In contrast, more populous neighboring cities such as Baldwin Park, with 44,000 residents, had received only 230,761 dollars in such revenues.[42] For the moment, the schools could live with the sales-tax imbalance—as long as Industry did not grab a disproportionate share of the revenues that the county and the state were levying from area real estate, including Industry's highly assessed properties.

A few local authorities suspected that this lull in the contest would not last very long. They had already watched the city of Los Angeles imple-ment a new governmental technology known as tax-increment financing, a system for diverting county and state property-tax revenues back to the city's Community Redevelopment Agency. By means of this technology, Los Angeles had already begun demolishing Bunker Hill's working-class tenements to make way for an ultramodern skyline. Despite the confusions inherent in the dissemination of these redevelopment plans, one reporter intuited a similar future for Industry, the "enigmatic municipality [that] sprawls across the map of the San Gabriel Valley like an underfed dragon," a menacing medieval allusion to the city's elongated shape on the map.[43]

Observers had guessed right about Industry's intentions. Approval of its bond issue was a first modest step in what eventually became California's most ambitious program of municipal borrowing. It also marked the start of Industry's long relationship with the municipal bond industry's attorneys, brokers, financial advisors, and underwriters. But now, at this early stage, the city needed a lawyer with expertise to guide it into the young field of redevelopment law. So in 1967 it hired Graham Ritchie, the same lawyer whom city council members had previously hired to defend them against voter fraud allegations, as Industry's second city attorney.

Enter the Technicians

In 1955, after a stint in the army, Ritchie had graduated from UCLA's law school, one year after the Lakewood plan had transformed Southern California's municipal landscape. The explosion in newly incorporated cities soon presented him with an opportunity: to construct the legal battlements, parapets, and redoubts behind which Lakewood-style cities could consolidate their gains. By 1970, three years after his appointment as Industry's city attorney, Ritchie's reputation had grown exponentially. He was leading the city of Lawndale's incorporation campaign and had secured city attorney positions in Hawaiian Gardens, a newly formed city southeast of Long Beach, and the city of San Gabriel. He had also collected the city manager's job in Baldwin Park, and appointments as urban development counsel in four other cities.

In Industry, Ritchie was credited with crafting contracts and orchestrating votes that would protect its officials from conflict-of-interest prosecution for decades, for initiating land confiscations via eminent domain that would pave the way for redevelopment, and for restricting public access to city government and records. He dispensed with the dissemination of city council agendas and reportedly said, "I really don't see any need for a [city] budget." He also applied the logic of subcontracting to his salaried positions. In fiscal year 1971–72, Industry allocated 168,033 dollars from its 2.3-million-dollar budget to the offices he then held: city attorney, city manager, and redevelopment agency director. The figure did not include secretarial salaries. Yet other than a 2,000-dollar monthly retainer that he admitted to receiving as city attorney, Ritchie's net earnings in that office could not be determined without also knowing the expenses he had incurred in performing his duties. The same went for his city manager earnings: he was paid on "an hourly basis for work not covered by the retainer." Meanwhile, during the same fiscal year, he had earned more than 26,500 dollars from the other cities and redevelopment agencies he represented; and his personal legal practice was billing private clients such as Jim Stafford while he was serving as Industry's city attorney and leading a city redevelopment agency that was purchasing Stafford's properties. Ritchie did, however, avoid a potential conflict of interest by appointing another attorney to represent Industry's redevelopment agency in the transaction.[44]

In April 1969, Ritchie returned to the unfinished business in Little La Puente Hills. He drafted an ordinance, summarily approved by the city council, requiring brothers Matt and Dominic Patritti to obtain a new permit for their landfill and pay 1,500 dollars in quarterly fees to stay in business.[45] In August, Ritchie announced that the city had passed the halfway mark in its acquisition of land for its wilderness park and exhibition center. He said the city had acquired more than three hundred acres and was negotiating to "purchase two large dump sites totaling 150 acres on the south side of the Puente Hills." Meanwhile, plans for a large hotel were added to the temporarily postponed project.[46]

Ritchie exuded confidence, but the legal battle was yet to be settled in the courts. That battle came to a head in 1970, when the Patritti brothers, in an effort to secure a higher price for their landfill property, filed a 3-million-dollar lawsuit against the city. They claimed that the value of their eighty acres had climbed to at least 1.5 million dollars since 1968, when the city had offered them 500,000 dollars. The lawsuit also challenged the city's motives for condemning their property, alleging that "the evil genius of James Marty Stafford," with aid of city officials, had devised a conspiracy to put them out of business and sell their property to Ben Kazarian, operator of a neighboring dump, or unnamed private individuals who were planning to develop a racetrack there.

But the lawsuit had incorrectly identified the dump operator who wanted to purchase the Patritti property as well as the means by which the city would continue to permit the operation of a dump inside its wilderness park and exhibition center. Moreover, evidence of Jim's control of the city and its officials showed only that he had the means to carry out a conspiracy, not that he had executed it. The lawsuit's failure cleared the way for the city to apply its regulatory powers, which it used to find the Patritti brothers in violation of the new dump permit regulations and to induce them to drop their lawsuit and sell their property.[47]

Rather than creating a legal history, the tactics employed by both sides maintained a well-crafted silence. In an earlier phase of the lawsuit, the city had obtained a court order striking the most inflammatory allegations from the Patritti suit.[48] By excising these claims of Jim's controlling influence over the city, Ritchie discouraged Industry's enemies from using them in future scandals.

The city's legal victories gave Jim the power to grant even bigger favors to his closest friends. In 1970, for instance, the city awarded large service contracts to three companies controlled by Vicente Perez and his sons. Perez, a Spanish immigrant and one of the Stafford mill's oldest customers, not only belonged to Jim's ranching culture but had also helped him recruit support for Industry's incorporation campaign. That important support, some insiders claimed, had given him the right to extract a promise from Jim. According to Stephen Stafford, Jim's son, his father had told Perez he would eventually get all of the city's trash business; and "Perez badgered Stafford about his commitment . . . until he finally came to him with an ultimatum, saying it was time he made good on his promise." Stephen did not specify this "ultimatum," saying only that Jim had told Rope and Ritchie "to put [the franchise] together for Perez."[49]

In June 1970, without holding any public hearings or inviting competitive bids, the city council inked a contract granting Perez's firm, the City of Industry Disposal Company, an exclusive franchise to "collect refuse, garbage or combustible or non-combustible rubbish" within the city. The agreement's terms required all firms operating in the city to switch over to Perez's company within one year. The ordinance effectively shut out fourteen other trash haulers who had been competing for Industry refuse, a lucrative proposition in a city with more than 450 manufacturers who were generating tons of salvageable rubbish. It not only "prohibited business owners from carting away" or selling "their own trash," but it also forbade businesses from salvaging trash they had received from other businesses.[50]

As Stephen Stafford recalled, when "word . . . leaked out that the Perezes would become the city's exclusive trash collectors," the news raised a furor. Stephen said that both Perez and Rope "received death threats," prompting Rope to try to withdraw his support for the plan "at the last minute," an attempt that infuriated Stafford and Perez. Nevertheless, at Jim's insistence, Ritchie pushed through the plan without Rope's support, after which, according to Stephen, "Perez and Rope never spoke to each other again."[51]

Stephen's version of events may or may not be precisely accurate, but there's little doubt about what happened next. In 1971, four of the ousted collection firms filed a 750,000-dollar lawsuit. The judge, however, ruled that Industry had the authority to award the contract to one firm if it wished to do so. Vicente Perez pressured city council to hire a full-time inspector to enforce his exclusive contract; and the city, in turn, withheld 50,000 to 60,000 dollars each year, or 10 percent of garbage-hauling fees, for serving as the City of Industry Disposal Company's bill collector.[52] The arrangement attracted a few fierce complaints from business owners, who claimed they were being forced to pay whatever the city-authorized monopoly demanded. "We are like prisoners here," said one plant manager, who also insinuated that a "tiny clique" ran the city for members' personal benefit.[53]

DISCOVERING REDEVELOPMENT

Still, the city's defense of the City of Industry Disposal Company's franchise was not Ritchie's biggest legal accomplishment of 1971. That year he also rolled out his bold new interpretation of California's redevelopment law, which had been on the books since 1952. In that year, Californians had voted to amend article 16, section 16 of the state constitution, otherwise known as the Community Redevelopment Act, a change that gave cities a new technique for financing urban redevelopment projects. The original Community Redevelopment Act had been an offshoot of the federal Redevelopment Act of 1945, which was intended to resurrect the big cities that had fallen into neglect during the war years. Soon after passage of the federal act, the California legislature passed its companion law, which permitted cities in the state to participate in the federally funded program. Participation came with several catches, however. To receive funding, California cities would have to agree to the federal government's housing agenda, which included alleviating postwar unemployment, cleaning up urban decay, and relieving an acute housing shortage.

Nationwide, a bitter ideological dispute had dogged the Redevelopment Act since the moment of its proposal. Around the country, as cities such as Los Angeles exemplified, developers and the political elite wanted federal money for their cities but not the federal public housing agenda, which they described as the "back door to socialism."[54] The contest over definitions of urban renewal turned particularly nasty in the late 1940s and early 1950s, when LA's first inner-city housing projects went up and local agencies began drawing ambitious low-cost public-housing plans for Chavez Ravine and Bunker Hill. Led by Norman Chandler, who had taken over the *Times* after the death of his father, downtown real estate developers campaigned to resist these initiatives and to subvert them by pushing for legislative remedies in the state capital.

Even in its original form, the 1945 Community Redevelopment Act took the step of removing the federal rationale for public housing while retaining the legal technology of urban renewal. The law gave local government the power to label specific neighborhoods as "blighted" and then allowed cities to apply for federal grant money to pay for redeveloping those districts. It gave statutory oversight and regulatory authority to the state and planning, financing, and implementation authority to local governments. Importantly, the law concentrated its power in local redevelopment agencies, a modification that fit neatly with California's home-rule laws and would soon complement the Lakewood plan's subcontracting technology. A city's redevelopment agency now had the power to condemn and assemble land into larger blocks, prepare a site for private development, impose conditions and restrictions on development, and orchestrate public and private financing for a project as long as it could justify that project under the vague rationale of blight removal and slum clearance.

Despite the acquisition of such formidable powers, cash-strapped cities recovering from World War II and the 1953–54 recession complained that they still needed a financing mechanism to free them from the federal government's "socialist" urban renewal agenda. The 1952 amendment to the Community Redevelopment Act resolved this shortcoming via tax-increment financing, a radical new system that involved paying for slum clearance by diverting property-tax revenues to local redevelopment agencies.[55] Tax-increment financing allowed redevelopment agencies to skim off all new tax revenues generated from increases in property value after the start of a redevelopment project. The new system assumed that redevelopment rather than market forces had increased those property values and their resulting tax revenues. As an added benefit, state law ensured that an agency could count on diverting this flow of newly minted revenue for the life of a redevelopment project, which could last up to fifty years—even longer if the project remained in debt. Forming a new agency with new land to develop could restart the process and divert a fresh stream of tax revenues. And now that redevelopment agencies were certain of harvesting these revenues, they could use their tax increments along with various bond instruments to incur and repay long-term debt.

Lax oversight in Sacramento allowed counties and cities, starting with Los Angeles, to fashion a perfect financial tool from these laws and thus expand the political-economic sovereignty promised by California's home-rule laws. The new system also gave municipalities the financial resources they needed to cut the last remaining strings binding them to the federal public housing program. Cities and counties, particularly those in Southern California, now possessed the legal authority, the financial resources, and the political rhetoric to rationalize the massive transfer of public wealth into the hands of private developers, all in the name of urban renewal.

The local press, however, continued to confuse the low-cost housing agenda of federal urban renewal programs with the new purposes of California redevelopment law. This confusion only helped the developers. When reporters highlighted redevelopment abuse as a violation of the program's "true" purposes, they took ordinary citizens' focus off the state law itself, which now was clearly aimed at urban renewal for the rich. Such a bait-and-switch confusion was guaranteed to frustrate homeowners, but that was a small price to pay to avoid public revelations of corporate welfare.

Cities found themselves able to pursue these corporate-friendly effects in the name of alleviating poverty. Los Angeles, for instance, took early advantage of the state law's vague definition of urban blight and its new financing technology to begin diverting millions of dollars to downtown redevelopment projects. In the mid-1950s, the local community redevelopment agency, at the direction of the city's developer elite, evicted the working-class, primarily immigrant residents and small property owners of Bunker Hill to make way for gleaming high rises for corporate attorneys and a high-class concert hall named after the Chandlers. But most cities did not exploit the new law's potential so quickly. Rather, California's redevelopment agencies tried to condition their investment of local property-tax dollars on their ability to secure federal urban renewal grants. By the late 1960s, however, a growing number of cities were coveting the hundreds of millions of dollars that Los Angeles's redevelopment diversions had generated—in great measure, from increasing property values. These cities realized that they, too, could fund projects without federal interference.

The law required that a legal challenge to a proposed redevelopment project be filed within sixty days of its adoption by a city. This caveat gave the city a virtually impregnable defense. Now a project need only pass muster in Sacramento, where friendly legislators, lobbyists, and real estate developers had formed an aggressive, pro-redevelopment consensus around the new technology. The new suburban cities founded, like Industry, after the mid-1950s did not discover tax-increment financing until the 1970s. When they did, however, it caught on like wildfire, sparking the formation of redevelopment agencies up and down the state. By the early 1980s, more than twenty other states, with the encouragement of Wall Street's municipal bond brokers, were imitating California's tax-increment financing laws.[56]

Ritchie and one or two other Southern California attorneys made a uniquely troubling contribution to spread the technology when they stretched the definition of urban blight to include Southern California's remaining pastures and orchards. Their interpretation, however, required them to invent a new lexicon of poverty, pointing to broken drainage pipes, abandoned orchards, weed-choked ditches, poorly designed roads, and irregular lots as evidence of urban decay. The state's redevelopment law did allow cities to represent properties as blighted if private developers had previously failed to develop those parcels on their own; but Industry's legal team attached new images, meanings, and qualifying exceptions that completely disconnected redevelopment from its intended urban context.

According to urban historian Gary Miller, one of Ritchie's earliest critics, it was hard "to see how Industry, which [was] either undeveloped or newly developed in its entirety, could benefit from blight-eradication programs."[57] Miller's critique, however, missed the point in one key respect. California clearly permitted Ritchie's interpretation of the law; and Ritchie, to his credit, did not try to hide the law's artifices when he called it "a gimmick every city ought to look at."[58] But his candor and its implications did not get much coverage. Instead, the press continued to stress his personality, his intelligence, and his taste in clothing and cars. That coverage, moreover, implicitly identified Ritchie, not Jim Stafford, as the mind behind the city's growth.

Expecting a newspaper such as the *Times* to exhibit a critical awareness of the broad significance of Ritchie's and California's reinterpretation of federal redevelopment law was also unthinkable. The newspaper and its parent corporation, Times Mirror, were themselves promoting the development of their real estate holdings through their continued support for publicly subsidized redevelopment. *Times* support proved to be especially crucial in subsidies for downtown real estate development because it reinforced the perception that redevelopment, by itself, would increase property values. In 1959, when redevelopment of Bunker Hill began, the assessed value of the area's twenty-five city blocks, which included twenty-two *Times*-owned parcels, was 20.3 million dollars. After thirty-two years of redevelopment, Bunker Hill's assessed property value had soared to 2.8 billion dollars; and by 1982, the *Times*-owned property inside the Bunker

Hill project area had climbed to 52.4 million dollars.[59] Clearly, any media criticism of redevelopment would have to occur beyond the city limits.

In Ritchie's case, *Times* coverage took the form of a morality tale tracing one individual's abuse of redevelopment policy. Thus, a 1973 feature profile led off with a description of the biting "sarcasm" and arrogance he had displayed during a city council meeting. The *Times* reported that he had lectured the school officials in attendance, telling them how little the schools had done for the city and how lucky the city was to have two maintenance men on its "redevelopment board" instead of "fuzzy-thinking educators." The educators, accustomed to being treated with deference, were shocked. One teacher, shaking with anger, told Ritchie he was "appalled" by his outburst.[60]

Ritchie's critics accused him of a creating a "1984" climate in which "everybody was in mortal fear of" opposing or criticizing the city. The *Times* reinforced the point, adding that Industry council meetings largely consisted "of monologues by Ritchie, punctuated by approval of his recommendations. Councilmen talk sparingly and anything but a unanimous vote is rare." According to the profile, the attorney's defenders saw his intelligence as his strongest asset, describing him as "the sort of man who can find a way to do things that other lawyers would say could not be done." The article quoted Ritchie as saying, "There are very few things a community needs and wants that it can't accomplish."[61]

Almost every detail of the profile viewed his accomplishments and policies through a moral filter. His sarcasm, his violin playing, his taste in fancy tailored suits, his red Ferrari, and his inability to hide his pride in his own intelligence signified snobbery and hubris, while the clever legalities he had devised to withhold information suggested deceit. The press was willing to hold up Ritchie's character and Industry's peculiarities for public criticism as long as they were represented as anomalies. By stressing the attorney's and the city's uniqueness, the *Times* profile discouraged comparisons with Los Angeles's own use of redevelopment to remove immigrant working families, many of them Latinos, from Bunker Hill or the fact that the city had spent millions of property-tax dollars on a few square miles of downtown property owned by the city's biggest corporate investors, including the *Times* itself.[62]

Ritchie, to his credit, did not hesitate to chide the *Times* for its hypocrisy. As he said many years later, "Look at Bunker Hill, where the *Times* benefited in a gargantuan way." Industry, he implied, could not be faulted for following LA's example. Anyway, he prophetically said, the so-called boundary between what is private and what is public did not apply to redevelopment. A city's transfer of public wealth to a private developer could be justified as long as it promoted a greater public good.[63] Still, there was little Ritchie could do to stop the press from projecting a personality onto his application of redevelopment technology. He and his colleagues, however, would tolerate that projection as long as the redevelopment "gimmick" did not become the most important issue, which was unlikely, given the pro-redevelopment agenda of the *Times*.

Meanwhile, Ritchie's legal innovations and his tamperproof trash-hauling monopoly were reinforcing Industry's insular culture. Each year, for instance, Vicente Perez and his sons organized Fourth of July, Christmas, and New Year's celebrations for their friends and supporters on "P Hill," the trash and salvage business they operated on the five hundred acres the city had acquired through eminent domain. The parties were communal events, with as many as 1,000 attendees. Jane Stafford's recollections of these affairs reveal both the class and cultural composition of Industry's resident population and the social chasm dividing husband and wife. She said that "she stopped going to these parties because she always ended up in the company of 'hookers, shack-ups, and drunks' as the evening wore on and her husband remained to party with his cronies." Jane added disdainfully that Jim preferred "[Mayor] Ferrero and the truck drivers and roustabouts who worked for him" to the company "of educated and cultured people" like herself.[64]

No doubt, Jim and his cronies relished their city all the more because the financial and legal barriers they had erected around it permitted them to be themselves without feigning respectability. And Jim, who had suffered the humiliations of public exposure during his father's rape trial, probably felt particularly justified in enjoying his success. So what if he had used irregular methods? He had lived close enough to his superiors and had admired them for long enough to know that they, too, had used brute violence and sublime deceit to acquire wealth and prestige.

CHAPTER 6

TRIANGULATING
THE THRONE

A captive always ends up being a captive of somebody else's words.
—Ariel Dorfman, *Heading South, Looking North: A Bilingual Journey*

According to Industry businessman Robert K. King, a wholesale dealer in rare and expensive hardwoods, admission to Jim Stafford's world hinged on how King chose to answer a question. In a series of interviews he gave after Jim's 1983 indictment on bid-rigging and kickback charges, King offered his tale of seduction and disgrace, beginning in 1968, a few years before Industry's redevelopment projects formally got off the ground, when the lumber dealer first explored the idea of relocating his business to Industry.[1] The episode offers an intimate look at the way in which Industry's officials served their railroad clientele and how one developer, Majestic Realty, formed its triangular relationship with the city and railroads. King's story also gives us a close view of the political culture in which Jim's bid-rigging, kickback, and money-laundering conspiracy flourished.

King discussed his relocation proposal with Ron Moyer, who worked in the Southern Pacific's real estate division. Moyer suggested that he first clear the way with city officials. Moyer arranged for King to lunch with city manager Bob Rope at the swanky California Country Club, where Stafford and Rope continued to hold court even after redevelopment money had financed a new palace of city government.

On the day of the meeting, Moyer picked up King at his place of business in the City of Commerce, a municipality that had been modeled on Industry's single-use plan.[2] At the country club, Moyer introduced King to Rope, who, according to King, carried himself as if he were Jim's equal. A big chair at the end of the bar had been elevated onto a throne-like platform; and there Rope sat, large and boisterous, presiding over three telephones: one red, one white, one black. As King recalled, "The red phone [was] Rope's hotline to Sacramento. The white phone [got] him to his office in city hall, and the black line [was] for outside calls."[3]

Moyer said, "Bob, I'd like you to meet Bob King."

Rope's reply, King said, was something like "Sit down, dumb shit. What do you want to drink?" King felt unnerved by the manager's gruffness and the collection of bank presidents, high-ranking county fire and sheriff's officials, and judges who witnessed his humiliation

But King persevered. "So now it's time for me to talk to the Almighty," he said. "I'd like to move to the City of Industry, Mr. Rope."

"'What kind of business are you in?'" Rope asked. After King explained, Rope said, "Yes, Bob, yes," signaling that he might be willing to consider the request. Then the manager said that King would have to buy property along Nelson Avenue, a gritty stretch along the Southern Pacific's main line. Industry's planners had reserved the avenue for businesses similar to his. King, however, told Rope that he had his eye on the commercially zoned property on Gale Avenue, which paralleled the Pomona Freeway. Easy freeway access and exploding suburban growth would ensure big returns if he were lucky enough to get a piece of Gale Avenue.

Although Rope's arrogance had offended him, King resolved to settle for buying the Nelson Avenue parcel, if that was to be his only choice, but not before speaking his mind to Moyer: "Who the hell does he think he is, sitting on a throne!"[4]

King recalled that Moyer told him, "Bob, relax. That's the way it is in the City of Industry. What did you spend today?"

"I didn't spend anything," King answered. "I had five drinks and I had lunch."

"That's right," said Moyer. "You don't have to pay here. He pays. You don't have to spend a nickel, and he's not trying to buy you."[5]

Although King did not admit it to Moyer then, his encounter with Rope had thrilled him. Something about both the California Country Club and Rope (whom he later described as a dear friend) had intrigued him: "I said, 'Screw it, I'm going to the City of Industry.'"

A year later, Moyer arranged another country-club meeting between King and Rope. According to King, Rope said, "We have a little parcel on Nelson Avenue, because it's where all the goddamn trashy outfits are. We are not going to have lumber yards on Gale Avenue." Gale was visible from the Pomona Freeway, and the city was planning to develop it with eye-catching shopping malls.

Rope's crude comments had a purpose: they were designed to kill King's interest in the Gale Avenue corridor, while making him grateful for the opportunity he was going to be allowed to get. But Rope didn't limit his comments to real estate; he continued to needle King in front of his friends and hangers-on. Eventually, he tossed out a trivia question: "What was Pancho Villa's real name?"

"Doroteo Arango," King said, naming the Mexican revolutionary who symbolized the ruthless man of action who imposed his will on women and men alike, a vibrant macho fantasy for this band of middle-aged white men faced with declining virility accelerated by heavy drinking and equality-demanding minorities.

This intellectual feat impressed Rope. Now the pair began to develop a mutual respect. King credited Rope with giving him a chance to buy the Nelson Avenue parcel and later letting him put up temporary storage sheds on the property, despite city policies that prohibited such structures. Apparently, Nelson Avenue, though trashy, was a profitable investment; and in later years King continued to express his appreciation for Rope's support.

His story about the property, however, was incomplete. In his press and FBI interviews, King omitted an important detail: he never bothered to explain that he and his partner, Richard G. Lapin, did not buy the property from the city. They bought it from the Southern Pacific, Moyer's employer. In other words, city manager Rope was helping the SP market one of its rail-connected properties.[6]

King and his partner moved their business onto the Nelson Avenue property in November 1969; and after the move, King's relationship to Rope underwent a transformation. In 1970, as King recalled, Rope asked him "if he would be interested in joining the Industry Manufacturers Council," the city's version of a chamber of commerce organization. Rope also told King that "he wanted him to meet Jim Stafford," whom he described as "an important man in the city." Until that moment, King had assumed that Rope was the "important man."[7]

After King had conveyed his interest in both propositions, Rope extended another invitation. "When's the last time you've eaten in a private dining car?" he asked.

"Shit, Bob, probably fifteen years ago," King answered.

So Rope told him to be on the spur track behind Community Bank "at seven o'clock in the morning."[8]

King recalled, "I show up. There are three people there I don't know, plus Jim Stafford, who I'd never met." Two of those people were Larry Peck, then executive director of the Industry Manufacturers Council, and Jay Long, a "troubleshooter" for the Southern Pacific. Long had arranged to have the dining car parked at various locations in the city, his way of doing public relations for the railroad's real estate business.[9]

The experience of sitting down to a sumptuous breakfast in a fancy dining car intoxicated King, and he thought the black steward that the Southern Pacific had hired to serve them was a particularly classy touch.[10] "It was impressive, and obviously I made a good impression [on Jim], so he asked me to serve on" the manufacturers council.[11]

The Industry Manufacturers Council functioned as both a traditional chamber of commerce, assembling businesses leaders to engage in ordinary backslapping and self-promotion, and an organization that advanced the city's political agenda. It dedicated its energies to manufacturing and disseminating legal and legislative arguments, which it reinforced with member campaign contributions to friendly elected and appointed officials in federal, state, and county government. For financial reasons, the city also maintained a corporate shell known as the Industry Chamber of Commerce, using it primarily to facilitate money transfers to the council and buffering the city from the council. Despite their different names, however, Jim Stafford directed both organizations as one entity. That's why King thought Jim's invitation to join the council was "a joke." The council members were "supposed to be elected," he said, but "no one's ever been elected." They were "all appointed," King said, per Jim's invitation.[12]

King's recollections of the dining-car encounter focused on Jim's ability to recognize intelligence, dispense political appointments, and display a showy command of power. That was Jim's intention. The Industry Manufacturers Council was his theater of influence. From at least the 1970s onward, and throughout the 1980s, the city allocated between 400,000 and 900,000 dollars a year to the council, while the Industry Chamber of Commerce, its odd silent partner, was surviving with "just a board, just enough to make it legal," according to a former chamber official.[13] Although the city did not explain why it was funding a membership organization with no members, the arrangement authorized the chamber's board to coordinate expenditures with the council and gave the council's staff enough resources to place advertisements in national business magazines, a way to highlight the city's strategic assets and attract Fortune 500 corporations that were scouting for branch plant locations. The council also trumpeted its favorite elected officials in the pages of the *City of*

Industry News, which the council published, and used its generous budget to organize lavish promotional events.

The council's executive director, Wilfred W. Steiner, was the former Southern Pacific land buyer who had made the timely property purchase that had sealed Industry's fate. In a candid 1984 interview, he clarified the organization's political methods: "Most of our politicking is *sub rosa.* We keep an eye on adverse legislation. We take a stand when someone notifies us to write to our congressman to oppose anything we determine as a bad bill. We send this information to our members."[14]

The council's way of cultivating relationships between its members and guest speakers made it an attractive venue for politicians who sought to market their services to Industry's wealthy industrialists. But its composition and agenda still reflected the presence of Jim's guiding hand. In addition to its members, he picked its administrative staff, signed off on their salaries, and recommended pay raises. According to some people, he later pushed the council into hiring his mistress, Janet Crowley, who, by the early 1980s, was earning more than 42,000 dollars a year as its assistant executive director.[15] Jim owned the building that the council eventually leased from him and used its members and events to funnel donations, some of them illegal, to his favorite candidates. The directors who performed these political tasks would later learn that they had helped Jim find recruits for his criminal conspiracy, as King's story explains.

After King had joined the council's board, Jim "called me up and said, 'Bob, I'd like to see you.'"

"I said, 'Yes, sir, Mr. Stafford. I'll be right over.' He said, 'No, no, I'll come up and see you.'"

At first, King interpreted Jim's insistence on inviting himself over as his folksy way of socializing. "It was always, 'Let me come and see you, son.' I'd say, 'No, Jim,' but he would not hear it. He'd bring over a crate of cantaloupes, a crate of lettuce, two lugs of tomatoes. Or 'Son, I have tickets for the Tex Beneke Orchestra this weekend. Would you and your lovely wife, Nancy, like to go?' Or 'Son, let's go to the Rams game [at the LA Coliseum] this weekend.'"[16] Although King usually closed his office door during Jim's visits, King's business partner heard King affectionately address Jim as "Pops" on several occasions.[17]

Eventually, King realized that Jim used his intrusions and favors to maintain the upper hand in his personal relationships. "So he came up here and said, 'You know, there's twelve guys on this board. We got too many guys on the board. There ought to be only seven.'

"I said, 'Mr. Stafford   '

"'Call me Jim.'

"'Well, Jim, I've never served on a board in my life, and I don't know anything about board procedure. But I know that a committee of more than one is too many.' He laughed. 'Well, I've been checking it out,' [Jim said.] 'You can call a special board meeting and call a vote to cut the board from twelve to seven.'"

Justifying himself, King said, "So, I [was] eager to please, and there [was] nothing wrong with it." At the same, however, he feared that the other board members would fire him for depleting their number and deny him a chance to show his leadership skills.

King wanted to serve and impress; he wanted to show that "a guy with a half-assed high school education" could do a better job as president than the "yahoos" who had preceded him. "So I called a meeting. I propose we cut down the number of board members from twelve to seven." Without even the pretense of a discussion, William Bryant, who ran the golf operation for the California Country Club, seconded King's motion.

"I said, 'OK. Let's vote on it.'" They did. Only one board member voted against the motion, the result of an oversight: Jim had forgotten to call him. "Meeting adjourned."[18]

King later concluded that reducing the board's size had served no administrative purpose. Reasoning that Jim could appoint and remove members as he pleased, he suspected that Jim had coached the board members to put on a show for his sake, but he could not figure out why. "I found [the experience] amusing because there was no real harm in it. Nothing had really occurred in that meeting. I just thought, Well, Jesus, it's a joke."

But it may not have been a joke. Reducing the size of the board reinforced Jim's control over the council's budget and the image of omnipotence he cultivated in the minds of the board members he had spared. The display had also impressed King, who saw his appointment as council president as a rare opportunity to receive public recognition for his intelligence and leadership skills.[19]

"You see," he said, "I grew up in a little town in Georgia. My mother kept house for rich people. My father was a dishwasher. I had three brothers and two sisters. I was the only one who finished high school. I tried to enroll in the University of Georgia with a major in journalism. I had to work nights, so I [dropped] out. I made a lot of money on my own, and moved out here. And through the good graces of a man named Bob Rope, a man I truly love, I got involved in the City of Industry." Then he added ruefully, "The wine got to taste too good. I'm the guy introducing President

Ford, President Reagan, Armand Hammer, Justin Dart [drugstore magnate, philanthropist, and key financial backer of President Reagan]. It got to be a kind of an ego trip."[20]

King claimed that Rope exploited his gratitude, his willingness to endure humiliation, his hunger for acceptance, and his eagerness to demonstrate his natural wit. Jim, however, seemed to identify with King's southern origins and his outsider status. He called King "son"; King called him "Pops." He flattered King, and incurred an emotional debt, by asking for his opinion and showering him with gifts, while King eagerly accepted his new identity and status.

Reflecting on why he had so willingly followed Jim into crime, King blamed his own moral weakness and Jim's irresistible personality. He portrayed Jim as a man who would charm, scheme, and bully until he got what he wanted. King even attributed the presence of the Southern Pacific's dining car to Jim's influence, not to the city's tacit agreement to market the railroad's real estate. King also credited Jim with introducing him to Edward P. Roski, Jr., the son of Industry's biggest developer. According to King, he and Roski became friends and business partners, a relationship that hitched him to the star of the city's fast-rising developer.[21]

Ed Roski came to Industry by way of his father, Edward Roski, Sr., who began investing in the city in 1968. No accounts directly describe Jim's introduction to either Roski. The family's only existing history in the city is the story of self-made success that Ed Junior fashioned for his father four decades later.

According to that story, after serving a stint in the U.S. Navy in World War II, Ed Senior moved from Oklahoma to Southern California. In 1948, he founded Majestic Realty Company, a real estate brokerage firm that operated in the City of Commerce, which, like Industry, was traversed by major railroad lines. The family business changed in the 1960s, when Ed Junior returned from the Vietnam War, where he had served in the Marines. He joined the firm and began to specialize in development and construction.[22] Soon Majestic Realty and its various offshoots became one of Southern California's biggest real estate developers, a success that Ed Junior credited in large part to his father's work ethic.

"He was the soon of a poor, immigrant family from Poland," he wrote in 2004 in his eulogy for his father. "He grew up in the emotional and financial hurricane of the depression. He never finished high school." He overcame humble origins by working "harder than the next guy," by learning his business "from what he saw, what he heard, and what he felt," not from any books.[23]

William Bizzel, a Roski business partner, offers a more mundane alternative to this success story. According to him, Majestic's achievements in Industry hinged on the role it cultivated as the Union Pacific's preferred developer. With Majestic's backing, Bizzel and Ed Junior had co-founded Commerce Construction Company, which was intended to serve as the design and construction arm of Majestic's development business. Bizzel was the company's general manager and executive vice president. In 1983, he told the FBI that "75% of Commerce Construction Company's business came from Majestic Realty salesmen who packaged properties for them to develop." Majestic organized investor syndicates that financed its projects, attracting major players such as Oral Roberts, the ultra-conservative evangelical minister, who was recruited by Ed Senior's brother Henry.

In interviews, Bizzel told the FBI that the Union Pacific only wanted land buyers who "would require rail service." Because Majestic could deliver that kind of customer, the railroad was "willing to sell their land [to the broker] for $40,000 to $50,000 an acre less than the market value."[24] Majestic's special access to the railroad also explains why the Roskis cultivated a relationship with Jim, who had the power to grease the connections among Majestic, the railroad, and the city. But their mutual interests, one might argue, also imposed its own discipline. In the emerging power triangle, Jim could not ignore the unwritten understandings with the Union Pacific and the Southern Pacific, which several sources alleged had led to the city's formation and continued development, without also putting his authority at risk.

His role as expediter and fixer, however, entitled him to a cut of the action so long as the city continued to procure land for Majestic's rail-friendly development schemes. By the early 1970s, Majestic Realty Company and Commerce Construction Corporation were fast emerging as Industry's preferred factory and warehouse developer, a trend not widely known beyond King's circle and the developers left standing outside the city's redevelopment banquet. Between 1971 and 1975, Industry's city council approved at least 1.2 million square feet of Commerce Construction building plans, far more footage than it approved for any other developer in the city at that time—and it did so without calling for competitive bids.[25] But even this impressive pace pales in comparison to what the Roski-owned and -controlled firms had in store for the city.

King knew about Ed Junior's success in leveraging his special relationship with Jim, the city, and the railroads; and soon he, too, joined their investment partnerships in warehouse developments. Yet no one, not even the FBI or the local press, ever convinced King to talk about his relationship with Ed Junior or about Ed's relationships with Jim or the railroads. King expressed trepidation at discussing his personal relationship with Ed Junior because it would violate a pact he had made with the Majestic scion in the early 1970s. "Eddie and I made an agreement 15 years ago," King said in his 1984 interview, "that what he did was his business, and what I do was mine." That pact, however, did not prevent Ed from prodding King to perform certain favors or from inviting him to invest in warehouse projects together.[26] King's insistent silence suggests that Ed Junior represented threats and rewards that exceeded even Jim's powers of intimidation.

Moreover, King's recollections do not portray the city as a manifestation of the state or acknowledge the governmental technologies that had helped concentrate so much wealth and power in one place. Instead, they moralize. According to King, "the program" (his code phrase for Jim's approach to running the city as a criminal enterprise) explained how and why everything occurred in Industry. King and the other insiders who served as city officials saw government from the "us versus them" perspective of outsiders who distrusted government and electoral politics. Even though he and his buddies *were* the government, he represented himself as just another politically alienated Joe, a viewpoint that colored his understanding of power and those who wielded it. For King, only strong men—charismatic authoritarian figures of ruthless ambition—could embody power.

No doubt, he granted press interviews in order to express his heartfelt contrition, an act that required him to show that he was cooperating with federal prosecutors. In the long term, the circulation of his story of wrongdoing reinforced the FBI's image of omniscience in the eyes of the news-consuming public. King talked because he hoped to win a lenient sentence and repair his reputation. Perhaps his friends, family, and business associates would judge him less harshly, maybe even forgive him, if he could recast himself as an unwitting conspirator and a foolish victim. But King's media confessions required an evil genius, and that role was Jim's. The more effectively he could represent Jim as a ruthless and all-seeing power, the more effectively he could blame his own deeds on his frailties.

His narrative strategy, however, hid Jim's limitations as a city father. King's story does not tell us how Jim failed to keep pace with what the City of Industry had become: a matrix of discrete governmental technologies, a micro-corporate state with its own social and cultural ecology. Despite Jim's best efforts to keep the city under perpetual surveillance, its expanding governmental matrix opened new spaces for others to explore schemes he had never imagined. The city's growing power matrix fostered environments and power effects in which new behaviors and personalities could flourish. Upgrading the city's financial technology, for example, created opportunities for other technicians to carve out power circuits to suit their own talents. As the city added to its repertoire of governmental technologies and contracted more specialists and businesses to operate its governmental apparatus, Jim exercised less control.

He probably did not immediately perceive that loss of control. But as Industry began subcontracting its governmental technologies to highly trained technicians, the number of people who were now serving as conduits and synapses of power also increased. The specialists' knowledge, in turn, entitled them to enjoy the invigorating results of their quiet, well-run technologies. Those persistent, repeated, heady experiences called for the technicians to invent new identities that reconciled their unknowing pasts to their knowing presents, to what they once were and who they were becoming. Warner W. Hodgdon rapidly emerged as the most visible and powerful specialist during Industry's acquisition of redevelopment technology. The city needed a financial guru who could exploit its redevelopment opportunities to the hilt. Hodgdon had cultivated a personality savvy and brash enough to fit the bill.

CHAPTER 7

SOWING A FIELD, CLIMBING A TREE

In that Empire, the Art of Cartography achieved such Perfection that the Map of one single Province occupied the whole of a City, and the Map of the Empire, the whole of a Province. In time, those Disproportionate maps failed to satisfy and the Schools of Cartography sketched a Map of the Empire which was of the size of the Empire.

—Jorge Luis Borges, *Dreamtigers*

It should come as no surprise to learn that the Southern Pacific's man in Industry, Wilfred Steiner, was also the man to recruit Warner W. Hodgdon. Steiner believed that Hodgdon could repeat the magic he had performed as director and financial consultant of San Bernardino's redevelopment agency, where he had quickly succeeded in qualifying that chronically depressed city for federal and state redevelopment funding.[1] Perpetually optimistic, Steiner was practiced at the art of can-do publicity, and he no doubt recognized the San Bernardino native as a kindred spirit, one whose winning personality had infected both community leaders and the area's news media with his exuberant boosterism.

Hodgdon later acknowledged to the FBI that Steiner and Loyd Lucy, a Southern Pacific employee, had invited him to Industry. He had gotten to know them during "his dealings with the Property Management Division of the Southern Pacific Railroad while he" consulted for the San Bernardino Redevelopment Agency. One former Industry insider believed that Steiner's interest in Hodgdon expressed the SP's desire to see the city take the plunge into redevelopment, an interest that coincided with a major course correction within the railroad's real estate division.[2] In 1970, faced with unrelenting competition from the trucking industry and a declining passenger business, the SP's directors announced new plans for their more than 3.8 million acres in U.S. real estate holdings. They appointed O. C. Linde to lead a new subsidiary, to which the railroad assigned about 23 million dollars' worth of land and 2 million dollars in cash. The goal was to spark development in markets in the Los Angeles and San Francisco areas.[3] Not surprisingly, Linde visited Jim Stafford at his mill during the early 1970s, perhaps to discuss the Southern Pacific's decision to sell 8.8 acres to Roski Senior's Majestic Reality at that time.[4]

Steiner introduced Hodgdon to Industry leaders as the visionary who would move the city beyond its piecemeal development practices. After his first meeting with city manager Rope and city attorney Ritchie, Hodgdon contracted with the city to draft a comprehensive redevelopment plan. He began by forming the Industry Urban Development Agency, which he structured in a manner that invested him, as the city's redevelopment coordinator and financial consultant, with the planning authority to administer the city as a single big redevelopment project. By subcontracting their planning authority to Hodgdon, Industry officials had followed the logic of the Lakewood plan. Hodgdon chose to exercise that authority by way of a joint venture with Hornblower & Weeks-Hemphill, Noyes, a municipal bond brokerage firm that had been hired to prepare and sell Industry's redevelopment bonds on Wall Street.[5]

Responses to Hodgdon's ambitious designs varied. Although some observers described him as "brilliant," "imaginative," and "inventive," his verbal slickness could also create problems; more than once Jim had needed to use his country charm to placate the plodding county bureaucrats whom Hodgdon had irked with his arrogance.[6] Nonetheless, Industry's new redevelopment coordinator made up for his impatience and brashness with an energetic lifestyle that impressed both clients and friends. The tireless networker could boast of not only his connections with high-powered Republicans and religious leaders, his generous philanthropy and community service, but also a passion for stockcar racing and his grandiose helicopter entrances.[7]

Hodgdon traced his genealogy of self-reliance back to rugged Mormon pioneer roots, and he loved to play up the image of himself as a self-made man, as in this 1976 *Times* article: "He went to work at 10. He finished high school and became an apprentice plumber and a journeyman carpenter. 'I started building buildings,' he says, 'and from that background, I got into the financial consulting business.'"[8] In time, however, he attracted critics who viewed his autobiography with suspicion. "Hodgdon," one San

Bernardino reporter politely observed, "is driven by a desire to leave as great a mark on the San Bernardino area as he can—as great as Jefferson Hunt, an early Mormon settler and—according to Hodgdon, Hodgdon's great-great-grandfather." Considering his audience, Hodgdon had chosen his ancestors well: "Capt. Jefferson Hunt, who led a party of Mormons into the territory in the early 1800s, became a state assemblyman and is the recognized 'Father of San Bernardino County.'"[9] By the time he arrived in Industry in 1971, Hodgdon had earned a reputation comparable to Hunt's. According to another reporter, "as chairman of the city's Redevelopment Agency, he played the key role in building the new civic center and is responsible for most of modern San Bernardino."[10]

But Hodgdon appeared in Industry with more than his Rolodex. In 1968, he had served a twenty-day jail sentence for failing to file an income-tax return for 1965.[11] Eventually, in December 1968, he resigned his San Bernardino redevelopment post under a cloud for making agency decisions that, among other irregularities, allegedly benefited his friends at the city's expense. The agency had selected a company partly owned by John Curci, uncle of Hodgdon's close friend Robert Curci, to build a mall project for the city of San Bernardino. But in a town with a reputation for gang violence and chronic economic depression, simple gratitude explains why officials and critics in San Bernardino went easy on him. On the same day on which he announced his resignation, he also obtained millions in redevelopment subsidies and low-grade bond financing for the city.[12]

Attorneys overseeing Industry's bond financing were not prepared to make Hodgdon's indiscretions an issue as long as his financial consulting duties did not authorize him to handle the city's money.[13] Still, his elevation to redevelopment architect irked some in the city, not least because it altered its division of intellectual labor. City attorney and acting city manager Graham Ritchie, who until then had enjoyed the run of the city, was one official who saw his powers being reduced.[14] According to some observers, this loss of power fueled a rivalry that saw its embarrassing denouement more than a decade later.

For his part, Jim Stafford both benefited from and was irritated by the new man's visionary skill, winning charm, and planning knowledge. Although Hodgdon began by implementing plans that were designed for Jim's benefit, he also proposed enormous, complex projects that would gradually reduce Jim's ability to direct development. In later interviews, Hodgdon insisted, for example, that he, not Jim, should decide which economists, bond brokers, and lawyers to retain to do the "actual planning for the development of the city." He also took sole credit for proposing and executing a series of large real estate purchases. Never, Hodgdon later declared, did he discuss the advisability of these purchases with Jim. Only once did he admit to Jim's help: when the two of them persuaded a Union Pacific subsidiary to discuss selling a property to the city redevelopment agency.[15]

"You Will Be Subservient!"

Hodgdon's formidable ego required Jim's vigilance. Stephen Stafford, a teenager at the time, was present during many meetings between his father and Hodgdon. He saw them as rivals. In 1982, Stephen told the FBI that the relationship between the two "was never clear" and that Jim struggled to maintain "the upper hand." The younger Stafford had witnessed "a few heated exchanges over some things involving the city, but his father always seemed to win out." On one occasion, Stephen recalled, "his father said to Hodgdon, 'You will be subservient!'" an order that revealed Jim's struggle to impose his will.[16]

Jim got what he wanted at first. In May 1971, Hodgdon delivered the city's first general plan, which included photographs that connoted Industry "blight" and thus invoked California's formidable redevelopment laws. The plan also revealed details about the city's proposed civic-financial center, a twenty-six-acre district anchored on its northern boundary by the Los Angeles County sheriff's substation, which had been built in 1961 on land purchased from Jim's milling business.[17] The plan did not explain why this part of the city was best suited for a new city hall, although banks and financial offices were already operating in other parts of Industry. It also failed to mention that Jim, his business partner Lefty Horst, their family members, and other city officials owned the designated land.

Three months later, Hodgdon advanced the Civic-Financial Center project when he scripted the formation of the Industry Urban Development Agency, which took its planning and financial directives from Hodgdon and its engineering and architectural directives from National Engineering Company, an engineering and architectural services firm. Despite Hodgdon's purported independence, the civil engineering firm's numerous Industry contracts provided the first clue that a third party was monitoring what was supposed to be a two-party relationship.

In 1954, Ellsworth Epperson had started National Engineering as a sideline to his day job as a civil engineer for the county. After its incorporation in 1957, Industry began to award engineering contracts to the firm. Eventually, Epperson's brother-in-law George O. Asch, a civil and mechanical engineer, joined the firm as a partner, with the task of handling more of the city's business.[18] State corporate filings show that, in February 1969, the firm moved yet another step toward becoming a full-time operation when Epperson and Asch added city attorney Ritchie as a partner.[19]

Jim's "Fair Haired Boy"

But former employees and Industry insiders have claimed that National Engineering owed its success to Jim, who rewarded Epperson for providing decisive advice during Industry's 1957 incorporation fight. What that advice was is unclear. But Ann Nowels, National Engineering's bookkeeper from 1962 to 1977, told the FBI during its subsequent criminal investigation that Epperson "became Stafford's 'fair haired boy' and got a contract to serve as" Industry's city engineer, a job that "soon became [National Engineering's] major source of income."

Jim's generosity, however, was predicated on certain expectations, which Epperson expressed in code. "For instance," Nowels said, "he would say things like, 'if we cooperate with Stafford, we will be taken care of.'" Although Nowels no longer had access to files that could support her claims, she said that cooperation meant paying Jim "rebates" from National Engineering contracts. According to her, Epperson used his gambling habit to hide these alleged kickbacks: "Epperson would withdraw money from the [firm's] account and deposit it into his own personal checking account. He would then cash checks at the Desert Inn [a casino in Las Vegas], and use that money to pay Stafford the 'rebate.'" Jim expected Epperson to do free engineering work on Jim's personal real estate development projects and "give priority attention to anything in which he had an interest," such as paying a higher monthly rent by moving his business to the new office building that Stafford had just erected in the Civic-Financial Center.[20]

Virgie Lee Epperson, who was Epperson's longtime companion until they married in 1973, corroborated Nowels's testimony to the FBI. She often went with Ep, as Jim called him, on his monthly gambling junkets. During one such trip, Virgie recalled, "she noticed her husband writing a check to the Desert Inn for $3,000 or $4,000 in cash," even though he was not losing at the tables. "She later looked in his checkbook and noticed he had written other large checks." After she confronted him about the checks, her husband told her "he used the cash to pay Stafford" and that he did so every month. Virgie also recalled accompanying Ep to Jim's mill to deliver a 7,500-dollar check. Later, as she went through her husband's canceled checks, she noticed a "check for cash at the Desert Inn in the amount of $4,100 with the notation, 'J.S.' in tiny letters." Virgie told the FBI that "her husband referred to Stafford as, 'J.S.'"[21]

Jim's expectations went beyond these alleged kickbacks. He assumed that Epperson would hire the people whom he recommended. In one case, Jim directed Epperson to hire Steiner and provide him with his own office after he retired from the Southern Pacific in 1972, the same year the city named the Monrovia resident an "honorary inhabitant" of the city.[22] It is not exactly clear why Jim wanted Ep to hire Steiner. Perhaps he was repaying him for ensuring the city's creation or trying to maintain good relations with the railroad. But when Nowels asked her boss "why they were putting Steiner on the payroll when he evidently performed no services for the company, Epperson told her, 'we are putting him on the payroll because Stafford wants us to.'"[23] By the time Hodgdon arrived on the scene, any developers who wanted to build in the city knew that National Engineering would need to sign off on their design work.

Clearly, Jim still held the reins of Industry. Hodgdon may have created the Industry Urban Development Agency, but Jim quietly selected the people whom the city council appointed to its board of directors, raising Industry's cronyism to a new level. Nonetheless, Hodgdon's contractual authority over the agency had introduced a competitor into the city's chain of command; and by concentrating the agency's engineering and design contracts with National Engineering, the new arrival had the oversight necessary for implementing Industry's comprehensive plan. On the one hand, Jim's alleged control of Epperson and of the friends he selected for the agency's board made it easy for him to monitor both the engineering firm and the agency without risking public exposure. But on the other hand, Hodgdon could control the actions and decisions of the board of directors: with only rudimentary knowledge of the intricacies of redevelopment and municipal finance, they were dependent on his instructions.

Swallowing a City

Under Hodgdon's direction, the Industry Urban Development Agency promptly proposed a 55-million-dollar project. Prosaically known as Project One, it encompassed about seven hundred acres, or one-third of Industry's area within its boundaries, and included the La Puente Hills landfill (now slated as the site of Industry's exhibition-conference facility) and sixteen acres owned by Jim and Lefty Horst.[24] At its public unveiling in July 1971, the project immediately triggered conflict-of-interest allegations, which were echoed in the local press. Dissenting property owners and schools claimed that the city's first redevelopment project would enrich a circle of unnamed individuals, authorize legally sanctioned fraud, toss properties within the project area into financial limbo, and pervert state redevelopment laws by treating rural properties as if they were urban slums.[25]

After Industry's city council brushed aside the allegations and approved the project, the Rowland Heights and Hacienda–La Puente school districts, which overlapped Project One's boundaries, announced their intention to file suit against the agency's use of tax-increment financing. The districts argued that their schools were being forced to "receive taxes based on the valuation before the land" was developed, while the city would reap all tax revenues from properties reassessed after it began. Because property values would continue to climb, the agency had engineered recurring tax windfalls while freezing school revenues just as student populations were rapidly growing.

Industry's redevelopment project, which was years away from completion, could not take credit for the city's 12-percent annual increases in property values during the early 1970s. Nevertheless, it still enjoyed the benefits of tax-increment increases.[26] The school districts' media and legal campaign did earn them a few modest concessions, though. In September 1971, the plaintiffs halted their lawsuit after the city agreed to return a revenue share to the schools that was proportionate to the size of the project area but was not the full amount they would have otherwise received.[27] Under the agreed-upon formula, the school districts received 68,787 dollars less in revenue but did not face the 1.85-million-dollar loss they would have suffered had they rejected Industry's most recent offer.

That year, the thirty-two schools and government agencies surrounding Industry lost 474,656 dollars in tax revenues diverted to Project One—or 405,869 dollars when adjusted for the agency's supplemental payments to the school districts. A handful of Industry's critics predicted that such losses would grow to 1.13 million dollars by the following tax year, reaching a projected 15.4-million-dollar loss in the 1981–1982 tax year. In other words, these schools and government agencies faced a 57.6-percent revenue reduction due to Project One alone.[28]

Turning a Blue Collar Brown

These projected fiscal imbalances coincided with demographic changes in the San Gabriel Valley, particularly in communities such as La Puente, which was well on its way to becoming a majority blue-collar Latino community.

According to the 1970 U.S. Census, the city's Latino population had grown to 46 percent, a trend that would continue for the next two decades. New arrivals from Mexico and Central America were joining the city's longtime residents, immigrants from previous decades, and the descendants of the nineteenth-century Mexican population that settled in the La Puente Valley. This Latino community was poorer and less well educated than its Anglo counterparts, and now Industry's explosion of commercial development and reorganized transportation grid was beginning to starve La Puente economically. Redrawn boulevards and the barrier created by the Pomona Freeway made access to La Puente's stores more difficult, while a new mega-shopping center south of the freeway in Industry offered a more attractive alternative to shoppers. Industry's civic center and commercial developments not only blocked north-south traffic but also made it easy to resegregate La Puente's growing Latino student population into separate but increasingly unequal schools.[29]

The predicted damage to neighboring cities did not stop Industry's leaders from approving the civic center project. In 1972, the Industry Urban Development Agency proposed two more project areas that would put more than 80 percent of the city's area under its redevelopment authority and launch 55 million dollars' worth of large and small projects. The city also entered into an agreement with the agency to spin off another redevelopment entity, the Civic-Recreational-Industrial Authority (CRIA), which would assume responsibility for planning the development of the La Puente Hills property. As illustration of how redevelopment could theoretically produce an endless succession of government entities administered by the same handful of elected and unelected officials, CRIA had been authorized by way of a new government technology called a joint powers agreement, an irresistibly attractive model for compartmentalizing government functions. Now the development agency and CRIA entered into a three-way joint powers agreement to co-fund a fourth entity called the Parking Authority, which issued 5 million dollars in redevelopment bonds to pay for the civic center's parking facilities.[30] That action was merely a preview of what was to come.

Warner Hodgdon, Jim Stafford, and the City of Industry had managed to yoke three bodies—the city council, the Industry Urban Development Agency, and the Civic-Recreational-Industrial Authority—into a comprehensive program to acquire millions in tax increments and then to leverage those funds into millions more in long-term bond debt. But coordinating these public agencies to function as quasi-corporate subsidiaries required a radical transformation of city government. Industry was no longer just a city; it was now one huge redevelopment mill, the largest in California, perhaps in the nation.

Again, the local press aired the grievances of school officials, who continued to challenge the fiscal fairness of Industry's redevelopment plan. Again, the press highlighted the troubles of homeowners and interviewed political leaders who claimed that the proposed shopping center would rob sales-tax revenue from neighboring cities with older commercial centers.[31] Industry mayor John Ferrero rejected the criticism as meddling, telling those city officials to "spend more time planning for the growth and success of their own communities and less time opposing the growth and development of their neighbors."[32] Meanwhile, Valdis Vilmis Pavlovskis, one of Industry's rare academic critics, predicted that the three project areas would accelerate the rate of property-tax diversions, siphoning off as much as 29 million dollars each year by 1983.[33] As it turned out, these predictions undershot Industry's actual annual increment funding by at least 10 million dollars, and its long-term increment revenues by even larger margins.[34]

With such frequent criticism appearing in the press, one might assume that the public was vigorously involved in discussing Industry's development plans. Most of the *Times* articles, however, were either very short, lacked contextual detail, or were restricted to the San Gabriel Valley's suburban edition.[35] More importantly, major elements of the city's plan, such as its twenty-six-acre civic center, received almost no press attention, even though the project mirrored the controversial sheriff's substation deal of the 1960s.

In August 1972, the Industry Urban Development Agency filed suit to acquire property for a new city hall, a post office, and office space for banks. Not surprisingly, Jim, Lefty, and their close friends (including the agency's chairwoman) had approved of the project from the start. In June, the agency announced its decision to purchase seventeen parcels for the new civic center, eleven of which belonged to Jim, Lefty, and their wives—a total of sixteen acres, or 64 percent of the center's project area.[36]

The court-appointed appraiser in the city's condemnation suit estimated the value of Jim and Lefty's 11.3 acres at 1.38 million dollars, an offer Jim and Lefty eventually accepted but only after they had failed to convince the court to go with the agency's 1.47-million-dollar appraisal for their property. But the partners had not exhausted their money-making options. The agency said it still intended to acquire the unsold 4.7-acre parcel where they operated their feed and warehousing business, arguing that it could not ignore Jim's rusting grain mill if it hoped to give Industry the much-needed facelift it required.[37]

In the local press, Industry's critics pointed to the Civic-Financial Center project as further evidence of redevelopment abuse that favored Jim, his friends, and his family at taxpayers' expense. Although Jim and Lefty accepted the court-appointed appraiser's lower offer for their 11.3 acres, the critics said the agency still overpaid the partners by more than 76,000 dollars an acre for property the county had only recently assessed for 11,000 dollars an acre. But city attorney Ritchie argued that one bank's willingness to pay $3.35 a square foot in 1971 for office space in the Civic-Financial Center showed that the agency had not paid too dearly.

In the second interview he granted to the press, Jim told the *Times* that the purchase price had been set by a Los Angeles Superior Court judge after he had "reviewed the facts."[38] Jim's laconic explanation relied upon a public assumption of court-arbitered truth, even if the "facts" that had led to the court's decision involved a series of deletions. Without a markedly lower property appraisal for comparison or courtroom allegations of Jim's undue influence over the city, the presiding judge was obliged to accept the court's appraisal as a "reasonable" asking price.[39]

In the article, the *Times* cited an unnamed source outside the court-room who saw Jim's favorable treatment as further evidence that the city's purported founder was the "dominant influence in Industry."[40] Jim reportedly "scoffed" at the allegation, which reiterated the mastermind motif of the boss who runs a city as his personal domain. "Jealous and idle people breed idle thoughts," he shot back. "If someone were to ask me, do I know the councilmen, the answer is yes, I've known them all my life." According to "blunt-talking Stafford," his longtime affiliations with the mayor and the other council members who had approved the land deal did not prove that he had sinister motives. He made his agenda clear: "If it's good for the area and Industry, I'm for it." His boosterish retort presumed that the region's manufacturing minority required special protection from the homeowning majority. If he and his fellow city founders had not acted, real estate speculators would have stepped in and built "instant slums."[41] It's hard to ignore Jim's disdain for the ordinary folks who also wanted to cash in on the local real estate boom. He reserved the sharpest edge of his disdain for the mill's closest neighbors. Readers with an intimate knowledge of local demography and Industry's recent conflicts with La Puente would have understood the subtext of his "instant slum" reference. It was a racial code for the need to contain La Puente's increasingly Latin working-class residents. Likewise, his portrayal of manufacturers as victims who deserved protection would not have withstood a public debate: considerable evidence was already available to show that Los Angeles County represented one of the nation's fastest-growing manufacturing zones, not a region hostile to industrial development.

Still, the contest over the civic center's future accounted for only a fraction of the redevelopment projects Hodgdon was quietly drafting for the rest of the city, the part the local media ignored as long as there was no clash of personalities to focus on. A review of property records, city planning proceedings, and redevelopment agency publicity shows that warehousing, manufacturing, and commercial development were feeding Industry's growth. Now Hodgdon had developed plans for a municipal airport, a free-trade zone, a massive shopping center with its own office complex, and a warehousing and office complex called the Crossroads Industrial Park, each larger than the Civic-Financial Center.

By completing just one project awarded in 1976, Ed Roski, Jr.'s, Commerce Construction could outstrip the total volume of redevelopment previously completed in the city. That project, part of the proposed Crossroads Industrial Park, would be located on the city's northeastern edge, at the cloverleaf junction of the Pomona Freeway and the San Gabriel Parkway and the Union Pacific and Southern Pacific rail lines, and would involve more than 2.8 million square feet of new construction. Commerce Construction and its investment partners, who included Robert King and Jim Stafford, had acquired their share of the site from the Industry Urban Development Agency on extremely favorable terms.[42] At first glance, however, the terms of the deal appeared to favor the agency at Ed Junior's expense. Commerce Construction had agreed to purchase 140 acres of the 188-acre project from the agency for 5.4 million dollars, a million dollars more than what the agency had paid to assemble the parcels from private owners. To fulfill its part of the deal, however, the agency agreed to pay for grading and filling in the rough spots, installing storm drains, realigning roads, and building a bridge over Pomona Freeway. The total cost of these improvements would top 30 million dollars; the bridge alone would set the city back by 6 million dollars, but those investments would also dramatically increase area property values.[43]

The agency took a no-nonsense approach to marketing the Crossroads project. In particular, it stressed the site's strategic transportation assets—a strategy that also reinforced allegations that the Roskis had a special understanding with both the city and the railroads. According to the literature prepared in support of the bond issue that would finance the project, "excellent rail facilities are provided by the Union Pacific main line. The location of the line within the Project Area provides excellent opportunities to serve future industrial development. There are few topographic problems [that] would prohibit construction of rail spurs within the Project Area."[44] The development's interested parties also focused on the project's proximity to the ports of Los Angeles and Long Beach, which were central to Southern California's growing importance in global trade. The attorneys who prepared Crossroads' 4-million-dollar bond issue therefore encouraged Wall Street bond brokers to view Industry's location and transportation infrastructure as tangible, proven assets.[45] Moreover, the project's location at the junction of the freeway and the parkway had the potential to attract as many as fifty local trucking lines, which could then provide "overnight delivery to a wide region," while "nearby Los Angeles and Ontario International Airports" offered future tenants "excellent air freight" service.[46]

In addition to the Crossroads project, Hodgdon had proposed the purchase of a 2,575-acre ranch outside the city's boundaries, where he intended to build a dam and a filtration plant in order to market Northern California water to Industry's thirsty factories and perhaps (if any water was left over) to its surrounding suburbs. Only one other city, Los Angeles, had made such large-scale land purchases to secure water for its residents. The press, however, continued to focus on the Civic-Financial Center, ignoring Industry's plan to purchase land outside its city limits. The press also overlooked a struggle that was unfolding among Industry's elite.

In 1973, National Engineering's Ellsworth Epperson lost control of his car and rolled it off the Pomona Freeway. He had just left a party at P Hill, home of the Perez family's trash-hauling operation, and was en route to a meeting at the Dal Rae Restaurant in nearby Pico Rivera, a watering hole for City of Commerce and City of Industry big shots. Although Epperson survived the accident, it was clear that he had suffered serious brain damage, which, his doctors said, would grow progressively worse. They told Virgie, his companion of eight years, that he would need someone to take care of him. As she later told the FBI, the two decided to marry, a move that "caused a furor with those in power [in Industry] because they were convinced that she would [now claim] ownership in National Engineering."[47]

The passivity of the local press, when combined with Industry's ferocious approach to information management, meant that Ep's condition would stay under wraps and that Industry's critics—the property owners facing condemnation, the developers thwarted from participating in redevelopment, and the revenue-starved public agencies—usually lagged a few steps behind the action. Because Industry's critics could object only to the information the city chose to release to the public, they failed to significantly modify the three-part, 102-million-dollar redevelopment plan that the city had announced in 1971. Their only short-term success was to halt the airport project and temporarily reduce the amount of land subject to redevelopment.[48] Apparently, however, Hodgdon had counted on these losses from the outset. At one National Engineering board meeting, he allegedly confided that the airport controversy "was a diversion" calculated to accomplish "something else behind the scenes. . . . Sometimes you have to create a diversion at the front door when you're trying to get in through the back door."[49] It is hard to know if this comment was braggadocio or simply a moment of candor, but available documents and records clearly demonstrate that the airport reversal did little to impede his immediate plans to engulf the city in redevelopment. And voter approval of Industry's comprehensive plan a year earlier, in 1974, ensured that the city would remain a virtually closed knowledge system and that its next big decision would be made without sparking a scandal.

In 1975, the Industry Urban Development Agency paid Jim Stafford and Lefty Horst 497,000 dollars for the mill's remaining 4.7 acres. In other words, the agency not only paid them nearly 150,000 dollars more than the county assessor's estimated market value for the property, but it also added 120,000 dollars to the sellers' 1972 asking price while allowing them to continue operating their mill on generous terms. In addition, the agency paid the partners an additional 10,000 dollars to cover their relocation costs. In all, Jim, Lefty, and their family members earned nearly 2.6 million dollars in the deal.

Nearly a decade later, when examples of such favoritism had become too numerous to deny, Hodgdon insisted that he was merely implementing plans that had already been in place before he had arrived on the Industry scene.[50] He did not, however, apologize for the 2-percent fee he charged on all new or refinanced bonds that he prepared, which, his critics alleged, was at least three times higher than the going rate of 0.25 to 0.5 percent. Such a discrepancy quickly turned into big money when the city began to issue hundreds of millions worth of redevelopment bonds. Yet city attorney Ritchie, overlooking his alleged differences with Hodgdon, defended the fee contract as "reasonable," arguing that Industry's bonds were difficult to sell, a claim flatly challenged by redevelopment directors and consultants in other cities, who were well aware of Industry's value to developers, manufacturers, and warehouse owners.[51]

Once the land deals were made, the civic center project entered a new phase. In April 1975, the Industry city council passed a resolution authorizing a firm known as S. & R. Investment Company to purchase a civic center parcel at $2.96 a square foot. Those initials stood for Stafford and Roski. The partnership promptly built a two-story office building, which it then leased to Bank of America. The Industry Urban Development Agency installed and maintained the parking lot and landscaping that surrounded the structure at no charge to the developer. S. & R.'s partners paid about sixteen cents a square foot more than what Jim and Lefty had sold it for in 1972, which might almost qualify as a fair markup. But not if you factored in the generous subdivision and site preparation investments the agency made in the property and the free landscaping and parking subsidy it threw in on top of that.[52]

The April agreement signaled a shift in the way in which Jim now began to profit from his power. Thanks to the Roskis, he acquired half-interests in two other Civic-Financial Center properties. One of them was an office suite at 220 North Hacienda Boulevard. Stephen Stafford later told the FBI that the Roskis had built those offices and then leased them to the First Federal Savings and Loan Association. Stephen learned about his father's involvement in the property several years later, when, in a "rare mood of generosity," Jim decided "to transfer his interest in the property . . . to him," even though Ed Junior was officially "listed as the sole owner." According to Stephen, his father told him he "no longer needed the income and depreciation," so he set up a rental-trust agreement that allowed Stephen to use the income to "pay off the mortgage" and split whatever was left over between Ed Junior and himself.[53]

Jim had another half-interest in a Roski property on North Hacienda Boulevard, a brick office building erected by Commerce Construction Company and leased by National Engineering and the Industry Manufacturers Council. Clearly, Ed Junior was helping Jim shift from orchestrating one-time real estate deals to the similarly lucrative but long-term strategy of extracting lease rents from city-subsidized tenants. Before the 1970s, California's local rentiers had played an intermediary role, doing the political and financial groundwork necessary to attract Fortune 500 corporations to Southern California. But the Roski business was redefining the role of the region's rentier class. By means of its proliferating real estate partnerships, innovations in building construction, financial backing from national banks, and preferential treatment from railroads and redevelopment agencies, the Roski development empire was garnering enough financial and technical resources to tap into the international trade that was already flowing from the ports of Los Angeles and Long Beach. The Roskis nationalized the business of building and leasing factories and warehouses, slowly but surely insinuating themselves into infrastructure of global trade in Las Vegas, Denver, Houston, and Atlanta.

But when left to his own devices, the Jim of the mid-1970s reverted to smaller-scale profit strategies on the feudal end of the capitalist spectrum. Across the street from his bank property, for example, Jim and Lefty were renting back the mill they had sold, paying their new landlord, the Industry Urban Development Agency, 2,500 dollars a month, half the agency's going rental rate. In essence, the agency was subsidizing the partners' mill, a business with a finite future, thanks to the relentless suburbanization of the San Gabriel Valley.[54]

Yet for Jim, the leasing arrangement was also a symbolic gain. The maps that National Engineering drew up during its campaign to widen and reorient the civic center's streets show how he had managed to preserve his privileged vantage point, now symbolized by the mill that towered over the city's seat of government.[55] With Industry's city hall on his doorstep, Jim validated his claims to ownership. Moreover, in a multivalent act of re-signification, the city rehabilitated the memory of Jim's disgraced father, C. C. Stafford, by renaming the street that stopped at city hall in his honor and thus establishing a founding genealogy that made Jim's role as the city's unofficial leader seem natural.[56] It is easy to imagine Jim standing at the window with a bottle of his favorite Corona beer in hand and savoring the ambiguity of a street name that could be read as both a public recognition of his father and a private reminder to city officials and property owners that Jim was watching them and that everything inside the Civic-Financial Center—its tenants and city employees—were objects under his personal surveillance.

For years Jim had seen the city as his personal possession, as an extension of his personality, a theater for dramatizing the power of his gaze. Now he not only began to believe the stories that his friends and enemies told about him, but he also let his power to rename a city street become visible to strangers beyond his immediate social circle. Each angry property owner, government official, or journalist on his or her way to city hall who recognized the Stafford name on the sign represented an opportunity for that person to feel Jim's gaze but also to question the family origin myth the city's publicity men had manufactured on his behalf. Allowing his naming power to become visible therefore suggested a crude grasp of how a well-crafted history could help his gaze appear natural and necessary. The commemorative event Steiner organized for that purpose in 1975 would have been more convincing if a respected historian had independently confirmed Jim's version of his father's life.[57] Permitting his watching to become visible, by contrast, gave individuals or institutions not subject to Jim's influence an excuse to read his story, whether inscribed in published or built texts, with a critical eye, a questioning tendency that might even undermine Jim's desires to protect himself from shame if allowed to spread in the press.

Consolidating His Powers

By 1975, Jim, perhaps emboldened by the success of his redevelopment ventures, had turned his attention to reorganizing the city's civil engineering apparatus. In a maneuver that briefly ruffled a few feathers, he helped Hodgdon acquire a majority interest in National Engineering.[58] During her interview with the FBI, Virgie Lee Epperson recalled the September day when Jim unexpectedly sent a driver to pick up her husband at their West Covina home and deliver him to a meeting in the offices of the accounting firm Frazer and Torbet in downtown Los Angeles. Among those present were Jim, Fred Gysi (his personal accountant at the firm), and Hodgdon. Virgie said her husband returned from the meeting in a shaken state. At first, she said, he told her he had decided to sell his business and had received inquiries from a buyer—Warner W. Hodgdon. But later she learned that during the meeting, when he had expressed reluctance about selling out to Hodgdon, Jim "told him to take the offer. . . . If he did not like it, he would not get anything at all. Stafford told him that he could not sell the company [to anyone else], and even if he did, the buyer would not get nothing [sic] because he would see to it that National Engineering Company never got another contract through the City of Industry."[59]

A witness at that meeting confirmed Virgie's account. Stephen Stafford, then about twenty-five years old, was also present at the showdown.[60] He said his father got right to the point: he told Epperson that Hodgdon wanted National Engineering. According to Stephen, Jim "said something like, 'Ep, this is the way it is. This man is coming in. Let's accommodate him.'" His attitude made it clear to Epperson that he had no choice; the only issue left to settle was the price. But when Epperson asked for more than Hodgdon was willing to pay, Jim cut him short: "Quit talking about the blue sky, Ep. If it wasn't for the city, you would not have any business." Stephen said, "Epperson nodded in apparent agreement, but he was not . . . enthusiastic."[61]

Virgie told the FBI that her husband sold National Engineering to Warner Hodgdon for 396,000 dollars to be paid in six yearly installments. In addition, Hodgdon guaranteed Epperson a 90,000-dollar annual salary and a new Lincoln Continental every year, free gas included, for as long as he lived. She said that Hodgdon lived up to his agreement, even though her husband survived for longer than anybody had expected.[62] But according to Stephen, when the meeting ended and the attendees began walking to lunch, Jim told the people around him, "That was not a bad price for that old goat, but that whore he is married to will get every penny of it."[63]

By 1979, when *Los Angeles Herald Examiner* reporter Scot Paltrow tried interview the seventy-nine-year-old Epperson, his neurological condition had greatly deteriorated. He was not able to corroborate Virgie's account of the sale. Hodgdon, however, insisted to Paltrow that he had not pressured Epperson or his brother-in-law George Asch to sell their business.[64] Hodgdon elaborated on that claim five years later, when he told the FBI that Epperson and Asch could not "keep up with the progress of the [city] planners."[65] He said "there was nothing [unusual]" about the way in which he had acquired his majority interest in the firm.[66] The result of his acquisition, however, was unusual.

By adding a major ownership share of the firm that monopolized Industry's engineering work to the list of redevelopment powers Hodgdon had previously acquired, he consolidated his formal control over the city's redevelopment apparatus. The situation alarmed James Warren Beebe, an attorney with O'Melveny and Myers, a law firm that served many members of the Los Angeles blueblood elite. Subcontracted to work on Industry's redevelopment bonds, Beebe "notified Hodgdon in writing that he should 're-examine his relationships with the City of Industry.'" If problems with the bonds arose, the attorney said, "the legal sufficiency of future bond issues could be challenged by the bond holders as invalid." Beebe made it clear to Hodgdon and city attorney Ritchie that he "did not want to assume" legal liability for any potential conflict of interest. In response, Ritchie requested a legal opinion from the law firm of Burke, Williams, and Sorensen, which concluded that Hodgdon's bond issues "would be 'clean,' although in the end of his opinion, Sorensen added, 'This is not a bond opinion,'" averting the legal consequences of taking an official stand on the issue. Soon thereafter, Beebe notified Ritchie and Hodgdon "that he could not continue as their bond counsel."[67]

Beebe's departure left the field clear for Hodgdon, who accelerated the city's land-buying program, a move that served not only his own ambitions but also Jim's and the Roski family's development agenda. Under the aegis of National Engineering, he not only participated in current development projects and designed the new manufacturing and warehousing parks sprouting up throughout the city (many of which the Roski family or its friends developed) but also implemented his own vision for the city, buying up acreage on the city's eastern extremities for an international free-trade zone as well as a 2,500-acre estate completely outside the city's boundaries.

The financial schemes he set in motion to pay for these projects were just as ambitious. In June 1975, the city gave Hodgdon permission to issue 84 million dollars in bond sales to retire 30 million dollars in previously issued bonds; he also had permission to secure a 54-million-dollar infusion of new redevelopment funds. The Industry Urban Development Agency used those transactions to redirect as much as 3.8 million dollars in tax-increment funds to Hodgdon's new projects and thus put off bond repayment to a later date. But he did not have to put off charging his financial consulting fee, which came to 840,000 dollars.[68]

By 1977, it became apparent that concentrating three executive functions in Hodgdon had the potential to invite unwelcome scrutiny. So in August, the city and the development agency issued new contracts with National Engineering that "clarified" their relationship with Hodgdon and rescued him from having to file financial disclosure statements with California's Fair Political Practices Commission. City attorney Ritchie explained that National Engineering would henceforward restrict itself to a consulting role; it would no longer have decision-making power over Industry's redevelopment program.[69] This technical fix, which took place more than a year after Hodgdon had taken the reins at National Engineering, was not as limiting as it might seem. He had already had plenty of time to design the city's financial and development plans for the coming years and to cement his relationships with the development agency's directors and the city's other government entities. Under the circumstances, any plan he proposed was already as good as a command.

CHAPTER 8

SCARING THE PESTS AWAY

Who isn't aware that beneath every great . . . showy flag quite often there are
several other modestly private banners that are unfurled and waving in the
shadow of the first, and ever so many times outlive it?
—Joaquim Maria Machado De Assis, *Epitaph of a Small Winner*

Industry's critics did not prevent the city from transforming into a redevelopment juggernaut. They didn't even slow it down. But the schools,
the good government types, the small business owners and homeowners
who had failed to curtail redevelopment in their own backyards heard
and felt those criticisms, though often in unanticipated ways.

In the mid-1970s, amid generalized anxiety about skyrocketing property
values, opponents of redevelopment either willingly lent their arguments
to critics of big government or saw them hijacked by those critics. The
media's "benign neglect" of redevelopment reporting during its first
thirty years of existence had the set the stage for this conflation. Press
criticism, when it occurred at all, had portrayed redevelopment as an
abuse of the concept's original intentions or as reckless overspending by
greedy individuals or city bureaucrats.[1] For example, between 1970 and
1974 (Industry's dynamic planning period), the *Times* published articles
that either criticized Jim and the city's leaders for perverting the intent of
redevelopment or attacked the unfairness of California's tax-increment
financing system. The abuse motif followed a predictable moralizing logic:
it painted the abusers as individuals, some of them private business owners
like Jim, some of them crafty officials like Ritchie, who had violated the
law's assumed noble intent. Not once during this period did the *Times*
or any other local newspaper portray specific corporations, such as the
railroads, as abusers. And the press rarely informed readers about the

differences between federal and California redevelopment law and the consequences that flowed from those differences.

Among leaders of the tax-revolt movement, these stories further illustrated the ways government overreached its authority and burdened citizens with taxes they had never bargained for. No matter that the tax rebels could not show a causal link between inflation and tax-increment financing or redevelopment: homeowners were absorbing the powerfully emotional message, and anti-tax leaders hoped their anger would trigger a stampede to the ballot box.

Over a span of four years, starting in 1974, the average price of a California home rose from 34,000 to 85,000 dollars, an inflationary spike that alternately thrilled and terrified homeowners, who saw their fantasies of sudden wealth undercut by the threat of higher property taxes.[2] Conservative demagogues blamed homeowners' distress on excessive government spending, an argument that resonated strongly among the San Gabriel Valley's newly indebted working class and fixed-income elderly. According to urban historian Mike Davis, "Frustration [had already been mounting] through the mid-1960s and the early 1970s, a period which saw angry San Gabriel Valley homeowners storm the board of supervisors, attempt a tax payers' strike, followed by failed attempts to secede from the county altogether."[3]

In Southern California, homeowners grappled with their choices for managing the crisis. They could devise a new formula to enable local government to build the infrastructure for future suburban growth, they could reevaluate the plausibility of limitless suburbanization, or they could turn their backs on local government and hope that the problem would just go away. The first and second options, however, required homeowners to come to grips with their own role in fueling suburban sprawl and to question industry's use of anti-urban narratives to market the region's farm and scrubland as virgin space. But hardly anyone in the press or in politics raised these issues.

That lack of curiosity left a tempting opening for a handful of tenacious ideologues. In an effort to shape homeowner discontent, fiscal conservatives such as Ronald Reagan, the TV spokesman turned perennial Republican candidate, and anti-tax gadfly Howard Jarvis qualified a series of ballot initiatives to cut property taxes in an effort to circumvent the legislature. The tax rebels were not trying to pass laws so much as to cultivate panic. Using the rhetoric of fiscal accountability heavily spiced with metaphors of family finance, they blamed the crisis on Sacramento's majority Democratic legislature and defended California's suburban dream as a non-negotiable entitlement, although they continued to ignore the uncontrolled growth that was making the state's mass-produced, faux-rural suburbs unlivable.[4] Nervous homeowners responded, lashing out at the 1974 energy crisis, at higher taxes in general, even at the fiscal technologies that were subsidizing suburban growth, but not at growth itself. The big government critics, meanwhile, now linked rising property taxes with the debt-financed construction of new roads, water mains, public parks, and Industry-style redevelopment projects.[5]

As the property-tax panic spread, a number of newly formed cities, hoping to assuage taxpayer wrath, decided to reexamine the tax-increment system that was financing redevelopment. But they approached the task with caution. The League of California Cities, a membership organization dominated by post-1950s suburban cities, had only recently discovered the advantages of using redevelopment to secure revenues in a tightening fiscal environment. As Michael Scott, a league staff assistant, told the *Times*, "cities see [redevelopment] as a very powerful tool to rehabilitate their deteriorating neighborhoods." His assertion of the redevelopment mantra marked the start of a collective crusade to defend new conquests. According to the league, the number of cities that had established redevelopment agencies had doubled since 1972; now 214 of the 229 projects underway in California were "using tax increment financing as their principal source of [funding]."[6]

Reforming Redevelopment

State assemblyman Joseph B. Montoya, an old-school Democrat whose district included the cities of El Monte and La Puente, knew that La Puente lacked the strategic assets to exploit tax-increment financing. A former La Puente councilman, Montoya had watched helplessly as his city's powerful neighbors had glutted themselves on factory and commercial development, and therefore tax revenue, while La Puente had starved. Industry's strategic exploitation of transportation infrastructure had deprived La Puente of commercial growth opportunities on its western flank. Immediately east of La Puente, the city of West Covina had used its access to the San Bernardino Freeway as a guarantor of commercial development. Meanwhile, La Puente's lower-middle-class homeowners paid the county property taxes that subsidized the industrial and commercial development of their wealthier neighbors. By 1977, the county was diverting 30,000 dollars in revenues each year for each of Industry's residents.[7]

In 1976, Montoya submitted four assembly bills that, if passed, would have implemented administrative and regulatory controls to reform redevelopment. His supporters included two young attorneys, C. Edward Dilkes and Peter L. Wallin, who agreed with his objectives, even though they politely questioned the assumptions upon which he and other reformers were waging their crusade. In written commentary supporting the passage of Montoya's assembly bill 2400, Dilkes and Wallin argued that the practice of redevelopment in California had nothing to do with the political rhetoric that justified it. Their critique focused on a key narrative, *The Use of Tax Increment Financing by Cities and Counties in California*, a 1975 report prepared by Ralph Anderson and Associates, which the redevelopment lobby had circulated in the legislature as an argument against reform.[8] After conducting a case-by-case review of California's redevelopment agencies, however, the attorneys found that not one of the projects cited in the report had built a single unit of new housing in a blighted neighborhood, despite their pledges of providing "slum clearance" and new jobs and increasing property values. The handful of new housing developments that had appeared in blighted neighborhoods were actually built with federal urban renewal funds and private capital, not local property-tax revenues.[9] Dilkes and Wallin claimed that the Anderson report also used naïve accounting logic to argue that redevelopment technology would increase assessed property values inside its project areas. The report's authors had calculated the effect on property values by subtracting total increased assessed valuations in 1975 from first-year assessed valuations inside project areas and then further deducting for inflation. They made no effort, however, to establish the rate at which property values would have increased without redevelopment, an important distinction in a state that was already registering dramatic increases in property value.[10] According to Dilkes and Wallin, the report also confused cause and effect to represent job growth as one of its benefits. Although the attorneys acknowledged that the practice could "have a substantial impact" on jobs in the immediate area, it had a minimal impact "on the absolute quantity of development within the region." Development, they wrote, is primarily a result "of demand factors beyond the control of the redevelopment process. While the tug-of-war between one city and another may result in a developer choosing San Fernando over Cudahy as a development site, the net effect on the Los Angeles Region is nil."[11]

Redevelopment, however, could take credit for real effects that its supporters had either ignored or failed to anticipate. First, it had from the beginning supplied generous subsidies for commercial and industrial development of vacant land that could have been financed with private money. Second, it encouraged redevelopment agencies to use tax-increment inducements to lure developers away from other cities. The practice turned into a game in which cities competed to see which could give away the biggest incentives to developers. Third, the technology for granting to private developers what Dilkes and Wallin described as "land write downs, lending of public credit, lending of the power of eminent domain, and provision of 'public improvements' such as city built parking lots for the developer's sole and exclusive use" transformed government functions into quasi-private commodities. In other words, the city's administrative functions became a kind of leasable property. The attorneys also saw the private developer as the principal beneficiary of a downward spiral of competition that would strain local government's ability to finance the growing suburban demand for schools, libraries, public parks, fire prevention, and other infrastructure costs.[12] Their arguments insinuated that, because California's redevelopment laws regularly facilitated these consequences, they could not be considered abuses.

The language of Montoya's reforms and his statements to the press did not echo the subtle contradictions that Dilkes and Wallin had detected in their critique. Instead, he exhibited the narrow pragmatism that typified his generation's style of Democrat leadership. Most of his bills tried to win modest concessions from more powerful opponents, as if he were hoping to impress them with his reasonableness and charm while forswearing any serious attempt to challenge the fundamental "facts" upon which redevelopment was debated. He also personalized his critique of Industry's interpretation of the law, singling out "the abuses of one Graham Ritchie. The city of Industry is Graham Ritchie personified."[13] As a maker of laws, Montoya identified Ritchie, an interpreter of laws, as the person responsible for molding the law to suit Industry's needs. Interestingly, however, he did not publicly subscribe to the Jim-as-the-power-behind-the-throne story, although he had allegedly feuded with Stafford.

Montoya's bills eventually introduced a few modest reforms, almost none of which had any impact on Industry's redevelopment practices or plans. One bill did narrow the legal definition of *blight,* but it only applied to agencies created after the bill's passage, thus automatically exempting Industry's redevelopment projects. Another, which eventually became law, required redevelopment agencies to submit annual financial reports to the state's Department of Housing and Community Development and to make the minutes of the department's board meetings available to the public. Yet another bill required redevelopment agencies to conduct annual independent audits and submit a budget and work program for the coming year.[14] Although these reforms did not explicitly single out Industry, they did establish surveillance systems for the state's redevelopment activities.

Three of Montoya's four bills were enacted, but only after substantial revision, thanks to the timely interventions of Republican state senator William Campbell, whose district included one-third of Industry and who acted as the city's "chief advocate in Sacramento." Democratic governor Jerry Brown vetoed Montoya's fourth and most ambitious reform package due to a drafting error the bill's co-author, state senator Alan Robbins, refused to correct in the closing minutes of the 1976 legislative session for procedural reasons no one believed. The press speculated that Robbins let the bill die because letting residents vote on new redevelopment projects for downtown Los Angeles posed an unacceptable risk to his chances of running for mayor against his Democratic rival, Tom Bradley, a strong supporter of downtown redevelopment.[15] Industry had already dodged an even bigger bullet: Montoya had proposed the establishment of a state agency empowered to cancel redevelopment projects that it saw as abusive or illegal. Campbell and his legislative allies made sure that this bill never reached a vote.[16]

Like Dilkes and Wallin, Eugene Jacobs, a former redevelopment attorney for the city of Los Angeles, supported Montoya's proposed amendment to require redevelopment agencies to file financial reports for their projects. After all, what could be more sensible than to establish a system for ensuring fiscal accountability? Now a law professor at Brigham Young University, where he specialized in redevelopment law, Jacobs argued that the public needed to monitor the investment of its tax dollars to determine whether that investment was having its promised effect and, if necessary, to assign blame to those responsible for an agency's reckless or fraudulent administration. But when Jacobs testified on August 22, 1977, before the conference committee assigned to iron out the differences between the senate and assembly versions of the bill, he was greeted with an orchestrated silence he did not expect. After all, the questions he asked from his written testimony seemed all too reasonable: "Why does the City of Industry object to an annual audit, an annual work program, an annual examination of the previous year's achievements and an annual budget?" Jacobs got his answer from Montoya when he finished. "Montoya stated that he agreed with Senator Campbell to support the exemption of the City of Industry from the bill," reversing himself on a position he had taken against the exemption only one month earlier.[17]

The words he heard from the man he had come to support, Jacobs recounted, shook his faith in the possibility of substantially reforming California's redevelopment law. He attributed the "loneliest time of my legal career" to the strength of Industry's lobbying campaign, the best-funded in the state at that time. He had gone up against not only state senator William Campbell but also Don Brown, the Sacramento lobbyist who also represented Howard Hughes's Summa Corporation, and former assembly speaker Robert Moretti, who received as much as 30,400 a year to defend the city in Sacramento. Not surprisingly, Montoya's reasonable reforms flagged in the face of such solid opposition. Marty Coren, the Montoya aide who drafted the reforms, later acknowledged that "cities with redevelopment agencies, including Industry, put up such opposition that legislators were forced to exempt already existing agencies."[18]

Montoya agreed to the exemptions so that he could pass a law requiring all future redevelopment agencies to accept a modicum of fiscal accountability.[19] And Industry insiders suspected that Montoya's alleged quarrel with city powerbrokers had been a show calculated to extract that reward. More than once during his reform campaigns, he had walked into P Hill parties to conduct private conversations with his "enemies." He had also met privately with Jim at his mill, visits that Stephen Stafford, then a teenager, later recalled as amiable.[20]

Some observers credited lobbyist Moretti with brokering the compromise between Montoya and the city. Whatever the case, city attorney Graham Ritchie did tell the *Times*, "I don't see the same kind of hostility that I saw in previous years"; and soon after that public statement, Montoya began to receive contributions from members of the Industry Manufacturers Council—a total of nearly 11,000 dollars between 1978 and 1984. That was a relatively modest figure compared to what council members were giving to their favorite legislative champion: between 1974 and 1984, they contributed roughly 61,000 dollars to William Campbell. Yet Montoya, perhaps not coincidentally, also obtained timely loans to launch his senate campaign from Los Angeles County supervisor Peter Schabarum, godfather of Republican fundraising in the San Gabriel Valley. For his part, the supervisor had received, between 1976 and 1984, more than 90,000 dollars from Industry manufacturers' council members to disburse as he saw fit.[21]

One of the most impressive displays of Industry's political dexterity occurred in 1977, when state assemblyman John T. Knox of Richmond submitted legislation that would change the rules under which cities could annex new territory. The proposed law gave requisite county agencies the authority to approve city-requested boundary changes without the consent of the people residing in those targeted areas. If approved without revision, the bill would technically have empowered La Puente to annex a portion of Industry without the consent of the city's residents. But timely intervention from Industry's legislative friends amended the bill's language to give cities with populations of fewer than 1,000 the authority to terminate a proposed annexation by passing a simple city council resolution.

Knox, who shared an apartment with Bob Rope until Rope's death in 1975, allowed the exemption language into his bill but credited Campbell for pushing through the amendment. In 1984, Knox explained the reasoning behind his decision to allow the exemption: "We took the amendment because we anticipated some very close votes on other parts of the bill and we couldn't afford to squander those votes. We decided, based on the political realities, that it didn't hurt anyone else, so why fight with them."[22]

As 1977 drew to a close, Industry city officials could take pride in having triumphed over the reforms. The city was continuing to tailor the technology of redevelopment to its needs. Its agencies had retained their authority to say when and how they would submit financial reports; suppress population; and continue representing "slum clearance," "property values," and "job growth" as expressions of a greater good achievable through redevelopment. These victories provided the cover that Industry needed to consolidate its position as the most ambitious and best-financed redeveloper in the state.[23] The city still needed to drum up customers, however—preferably Fortune 500 companies that had so far been reluctant to expand in an uncertain economic climate. Industry's promoters therefore continued to jump on every chance, small or large, and to portray it as a desirable growth opportunity.

Already, in April 1976, the *City of Industry News* had announced that the Union Pacific and the Southern Pacific had linked their computers to facilitate a "wider range of direct data exchange" to "smooth operations and improve the efficiency of both railroads."[24] The item did not say exactly how rail service to Industry's business and factory owners would improve, but it did remind readers of the railroads' presence at their doorsteps. The newsletter also promised the May 3 completion of a new Bank of America branch office, a 25,000-square-foot structure with parking space for twenty-eight cars, calling it the "theme building" of the new civic center. The item did not explain that the city's redevelopment agency had subsidized the bank's parking lot and landscaping or that Jim and Ed Junior were leasing the building and its property to the bank.[25]

The newsletter's 1977 issues continued to boost the city's friends and powerful clients. Among other articles, the paper published an obituary for a retired SP official and celebrated Industry's twenty-year anniversary with a cover story about the dedication of the city's recently completed city hall. According to the *News*, that ceremony gave Supervisor Schabarum a platform on which to rail against the dangers of illegal immigration. State senator William Campbell and Los Angeles district attorney John Van de Kamp also said a few words at the event, further cementing their relationship to the city and the Industry Manufacturers Council's generous members.

Later in the year the *News* published a special edition lauding the 625 industrial firms now operating in the city and the more than 9 million dollars in new building permits issued since 1976. The article said nothing, however, about the more than 100 million dollars in bond debt that the city and its agencies had incurred by 1977 to subsidize that development, a sum that nearly equaled the bond debt of the city of Los Angeles, even though Industry reported a population of only 720 residents. State and federal redevelopment law permitted Industry to increase its bond debt in step with its increasing flow of revenues from county property-tax increments (a total of 20 million in 1977) without requiring voter approval.[26]

The year's final edition featured highlights from former governor Ronald Reagan's November 30 speech to the friends of the Industry Manufacturers Council. Reagan's talk, held at the California County Club, elaborated key motifs of the property-tax revolt, lashing out at "government meddling, high taxes, the excessive costs of administering the many bureaus of government, the needless federal regulations, the tons of meaningless paperwork and the erosion of property rights and freedoms." His comments to Industry's capitalist class capture the moment at which the libertarian drift of his thinking, which increasingly portrayed government as an oppressive enemy, began to be accepted as mainstream Republican dogma.[27]

Also in 1977, courtroom gadfly Russell W. Bledsoe tried to revive allegations that Industry was "merely a sham and alter ego of one James Stafford and certain co-conspirators." Alleging a conspiracy to explain the absence of concrete evidence or named co-conspirators, Bledsoe argued in his suit that "the facts of Stafford's numerous crimes were known but his penchant for threatening prospective witnesses with death was equally notorious and the problem of obtaining admissible evidence was thereby made almost invulnerable." The plaintiff's only success, however, consisted of using the court record to reiterate the Jim-as-criminal-mastermind motif.[28] Nothing in his suit suggests that he had the faintest clue as to the actual conspiracy that Jim had set in motion earlier in the year with a general contractor named Frank C. Wood.

On the Beach

After months of coaxing and plotting, Jim had, in early 1977, persuaded his longtime friend to join a bid-rigging and kickback scheme that would add more than 2.5 million dollars in padding to more than 12.7 million dollars in construction contracts, most of them for work performed at Industry Hills. Wood, who eventually pleaded guilty to conspiracy charges, told investigators that Jim had befriended him twenty-seven years earlier on the beach at Carpinteria, then a sleepy resort a few miles north of Ventura. After that initial meeting, Wood began to time his annual beach vacations with the Staffords'. Their wives and kids "got along well"; his daughter loved taking horseback rides along the beach with Jim's daughter. Their friendship made it easy for Jim to track the decline of Wood's once flourishing business. By the 1970s, he no longer maintained work crews, equipment, or an office staff, "except for book-keeper George Jacques, and a very small office."[29] But Wood did have one thing that Jim needed, a general contractor's license, which allowed Wood to insert himself into projects as an extra, if unneeded, manager. From that position he could hide the pair's schemes to fraudulently extract redevelopment funds. Moreover, Wood ran more than one company, which gave Jim several ways to repackage those schemes without linking Wood's name with the names of Industry insiders.

At least since 1976, Jim had been looked for ways to begin siphoning money from the millions of dollars being spent on Industry's redevelopment. He got his chance when National Engineering employee C. Ronald Rabin informed him about a new project coming up for bid. A New York Jew, Rabin might have seemed to be the person least likely to collaborate with Jim, a white Catholic with deep southern roots and thinly disguised prejudices. But surprisingly, Jim liked Rabin immediately. His heavy drinking and willingness to ramrod projects through National Engineering impressed Stafford, who soon brokered an understanding: Rabin would "bird-dog" projects that might be suitable for Jim's schemes.

The conspirators finalized their plan about six months before earth-moving started at Industry Hills, one of their early targets. Wood bid for the projects and then subcontracted them to someone else who did the actual work. In the submitted bids, however, Wood did not acknowledge his silent partner's presence. The arrangement added a third layer of cost, but no one seemed to care—not the handsomely paid subcontractor; not National Engineering, which was supposed to monitor the project's finances; not the redevelopment agency, which paid the bills. The city, now swimming in redevelopment money, appeared to be more concerned with meeting deadlines for a growing list of projects than with saving the public's money. Still, Rabin took some precautions. He told Wood to encourage other contractors to submit "bids to create the impression" of competitive bidding. Wood obliged. For instance, in the case of one project, he got another contractor to submit a "collusive bid"; but Industry's redevelopment agency nonetheless awarded the contract to one of Wood's companies, Clyde W. Wood and Sons, which then submitted change orders adding 815,000 dollars to what was actually a 209,000-dollar job.[30]

With cash to play with, Jim implemented the next, longer-term, phase of his plan. He instructed Wood to start spreading money around to buy more influence in the city and to give Jim a cut of that influence money. Wood began feeding kickbacks to Jim through checks paid to bogus out-of-state companies for phantom building supplies and services. As another layer of protection, Wood used false names and company titles to open bank accounts for laundering money. And at Industry's Bank of America branch, the tellers let Jim cash checks written to other people on accounts for which he was not a signatory.[31]

Jim's bid-rigging and kickback conspiracy coincided with the city's most explosive period of growth; and Industry's redevelopment projects offered a forest of laws, bureaucratic procedures, regulations, documents, plans, contracts, resolutions, and ordinances in which to hide his schemes. Without delegating duties, however, he could not negotiate and sustain this useful complexity. For assistance, he turned to the trusted network of loyalties he had built over time. But no matter how hard he tried, Jim could not see, hear, or comprehend everything that touched or went through the city.

EVADING THE MOB

Warner Hodgdon, Industry's redevelopment guru, recommended in 1978 that the city acquire the more than 2,500-acre Tres Hermanos Ranch, which lay a few miles south of the city's boundary. As Industry sewed up the ranch deal, a new threat arose, forcing the city to engage on another front. On June 20, 1978, the revolt the right had so assiduously cultivated bore fruit with the passage of Proposition 13, a law that could conceivably deprive Industry of as much 12 million dollars a year in property-tax revenue.[32] The city's redevelopment ambitions would be nipped in the bud if it did not act before the proposition took effect on July 1, for after that date cities would not be able to levy new property taxes without voter authorization.

City attorney Ritchie drafted a ballot measure that asked Industry's voters to approve the sale of 250 million dollars' worth of bonds, enough to fund all the redevelopment projects the city had on the books and some it might think of later. The fundable projects and their projected costs were listed in the measure; they included 66.8 million dollars for the Industry Hills Exhibit-Conference Center, 6.6 million dollars for Industry's historical cultural landmarks project, 96.7 million dollars for its foreign trade zone project, and 16 million dollars for the reservoir and water reclamation project that Hodgdon had in mind for Tres Hermanos Ranch.[33] Predictably, voters passed the mail-in ballot measure by a margin of seventy-one to twelve. The city could now keep its commitment to raise property-tax rates to meet the growing debts it planned to incur.[34] Industry's guaranteed access to property-tax revenues and debt-financed redevelopment bonds also gave it the legal tools it needed to keep its redevelopment machine running, even as other California cities were grappling with the debilitating effects of Proposition 13. Moreover, passage of the bond initiative entitled Hodgdon to a tidy windfall—2.5 million dollars, or 2 percent of the bond's value—as the fee for his financial consulting services.

But the bond measure and Hodgdon's financial consulting arrangement proved to be divisive. According to a few Industry insiders, the special election's aftermath opened a rift between Hodgdon and Ritchie, who reputedly resented not being able to receive a similar 2-percent cut for services. Ritchie began to raise legal questions about the city's purchase of Tres Hermanos, angering Mayor John Ferrero, who, as one source claimed, "demanded Ritchie's resignation." According to the same source, one of those legal questions had concerned the propriety of allowing the mayor to graze cattle on the ranch as if it were his private reserve. Without going into detail, the *City of Industry News* tactfully reported that Ritchie had resigned his post on October 1 "to devote more time to his law firm." Glenn Watson, his predecessor as city attorney, promptly filled the vacancy.[35]

Meanwhile, enraged better-governments groups, some funded by a handful of disgruntled business owners inside the city, were alleging that Industry had encouraged or failed to prevent voting improprieties that had skewed the special election's results. The Los Angeles district attorney's office assigned deputy district attorney Robert Kuhnert to investigate the matter. Kuhnert reported that he could find no hint of wrongdoing.[36] Evidently, he did not know that, while he was investigating Industry's special election, the Industry Manufacturers Council was making a "big contribution" to the reelection campaign of his boss, district attorney John Van de Kamp.

Robert King, the council's president at the time, said he witnessed Van de Kamp accept the first of a series of contributions in June 1979 at a luncheon the council had organized in his honor at the California Country Club. Speaking to the FBI in 1983, King said that a handful of council directors, including himself, had announced on that occasion that they would support Van de Kamp's reelection bid with a combined contribution of 5,000 dollars. They planned to hand the check to William Martin, Van de Kamp's field deputy and one of Ed Junior's real estate investment partners.

According to King, "Jim told Martin, 'We want to give a contribution to Van de Kamp,'" whereupon Jim produced the check. Some one had "typed the name of the payee, the date, and amount, and needed only a signature." Jim asked King to sign it, but King said he was not a signatory for the council's Bank of America account; only Wilfred Steiner, the executive director, and Janet Crowley, a staff member, were authorized to sign council checks. But Jim told King "to go ahead and sign the check anyway as it would clear" at the bank's Industry branch. He then advised King to see Ken Derr, the bank's branch manager, or his secretary to get his name added to the council's signature card. King signed the check and gave it to Martin. It cleared, just as Jim had said it would. But King did not add his name to the account's signature card. When later confronted by the FBI, Steiner did not deny the essential details of King's account. He said that the council had wanted to reward Van de Kamp for being consistently tough on crime, an understandable expression of gratitude for an organization that represented the interests of property owners.[37]

The district attorney's office wrapped up its investigation in 1979, reporting that it could find no evidence of voter fraud. Van de Kamp, when questioned a year later by *Los Angeles Herald Examiner* reporter Scott Paltrow, maintained that he knew nothing about "his office's voter fraud investigation" when he received the council's contributions. He also reminded Paltrow that he had properly disclosed the contributions. The council did not disclose them, however. Paltrow's embarrassing questions therefore pushed Van de Kamp to request that the state's Fair Political Practices Commission investigate the matter. In 1981, the commission fined the council 2,000 dollars, giving the city's critics new reasons to question the independence of the county's top prosecutor.[38]

CHAPTER 9

THE OTHER CHINATOWNS

He erected his fortress over two dead Wobblies
The way a wasp deposits her egg
On its stung moribund host,
And thereafter bequeathed his protégés
Command of the Words.
With these they abducted a river,
Subdivided a desert,
Walled families with velocities.

—Victor Valle, "Los Angeles"

When interviewed years later by the FBI, Hodgdon made it clear that it was his idea, not Jim's, to pull off the biggest land buy the city had yet attempted: the 2,500-acre Tres Hermanos Ranch that straddled the Los Angeles, San Bernardino, and Riverside county lines. It was his prize and, until its sale, had been a historic chunk of *Times* mogul Otis Chandler's family real estate empire. The texts of that deal—letters, memoranda, property appraisals, city resolutions, and dozens of other documents—show that Hodgdon was working to acquire it as early as 1978, the same year in which the city skillfully skirted redevelopment reform.

The personal connections that Hodgdon had cultivated may have helped him close the deal. As he was orchestrating the purchase, he was simultaneously enjoying close friendships with both Chandler and powerful religious leader Bill Bright, a competing bidder. That Hodgdon would run in Chandler's circles isn't surprising. He had ownership stakes in several racetracks as well as the Junior Johnson Racing Team, once NASCAR's "most successful [stockcar] racing operation," which naturally brought him to events such as the Times-Mirror Grand

Prix in neighboring Riverside County. This annual affair, which had been held at the Riverside International Raceway since 1958, allowed him to rub shoulders with other well-heeled racing enthusiasts, including the raceway's biggest fan, Otis Chandler.[1]

The *Times* scion, who had inherited the event from his father, Norman, used fat purses, hundreds of *Times* advertisements and articles, and corporate sponsors to defend the raceway from the encroaching suburbs.[2] Hodgdon, who took pride in discovering the needs of his friends and business prospects, quickly noticed Chandler's auto-racing agenda. Their converging passion became increasingly evident after 1977, when Hodgdon began sponsoring dozens of cars and races at both the Riverside Raceway and the Ontario Speedway in northern San Bernardino County, which Chandler had also tried to save from the wrecking ball. In 1981 and 1982, Hodgdon even let Chandler's son Michael drive one of his cars in the Indianapolis 500. This display of racing enthusiasm earned Hodgdon plenty of media coverage: the *Times* ran at least three feature profiles on him between 1976 and 1981.[3]

Hodgdon's zeal for knowing the right people also led him to Reverend Bill Bright, founder and director of the politically powerful Campus Crusade for Christ International. Headquartered in the San Bernardino Mountains near Lake Arrowhead, the crusade at its height boasted a 5,000-member staff in eighty countries, a 30-million-dollar annual income, and access to the wealthy and powerful via the Christian Embassy, a lavish Washington, D.C., mansion that Bright's friends had purchased for him in 1975 from the Catholic archdiocese. Bright used the embassy, a separately incorporated entity that shared the crusade's officers and directors, to stage prayer breakfasts and religious counseling sessions with conservative legislators and corporate powerbrokers, a way of promoting his goal of "saturating every country in the world with the gospel of Jesus Christ" by 1980.[4] Although he denied practicing partisan politics, Bright injected cold war–style anti-Communist rhetoric into his sermons, pushed for the election of "men and women of God to public office," and openly allied himself with South Carolina's far-right stalwart, Senator Strom Thurmond.[5] By 1976, his message had become so extreme that even middle-of-the-road *Newsweek* found it necessary to note that his rightwing Christian ideology "excludes most Roman Catholics, mainline Protestants and political liberals of any religious denomination."[6] Hodgdon, for his part, made generous contributions to the crusade, and a copy of his 1978 résumé documents his position on the Christian Embassy's board of directors and lists Bright as a personal reference.

Roots of Water and Blood

Hodgdon's ambitious networking, however, does not tell the whole story of how Industry acquired the Tres Hermanos Ranch. We also need to consider the history of the ranch's administration and ownership if we want to expose capital's role in planting the technological rhizomes that made Southern California's suburban landscape and that energized on of its most powerful twentieth-century media dynasties. In 1914, after marrying into ownership of the *Los Angeles Times*, Harry Chandler organized a real estate syndicate to acquire one of Southern California's last Mexican-era ranches. He recruited Tom Scott, a wildcat oil driller turned elite attorney, and William Rowland, a former Los Angeles County sheriff and descendant of wealthy La Puente rancher John Rowland, to acquire property at the southern tip of Los Angeles County, which they named after themselves: the Tres Hermanos, or "Three Brothers." But like the other real estate syndicates Harry organized, theirs could not prosper without the lifeblood of water and the governmental technologies that ensured its supply.[7]

At least a dozen years earlier, Harry Chandler, Otis's grandfather, got the Los Angeles economic and political elite to join forces to find water to fuel another real estate boom. Their grand enterprise began when the private side of the partnership relinquished control of the city's water supplier, the Los Angeles Water Company, and gave it to the city's newly formed Board of Water Commissioners. More than a transfer of property, the arrangement planted the partners' friends and their expertise inside the city's new utility. William Mulholland continued as the commission's superintendent, the position he had previously held in the private water company. Fred Eaton, the city's recently retired mayor and architect of the transaction, became the commission's new consulting engineer. Streetcar owner Moses Sherman, "Harry Chandler's friend and intimate business associate," represented the real estate developers on the commission.

The new utility began to search for a water supply it would not have to share with any other Southern California city. Eaton recommended constructing an aqueduct that would redirect the Owens River, now located in the eastern Sierra Nevada Mountains 223 miles due west, through the Mojave Desert and two other mountain ranges to reach Los Angeles.[8] Meanwhile, Joseph B. Lippincott, an engineer who shared Mulholland's enthusiasm, accepted an appointment in 1902 to represent Los Angeles in the newly formed federal Bureau of Land Reclamation, which intended to develop the Owens River for local ranchers. Now a paid consultant for the city, Lippincott told the water commission of the bureau's plans to bundle tens of thousands of Owens River frontage and water rights for a reclamation project there. Soon, more than 90 percent of the ranchers along the river agreed to relinquish their water rights, believing that they would benefit from the federal project.

In 1903, General Otis and Harry Chandler quietly recruited the Southern Pacific's E. H. Harriman, water commissioner Moses Sherman, and other local big shots to form the first of two real estate syndicates and take an option on the 16,000-acre Porter Ranch in the San Fernando Valley, a few miles north of Los Angeles. Because Sherman was privy to aqueduct route maps and the project's latest developments, he would be able to tell his syndicate partners when to pull the trigger on the option. In 1904, with almost all the water rights consolidated, Lippincott, who remained on the city's payroll, treated his friends Eaton and Mulholland to a series of camping trips through Inyo County, a roughly 5,000-dollar expense that Lippincott put onto the city's tab. Their intent was to investigate the feasibility of Eaton's aqueduct idea. Sherman must have heard good news from the expedition because in November the syndicate made a 150,000-dollar down payment toward the purchase of the 500,000-dollar Porter Ranch. Meanwhile, Eaton bought up the remaining Owens River frontage and water rights, while Lippincott lobbied the reclamation agency's chief to suspend its project and let the city of Los Angeles take over the river's water rights.

In May 1905, Eaton resold his river frontage and water rights to the city; and in July, the bureau agreed to Lippincott's proposal. The water commission then tasked its engineers with designing the aqueduct and coordinating right-of-way acquisitions to Los Angeles. Sherman must have also continued to feed his friends information because a second syndicate was formed. It snatched up another 28,000 acres in the San Fernando Valley at bargain prices, thanks, in part, to the *Times*, which played up drought news. The newspaper later ginned up a water panic that convinced already receptive voters to approve 23 million dollars' worth of municipal bonds to pay for the aqueduct's construction. No dummies, the voters also hoped to cash in on the real estate boom that was sure to follow.[9]

But no one made out as well as the syndicates. After the aqueduct's completion in November 1913, the Chandler-led syndicates netted more than 107 million dollars from San Fernando Valley real estate sales. Robert Gottlieb and Irene Wolt write in their classic history that the Chandlers used this enormous windfall "to dominate Southern California for the next three generations" and fuel a new round of population growth. In less than a decade, the city of Los Angeles grew from a city of 500,000 to one with 2 million residents.[10]

Harry Chandler, meanwhile, resumed his strategic storytelling as the Owens flowed into Southern California. In 1914, he portrayed the purchase of Tres Hermanos as a place where La Puente ranch hands taught his sons "the joy of sweaty toil" during supervised weekends of roping and cattle branding.[11] In 1917, when General Otis died and Harry took over the family business, he preserved the ranch's anonymity by keeping family business affairs out of the *Times*.[12] In the 1930s, he transferred his share of the ranch to Chandis Securities, the family-owned land-holding subsidiary of the Times Mirror Corporation.[13]

Despite the media empire's corporatization and evolution to a less reactionary style, Harry Chandler's death in 1944 did not alter its role as a Southern California real estate booster. The *Times* remained a more or less consistent backer of giant water and transportation infrastructure projects and, just as importantly, the ideology of limitless growth. The influence and reach of that ideology, however, did not depend on one individual but on the governmental technologies that remade local public institutions to satisfy developer needs. His maxim "Think of what is good for real estate" perfectly expressed the arrangement.[14] He could not have realized his vision alone or with only the help of his elite friends. They needed to create a story for a new class of real estate entrepreneurs, one that convinced local government to use its revenues to pay for moving water to an arid environment and populating and financing a market big enough to buy the entrepreneurs' goods: new homes, newspapers, and factories.

Times editorial policy helped close this reinforcement loop. While Chandis Securities continued to exploit the development opportunities generated by the completion of new freeways and water projects, the *Times* mobilized news coverage, commentary, and strategic silences to promote them. Chandis's development of the Tejon Ranch, a former Mexican hacienda acquired by a Chandler-organized syndicate in 1911, illustrates this circularity. The 281,000-acre southwestern San Joaquin Valley estate stretched from the Tehachapi Mountains to the outskirts of Bakersfield and doubled as a cattle ranch and a family hunting reserve. But it would need more water if Chandis expected to exploit its ranching, farming, and perhaps its home-building potential.

The *Times* water imperative neatly reinforced what Southern California real estate developers were already clamoring for: more water for more suburban growth. Southern California agribusiness and suburban developers identified the Feather River north of Sacramento as the next likely source of cheap, publicly subsidized water. The *Times* published editorials and news stories that extolled the virtues of a state water project. Its media campaign, however, did not tell readers that the project would traverse the Tejon Ranch and secure the careers of those political leaders, from the governor on down, who were helping the press sell the aqueduct by means of the familiar all-or-nothing verbiage of previous water campaigns. The project's engineers and legislative proponents represented the southern part of the state (which held the most promise for suburban, agricultural, and manufacturing growth) as a desert that would soon exhaust the little water it had. They represented the northern part of the state as a region with more water than it could use but with limited growth potential. The project's proponents did not mention that the effort to put the aqueduct through the Tejon Ranch was a replay of the *Chinatown* technology that had made the Owens Aqueduct such a lucrative investment opportunity.

In 1959, after Governor Edmund G. "Pat" Brown tried several times to strike a compromise between farmers and developers, the state legislature approved a ballot initiative that would authorize the formation of the 1.75-billion-dollar state water project. Water dammed at Oroville, in the northern Sacramento Valley, would be diverted 442 miles, around the San Joaquin Delta, and continue south, down the coastal range's inner ribs, over the Tehachapi Mountains, before reaching Lake Castaic, northeast of the Los Angeles County line. In 1960, the *Times* rallied its friends and resources behind the governor to ensure the initiative's passage. Success hinged on removing a 160-acre ownership limit on property adjacent to the aqueduct to win over Southern California's biggest landowners, who envisioned massive factory farms fueled with plenty of cheap water. The paper counted on Norris Poulson, whom it had groomed for Los Angeles mayor, to chair its campaign. Taking nothing for granted, the newspaper gave the campaign its "full editorial backing," while the Southern Pacific and Tejon Ranch, in which Chandis Securities held majority interest, paid out enormous campaign contributions.

The *Times* also supported Poulson's appointment to the California State Water Commission to ensure project oversight. Serving from 1963 to 1969, Poulson helped shape water policy at a time when, writes Dennis McDougal, "the multibillion dollar State Water Project siphoned Northern California's water to Los Angeles on a scale that made the Owens Valley look like a radiator leak."[15] Not surprisingly, the *Times* and Southern

Figure 1. Sanborn Insurance Map of "Puente Quadrangle," Los Angeles County, Calif., 1927 edition. Courtesy of Geography Map Library, California State University, Northridge.

Figure 2. North side of "C. C. Stafford Feed Mill, Puente Calif., H. & H. Photo," photographed from Valley Boulevard, circa 1940. Courtesy of La Puente Valley Historical Society.

Figure 3. East side of North side of C. C. Stafford Milling & Warehouse Co. Courtesy of La Puente Valley Historical Society.

Figure 4. Portrait of "Miss Rae Schade and her father, Mr. Schade" at court appearance photographed by the Los Angeles Evening Express *on October 26, 1929. Courtesy of Herald Examiner Collection, Los Angeles Public Library.*

Figure 5. "C. C. Stafford, her wealthy employer, pictured below, at his trial here on charges of attacking her. She has been under guard since attempts by three men to take her from a train," Los Angeles Evening Express, *October 30, 1929 Courtesy of Herald Examiner Collection, Los Angeles Public Library.*

Figure 6. *Courtroom portrait of "Rae Schade,"* Los Angeles Evening Express, *October 30, 1929. Courtesy of Herald Examiner Collection, Los Angeles Public Library.*

Figure 7. "Main Street in La Puente, 1930s." Courtesy of La Puente Valley Historical Society.

Figure 8 July 4, 1943 photograph of C. C. Stafford, right, and Pete Lamaison, left. Courtesy of La Puente Valley Historical Society.

Figure 9. A July 27, 1961 "Portrait of James Stafford," seated right, looking into camera, and unidentified person, seated left, most likely at a Los Angeles County Board of Supervisor's meeting photographed by the Los Angeles Times. *Courtesy of the* Los Angeles Times *Collection 1429, Department of Special Collections, Charles E. Young Research Library, UCLA Library.*

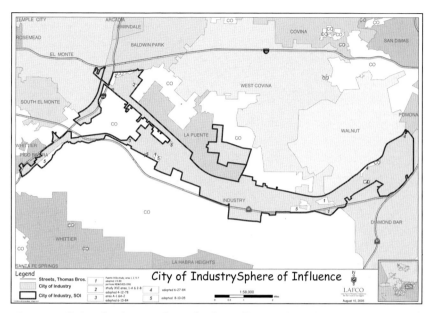

Figure 10. *"City of Industry Sphere of Influence" map adopted on August 10, 2005 by the Local Agency Formation Commission for the County of Los Angeles.*

Figure 11. *Overview of the City of Industry and the La Puente Valley.* © 2006 Google.

Figure 12. Union Pacific (formerly Southern Pacific) rail yards in the City of Industry, below, Pacific Palms Conference Resort (formerly Industry Hills Exhibit Conference Center) above. © 2006 Google.

Figure 13. Evergreen Los Angeles Terminal. Courtesy of Cooper Brislain.

California's biggest real estate developers dominated the project's purposes and rhetoric. They framed California's water resource debate as a competition between a wet desolate north and a dry populated south, where big factories, big farms, and big housing developments waited for Governor Brown to make good on his promise to supply them with much more water.[16] Fueling regional growth was not enough for the *Times*, McDougal writes in his excellent biography of Otis Chandler. The conscience and voice of the developer class wanted Poulson, their man on the state water commission, to make sure his colleagues voted to "bring cheap water to L.A. directly through the Tejon Ranch, giving the Chandler-owned property ample irrigation for fire-sale prices."[17] The *Times*, of course, did not tell its readers how an aqueduct big enough to be seen from an orbiting satellite would benefit farming operations on their ranch or how that shimmering ribbon would someday spawn corporate fantasies of new housing developments.[18]

Later, when the paper threw its support behind the Peripheral Canal, a project that would double the amount of water carried by the California Aqueduct, and did not disclose Chandis's interest in the Tejon Ranch, a few out-of-town newspapers finally began to notice the resounding silence and to press their rival for an answer. The *Times* replied "that [it] did not consider the paper's staunch editorial backing of the canal . . . to be a conflict of interest" because its editors had taken their positions "independently of the economic interests of the Times Mirror Company."[19] The reply ignored common historical practices among newspaper owners, who cherished the prerogative to voice their political and business ideas in their own opinion pages. Meanwhile, the *Times* editors and reporters did not appear inclined to demonstrate their independence by publishing news stories that challenged the newspaper's pro-growth editorials.

They couldn't take that risk when so much more needed doing. After the California Aqueduct reached completion in 1972, someone would have to build a network of canals, pumping stations, tunnels, reservoirs, and filtration plants to distribute the northern water throughout Southern California. The local developer class did not need to look far for help. The region's Metropolitan Water District, founded in 1927, had grown into a super-regional agency large and rich enough to meet that challenge. In 1941, it had completed a 242-mile aqueduct to transport Colorado River water to its member cities and water agencies and secure enough water to sustain Southern California's astounding suburban and industrial growth rate for a few more decades.[20] By the time the state legislature previewed its plan to divert Northern California's biggest untamed river, the Metropolitan Water

District was already supplying several million customers in six Southern California counties, more than 130 cities, and dozens of water utilities.

Like its predecessors, the Metropolitan Water District embodied and disseminated the ideology of limitless growth. Its practices and policies enabled a growing real estate development industry to practice the economics of place speculation on an ever-larger scale. The agency, after all, had borrowed from and then improved upon the governmental and engineering technologies that the Owens Aqueduct project had innovated. Their differences came down to matters of scale and application. Whereas the Los Angeles Department of Water and Power had secured water for the biggest city on the west coast, the Metropolitan Water District had built a system to supply most of Southern California, a region whose economic sphere of influence went far beyond the state's borders. The upstart agency further illustrated the ease with which governmental technology flowed beyond jurisdictional boundaries and the role that developers played as vectors for these knowledge transfers.

The developer class had implanted the DNA of city and statewide water policies and legal technology into a new hybrid agency, one that blurred the lines among a public utility, a natural resource manager, a city planner, and a corporate developer. No one agency or entrepreneur, not even the Chandlers, could claim exclusive paternity. The agency's creation could thus be understood as a kind of library that archived the technological contributions made by many cities and water agencies. For the scale and character of Southern California's place-making economy and the ambitions and culture of its developer class were embodied in the representatives of the cities and water utilities and the developers who directed the Metropolitan Water District's policies and plans. Its member agencies and directors had more than naming rights. During the water district's first fifty years of existence, their combined governmental and economic power advanced suburban growth to unprecedented levels. We might even say the Metropolitan Water District had succeeded in generating its own force field, one that guaranteed a fertile environment for its policies for decades afterward.

The Metropolitan Water District's Recipe for Growth

The Metropolitan Water District depended on at least five governmental technologies for growth. First, to foster its distinct culture, it selected its policy and administrative leadership from the region's elite developers and their supporters and appointed major property owners and developers to sit on its board of directors. The board's class composition did not become fully apparent until 1980, a decade after it had been forced to admit a wider spectrum of members. In that year, belated enforcement of economic-interest filing laws revealed that more than half of the water district's fifty-two-member board still had substantial interests in land development, real estate, banking, insurance, oil drilling, construction, and engineering—businesses that directly and indirectly enjoyed the fruits of agency policies and projects. Longtime board chair Preston Hotchkis, who owned as much as 30,000 acres of Southern California real estate, including warehouses in the City of Industry, typified the director demographic of the agency's first fifty years.

Hotchkis had earned his position by representing San Marino, a tiny, rich, Anglo municipality south of Pasadena that had been tellingly named after a European micro-kingdom. He came to the water district board with elite and impeccable credentials. Chairman of the Bixby Ranch Company, he sat on boards with *Times* publisher Norman Chandler and served as a University of California regent and as president of California's state chamber of commerce, venues that allowed him to promote the agency's pro-development agenda while his businesses funded pro-water development initiatives.[21] The quantity and quality of *Times* news coverage about Hotchkis between the early 1950s and the early 1970s suggest a significant investment in his public image. No part of his personal, business, or political life seemed to be unworthy of recognition. The newspaper's social pages reported his marriage and charity work; the front page trumpeted his forays into international diplomacy; the inside pages allowed him to promote the paper's favorite water policies and projects.[22]

In short, no one needed to tell the agency's directors how to vote; they already owed much of their wealth to the institutions and technologies that promoted the ideology of growth and knew in advance that their colleagues could be counted on to vote for projects that increased agency water supplies. Thus, outsiders found it difficult to accuse any one director of committing a blatant conflict of interest. The director could easily argue that, because the board's decisions were benefiting a whole region, the private gains he had had happened to derive were purely incidental. The agency's directors maintained their political and administrative control by way of an unwritten policy that granted them lifetime appointments, despite agency bylaws restricting them to two-year terms of service. By allowing cities and other water agencies to routinely reappoint their board representatives, the directors reinforced a country club culture that encouraged conformity, suppressed dissent, and discouraged electoral competition.

Second, the Metropolitan Water District's growth narratives prefigured and reinforced arguments that state water project officials would make a decade later. During the water district's "aggressive postwar expansion," Joseph Jensen, the Getty Oil Company executive who doubled as its board chairman, noted with Mulholland-like understatement that "land is just land until it gets water on it."[23] His comment echoed the all-or-nothing reasoning favored by his colleagues, who liked to invoke biblical drought imagery when they argued that Southern California, that sunny and prosperous Eden, would fail without more water.[24]

Third, the agency could not have grown so quickly if it had relied on rate-paying customers to finance its construction projects. Knowing that the new suburban coastal zone stretching from the Los Angeles County line to the Mexican border could not be built or sold if developers did not first have a reliable water supply, the Metropolitan Water District, even before 1971, had assessed property taxes and other fees to raise needed capital. Its strategy was to harvest revenues from the most developed and thus more expensive real estate inside Los Angeles County to pay for development outside the county. The bigger cities could afford the expense because growth in the new suburbs would only increase demand for the governmental and corporate services they provided.[25]

Fourth, the circularity of the Metropolitan Water District's development effect amplified the reach of its fiscal and discursive technologies. Moving water beyond the suburban periphery fueled development, which increased population densities, which increased customer demand for water. Supplying water to new suburbs also increased development and therefore raised property values, which increased agency revenues. This seemingly natural reinforcement loop enabled the agency to portray itself as the humble servant of its thirsty customers. Representing the growth industry's needs as community needs allowed it to maintain an illusion of distance between its projects and developer interests. The water district's image of benign disinterest also allowed the agency to shield its state-granted taxing authority from public criticism until the 1970s, when it finally adopted another revenue-collecting system.

Fifth, the Metropolitan Water District employed a well-funded communications apparatus to shield the directors and their policies from public scrutiny. Its trained staff of engineers and public relations operatives used a blend of technical hydrological language and quasi-biblical rhetoric to connote scientific-spiritual truths. As they informed the state's political leadership about agency projects, they taught politicians to speak the water district's seductive language. They also transmitted it to the press, which translated it into the public vernacular, thus further naturalizing the agency's control over the "the flow of information."[26]

Growing Its Tree of Water

Thus, the Metropolitan Water District had all the necessary tools and resources when construction of the California Aqueduct began in 1966. Anticipating that moment, the agency had begun preparing in 1962 during the design phase of the Foothill Feeder, a more than 500-million-dollar interurban water delivery system "capable of conveying over 2 million acre-feet of state project water." The feeder's planned ninety-one-mile-long capillary system of tunnels, siphons, and pipelines would extend in a southeasterly arc "through the Castaic Hills, the eastern fringe of the Santa Susana Mountains, the Verdugo Mountains, and the south flank of the San Gabriel Mountains" until linking with the last section of the California Aqueduct below the Cedar Springs Reservoir.[27] From there, the Metropolitan Water District would distribute its cargo via a network of tunnels and pipelines to southern Los Angeles County and the growing suburbs of Orange, San Bernardino, and Riverside counties.

At about the same time, the agency charged William Lundy and his fellow engineers with designing and building a pipeline that would tap the Foothill Feeder's water and divert it to the giant Diemer Filtration Plant near Yorba Linda in northern Orange County. After reviewing several potential alignments, Lundy and his colleagues recommended "a straight shot" to Yorba Linda, concluding that the La Verne to Diemer route was the best" in terms of cost, although Lundy could not offer comparative estimates to support his claim. He said, "We probably came to the decision . . . in 1965." The alignment they chose dropped the feeder line from Devil's Canyon, near the city of San Dimas, and continued in a southwesterly direction through the city of La Verne and up into the Chino Hills until arriving at its Yorba Linda terminus. The water district's Yorba Linda feeder, a ten-by-ten-foot artery big enough to accommodate a small car and carry six hundred cubic feet of water per second, also happened to pass through the Tres Hermanos Ranch. As Lund said laconically, his recommendation "was pretty well accepted by Chandis. We had to construct the whole distance. We had to pay to go on the property."[28] Pay indeed. The Metropolitan Water District paid easement and right-of-way fees to get Chandis's permission to put an aqueduct carrying state-subsidized water through the ranch, a deal that soon made the property very attractive to potential buyers.

According to the water district, the agency first contacted Chandis Securities by letter on March 24, 1966. Construction began in 1972 while O'Melveny and Myers (the law firm representing Chandis) and the agency were still negotiating fees. Chandis wanted 1.5 million dollars for allowing the agency onto its property. The water district countered with an offer of 315,000 dollars. On October 1, 1976, they settled on 513,177 dollars in fees.[29] These fees, however, represented a fraction of the value the feeder could add to the ranch.

The *Times*, not surprisingly, did not report on the Yorba Linda extension project, which is not to say it went unnoticed. In 1972, the Pomona Valley Municipal Water District published a "Technical and Feasibility Report: Tonner Canyon Water Project," in which it proposed buying the ranch and building a water system there to handle suburban population growth in and around the Chino Hills that straddle the border between southern Los Angeles and northern San Bernardino counties. The report discussed the idea of building a reservoir at the mouth of Tonner Canyon and filling it with 4,500 acre-feet of water diverted from the Metropolitan Water District's feeder line. Because water from the California Aqueduct would need to undergo further treatment to meet drinking standards, the district proposed building a filtration plant on the property below the reservoir.

As early as 1970, the Pomona Valley Municipal Water District had been making preparations to secure the ranch and adjacent properties in Tonner Canyon. This interest was no surprise: the district had been a member of the Metropolitan Water District's governing body since 1950, so it was privy to the agency's project agenda.[30] In 1975, the Pomona water agency asked voters to pass a 35-million-dollar bond to finance the reservoir and filtration project, but they rejected the proposal. Then in 1977, the district resubmitted a scaled-down version of the project to voters, who again rejected it, opening the door for other suitors.[31]

If water made the property worth buying, it also made it worth selling. As Richard Hansen, general manager of the Pomona district said in 1985, "anytime you have an undeveloped piece of property and you have access to water, it will increase the value of that property." How the water got onto the property did not seem to matter, as the Chandis partners also apparently realized. In 1975, while the Pomona agency was trying to acquire the ranch and Chandis Securities was negotiating with the Metropolitan Water District, the Chandis partners themselves were applying to obtain rights to the water stored in the ranch's largest reservoir. Named after L. C. Arnold, a rancher who had leased the acreage since the 1940s, the 125-acre-foot Arnold Reservoir had been built in 1918 to water cattle and attract wildlife for the Chandler boys to hunt. In their application to the state's Water Resources Control Board, the partners argued that rights should be granted to them without a lengthy environmental impact review because the dam had not had any adverse effects on wildlife and would continue to be maintained in its current benign state.[32]

The opportunity to avoid the expense and public scrutiny involved in submitting an environmental impact review would be attractive to any would-be buyers, whatever their development plans. Two years later, William Keith Scott, a Chandis partner, submitted a plan to appraisers that played up the ranch's three "man-made lakes," which, if "filled to capacity," could cover thirty surface acres. Scott's plan recommended filling them "to take advantage of their obvious recreational potential and future impact on surrounding land values." It also represented the ranch as an ideal location for "planned urban development," contradicting the objectives of wildlife preservation promised in the water-rights application.[33]

Meanwhile, as the state weighed the application's merits, the realtors representing Tres Hermanos hunted for information to help them market the ranch to a buyer other than the Pomona water district. On August 18, 1978, per the request of the Wesley N. Taylor Company, Stan Kawa, then general manager of the Pomona district, sent the realtors a letter and a map showing where the water district had intended to build a reservoir on the ranch.[34] Tellingly, the application that Chandis had previously submitted to the state water control board and their subsequent correspondence with that agency had failed to mention their right-of-way negotiations with the Metropolitan Water District, their development plans for the property, or the Pomona water district's plan to tap the feeder line. That reticence was understandable. Acknowledging these developments in their application may have invited more questions from the state agency, perhaps even a request for an expensive and lengthy environmental impact review.

The realtors, however, did not share that reticence when they marketed the ranch. A Taylor Company representative sent his own copy of the map of the proposed reservoir to Harold Arnold, son of the former leaseholder, who had continued to lease the ranch after his father's death in 1964. The realty firm had mailed the map at Arnold's request, after he had given them a tour of the property.[35] It is important to note that Arnold was more than just a leaseholder. Not only was he subleasing the ranch to Industry mayor John Ferrero's cattle ranching outfit, but he had founded the City of Industry Security Company in early 1975, a business that permitted him to become a city contractor five months later. In 1976, the company was paid 85,973 dollars for taking undertaking city hall security; about 24,000 dollars of that sum was Arnold's own salary.[36]

Arnold, a former Los Angeles County sheriff's deputy, started the venture after then city manager Bob Rope recommended he get a state contractor's license. Rope had known Arnold's father and gave the younger Arnold a security position in the city until he could receive his license.[37] Arnold thus had at least two good reasons for sharing the map with the mayor. Whether he was acting as the property manager who leased the ranch to Ferrero or as the city's hired spy, it was his duty to tell the mayor about anything that might affect his ranching business.

A Web of Contracts

More intriguingly, the contractual ties between the two suggest a quid pro quo arrangement. Arnold told the FBI in 1983 that, as early as 1976, he began subleasing the ranch to Ferrero at 15,000 dollars a year, at the same rate at which he leased it from Chandis. Ferrero and a partner had already been leasing acreage from Arnold for farming purposes at three to four dollars an acre; an Industry feed yard leased the balance of the acreage. But the dual-use leasing scheme was proving to be less profitable than Arnold had expected, which made him receptive to Ferrero's offer to lease him the whole property. When the FBI asked him about his arrangement with the mayor, Arnold explained that it "relieve[d] him of any concern about losing money on the farming and grazing rights during a bad year when he [stood] to make less than the $15,000 lease amount." The mayor sweetened the deal by agreeing to maintain the ranch's boundary fences and access road, further reducing Arnold's costs of meeting the terms of his Chandis lease agreement.[38]

When Arnold opened a channel of communication between the City of Industry and Chandis, news of the feeder line soon reached Warner Hodgdon. In a January 10, 1978, letter addressed to Chandis partner Scott, Hodgdon complained about delays in obtaining information "to culminate [in] any property acquisition." The letter demonstrated Hodgdon's active role in property acquisition negotiations, and its reference to the Yorba Linda feeder line shows that he, too, knew about the Metropolitan Water District's project. A second letter with the same date, this time from Hodgdon to Richard S. Volpert, an O'Melveny and Myers attorney representing Chandis, acknowledges receipt of documents that Volpert had previously sent him as well as those received from Scott. The most important of these documents included Metropolitan Water District maps showing "the Yorba Linda Feeder Line which traverses the Tres Hermanos Ranch" and the development plan for Tres Hermanos "received from Mr. Scott."[39] When questioned by the FBI in 1986, Hodgdon said he could not recall exactly when he had initiated those discussions, though he did recall meeting Scott. He recalled that he had "reported the results of these contacts to Graham Ritchie" and had noted "the reasonableness of the [Chandis] asking price. Ritchie handled the transactions from there," a statement that seems to insulate Hodgdon from conflict-of-interest allegations.[40]

In a January 25 letter to Industry city engineer John Radecki, Hodgdon had communicated his reasons for recommending the Tres Hermanos purchase, carefully weighing the advantages that the feeder line would bestow on the property. The letter tried to address a strategic weakness in the city's position: unlike the Pomona water district, Industry did not have a vote on the Metropolitan Water District's board of directors. With a feeder line on its property, the city was entitled to approach the almighty agency and ask for some water. But the agency could deny the request if its engineers concluded that the project did not mesh with its overall plan for Southern California. Hodgdon's letter to Radecki anticipates this possibility, sketching out an alternate proposal for developing the ranch as part of a larger city-run water utility. In this scenario, the reservoir could not only collect runoff but also store reclaimed sewage water purchased at a nominal fee from the Los Angeles County Sanitation District. That district's San Jose Creek plant, at the city's northern tip, could pipe the partially treated water up to the reservoir. The reclaimed water, suitable for industrial and recreation uses, such as watering the greens of the Industry Hills golf courses, would reduce purchases of costly drinking water in times of dwindling supplies. In addition to invoking the drought motif to justify new water projects in California, Hodgdon cited the "struggle between the Los Angeles County Municipal Water District and Inyo County over groundwater depletion in the Owens Valley" as a policy rationale for his reservoir-building scheme.[41] By drafting a property development plan that could proceed without the Metropolitan Water District's participation, Hodgdon presented the city and its officials with a deal they couldn't refuse. The city would not need to rely on district water to store reclaimed water on the ranch for its comprehensive water utility, so it put off its request for district water.

His correspondence, however, does not disclose Chandis's "reasonable" asking price. We only have the figure for the city's initial offer: 4,000 dollars an acre, or 10.3 million dollars for the whole ranch. When the city discovered that it did not have enough cash on hand to swing the deal, it routed the offer through the Industry Urban Development Agency. In the meantime, a handful of private individuals submitted higher offers for the ranch. A January 27 letter from a Caldwell and Toms realtor to Chandis attorney Volpert states that "Dr. Bill Bright, President of Campus Crusade for Christ, Inc., offered to purchase an option on the property" for 12.1 million dollars. According to the letter, Bright had made his offer orally the day before. In another letter, also dated January 27, Volpert informed city attorney Ritchie that Howard Goldstein, vice president of Watt Industries, had telephoned in an 11.8-million-dollar offer.[42] The letter does not explain how Goldstein and Bright had learned that Chandis was selling the ranch; nevertheless, the city quickly matched Bright's (the higher) offer. Observers may wonder if Bright had collusively submitted his bid to help Hodgdon boost the price and benefit his friend Otis Chandler, but no evidence supports that theory. It's more likely that a sizable property straddling Los Angeles, San Bernardino, and Riverside counties simply had straightforward attractions for the Campus Crusade's student-oriented ministries.

In any case, on January 30, Ritchie advised the city council, per the appraiser's recommendation, that the higher (4,700 dollars an acre) asking price was "well within the scope of reasonableness" and that, in the city engineer's opinion, a reservoir was "a technically feasible use for the property." Matching Bright's offer meant that the city would pay 1.8 million dollars more than its initial bid. Ritchie's next piece of advice to the council sheds further light on the benefits of the Chandis partners' water-rights application for the ranch's largest reservoir. He told them the city could forgo the messy business of preparing an environmental impact review because it had not officially submitted a reservoir engineering plan, which meant that Industry did not have to gauge the project's environmental impact, at least not yet. The city could also offer the partners' water-rights application as further evidence that the proposed use, which the city had inherited, posed no danger to wildlife.

According to Ritchie, the council still had to address another matter if it intended to go ahead with the deal. Mayor John Ferrero and his son, Councilman John P. Ferrero, Jr., would have to disclose "their possible interest" in the ranch and "abstain from voting" on the matter. Ritchie advised that "since neither the Mayor nor Councilman Ferrero have any direct financial interest in the purchase of the property, abstaining and disclosing the nature of the interest would satisfy [the law]."[43]

So assured, the non-abstaining council members promptly approved the acquisition. The Industry Urban Development Agency's board of directors then declared the construction of a reservoir on the ranch to be a valid redevelopment objective. The city would assume responsibility for obtaining the state's go-ahead on the Chandis partners' water-rights application, which it obtained shortly afterward. The city council also felt compelled to request a legal opinion from Ritchie to assess the city's legal standing in acquiring property.

In the memo he drafted on January 30, Ritchie rendered a legal opinion that reiterated a *Chinatown* motif in the form of a proposed legal precedent. The city could legally purchase property three miles outside its city limits if it satisfied a municipal purpose. "Pursuant thereto," Ritchie continued, "the City of Los Angeles owns numerous real property interests in the Owens Valley and elsewhere for water and power purposes."[44] In other words, what was good enough for Los Angeles was good for Industry, even if that meant imitating one of California's most detested water projects. The Owens Aqueduct, its critics remind us, fueled decades of uncontrolled growth, destroyed a farming community, damaged a pristine wild trout fishery, and institutionalized a quasi-privatized water utility.

Industry got more than pastures, reservoirs, and legal technologies when it purchased the ranch. Its purchase reinforced a social network that had expanded during several decades of property relations and the knowledge communicated through that network. Those relations become evident in the exchange of knowledge among buyers, sellers, and tenants, communications defined by the cozy exclusivity of shared interests. The Pomona water district, for example, probably acquired its knowledge of the feeder project via its representative on the Metropolitan Water District's board. Industry's chances to learn about the feeder line could be traced back to the Pomona water district's efforts to build a reservoir on the ranch or to Arnold's business ties to Mayor Ferrero. Hodgdon may have discussed Chandis's plans to sell the ranch with friends such as Otis Chandler or his son Michael, members of his racing circle. That knowledge, however acquired and communicated, spread to Bright, one of Hodgdon's dearest friends and confidants.[45]

The city's acquisition of the ranch, in other words, consummated a simultaneous transfer of property and knowledge, a transfer of seemingly intertwined genetic qualities. For the rights of ownership not only gave the city access to the feeder line, but they also meant that it immediately inherited the new strategic meaning the Metropolitan Water District had already assigned to the property. And the new knowledge, in the form of reservoir engineering studies, the environmental impact exemption the city obtained, and the defensive possibilities of the Owens Aqueduct's legal precedent conferred to the ranch, promised to spawn other consequences. Like so many knowledge seeds, the conceptual technologies transmitted with the ranch contained the coded rationales the city would someday need to develop the property.

CHAPTER 10

JIM'S BUSY PERIOD

Bertolt Brecht used to say that robbing a bank is a crime but the greater crime is to found one.

—Eduardo Galeano, *Upside Down:*
A Primer for the Looking-Glass World

Jim's apparent disinterest in the Tres Hermanos acquisition coincided with a very busy, you might even say chaotic, chapter in his life. He had his hands full: he was engineering his divorce, hiding his wealth from his estranged wife, feeding his raging alcoholism, managing his deepening partnership with Ed Roski, Jr., and staying on top of a bid-rigging and kickback scheme that brought him more phony checks than he knew what to do with. If that were not enough, somewhere in the middle of a jumbled three-year period beginning in 1977, he began indulging in even more grandiose schemes, playing the city's political kingmaker and launching his own bank—a pursuit that, perhaps unwittingly, soon became the focal point of his criminal enterprise.

According to Jane, her husband had given her plenty of reasons to divorce him. But by 1977, after thirty-five years of marriage, his behavior had worsened. His violent outbursts and heavy drinking drove her to seek marriage counseling from a doctor the FBI's records identify as Dr. Gerty, a physician at Huntington Hospital in Pasadena. The doctor advised her to take assertiveness training courses to help her stand up to Jim and to bring him to one of her counseling sessions. But as Jane later told the FBI, the doctor rescinded his advice when Jim "went into one of his rages . . . during a counseling session which left both [Jane] and Dr. Gerty frozen with fear." Dr. Gerty diagnosed Jim as "paranoid" and flatly told Jane to leave her husband if she cared about her physical safety.[1]

Meanwhile, the tension at home had escalated. Jane said that Jim began carrying a shotgun and shells in his car. She recalled one incident in early 1979 that left her dazed and terrified, when "she and her daughter and son-in-law were watching the New Year's Day parades on television in the den of their Whittier home when Jim walked in with his shotgun. . . . He made a comment that a gopher was in the backyard and suddenly opened the door and fired a round from the shotgun from inside the doorway without warning anyone." Jim had discharged his gun only a few feet behind his wife. Her ears, she told the FBI, "rang for weeks afterwards." Shocked and horrified, she thought Jim had become "mentally deranged."[2] His drinking had also worsened. During the waning days of the summer of 1979, he began to suffer classic blackout symptoms, remembering nothing of what he had done before passing out.[3]

Jane also, however, recognized his attempts to dissemble. Before their separation, she found a forty-two-page document "in one of her husband's sweaters" giving detailed instructions for "depositing money in foreign bank accounts." He had circled a section titled "How to Hide Money from Your Spouse." She tried to use the discovery to bargain for a greater share of her husband's assets, but her lack of knowledge left her at a disadvantage. Over the years, Jim had told her very little about his business partnerships and investments, and she had no idea about what her cut of their estate might really be worth. She only knew, from overhearing his telephone conversations, that when he talked about money, the figures were "always in 'millions of dollars.'" She also heard enough to understand that "her husband was 'playing a shell game'" with those millions.[4] Of course, this is her version of events, one that implicitly casts her in the victim's role.

To break Jim's information stranglehold, Jane pestered him to write a will. She hoped, perhaps naïvely, that love of his children or even plain guilt would move him to fully disclose his assets before she could haul him into court. But the will he made, dated September 29, 1978, and prepared by a partner in Graham Ritchie's law firm, did not estimate the value of their estate; it simply listed his executors and trustees and explained how the estate would be divided. His son Stephen and his business partners Gary Bryce and Ed Roski, Jr., were named as trustees and executors of the estate. The will granted them the power to nominate their replacements and to distribute or invest his fortune.

Jane didn't understand why their son had been named a trustee, given the bad blood between Stephen and his father. In the months leading up to Jane and Jim's divorce, father and son repeatedly quarreled and fought for reasons that Jane never fully explained. She feared that Roski and Bryce would eventually remove Stephen as a trustee, although she knew why Jim had asked his two most important business partners to watch over his money. Her husband, she claimed, treated them like his own blood, like sons, or at least he wanted them to feel that way. She said that Bryce had even boasted that he had won Jim's favor at Stephen's expense. And Ed Junior would also have known how to play up to Jim's fatherly needs, as he had already learned to handle another powerful elder in his life—his own father.

The will gave the trustees the discretion to decide how much Jane would need for her "health, support, or maintenance," which meant that they could reduce her allotment if they reckoned that she could draw from "other income or assets." That other income, in this case, consisted of a 1,000-dollar monthly check that Jane got from her father's trust fund.[5] At the same time, Jim tried to claim her monthly trust payments as community property, which theoretically would entitle him to some of her money. His attorney went so far as to get Jane's bank account number and to file papers making Jim the executor of her trust fund account, a move that forced her to hire an attorney to regain control over her account.[6]

Jane refused to sign any papers that Jim put in front of her. Although she hoped that obstructing his business dealings would slow his efforts to liquidate his assets, it didn't. She said he recruited Bryce to do some arm twisting on his behalf and told the FBI that Bryce had asked her "to sign some documents in connection with the sale" of a 1,846-acre ranch in Blythe to the Mormon church for 5.6 million dollars in cash. One of the documents included "a 'continuing guarantee' for three million dollars at the Bank of America in the City of Industry." Jane said she had already signed the documents approving the sale of the ranch but drew the line at signing anything that made it easier for Jim to convert the proceeds of the sale to cash. Her refusals provoked an unexpected response. Bryce's "impassioned" pleas, she said, "went from tears to anger" and then further. He told her "she should 'get out and go live on the money you got from your father,'" a remark that showed her just how far Jim had taken Bryce into his confidence.[7]

In her FBI interviews, Jane painted herself as an "old-fashioned housewife" but did not acknowledge her complicity in Jim's quest for money and power. Instead, she represented herself as a battered wife who had paid the price for trying to stand up to her husband's threats and pressure tactics. Further resistance, she suggested, would not only have compromised her personal safety but also went against her upper-middle-class upbringing.

She claimed that she followed her husband's instructions out of habit and fear. She "had always signed whatever he put in front of her as she really had no choice in the matter." She believed he would throw her on the street and leave her with nothing if she resisted. That habit of submissiveness, combined with Jim's erratic, violent behavior and pressure from Bryce, finally made staying in the marriage too much to endure. Jane filed for a divorce soon after Thanksgiving 1979. Jim moved out of their Whittier home sometime afterward.[8]

The divorce settlement estimated the Stafford estate's cash deposits at slightly more than 1 million dollars. These deposits did not include Jim's interest in an Alabama oil well, a 45,000-dollar promissory note due to him, life insurance policies on himself and family members that had a 138,424-dollar surrender value, 40,000 shares of Birtcher Corporation stock, or his 116 shares of C. C. Stafford Milling and Warehouse Company common stock. The settlement did show his participation in six different business partnerships and major holdings in farmland and industrial property. It listed a 2,264-acre alfalfa farm that Jim owned in Blythe, on the California side of the Colorado River, and at least eleven commercial and industrial properties in the City of Industry. Jim, for example, held a 100-percent interest in the office building located inside the Civic-Financial Center that housed National Engineering, the Industry Manufacturers Council, and a jewelry store. But he split the "Chrysler Building" and the Bank of America building next door with Ed Junior. Jim and Ed also owned the property and building called the "Sofa Factory" and more than thirteen acres of undeveloped land outside the civic center. His other properties consisted of several warehouses near the San Gabriel and Pomona freeway interchange, inside the 140-acre Crossroads Industrial Park. He split six buildings in the park's Crossroads I and Crossroads D-I sections three ways with Ed Junior and John Curci, Ed's Sheraton Hotel partner at Industry Hills.

Aside from listing his cash deposits, the Whittier home, and a few undeveloped resort lots, Jim did not volunteer any information that would have helped Jane estimate the value of his other assets. In other words, he let her bear the onus of estimating what was hers, which, after a brief negotiating interlude, came out to about 2.6 million dollars. Her attorney conservatively estimated the value of what Jim had allegedly denied her at 10 million dollars. In the end, she got the house in Whittier, the beach and mountain lots, Jim's cars, his clothes, his personal jewelry (which consisted of a watch and a wedding ring), his Birtcher stock, and the cash in his bank accounts.[9]

No Jim without Junior

It is hard to imagine how Jim might have built his Industry fortune without the help of the city's biggest developer, Ed Roski, Jr. But apparently Ed also needed Jim to realize his goals in the city. No document has yet surfaced showing that Jim had promised Ed the biggest slice of the city's redevelopment program in exchange for choice investment opportunities, but the pattern of their dealings provides sufficient evidence of at least an unwritten understanding that allowed both of them to become prosperous, even though Ed enjoyed far bigger rewards.

A search of Roski's property holdings during this period found that "virtually all [property] transfers from the City of Industry or the Industry Urban Development Agency" went "to Edward P. Roski Jr., or one of his personal or corporate affiliates." That search was conducted by Sandra Lea Hobbs, a professional title researcher working on behalf of a client who was suing him. Hobbs identified "eighteen transfers from the City or Agency" occurring between 1975 and 1980, all of which were to Roski. Ed, in other words, was Industry's sole buyer of city-owned real estate after 1975, the year in which he formed his first business partnership with Jim. The Crossroads Industrial Park was one of the biggest of such transfers to a Roski-owned firm.[10] Hobbs's search also showed that Ed was the largest recipient of transfers from private property owners, most of which occurred after 1974. These transfers totaled more than four hundred acres and accounted for 30 percent of "all sales within the city" until 1980. Roughly thirty-six acres of these transfers consisted of property owned by the Southern Pacific, the Union Pacific, and their affiliates.[11]

The redevelopment agency made these transfers so routinely that it anticipated the resistance they would provoke, entering into deals with Roski's Majestic Realty even before acquiring the property through condemnation. According to the agency, no other competitors could match Majestic's warehouse and factory design expertise, understand the city's special needs, meet its high standards, or produce the financial wherewithal to handle big projects so reliably. Price rarely seemed to enter into the agency's selection rationale.

As a practical matter, the redevelopment agency had the authority to rely on a handful of contractors because it had put most of the city's land area under its own authority. Its property transfers often involved something called an owner-participation agreement. State law holds that if property is condemned by a redevelopment agency, that agency must offer property owners inside its designated project area a chance to participate in its redevelopment plan. For years, however, only Roski-owned firms had enjoyed the sole privilege of being offered owner-participant deals. Moreover, at least a dozen disgruntled property owners complained to the FBI in the early to mid-1980s that the city used its zoning and planning authority and its refusal to offer them the owner-participation option to force them to sell their properties to Majestic Realty.[12]

Only Francis Chan, a Taiwanese immigrant, had the temerity to sue and, miraculously, to wrest an owner-participation agreement from the Industry Urban Development Agency, but only after waging a protracted legal battle. The agency was planning to commercially develop a 116-acre strip on Industry's western boundary, a corridor running parallel to the Pomona Freeway. But in 1976, Chan had purchased a twenty-nine-acre parcel inside the corridor for the same reason. He saw the potential to make big money and earn the respect of his father, who had sent him to the United States to seek his fortune. With his attorney's help, Chan cleverly recast his experience in terms the press could understand: the underdog immigrant who battles city hall to fulfill his American dream.

For its part, the city, already armed with the power of eminent domain, moved to condemn Chan's property in early 1978, while the redevelopment agency worked hard to discourage him from becoming an owner-participant. According to Chan, the agency put off giving him the necessary owner-participant information for a year. When it did finally provide him with the information he needed to submit plans that were consistent with the agency's goals for the corridor, the agency did not process those plans and rejected his applications for building permits. The city also informed him that it planned to build a municipal service center on his property, which would allow the city to overrule the redevelopment agency's authority to recognize him as an owner-participant because Industry did not need a private partner to build a municipal building.

Discouraged, Chan attempted to sell the property for 7.5 million dollars. Yet the city, he claimed, sabotaged the sale, threatening to condemn the property as it went through escrow. Eventually, after scaring off a buyer who had expressed interest in the parcel, Industry offered to buy it for 1.3 million dollars under the threat of condemnation. Richard Richards, a former state senator and the attorney who represented the city in Chan's lawsuit, later said, "Chan knew there was a building moratorium in the Gale Avenue Corridor when he bought the parcel, which should have told him something." But the plaintiff's attorney, C. Edward Dilkes, said that the parcel had gone into escrow on November 23, 1977, four days before the building moratorium went into effect. He successfully argued that the city's belated actions, starting with its failure to notify his client of the owner-participant opportunity, smacked of a conspiracy intended for Roski's benefit.

Dilkes had learned the subtleties of redevelopment law as an associate attorney in the Richards law practice, and he based his conspiracy charge on a February 20, 1978, letter written to Chan by city attorney Graham Ritchie. Ritchie's letter expressed the agency's decision to condemn and sell the Gale Avenue corridor to Majestic Realty: the agency "is interested in the Roski proposal, since he is already developing a portion of the area with the Sofa Factory store. There was at least an informal understanding that the agency would give [him] first priority to develop the balance" of the corridor's property.[13] The agency formalized this understanding in June 1978. But Dilkes suspected that the Chan property was not the only parcel affected by the city's "informal understanding" with Roski. Therefore, he contracted Hobbs's study of Roski's property holdings in the city. Dilkes later told the FBI that Ed Junior, Jim Stafford, the City of Industry, and other parties had conspired to violate anti-trust laws "in connection with their real estate dealings," violations he would try to prove on appeal if the presiding judge had ruled against him.[14]

But he didn't need to. Dilkes won a ruling that saved Chan's property from condemnation and asserted his right to become an owner-participant a few years later. The judge who presided over the case had sent a message: Industry did not have the authority to ignore "inconvenient" parts of California redevelopment law. The judge did not, however, sustain Dilkes's conspiracy claims. As a result, the attorney never got a chance to present evidence claiming that Roski, thanks to Jim's influence, operated what amounted to a city-wide development monopoly.[15]

The will that Jim's lawyers drafted for him in 1978 would probably have helped Dilkes build such a conspiracy case. By naming Ed Roski, Jr., as a trustee of his estate, he granted him legal privileges usually reserved to heirs. The 1979 desk calendar that Jim's secretary maintained for him at the mill would also have helped Dilkes characterize his relationship to the Roskis. That calendar not only reveals that Jim constantly sent directives to Industry officials on highly sensitive municipal issues but also records the diligence with which the Roskis communicated with him. Of course, Jim had connections everywhere. Even former California attorney general, George Deukmejian, a staunch law-and-order Republican who would be elected governor in 1982, returned Jim's calls, eventually helping him settle a jurisdictional dispute on the California and Arizona border that clouded the deed to the ranch in Blythe that Jim co-owned with Bryce.[16] The calendar shows, however, that the Roskis communicated with him the most frequently in 1979, calling him at the mill at least forty-five times. Ed Junior made thirty-three of these calls; Roski employees made four or more of them.

An October 23 entry reads, "Roski wants to see you tomorrow at 11:00–11:30 to sign some papers."[17] The papers in question could have referred to any number of ongoing deals involving Jim and a Roski-owned firm, among them the continuing construction of the Industry Hills Exhibit and Conference Center. April 1979 saw the grand opening of the 18-million-dollar, three-story, 170,000-square-foot complex, which housed lavish restaurants, shops, offices, a ballroom, several conference and exhibit rooms, and a golf-course clubhouse replete with five hundred lockers as well as showers, saunas, and massage and steam rooms. But this achievement only represented the initial phase of a more than 60-million-dollar development plan. The project still called for the construction of two golf courses, two Olympic-sized swimming pools, fourteen tennis courts, an equestrian center with eight and half miles of fenced trails, an Austrian-built funicular to carry golfers up the four-hundred-foot gap between the ninth green and the tenth tee, and an eleven-story hotel on top of the conference center.[18]

In April 1980, the Civic-Recreational-Industrial Authority, the redevelopment agency that was overseeing the Industry Hills project, gave Ed Junior and John Curci, uncle of Hodgdon's close friend, the go-ahead to build the 284-room luxury hotel without the fuss of competitive bidding. The partners agreed to sink more than 15 million dollars into the new hotel and pay 71,000 dollars a year for the first five years of their fifty-year lease (and 3 percent of their gross thereafter) in exchange for giving the city's corporate clientele the run of the hill's publicly subsidized luxuries. To better capitalize on the city's investments in the 650-acre facility, Roski and Curci agreed to a second project phase that would expand the hotel to 316 rooms.[19] The hotel project's terms not only appeared to be generous but also allowed the city's critics to affirm what they had already perceived as an emerging pattern: this was the seventh of a dozen current redevelopment projects that had gone to a Roski-owned firm. And it would not be the last.[20] Clearly, Ed would not have enjoyed his role as Industry's preferred developer without Jim's approval, an arrangement that seemed to make him vulnerable to Stafford's demands.

But the redevelopment-financed construction boom that gave Jim opportunities to run his bid-rigging and kickback schemes came with risks.

"Our Little Bank"

It is hard to know which came first: Jim's obsession with creating a banking monopoly or his desire to open a bank in order to launder kickback checks. Whatever the sequence, his success in skimming money from Industry's redevelopment projects gave him a new set of problems. To begin with, asking his co-conspirators to write out checks in his name or to his businesses was like pointing a big arrow at himself. He wanted other people with credible corporate credentials to take the risk of letting him turn funny checks into untraceable bills. One by one, however, the banks that cashed his checks began to turn him down, leaving him with a growing pile of uncashed checks. He needed a long-term solution.

Businesses such as banks and casinos, which handle large volumes of cash, offered the best way to invent new pedigrees for his ill-gotten money. Like any modern mobster, Jim could try to hide a stream of kickback checks in an ocean of legitimate transactions or move the transactions offshore beyond the gaze of federal banking authorities. We know from his deeds and words that he weighed the advantages and liabilities of both options. While offshore casinos offered reduced regulatory oversight and impoverished governments susceptible to bribery, both had reputations that invited suspicion. Jim, who wanted to give his casino deals a semblance of legality, therefore made efforts to recruit legitimate investors. Banks had the advantage of staid reputations that put their affairs above suspicion.

Despite all his attempts at secrecy, Jim's casino and bank schemes left a crucial evidence trail, one that allowed his critics to construe him as the criminal mastermind who decided everything that happened in Industry. Prosecutors would later blame Jim's fall on his flawed character, his megalomania, his hubris, his contempt of the state. The local press embellished all these moral defects, portraying him as the brains behind the enterprise.

The evidence used to indict him, however, contradicted this omnipotent image. Jim seems, in fact, to have been a lousy gangster. His words and deeds suggest that he did not understand the legal, symbolic, and economic technology of corporate finance well enough to rob Industry's redevelopment projects without getting caught. Despite his reputation as a city builder, he lacked the organizational and technical expertise that real gangsters rely upon to hide their illegal dealings and enforce discipline in the ranks. He was also susceptible to his own stories and to his drinking. When we unravel and retell the tale of Jim's demise, we make room for other uncomfortable interpretations of both his role in Industry's development and his heroic capitalist identity.

Like a Godfather

By all accounts, Jim hatched the idea for the Bank of Industry during a series of 1977 lunch meetings at the California Country Club. He summoned about a dozen of his closest associates to discuss the bank's formation and ran the show form the start. "He sat there, in the middle of the table, firing questions like a godfather," said Stephen, who was twenty-seven at the time.[21] The literature that the organizers subsequently circulated to investors affirmed that "our bank will emphasize meeting the banking needs of small and medium-sized business firms, and the personal banking needs of business executives and professional persons located in the City of Industry and surrounding communities."[22] In other words, the Bank of Industry would market its services to Jim's people, Industry's small businessmen, and city employees who were his friends.

Jim's bank idea went beyond being merely a sweet deal for his friends. It may have expressed a private desire to wield the kind of financial power the banks had used against his father during the Depression. He already knew that founding and running a city gave him the right to thumb his nose at judges, lawyers, and journalists, that class of people who had humiliated C. C. Now, by forming his own bank, he could exact some revenge on the big-shot bankers who had nearly shut the mill down after his father's death.

The emotional roots of Jim's bank obsession expressed themselves in monopolistic fantasies. Stephen recalled hearing his father tell his buddies that "they were the only ones who were going to be allowed to have [the next] chartered bank in the Civic-Financial Center." Yet as his earliest selection of proposed bank directors would make clear, he still had a lot to learn about the banking game.

Robert King, who was a director and one of the bank's early organizers, said that Jim wanted to monopolize banks in the city's Civic-Financial Center. At first, he believed the scheme would work. "I fully thought we would start a bank and keep other banks out," King said, "and, after two to three years, we'd be approached by a [big] bank. We would say fine,

buy our little bank, at five times our investment."[23] Jim also invited Ed
Junior to serve on the board.[24] Ed was a sensible choice: his responsibilities
as Majestic Realty's executive vice president had increased as the family-
run business had prospered, and so did his reputation as the leader of a
growing corporation. Clearly, Jim appreciated his own role in Majestic's
success and felt entitled to ask for certain favors.

Behind his back, however, many of Jim's banking buddies laughed off
the scheme as naïve. Unlike place entrepreneurs, whose investment strategies try to attain a relative advantage by guessing the next location where
market demand will rise, corporate bank chains do not rely on their own
branch properties to make money. On the contrary, some regional and
national banks were already beginning to suffer liabilities from owning
redundant branch offices, collapsing property values, and advances in
automated banking. Jim didn't seem to grasp the idea that real estate
developers of his size still had to go to wherever the money already was.

His friends' reservations, if he ever heard them, did not deter Jim from
pushing forward. The Industry city council passed two ordinances in 1977
that restricted banking businesses to its civic center, a key piece of Jim's
plan for cornering branch expansion in the city.[25] His plan assumed that
banks would complete for a toehold inside the Civic-Financial Center just
as other developers had competed before. He based his actions, in other
words, on lessons learned from selling his property to the city, not on
knowledge of the banking business. "In his own mind," said King, "he truly
believed he had enough power to do this."[26]

It's not hard to see why Jim had become so impressed with his own
influence. He now enjoyed an entourage of toadies who did his bidding,
retold his deeds, and praised him so often that he had come to believe
the hype. So what if his buddies recounted his exploits for their own
personal gain or if they even believed them? Inside the recently completed
Industry Exhibit-Conference Center, he drank in his own myth, along with
increasing quantities of alcohol. The center's posh appointments, its mute
luxuries, the deference of its employees, and the money he still skimmed
from its unfinished construction projects spoke to him more convincingly,
more viscerally than did mere words. They reinforced whatever he wanted
to believe about himself.

Surely his new knowledge of finance capital and its impressive signifying
powers was just one more of his many talents. After all, he had learned
enough from the business world to see that corporations cultivated their
reputations in order to re-signify other products or business ventures.
He also knew that banks were powerful symbols of fiscal solvency and

trustworthiness. Why couldn't he hijack this symbolic power for his own purposes? If he couldn't use the Civic-Financial Center to extract bribes or special favors from the banking industry, he could at least run his own bank, direct the techniques that banks use to create an aura of respectability, and so hide his conspiracy.

Jim's efforts to apply his understanding of banking practice ran into problems from the start, however. It appears that the California State Banking Department rejected his first application for a bank charter (submitted sometime before 1977, although a full account of the department's actions no longer exist because it has destroyed its pre-1977 records). Then in 1977, state banking regulators turned up information that made them leery of his company's second charter application. In rejecting that application, the department cited the unacceptability of the bank's proposed president and a lack of evidence showing that the bank could attract enough local trade to be viable.[27] The bank's organizers also gave regulators other reasons for suspicion. William Adams, the assistant deputy in the banking department who reviewed the Bank of Industry application, said that not one of the investors identified as prospective bank supporters "expressed any interest in switching [their money] to the Bank of Industry." More importantly, Adams said, the corporate leaders whom the organizers had identified as their bank supporters acknowledged that "James Stafford was behind [the bank's formation] and that he would control it." Bank regulators began to wonder if Jim and Ed Junior would be able to resist the temptation to leverage their combined wealth and influence to overwhelm the other bank directors and thus undermine the bank's ability "to operate independently." The regulators told Jim and his associates that their next charter application would have to include board members with credible corporate credentials, more convincing expressions of support from the local business community, and a full-time bank president with a certifiable reputation for honesty and independence.[28]

Ed, who was serving as point man for the bank's organizers, turned to his growing business network to recruit a bank president with the appropriate credentials. That man was Dale E. Walter. Walter recalled that Roski had mentioned the bank idea to him in passing, at the time when organizers were first trying to get it off the ground. "Sometime later, during a casual conversation, [he] asked Roski how his bank was coming along." According to Walter, Roski told him about the failed applications, to which he replied with an alleged jest: "Ed, I could get that bank off the ground for you." Walter insisted that he had never intended to leave his position at the Redwood Bank, a small operation that occasionally financed Roski's construction projects. But the impending sale of the Redwood Bank in Northern California gave Roski a chance to remind Walter of his earlier offer. Walter told the FBI that "he accepted Roski's invitation to come to Los Angeles and meet with him and Robert [King]" in September 1979. Although Walter still held out hope of staying at Redwood, he took the prudent step of giving Roski permission to list his name as a prospective president when the organizers resubmitted their final application in January 1980.[29]

The sale of Redwood Bank three months later put Walter's career in limbo until the Bank of Industry's organizers received the California State Banking Department's May 31 reply. The department reported that it would consider the third charter application if organizers listed Walter as their firm choice for bank president and chief executive officer. A few days later, Walter flew down from Northern California to introduce himself to the bank's board of directors and to Jim, who held no official position on the bank's board of directors. They met inside the lavish new digs at the Industry Hills Exhibit-Conference Center, where Jim and his associates now held court.

The bank directors quickly let Walter know that Jim ran things in the city. They were not exaggerating. When the time came to negotiate his contract, Walter discovered that the bank's hiring committee included Jim; and from the start, he balked at the five-year, 80,000-dollar annual salary with perks that Walter had requested for his services. Walter patiently reminded him and the other committee members that they could not get their charter without his name on their application. Jim's reply was patronizing, to say the least: "Dale, don't worry about this little thing. Do a good job and you will be taken care of."

The negotiations also illustrated the extent to which Roski relied on Jim's help to broker an agreement. When Walter refused to yield, the hiring committee appointed one of their committee members, John J. Stanko, former president of Douglas Oil Company and a partner in another Industry-funded consulting firm, to engage the banker in one-on-one talks. According to Walter, Stanko tried to wear him down by haggling over every contract detail. He knew that Walter did not have a job waiting for him in the Bay Area. But Stanko's attempt to chip away at his resolve only exasperated Walter, who said that he "called Ed Roski at Industry Hills to tell him to get Stanko off his case or else." His threat appears to have caught Roski off guard. Roski asked Walter "to hold on a moment" but did not explain why. The reason became clear a few minutes later.

"The next thing [I] knew," Walter told the FBI in 1983, "James Stafford was on the line." Jim tried "to make light" of Stanko's meddling by offering an awkward non sequitur: "Just think how difficult it would be if we had an oil shortage."[30]

Walter eventually got the salary he wanted, even though it was more than Jim wanted to pay. And on May 30, banking authorities gave the bank's supporters official permission to begin seeking investors while they applied for their charter. The California Superintendent of Banks authorized the Bank of Industry to open for business on March 17, 1980.[31] Organizers promptly pulled together more than 6 million dollars to open the bank, nearly 2 million dollars more than they needed to get it off the ground.

The names on the bank's board read like a directory of Jim's best friends and the city's richest men. King, an active co-conspirator in Jim's fraud scheme, presided over the Industry Manufacturers Council as its president. Stanko, a partner in Municipal Research Analysts, did consulting work for only one client: the City of Industry. Robert H. Brown chaired the El Encanto Convalescent Hospital's board of directors; its patients had played a decisive role in Industry's incorporation. G. William Bryant, thanks to Jim's nod, had gone from a 30,000-dollar annual salary managing the California Country Club to a 300,000-dollar annual salary managing the Industry Hills Exhibit-Conference Center. Jim also recruited Owen H. Lewis, a real estate investor and former Los Angeles County regional planning commissioner, who had used his influence (improperly, some alleged) to help Industry acquire land for its foreign trade zone. Mayrant Dorsey "Mac" McKeown, Artesia's city manager, was Stanko's partner at Municipal Research Analysts. Donald R. Wheeler, a partner in the Lewis-Wheeler Company, was Ed Junior's investment partner. Only two of the bank's directors did not appear to be directly linked to Jim or Ed: James E. Brown, chairman of the board and chief executive officer of California Steel and Tube, and James E. Williams, president and chief executive officer of Golden State Foods Corporation.[32]

Roski, King, and Bryant purchased 40,000 shares at ten dollars a share, or about 8 percent of the money needed to capitalize the bank. Those three men, together with twenty-nine other investors, owned 70 percent of the bank's stock; two hundred other investors purchased the remainder.[33] Jim waited at least three months before he bought about 275,000 dollars' worth of stock, or 3.2 percent of the bank's total shares, through one of his accountants. His former daughter-in-law held the stocks under his grandson's name.[34]

In the meantime, Jim continued to attend the bank's organizational meetings. After one bank organizer complained about his attendance, Walter barred him from the meetings. Needless to say, however, that action failed to reduce Jim's meddling or derail his check laundering. He bypassed the restriction by pumping friendly bank directors for information. Sometimes he didn't even wait for meetings to end but telephoned the directors for in-progress briefings.[35] Nonetheless, the flow of kickback money that Jim laundered at the Bank of Industry must have been unsatisfactory because he began to run a second laundering stream through another local bank as early as May 1978.

Jim's Favorite Teller

Lucilla Rowlett, a teller at the Bank of America's Industry office, who would later figure in Jim's check laundering across the street at the Bank of Industry, told the FBI that the bank's officers made sure that the staff treated Jim like a VIP. She said that the branch's vice president of operations and its operations officer had told her more than once "to treat Stafford 'right,'" instructions that she believed expressed the bank's "special relationship" with him. She acknowledged that the other bank employees believed "she was personally connected with Stafford," but she blamed that "mistaken impression on her natural friendliness and inclination to flirt with" the bank's big shots. According to Rowlett, her friendship with Jim started after she and her husband rescued him from an embarrassing situation at the Chalet Basque Restaurant in La Puente, a few blocks from the bank. They drove Jim home after finding him totally smashed after lunch. She said Jim interpreted her rescue as a kindness he should repay. Her Louisiana roots also told him they had something in common. So he invited her into his universe. She accepted his invitation, attending parties with his Industry buddies and lunch dates with the bank's directors.[36]

Still, she claimed, socializing with Jim did not influence her actions on the job. Those were dictated by bank policy. All the tellers were "expected to know him on sight and to treat him with deference." They all knew that Jim owned interests in the pair of buildings that housed the bank's branch offices inside the Civic-Financial Center. Rowlett went a step further, however. To her, "treating Stafford right" meant cashing checks made out to other individuals. She did follow bank policy by at least asking Jim to have "the party to whom the check was made out present" when she cashed those checks.[37] But she also acknowledged cashing Stafford-endorsed checks made payable to businesses with which he had no official connection.

Rowlett and her fellow tellers conducted these transactions in the vault area, a space reserved for customers with cash transactions too big for the regular tellers to handle. She said that the checks she cashed for him ranged from 9,000 to 11,000 dollars. Per Jim's request, Rowlett paid the checks out in fifty-dollar bills, which she stuffed into envelopes she then sealed. He often called her in advance to let her know he would be cashing a check, an apparent attempt to keep the transactions under the bank's radar. Rowlett acknowledged that she knew these practices violated bank policy. But she did them anyway, she said, because, when she alerted her superiors to Jim's improper requests, they told her "to 'give Stafford what ever he wants.'" Rowlett believed that the bank's president, Kenneth Derr, knew of these exceptions, even if she couldn't prove it.[38]

Rowlett, for unexplained reasons, thought it would be prudent to make copies of the checks she cashed for Jim and then wait for the right opportunity to produce them. She created that opportunity when she asked a fellow employee, perhaps her boss, a question about the bank's check-cashing policies. Although she did not say as much to the FBI, her actions suggest anxiety over her role. The testimony of her superiors, however, adds a layer of fog to this cloudy episode. Derr told the FBI that "he somehow learned," perhaps from Rowlett, perhaps from someone else, that she was concerned about cashing corporate checks for individuals. Derr could not recall when he learned about her actions or whether they "concerned James Stafford in particular," but he said that he pulled her aside to instruct "her never to cash these types of checks unless they are approved by a bank officer." But he told the FBI that he could not recall her ever giving him copies of the checks.[39]

Rowlett did not suffer a similar memory lapse. She claimed that she clearly remembered approaching Derr with copies of the canceled checks. "I thought I should show [the photocopied checks] to them because I didn't want my job to be on the line."[40] According to Rowlett, Derr "became upset that the checks had been cashed and criticized [her], even though she had cashed similar checks" for Jim on previous occasions "with Derr's knowledge."[41] When the FBI questioned him later on this point, Derr denied that he had ever allowed tellers to violate bank check-cashing policies. If it happened, he insisted, it occurred without his knowledge or consent. All that Derr could offer in Rowlett's defense was that she did not try to hide what she had done and that she and two other tellers agreed to follow bank check-cashing policies in the future. By June 1980, the Bank of America's Industry branch had stopped cashing Jim's kickback checks.[42]

CHAPTER 11

ASSEMBLING
JIM'S PORTRAIT

And the island of the future, where the only time was the future, and the inhabitants were planners and strivers, such strivers, said Ulises, that they were likely to end up devouring one another.
— Roberto Bolaño, *The Savage Detectives*

The details of Jim's portrait had begun to accumulate since Industry's incorporation. Pieces of that identity had sporadically appeared in the local press but, like jagged bits of tile, had not yet formed into public mosaic we would later accept as his likeness. Nor had the local press made the city's image synonymous with Jim's or even made up its mind about his place in the city's hierarchy since it had previously portrayed city attorney Graham Ritchie as the architect of Industry's injustice.

Everything changed on June 26, 1980, when the *Los Angeles Herald Examiner* published the first installment of a nine-part series titled "The City of Insiders," a comprehensive account of how Jim and his business associates ran the city. Reported and written by Scot J. Paltrow, the articles collected characteristic populist narratives to introduce Jim and the City of Industry to the paper's blue-collar readers. Although more critical than any reporting that had preceded it, the series, by stressing the significance of Jim's influence and charisma, reaffirmed the concept of power as personal property. Its secondary attention to the city's governmental forms did not ask if those technologies had generated Jim's power or molded his personality.

The lead article, "How the Rich Get Richer," initiated the series with a populist cliché; and both this article and the ones that followed it reiterated several character-affirming narrative motifs. To begin with, Paltrow portrayed Jim as the city's pater familias, who had used his position as a Los Angeles County planning commissioner to win support for the city's formation. The reporter also represented Jim as the ultimate unseen powerbroker, who ran the city as his personal kingdom. According to Paltrow, "many who are knowledgeable about Industry's affairs claim that Stafford, the city's founding father, has never relinquished his considerable influence over his offspring." The lead article shared details of Jim's personality, his brutality, and his penchant for secrecy, noting that "Stafford is more than 6 feet tall, and despite his age and a slight paunch, is powerfully built. He has thick calluses on his hands, and is rarely seen outdoors without his Panama hat. . . . Stafford has refused repeatedly to be questioned by the *Herald Examiner*, and once ran after one of the newspaper's photographers in an attempt to stop him from taking pictures."[1]

For readers, such a characterization connoted brutality, avarice, and secrecy. Yet even though that representation was damning, it stressed the anomalous extremes of his monstrous personality, not his membership in a class that commits monstrous deeds. Paltrow and the reporters who followed him did not challenge these biographical assumptions. Rather, they magnified the significance of Jim's personality to explain why so much wealth was concentrated in such a tiny, evil city.

The series also attempted to show that Jim was running the city with the help of willing buddies and business cronies. In addition to repeating the idea in the series title, "The City of Insiders," Paltrow identified Ed Roski, Jr.'s, Majestic Realty Company as Jim's most recent collaborator, noting that "Stafford has direct financial interests in several of [Majestic's] Industry projects."[2] "How the Rich Get Richer" includes a flowchart in which the major players' names and titles appear in black print on a white field and Jim's personal ties appear in white print on a black field. The column is headed by title boxes using the same black-white, white-black motif—the left one titled "City of Industry," the right one "Stafford." A solid black line on the left connects each city official's title to the "City of Industry" box; a dotted black line on the right connects the official's summarized ties to Jim's name. The connotations are clear and sinister.[3] Yet the article does not explain how Jim and his cronies had fashioned their identities as men of action, vision, and power; it simply accepts these qualities as innate features of their characters.

Paltrow's series employed the "abuse of redevelopment" theme to address the legal technology that made the city resistant to reform. Here again, however, it failed to question the conventional moral frame or to ask if these laws, including legislation that the city had secured to protect its interpretation of those laws, had ever been used for anything other than permitting huge transfers of public wealth into private hands. Nor did the series explain how the confluence of contract-city technologies and the state's innovative redevelopment laws made Industry's formation possible in the first place.[4] It instead interpreted Industry's governmental technology as a perversion of something intended for another purpose, naïvely implying more honest, more impartial uses of redevelopment that did not amount to corporate welfare.

Moreover, the series did not explore the city's genealogies of governmental technology as a separate theme. The *Herald* did not ask its cross-town rival, the *Los Angeles Times,* whether Chandis Securities, Times Mirror's landholding subsidiary, had used its special access to the Metropolitan Water District's water to boost the value of its Tres Hermanos Ranch real estate holdings. Nor did the series explore Industry's decision to borrow from Los Angeles's governmental technology when it cited the Owens Aqueduct as a precedent. Paltrow, in other words, did not ask whether events in Industry might shed light on a few of California's most important historical controversies. Did the Tres Hermanos transaction, for example, offer fresh confirmation of another *Chinatown*-like water deal?

The series also only glanced at the relationship between the city's corporate clientele and the significance of its transportation infrastructure, as Paltrow's treatment of the railroads illustrates: "In the early '50s, Stafford, whose family owned hundreds of acres, and other area landowners decided they could boost their property values by incorporating the land and reserving it exclusively for industries and businesses. The site itself was ideal for businesses; it was bounded by the mainline tracks of the Union Pacific and Southern Pacific railroads."[5] Here, Paltrow accepts the symbiotic nexus between railroads and real estate development as natural, mentioning it only to stress Jim's power and thus relegating the railroads to the role of bystanders. Ironically, his only other mention of the railroads portrays them as victims of a city that forced them to let the mayor run cattle on their properties or suffer the consequences of slow siding authorizations and project approvals.[6] Yet the Southern Pacific's role in rescuing the city's incorporation, the railroads' and the city's lavish methods of marketing their real estate holdings, the city's willingness to overlook the SP's zoning infractions, and the city's strict enforcement of zoning ordinances, which protected the uses and value of railroad landholdings, hardly resembled a victimizing relationship. Making these connections explicit could have given readers a chance to reflect on California's history and to raise some new questions. For instance, did the Southern Pacific's role in Industry's creation revive its image as the octopus that once ran the state? Did Union Pacific and Southern Pacific investments in the city illustrate their resurgence as industrial developers, particularly as players in the growing warehousing and distribution sectors?

The series instead preferred to emphasize Industry's anomalies. For example, one inset caption explains, "The City of Industry has been an oddity since it was created in the mid-1950s" and then lists its other unusual qualities.[7] A later article focuses on redevelopment abuse and Jim's strongman image to reinforce Industry's uniqueness rather than its common use of regional governmental technologies or its sisterhood with other single-use industrial cities, which not only shared governmental technologies but also, in many cases, the same developers and cast of legal experts.

I do not list these narrative motifs to underscore an individual reporter's deficiencies. On the contrary, Paltrow's work is a well-realized literary portrait of the way in which his profession understood and coded political leadership, municipal corruption, and redevelopment in the early 1980s. Like most members of the mainstream news media at that time, Paltrow and his colleagues had not yet attempted an explicit description, let alone a critique, of how the technologies of power had affected the corporate privatization of a U.S. city. Instead, he uncovered what he was trained to see: the Industry Manufacturers Council's illegal 18,000-dollar contribution to Los Angeles County district attorney John Van de Kamp and the timing of that gift.

Like other members of the mainstream news media at that time, Paltrow had not yet attempted an explicit critique of the corporate privatization of government, let alone call it *neoliberalism,* the name intellectuals from Mexico to Argentina used to describe the corporate acquisition of Latin America's state-owned utilities and natural resources. Still, Paltrow did a thorough job of describing the relentless privatization of the local electoral system. He had uncovered the Industry Manufacturers Council's illegal 18,000-dollar contribution to Los Angeles County district attorney John Van de Kamp and the timing of that gift. Paltrow disclosed that the council had made its contributions while Van de Kamp's office was investigating allegations of voter fraud during the special 1978 bond election that permitted Industry to break Proposition 13's fiscal stranglehold.[8] These revelations gave his editors enough ammunition to boldly challenge local law enforcement. In a scathing opinion piece coinciding with the last installment of the series, they wrote, "The City of Industry could only go on with a law enforcement community that either does not care, or prefers to look the other way."⁹

Paltrow's Ideal Reader

One FBI agent noticed the newspaper's warning.¹⁰ Special agent John F. Keller, known to his friends and colleagues as Jack, had already been assigned to investigate redevelopment, gambling, and other types of fraud in the single-use cities of southeastern Los Angeles County. Paltrow's articles, despite their evidentiary and conceptual gaps—or more precisely, because of their particular way of telling Industry's story—were perfectly coded for Keller's purposes.

Quietly the agent explored the possibility of building a case against Jim, the city, or its officials; and in 1981, he got the green light to launch a formal investigation. Keller conducted interviews, collected public and private records, and prepped his confidential observers inside the city. He methodically entered the testimonies he collected in FD 302 reports, an agent's principal means of organizing narratives of suspected criminality. The case was his baby from the start, and he conducted more than 90 percent of the investigation's interviews. He knew he'd get the glory if he succeeded and lose the respect of his superiors if he failed. For four years he let the investigation take over his life, an obsession that eventually cost him his marriage.

The series triggered other effects as well. A few of Jim's closest associates and a few of the city's most important clients quietly began to pull away from him and the city. For example, Upland Industries, a Union Pacific subsidiary, which had agreed to sell off a seventy-six-acre parcel to the city's redevelopment agency before the *Examiner* series appeared, decided to sell all of its Industry holdings (about 370 acres) after the 1980 series ran. Donald E. Clark, Upland's director of real estate operations, later told Keller that the directive came from the firm's president, L. B. Harbour. Clark believed that Harbour called Jim a few months later to arrange the sale. He chose not to contact Hodgdon, who wanted the property for his foreign trade zone project, because, according to Clark, Hodgdon rarely followed through on what he had promised. "Stafford, on the other hand, was always good on his word and got things done."¹¹ Getting things done in this case meant that Upland got an excellent price for its properties with little negotiating. The company received 30.3 million dollars for its parcel from the Industry Urban Development Agency, plus the firm expectation of future freight-hauling profits for its parent corporation, because the trade zone's design featured Union Pacific and Southern Pacific sidings running through the more than five-hundred-acre development.[12]

The railroad's decision to sell its property showed that Paltrow had touched a nerve. The railroad executives who read his series now saw their business dealings with Jim the way other reporters or prosecutors might if they ever came to light. Their actions showed that they worried that the series might tickle the curiosity of other nosy reporters or spark a criminal investigation. It did just that, the railroad executives soon discovered, and from Paltrow's ideal reader. For Special Agent Keller's power to watch, interrogate, and report his observations could indeed transform almost anyone into a target of government surveillance. He could arrange searches, wiretaps, and arrests; convene grand juries; trigger indictments—and all were narrative opportunities that the media could use to paint a suspect's identity. Just as often, the agent's writing could lead to convictions, the court's most powerful way of confirming a truth of its own making and the media's best excuse for outfitting the accused with a new identity.

Historically, the FBI has ranked a would-be agent's mental capabilities higher than his brute athleticism. A new recruit can develop or learn strength, stamina, and martial-arts skills but not mental aptitude and what the bureau defines as moral character. Preferred candidates have exceptional intelligence, a rigid sense of right and wrong, and a fanatical devotion to country; and with the hope of molding such people into secular Jesuits of law enforcement, the FBI has recruited lawyers, accountants, and others trained in technical professions that demand close attention to written and spoken detail. Historically, the bureau has also molded agents' appearance. They should "look like a young businessman, dressing in dark suits, white shirts, and snap-brimmed hats"; they should look "all-American," which, for much of the FBI's history, has meant male and Anglo, without a hint of foreignness.[13]

Keller fit the bill. Tall, lean, with blue-gray eyes and hair so blonde it seemed to verge on silver, the Illinois native still spoke with a discernible midwestern twang. He wore his uniform, the special agent's typical dark-blue business suit, with impeccable neatness. Since joining the bureau in 1974, he had distinguished himself as an expert in white-collar crime, showing a talent for breaking loan-fraud cases, bank embezzlements, and telemarketing scams. After graduating with a political science degree from Southern Illinois University in 1964, he rose to a captain's rank in the U.S. Air Force before earning an honorable discharge in 1968. He later earned a law degree, passing the California bar in 1975, less than a year after having completed his training at Quantico. In time, he would win several annual

FBI exceptional performance awards, serve as an expert witness in Ponzi con schemes, and act as an FBI legal advisor, a police instructor, and a civil rights investigator.[14]

Keller was especially adept at detecting financial fiction, the elaborate stories that disguised the theft of public or private funds. And he had a talent for reading facial and verbal deceit as well as financial fraud coded in words and numbers. He poured over ledgers, inventories, contracts, memoranda, purchase orders, change orders, birth certificates, lawsuit paperwork, and countless other documents, hunting for clusters of words or ciphers that might reveal a suspect's motives. He looked for a soft spot, that point at which the force of the law could bear down on a suspect or a reluctant witness.

Importantly, Keller believed in his ability to let his training direct and validate his actions. His interview reports demonstrated this faith. His 302s show a deliberate use of language, one schooled in the rules of evidence and the legal definitions of proof accepted under federal law. He followed the bureau's standardized forms for reporting interviews and its instructions for composing and filing these reports, as listed in the *Manual of Investigations*, which ensured that any agent from any field office could find and understand them. Keller also understood that any letter he sent outside the office would be checked by as many as eight pairs of eyes, and he knew that no error was too small to be corrected.[15]

The Agent As Author

The agent's relationship with his readers was premised upon an unspoken covenant. He wrote his chronicles for an exclusive audience of fellow agents, prosecutors, and judges. These reports offered his superiors a window into his thinking, a way to monitor his questions and check the progress of his investigations. Keller understood the conventions and procedures of his police culture and accepted that culture's definitions of truth and its methods for obtaining it. The bureau's investigative protocols gave his writing legal legibility and coherence, a language his readers in the bureau and the justice department understood. They had the power to decode the evidence that he collected, to prosecute the crimes indicated by the evidence, and to recognize his unique contributions. Their mutual expectations hinged upon the blank underlined space reserved for his name on the first page of each 302 he filed. The name he wrote there guaranteed his authorship, a status that permitted the bureau's librarians to distinguish his reports from thousands of others.[16] Meanwhile, the system he used to classify each report he filed ensured that his colleagues in the bureau and justice department could always recover his writing. The letters, "LA," that initiated the series "LA 194C-143" stood for Los Angeles, the office where his report originated. The number "194" classified his investigation as a public corruption case; the "C" meant that his investigation targeted a private, non-elected individual. The "143" indicated that his investigation represented the 143d public corruption investigation underway in the bureau at that time. The numbers he wrote by hand after "LA 194C-143" assigned an individual serial number to each report he filed. Like Paltrow's in his world, Keller's reports bound him to a particular literary tradition, to a specific way of reading and writing but also to the FBI, which made his special form of authorship possible.[17] It had provided him with the ground to plant the seed of a literary persona, one that he would gradually discover and then cultivate inside the invisible cell of his professional and legal obligations. But the rules that walled the agent in still left cracks of meaning not governed by the bureau's manual, miniscule domains it could not always anticipate and therefore control. He slowly widened and filled these gaps with his own inventions, the seeds of his own voice.

In contrast to other agents, for example, Keller wrote up outlines that would guide him through his dictation, believing this strategy gave him the freedom to use strict chronology to organize his reports. Early on, he had made a deliberate decision to avoid the thematic reporting practiced by the other agents. They often wrote down their interviews as if time did not exist, as if all events had occurred in a perpetual present that made it easier to perceive plausible connections that chronology would later prove improbable. Keller had learned the importance of chronology in law school. It gave him a method for discovering and reconstructing patterns of fraud that suspects might have taken years to hide.

A careful reading of his reports shows that he plotted statements of witnesses and suspects and the discovery of documents in the sequences in which they occurred, even if he did not always grasp the implications of what his suspects or witnesses had said or done. Keller did not need to be omniscient as long as his chronology was accurate. Once he had made a written record, he could return to the testimony to reflect on what the witness or the suspect knew or did not know at a particular moment in time. The answers he gleaned helped him inhabit his characters' thinking and to test a theory of criminal opportunity and motive.

Keller's readers, particularly the prosecuting attorneys, preferred to read reports written as stories because evidence organized in narratives is easier for jurors and judges to understand. That preference, along with the success of his investigations, reinforced Keller's literary practices. He quickly learned why assistant attorneys tended to choose his cases over those of other agents: with mounting caseloads, they did not have time to reorder poorly organized evidence. Whether Keller realized it or not, however, the writing style that helped his readers visualize a complex case also required a degree of literary invention. Sometimes his inventions consisted of subtle inflections in tone that did not come from his training or his personal experience. Perhaps they arose from a mixture of obsession and imagination that awakened as he rehearsed his dictation. But for whatever reason, that voice grew stronger and more distinct with time. After years of writing for the bureau, Keller had created an author's voice that was subtly different from his speaking voice—an accumulation of seemingly insignificant improvisations, the result of listening for and recording his sources' convenient metaphors or of capturing the rhythmic fluctuations of emotional speech.

Keller admired investigative reporting and understood the importance of journalistic narration in painting a convincing portrait of criminal character. A meticulously rendered character portrait could help prosecutors develop a theory of a suspect's criminal motives. Paltrow's series gave him a both a complete character study and enough leads to test several theories about Jim's criminal methods. Identifying those opportunities and putting Jim at the scenes of the crimes would come later. But Keller's hypothesis—that Jim had committed crimes against the city he had created, which was both the means and the target of his transgressions—invited a literary conceit. Narratives about Jim, whether written or spoken, stressed the pervasiveness of his corrupting influence, the city's spatially reduced and intimate dimensions, and his role as founding patriarch. Jim was a symbol of primogeniture, a story that not only established a line of descent between the founder and his people but also implied the privileges of kingship, including dominion over territory. With such stories, Keller could equate the power of Jim's personality with a city's corruption and imagine the force of Jim's personality filling all of the city's territory.

Jim, however, did not anticipate the power that Keller's narrative would mobilize. Instead, he played a classic tragic figure. He continued to run his redevelopment scams and to scout for new ways to launder and hide what he and his collaborators were skimming. Federal court records show that one of these opportunities ripened when the Bank of Industry received its state charter in April 1981. Soon afterward, Jim began laundering checks through a series of bogus accounts made out to bogus employees. By September, he had cashed about 123,000 dollars in kickback checks at his bank, when the stream of checks finally caught a bank official's attention.[18]

Jim Plants a Seed

Jim had planted teller Lucilla Rowlett at his new bank even before it opened for business. He sang her praises to Bank of Industry president Dale Walter, describing her as a "very competent employee" who will bring new accounts "because she knew a lot of local businessmen." He did not tell Walter that she was one of several tellers who had cashed his kickback checks at the Bank of America, which had fired her. Rowlett impressed the bank's operations officer enough to get herself hired as head teller with a hundred-dollar-a-month raise over her pay at Bank of America. According to Walter, "he had no idea at the time that Stafford" had put "a 'plant'" inside the bank to launder checks and "report" back to Jim about bank business.[19]

Rowlett would have kept her new job if her supervisor had not handed some of the bogus checks to Michael K. Jones, the bank's chief financial officer at that time. In an interview with Agent Keller, Jones said that the checks were "made payable to a company he had never heard of." Jim "refused to further identify the company, so the checks were rejected." Walter and Jones confronted Rowlett about the checks and accused her of leaking confidential bank business to Jim. The confrontation prompted Rowlett to resign and return with her husband to her native Louisiana.[20]

Now Walter called King into his office and showed him a desk drawer containing several uncashed kickback checks. King, who later pleaded guilty to mail-fraud charges in connection with the kickback scheme, said he was shocked to learn that Walter knew about the checks. Realizing that a third of that money was earmarked for himself, King told Walter, "Dale, don't cash them. You're gonna wind up like me. I can't get away."[21]

When Walter ordered the tellers to stop cashing Jim's checks, Jim turned to Ed Junior for help. Roski complied, asking Walter "why he would not cash Stafford's checks." The banker told him he had to follow banking laws, to which Roski replied, "'I couldn't agree more,'" saying he would explain the situation to Stafford."[22]

But Jim ignored Walter's message. He soon returned to the bank "with a half dozen checks made payable to 'some company' [Walter] had never heard of before. All of the checks were under $10,000." In other words, they were under the limit that banks are required to report, "an obvious effort" to skirt bank reporting laws. Walter said the request made him "uncomfortable." He told Jim "he would cash the checks that one time, but no more." Jim didn't like what he'd heard, however. He left "in a 'huff'" and, according to Walter, began plotting to "force [Walter's] resignation."[23]

Jim decided to remove Donald Wheeler, the bank's board chairman, as way to get to Walter. According to King, Jim and Ed Junior told him that they wanted him to succeed Wheeler as bank chairman. During a fishing trip in Mexico in late 1981, "Eddie says to me, 'We're gonna make you, Bob King, chairman of the board,'" he recalled.

"And I says, 'I'm not interested in being chairman. . . .'"

"Eddie says, 'What Jim wants, we're gonna give it to him.'"

In a 1998 interview granted to an *L.A. Weekly* reporter, Roski said that he did not recall that King had ever been on the bank's board of directors nor that Wheeler, whom he described as a "close friend," had ever been forced out of the bank's chairmanship.[24] Bank documents, however, list Wheeler as the bank's first chairman of the board and King as a founding director. Bank records also show that Jim's allies on the board voted to oust Wheeler and elect King to the chairman's post.[25]

CHAPTER 12

JIM'S HOT VEGAS TIP

Camillo threw himself on the mercy of other animals, with no better luck, and all the winnings went into the bookie's cash drawer. He saw it would be better to rest for a while. But there is no eternal rest, not even in the grave. One day, along comes an archaeologist digging up bones and eras.
—Machado de Assis, "The Animal Game"

Jim's next big chance to extend his money-laundering operation came in the spring of 1981, when Bank of Industry director Owen H. Lewis told him about the hot investment tip he had received from his pal Clifford Aaron Jones, one of the most storied and politically connected casino lawyers in Las Vegas history. Desperate for new places to hide his money, Jim liked what he heard from Nevada's former lieutenant governor. His ensuing casino adventures, filled with international political intrigue and even the furtive delivery of a paper bag stuffed with hundred-dollar bills, offers a rare peek at dealings that Jones usually hid from public view. Thanks to the interviews that Jones gave to Agent Keller in October 1983, the episode also reveals that the bank had turned into a sort of social club for wealthy shareholders, with Jim, its social director, hustling colleagues to make casino investments and tag along on jet-setting excursions to Hawaii, Europe, and East Asia. But Jones did not open up to Keller because he liked him. He did it to avoid incriminating himself in Jim's money-laundering scheme. The shadow dance of his interviews shows that he came to that decision slowly, one calculated revelation at a time. His actions had nothing in common with the promising slip of the tongue that first brought Jim to his door.

Jim got the tip from Lewis, who got it from his old friend Jerome Louis Block, an insurance broker who had been Jones's longtime friend and business partner. The deal, Jones told Lewis, involved taking over a hot gambling casino, a "big moneymaker," in Colombo, capital of the island nation of Sri Lanka. American dollars, Jones said confidently, could buy a lot more casino action outside the United States than they could in Vegas, where gambling had gone tamely corporate. Like a devotee who had been allowed into Sin City's temple of secrets, Lewis eagerly spread the word to Jim and the other Bank of Industry directors. Several of them said they wanted in. The Industry crowd's enthusiasm inspired Jones to offer them a bigger, more expensive casino investment tip several months later.

Jim shared a history with Lewis that made his pal's tip seem credible.[1] Like Jim, Lewis was a wealthy real estate developer in his own right and an unapologetic, bare-knuckle promoter of Southern California's development industry. He had also represented the first supervisorial district on the Los Angeles County regional planning commission, as Jim had. And like Jim's, his dealings had attracted controversy and the epithet, the "official sprawl champion" of Los Angeles County.[2] After serving for eighteen years as planning commission chair and vice chair, Lewis resigned from his post in late 1980. Although the seventy-three-year-old blamed his departure on his bad heart, the report that the Los Angeles County district attorney had forwarded in August to the state's Fair Political Practices Commission mentioned suspicions of criminal self-dealing. The district attorney had investigated Lewis's failure to report a 315,000-dollar promissory note he had received from a mobile home company, "alterations of an ownership affidavit filed on property Lewis owned" in the city of Claremont, and possible "improper influence on planning department employees who were reviewing [his Claremont subdivision]." The affidavit in question, dated May 18, 1978, "listed Lewis as owner of the property." But Wesley Lind, the engineer who had subdivided the forty-two-acre Claremont property, stepped forward to rescue the commissioner's reputation. Lind, who would later lend a hand in Jim's money-laundering enterprise, said that he himself had innocently erased Lewis's name from the affidavit and signed his own in its place after he had reached "an oral agreement to purchase the property from Lewis." These explanations helped Lewis escape criminal charges, but the conflict-of-interest probe that the district attorney was preparing forced him to cut a deal with the county board of supervisors and announce his resignation.[3]

Lewis's condition had apparently improved enough by April 1981 for him to invite Jim, Ed Junior, and Lind, now on the Bank of Industry's board of directors, to join him in the Sri Lankan casino deal. Clearly, Jim, the leader of this pack of investors, saw money-laundering possibilities in the deal. Jones's promise of fantastic profits and the way in which he presented himself as both a son of Nevada's first pioneer families and a politically connected attorney with twenty-five years of international casino consulting experience only sweetened the project.

A Juicy Biography

But if the investors had consulted some of Nevada's old-timers, they would have discovered another side to the Jones reputation. Many Nevadans knew him as the "Big Juice," because he had the "juice" to get things done in Vegas. The twentieth-century annals of Nevada history confirm the appropriateness of that moniker. Jones emerged in the 1940s as the state's most powerful political boss, second only to Senator Pat McCarran, the infamous Democrat who had drafted the onerous immigration laws used to root out Communists and their alleged sympathizers during the McCarthy witch hunts.

Jones, who started out as a no-name attorney, had figured out how to invest in Nevada's growing gaming industry; and he did his parlaying with a uniquely western flair. His idea of business attire, at least in his early years, was "a calfskin vest with cowboy boots." His idea of an investment strategy was buying and selling percentage points in Nevada's gambling establishments. At one point, Jones owned percentages in seven different casinos, the most lucrative of which was the Thunderbird, "which opened in 1948, the year he became lieutenant governor." Jones and a partner owned about 51 percent of the casino they had built. Because gambling was legal in Nevada and the state had not yet passed laws to effectively regulate the gaming industry, Jones could sell a share of the Thunderbird to whomever he pleased. Historical accounts agree that Meyer Lansky and his brother, executives of Murder Incorporated, secretly held the remaining interest in the Thunderbird via George Sadlo, a known Lansky associate.[4]

Organized crime owed Jones, McCarran, and the state's ruling elite a favor for standing by as the Chicago and New York mob syndicates set up shop in Vegas. Their failure to regulate the gaming industry allowed Bugsy Siegel; Benny Binion, "one-time king of the rackets in Dallas"; and Moe Dalitz, "an old-time bootlegger and gambler," to invest in and open casinos there. Jones meanwhile earned McCarran's trust as a political operative by allowing him to draw cash advances at the Thunderbird, giving him all the complementary rooms and meals he and his family could want, and amassing a ready supply of campaign contributions from his Vegas connections.[5] Jones collected on his favors to win a federal district judgeship and then a stint as majority leader of the state legislature, followed by terms as lieutenant governor from 1946 to 1954.

His casino dealings also earned him an invitation to testify before the Special Committee to Investigate Organized Crime in Interstate Commerce in 1950. The committee's hearings exposed Jones's outrageous conflicts of interest, forcing him to divest himself of those interests, at least while he remained in office. His testimony also contributed to the passage of gaming laws that he and his friends had failed to enact.[6] In a state like Nevada, however, bad publicity was often good résumé copy. Stories of how "Cliff" had opened up dozens of casinos, had beaten a federal perjury rap in 1972, had kept state legislators in line on gaming issues, and had wined and dined President Harry Truman strengthened his credentials among members of his unique clientele. He cemented his macho credentials by talking about how he had worked the rodeo circuit in his youth, risked his life pouring cement into Hoover Dam's cavernous entrails, and married his movie-star secretary. Even the photographs of him in Roy Rodgers attire posed next to his horse could prompt questions from prospective clients. Yes, he owned horses and a ranch where he relaxed with casino owners, entertainers, and European presidents; yes, he had crisscrossed the Caribbean, Asia, and Africa bird-dogging casino investment opportunities; yes, he had bounced back from bankruptcy to become Nevada's ambassador of gaming.[7]

It is not clear if Jim and his pals knew part or all of the attorney's unofficial biography when each of them forked over 131,250 dollars to invest in a Sri Lankan casino called the Palm Beach Club. Jones's reticence during his interview with Keller suggests that he did not divulge more to him than was necessary, a favor he returned to his partners when they made the deal. Nor did Jones, ever the gentleman, ask Jim and his pals to produce pedigrees for their own money. He simply said that the 656,250-dollar investment would bring each investor a 9.375-percent ownership interest, which he would return a year later with the profits. Jones did not risk his own money, however. Instead, he offered his partners the kind of deal he had set up for his other clients: he received a 25-percent stake in the casino for letting the partners use his Las Vegas reputation, legal savvy, and industry contacts.[8]

A Second Casino Deal

The casino, as Jones had initially predicted, returned a hefty 215,000-dollar profit after the first month of the partnership's investment. The heady prospect of realizing comparable monthly returns set up Jim and his pals for the next deal. In February 1982, Jones offered them a piece of a Greek gambling establishment on the outskirts of Athens, at Mount Parnassus. Since 1975, Jones had been trying to buy part of that casino from Detroit native Harry Dimetrio, but Dimetrio would not sell. Not to be denied, Jones obtained a license from the Greek government (then under the control of a rightist military junta) to open his own casino. Dimetrio still would not sell.

The October 1981 landslide that brought Andreas Papandreou and his Panhellenic Socialist party to power suddenly made Dimetrio receptive to Jones's overtures. He sold the Mount Parnassus Casino to Jones for 6 million dollars in early 1982, citing family squabbles over the casino's management. Jones paid 3.5 million dollars up front to take over the casino, which featured forty live games compared to the Sri Lankan casino's seventeen. He agreed to pay the balance later, which gave him time to hit up Jim and his buddies for the difference. Jim, flush with kickback money, promised 405,000 dollars for the venture. Lewis matched Jim's number. Janet Crowley (Jim's mistress), Ed Junior, and three others, including Industry Manufacturers Council director Julian Lobosky, kicked in 135,000 dollars each. Surprisingly, Lind, the newcomer to the party, put up 675,000 dollars.[9]

The size of Lind's share might suggest that his engineering firm and his directorship of the Western State Bank were going so well that he could afford to play with the big boys. Not really. After raiding the family trust he had recently set up, Lind still came up short. His desperation conveys how deeply he wanted to impress the other investors and how much he believed in the sure thing that Jones was offering. Noticing his distress and sensing an opportunity, Jim took Lind under his wing in March, helping him "secure a $316,000 loan to invest with him in Sri Lankan and Greek gambling casinos." That "help" consisted of a loan-fraud scheme that Jim devised for Lind and himself. According to Jim's reasoning, the more investors he could bring to Jones, the easier it would be to have other people invest his kickback money in the casinos.

Jim and the ever-eager Lewis accompanied Lind to the Bank of Industry, where he submitted a loan application to bank president Dale Walter. Lind said he needed the money "to launch a new business in La Puente," a request that was apparently designed to remove suspicion, given Jim's history of bad blood with that city. Lind's loan application listed a 35,089-dollar account to bolster the illusion of his fiscal solvency. He later admitted, however, that Jim had given him that money from kickback proceeds. He also allowed Jim to use the personal account he opened to deposit the loan money to launder another 90,000 dollars in kickback checks.[10] Jim, in other words, had found a way to outsmart Walter.

Meanwhile, Lind persuaded other business partners to invest the 149,000 dollars that the partners still needed to swing their 2.5-million-dollar share of the Greek casino deal. Jim followed suit. In May 1982, he invited Robert King and his wife to attend "the famous annual flower show in Chelsea, England." He also invited Ed Junior and his wife "to accompany him and Janet Crowley" on his British tour. Jim's invitation did not make King suspicious. For the past several years, the Industry Manufacturers Council had made a habit of holding seminars in posh resorts as an excuse to party on the council's tab. Still, King said that he still felt torn: he could not justify the extravagance of the seminars, yet he lacked the courage to challenge their "appropriateness" before the council's board of directors. So now he looked for a way out. According to King, "he told Roski that he wanted to pass on making the trip as he did not want to be around Stafford anymore than he had to. . . . However, Roski told him [that] neither of them had a choice."[11]

King had to give in one more time, he said, because Jim "had the power [in the city] to put him out of business altogether if he wanted to." Before leaving, however, he went to dinner with Janet Crowley at an Italian restaurant in nearby Whittier. At one point during their dinner, he said, Janet came out "of the ladies room with tears in her eyes." Ever the gentleman, he asked why. She answered that "she did not want to go on the London trip [with Jim]. 'I'm tired of him physically abusing me,'" she reportedly told him. King didn't want to go either, "but neither of them had a choice," he told Keller with a touch of fatalism. "Stafford had his mind set on it," although King didn't know why.

King said that Jim pulled him aside on the flight to England to pressure him to buy into the Greek and Sri Lankan casinos. King tried to beg off, saying he had money problems, but Jim had a ready answer. He offered to "loan him the money and he could pay it back with no interest." King said he resisted until Jim gave up. Then he saw Janet crying again in London's Pan Am Clipper Club as they waited for their return flight. When he asked her why, she revealed that Jim had forced her to join his money-laundering operation. Then she told him something more: "I'm sick of it. I don't want to go to prison. I thought having him as a boyfriend would put me on easy street, but now I'm going to have to go back to Sarasota. He would not let me pay for the repairs on my house even though I wanted to."[12]

King did not ask Janet about her home repairs. He didn't want to know. But when he later acknowledged to Keller that Jim had sent a landscape contractor to install a new sprinkler system in his home and to deliver each month thereafter an envelope containing a pair of hundred-dollar bills, the agent began to suspect that Jim was not using kickback money to pay for these services. Perhaps the trail of renovations and envelopes of money led back to another ongoing scheme.

ANOTHER OMEN

Meanwhile, the Sri Lankan casino partnership was moving along at a re-assuring pace. In August 1982, the partnership paid out 85,000 dollars in dividends. That development gave Jim, Lewis, Lind, and Roski the confidence to kick in another 90,000 dollars to cover the club's operating expenses, raising their investment in the casino to 640,000 dollars. Jones said he needed the money so that he could replace the Sri Lankan crew with trusted people culled from his Vegas contacts. Spirits were high when Jones flew Jim, Janet, Lewis, and Lewis's wife to the casino's 1982 grand opening on the partnership's dime.

But the club, Jones later confessed to Agent Keller, "opened under a bad omen when a full page newspaper advertisement" slamming the club's new management appeared in Colombo's newspapers. The Palm Beach partnership's move into the casino had triggered "a political furor." The owners of the two other government-sanctioned casinos operating in the capital pressured the government to stall the grand opening from a Saturday to a Monday, a delay that "peeved" Jim so much he booked the next flight out with Janet.[13]

The reversal required Jones to do a hell of lot of explaining—first to his associates, later to Agent Keller. Jones told Jim that a man named S.M.A. Aloysius, one of the Palm Beach casino's previous owners, was leading the effort to ruin their grand opening. Also known as the "Little King," Aloy-sius told Jones he would have to sell the partnership's controlling interest in the club because foreigners "cannot own a gambling business in [Sri Lanka]." Clearly, Jones had not warned Jim and his pals about the risk of pushing the Little King, a "very influential" player in the government's Buddhist-dominated circles, out of his casino.[14] But Jones distracted the partners from the fiasco by blaming it on a malicious translator who had turned Aloysius against their takeover deal. His excuse reminded them of their linguistic ignorance and how much they needed his participation. Yet they also began to realize that they had put their money into the hands of a master storyteller.

Jones hoped he could set things straight by convincing Jim and his pals to accept Aloysius as a partner. Several unproductive rounds of negotiations ensued in Colombo, Washington, D.C., and Los Angeles. Jones told his partners not to despair, reminding them that he had "personally guaranteed the loans" they had made to the Palm Beach Club and that he intended "to repay them" no matter what. He told them he was "doing everything within his power," including asking the U.S. State Department to intercede to "protect the investments of American citizens."[15]

Jim was tired of his assurances. But when he tried to remove Jones as head of the partnership, Jones, revealing his true Vegas colors, cut him short, telling Jim he would rescind his loan guarantee if the partners tried to unseat him. Jim then pressured Jones to accept Lind as his chaperon during his ongoing negotiations with the Sri Lankan government. Moreover, Jim and Lewis refused to select the casino's new management team from the list of 150 gaming employees whom Nevada gaming authorities had already cleared through background checks. Refusing "to heed [Jones's] advice," they sent their own team to approach the Sri Lankan government. The mission failed miserably: the government "barred" the management team from ever stepping foot in the club again. A year had passed, but nothing had been gained.[16]

Meanwhile, with Papandreou's electoral victory, which signaled Greece's rejection of U.S. realignment with Turkey and a rising socialist agenda, news from the Greek casino front was also grim. The previous owner of the Mount Parnassus Casino had moved quickly because he realized that the new administration would not be hospitable to U.S. investors. Now Dimetrio was hoping that the deal he had put together with Jones's partnership would hold and that he could keep his 6 million dollars.

Hostilities did erupt, however. They came, according to Dimetrio, from former employees he had fired for skimming casino profits. These ex-employees persuaded the Greek investors still serving on the casino's board of directors to ask the government to take the club back from Jones "and declare his contract with Dimetrio null and void." Dimetrio got wind of the scheme in time to dismiss the board, withdraw the casino's stock from the bank, and sell it to Jones and his clients, a shrewd but sketchy move that quickly put him into hot water. "The Greek government," Jones later explained to Agent Keller, "brought criminal charges against Dimetrio saying he had no right to sell the casino in the first place" and then moved to "nationalize it." According to Jones, he himself took a 120,000-dollar loss in the form of legal fees, which he had run up while trying to recoup the 3.5 million dollars he had invested. After settling his differences with the new government, they paid him back 70 percent of the money he had invested in the casino before June 1983.[17]

At least that's the story Jones chose to tell when he began his interview with Keller in 1985, coolly steering the agent away from what Jones preferred not to disclose by offering a profusion of harmless details. Anyway, there were no real victims, Jones suggested. He had paid back most of the money that the Industry crowd had invested, and he would try his best to pay back the balance of what he owed. All of the investors, he led Keller to believe, blamed their bad luck on the vagaries of politics in the developing world. Their grumbling acceptance, even Jim's and Lewis's, implied that there were no hard feelings, surely not from Jones, who related his story so calmly that he did not need to tell Keller that he knew how to accept the risks of his trade like a pro.

But the agent's questions soon made it clear that he had not called on Jones to quiz him about his business ethics. Keller did not care if Jones had given his partners bad advice on purpose or through sheer incompetence. Instead, he wanted to know how Jim and his buddies had paid him.

They had all paid by check, Jones told Keller—that is, all but Jim. Jones had to fly to Ontario International Airport, south of Industry in San Bernardino County, to take personal delivery of Jim's share of the Greek casino investment. He met Jim and Lewis at a restaurant two blocks from the airport. After talking for about an hour, Jim invited Jones out to the parking lot, where he opened the trunk of his car and handed Jones a paper bag filled with 405,000 dollars in cash. Jones said he had expected Jim to hand him a check, not bundles of hundred-dollar bills. Nonetheless, he had the presence of mind to promptly transfer the money to a suitcase.[18]

There, he had said it, disgorging what had troubled him most about the casino debacle, an episode he had tried to avoid until that moment. Jones followed one awkward disclosure with several others. He promptly added that "he sent Stafford a receipt for the cash when he returned to Las Vegas." Then Jones, responding to a question Keller does not record in his log, declined to "identify anyone else who" witnessed the delivery of Jim's suitcase. Sensing the slippage, Jones sallied forth with details that invited more questions. He said he followed Jim's investment instructions to the letter, except that "the amount of the investment is not reflected in his books on the casino." Jones stopped himself, declining to specify exactly "how the transaction was handled from the time he picked up the money from Stafford until . . . it was actually invested in the casino operation."[19]

Realizing that refusing to go into details would give Keller license to spin theories of criminal motives at his expense, Jones tried to clear the record by anticipating the agent's next question. Jones said that he "did not" return to Jim any of the money he gave him that day in the parking lot. There could be no evidence of money laundering, Jones suggested, if he had not completed the wash cycle by writing Jim a check from one of his own accounts, one disguised as a legitimate payment of interest earnings, let's say. But Jones still had to account for the bagful of bills Jim had given. It is at this precise moment in the interview that the smooth-talking attorney hesitated to say what he did with the money. What did his reluctance to explain his handling of the money suggest? Was Jones pulling himself from the brink? Suddenly, it seemed, he had a great deal to answer for. If Jim had told Jones to put the bagful of cash in their casino partnership, did Jim also tell him to keep his money off the books to make it untraceable? And why, if Jim's investment motives were really aboveboard, didn't he write Jones a check instead of stuffing bills into a paper bag? Any bank would have confirmed Jones's story by automatically recording a transaction of that size.

Jones sealed these silences with assurances that he would hand over his records only on issuance of "a grand jury subpoena." As far as he was concerned, he had "done nothing improper or illegal." With that remark, the tone of the interview suddenly changed. Jones had dropped the pretense of friendly cooperation. Keller would not get any more out of him unless he dragged him before a grand jury. Otherwise, as Jones told Keller respectfully, he was "reluctant to expand upon the cash transaction involving Stafford because he want[ed] to think through the entire episode and refresh his memory before he [went] on record as to exactly what happened."[20]

The abrupt change, which Keller transcribed in short paragraphs, shows Jones pausing to reflect on whatever privilege of privacy he may have promised his clients. Then he proceeded to tell Keller that he would perform his professional duty and tell Jim, Lewis, and the other partners that the FBI had contacted him. Keller could take his last comment as a threat: such an action would give the partners advance warning that would buy them time to get their stories straight. But Keller, for his part, had already turned several of Jim's conspirators, including key informants, into grand jury witnesses. They would soon give assistant U.S. attorney Gary Feese enough evidence to draft the first of several indictments. So Keller's refusal to back off from his line of questioning was as good as calling Jones's bluff: go ahead and tell them, his non-reaction to the lawyer's threat seemed to suggest.

The agent counted on his interview with Jones to trigger a new round of anxious guessing, followed by incriminating telephone calls between conspirators and hasty attempts to destroy evidence, which the FBI would try to record or observe. And Keller had another reason for ignoring Jones's bluff. He had already interviewed the unnamed source, Jerome Louis Block, who had witnessed Jim's money drop; and he would soon flip the weakest link in Jim's money-laundering operation.

That link was closed when Lind admitted to cashing at least two bundles of Jim's kickback checks on two different occasions and to lying in his applications for the 406,000 dollars in loans he had secured for his casino investments. Jones also became more cooperative in his next interview, soon after informing the FBI that Jim and Lewis had indeed been angered by his failure to recover their money. He believed they had been about to threaten him when he informed them at an October 1983 meeting inside his Las Vegas law offices that he had told the FBI about Jim's bagful of cash. "That doesn't concern me a bit," Jim had replied. But the disclosure did concern Lewis. The septuagenarian suffered some kind of a "fainting spell" or seizure, Jones said: he "went limp, grabbed his chest, and said, 'wait a minute.'" Jim did nothing to "aid his friend," which suggested to Jones that such "attacks" were a "more or less habitual" reaction to bad news.[21]

Lind, meanwhile, tried to sell Keller on the notion that the check cashing he had done for Jim was the kind of favor one did for a true friend. He called it "a friendship deal," the kind of ingratiating gesture an ambitious banker might make to win the trust of a wealthy depositor.[22] But his argument sounded less and less convincing as he confronted the evidence Keller put in front of him. In the interview, Lind struggled to explain the ease with which he had performed his sketchy errands. He was in a hurry, he said. Lewis, he added, "probably knew" that he was serving on Western State Bank's board of directors. Without explaining the significance of that statement, Lind jumped to his conclusion: he "figured the checks were legitimate, as he had no reason to think otherwise."[23] He did say that he had noticed that the Michner Corporation was the payee of the checks. And Keller knew that this bogus firm had been created to funnel redevelopment money to Jim and his associates.

Lind told the agent he had asked an employee at Western State Bank to deposit the checks into his account. He thought the checks "would be deposited in an old account." They were instead deposited into a new one opened without his instructions. Lind said he did not notice if someone had endorsed the checks, as he had fallen into the habit of depositing unendorsed checks from his rental property. According to Lind, he withdrew the cash from the new account and gave it to Lewis without asking any questions. Lind, trying to gauge the trouble he was in, gave Keller vague replies during his December 1983 interview, omitting dates and reasons for his banking decision. Keller helped him remember, providing him with a list of the twenty-one checks Jim laundered at his bank.

Federal prosecutors said they would allow Lind to fill in the missing details as long as he would agree to a plea deal that required him to stand before the grand jury and testify against Jim. At the same time, the prosecutors were noticing a common dominator in the giving and receiving of favors: they were planned and plotted inside the members-only clubroom, bars, and golf greens of the Industry Hills Exhibit-Conference Center. Lind told Keller, for example, that he had attended weekly lunches with Jim and Lewis at Industry Hills "when the casino deals were being put together in 1982." Lind acknowledged getting to know Jim on a personal level during these lunches, so much so that Jim felt confident enough to ask for another favor: after one lunch, Lewis "asked him if he would cash some checks for Stafford." And Lind did.[24]

The Industry Hills effect should be factored into Lind's seduction. Its pair of golf courses, its golf museum, Churchill's funeral car, its Olympic swimming pools, its equestrian center and bridle paths, its lavish conference halls, and its white-linen restaurants spoke as loudly as the alcohol and the ambitions of Jim's friends and hangers-on. To people like Jim and his agrarian, Depression-era peers, the center's appointments would have been a sumptuous materialization of all their unmet desires—in other words, their idea of heaven. Industry Hills employees told Keller that they ran the place like a private club for Jim and the city's insiders. They mentioned the list of asterisked names kept at the cashier's desk, which identified the big shots who were allowed to run up drinking tabs. They talked about the girlfriends these men put on the center's payroll; about the employees who sold liquor out the back door; about the drunken carousing of Jim and his friends; about the county sheriff who protected sloshed Industry insiders from being busted on driving-under-the-influence charges; about the National Engineering officials who met with developers while completely smashed; about the luxury hotel suite, complete with sunken bath and mirrored ceiling, reserved for Ed Roski, Jr.; about Hodgdon's helicopter landings on the hotel's rooftop.

Employees told Keller that they were instructed to treat Jim like a god, even if he dressed like a farmer in khaki slacks and long-sleeved white shirts, when he went to the Top of the Brae, his golf-themed, wood-paneled refuge perched on a mezzanine balcony with a view of the exhibit center's foyer below, a smallish (read, "exclusive") place where he lunched with Ed Junior, the only person who routinely got a private audience with the old man. They revealed that Mayor Ferrero had put his son's lavish wedding on the Industry Hills tab, an expense that the city attorney had justified as legitimate because it promoted the city's image to prospective business owners. Keller's undercover eyes also told him about the national and local political officials who were feted at the center and at least one of them who was bribed there. They discussed the former laundry room that had been turned into a meeting room reserved exclusively for Jim and the Industry insiders. They talked about Jim's hopes that gambling would be legalized in the state and his reputed plan to turn the hotel's third floor into a casino, until the Sheraton people shot down the idea because it violated their anti-gambling policy.[25]

Life inside Industry's palace of vanities could not have contrasted more sharply with what was going down inside and outside the city's factories that year. Press reports and the *corridos* of Immigration and Naturalization Service (INS) raids of Mexican undocumented workers broadcast over the radio in 1982 were filled with stories about Operation Jobs, one of the state's customary cleansing rituals. The press reported a "sweep" of 5,635 suspected "illegal aliens," actually Mexican and Central American immigrant workers, not shop-floor trash or invaders from outer space. That April, the program, which was coordinated by the INS, targeted factories in nine cities across the county, including the manufacturing zones of greater Los Angeles, as a way of opening up "'higher-paying' jobs for unemployed American [another unexamined cultural construct] and legal residents." The raids failed miserably, however. The national press reported that "80 percent of the suspected illegal aliens apprehended in Los Angeles and Orange County" were back at their jobs in a few days.[26]

The operation's disciplinary effects were another matter. Captured and deported workers did not soon forget the experience of suddenly being stolen from their lovers, husbands, wives, and children—from the lives they had begun to build for themselves in places such as La Puente. They did not forget being humiliated at the hands of immigration and border patrol agents. "Of all the people arrested in the raid, we suffered the most," said a forty-two-year-old Mexican immigrant who was separated from his wife and six children for sixteen days. "We suffered physically, we suffered

spiritually." In recalling the raid's punishing effect, Aurelio Norte (fictitious name invented to protect his identity) said, "You feel bad, you feel
bound, you feel very small."[27] The raids were designed to make him think
twice about joining a union, demanding fairer wages or medical insurance,
reporting factory conditions in which workers lost their limbs in giant
meat grinders, or sharing his given name with curious strangers.

In the city of Industry, INS agents grabbed 146 workers at three different
factories: El Rey Mexican Food Products; Kern Foods, which canned
the guava and mango juices still popular in the Latino community; and
Acme Lighting and Manufacturing Company. The manufacturers, who
complained about lost production time, themselves reflected a global
transformation in industrial production. More of the city's factories now
consisted of light manufacturers of nondurable goods, firms that jettisoned
health benefits, job security, unions, and living wages and embraced pliant
"illegal" immigrant workers who could compete with other desperate
workers in Asia and Latin America.

Wilfred Steiner, still executive director of the Industry Manufacturers
Council and the voice of Industry's factory-owning class, responded to
questions about the grim drama rather peevishly. Steiner, who edited
the newsletter that weighed in on all sorts of industrial issues in the city,
including illegal immigration, said he could not express an opinion on the
INS raids until he had talked the matter over with the council's members in
June. But it is hard, given the turmoil inside the highest levels of Industry
society, to imagine that Steiner ever found a chance to discuss the raid's
policy implications with council president Robert King or council boss Jim
Stafford. "I guess the INS knows what they're doing," he finally ventured.
"At least we haven't got any complaints about the raids, and no one has
said they're in favor of them either," he said, covering his bases. "But we do
have a lot of Mexican workers here in the city and in La Puente."[28] Steiner
was right: Industry's workforce and the city's adjacent suburbs were fast
becoming majority Latino.

CHAPTER 13

A PUNISHING GAZE

For days, it was as if I weren't there, turning things over and over in my mind,
wanting to leave, ashamed and frightened, sure there would never be another
peaceful afternoon, that I would never be free of my disgust and fear.
                                      —Angeles Mastretta, *Tear This Heart Out*

Special Agent Keller's power to inspect the most intimate moments of Jim's life and Jim's anxious anticipation of that surveillance had begun to take their toll. We can detect that stress in the text of Jim's actions and statements, in his desperate efforts to cover his tracks. One might even say that Keller, in tempting Jim to interrogate his every action and thought, was making him sick, although no doubt Jim's lifetime of drinking and steak-and-potato eating had also aggravated his growing cardiovascular problems.

Still, it is hard to pin down exactly when Jim realized he had to do something about Keller's watching and asking. The date had to have been after October 19, 1981, when Keller conducted his investigation's first formal interview. Certainly, Keller had clearly telegraphed his intentions by September 1982, when he asked one of Jim's best friends, current city manager Bob Baker, if he would like to "discuss the Federal Bureau of Investigation's interest [in Jim] as a possible conspirator."[1] Keller knew that Baker's friendship with Jim went back to the days when they both worked in county government for Supervisor Herbert Legg and that Baker had the reputation of being a toady who would not hesitate to report the meeting to Jim. Keller had picked him for exactly that purpose.

But Baker's report would not necessarily have justified Jim's alarm. Keller, after all, was just using Baker to rattle his cage. Jim must have steadied himself by remembering that Industry had gone through this drill before. At least two district attorneys had taken investigative shots at the city and come up short. Others had sued Jim and the city with the same result. To play it safe, Jim and his city hall friends had already befriended high-ranking officials inside the district attorney's office and the sheriff's department, who would warn them if trouble came again.

Keller, however, scrupulously detailed each step of his investigation: the people he tailed, the questions he asked, the dates and places of those questions, and what the subjects did after he had confronted them. Jim must have made some guesses about who those people might be. For instance, given his nasty divorce, he must have expected the agent to talk to Jane Stafford. And eventually, Jim became aware that Keller had begun to unravel his network of conspiracies. His law enforcement pals, his attorney, and the city's security staff informed him that federal prosecutors had convened a grand jury to review the evidence the agent had collected. Jim could guess from the people Keller had questioned and those asked to testify that his own name would top the list of those who stood to be indicted.

One by one, his friends assured him that they had told the grand jury nothing, that they had closed ranks around their friend. But by 1982, Jim had realized that the people in his inner circle were feeding the agent incriminating evidence. The slow trickle of knowledge the agent had trapped with such tenacity would soon cascade into a series of confessions leading directly back to Jim. Not surprisingly, it appeared that the incremental effect of each betrayal, of each unwelcome surprise, began to affect Jim's physical and emotional stability. So in an attempt to neutralize Keller's threat, Jim reasserted his authority in the city. During the summer of 1982, in the midst of his offshore casino adventures, Jim plotted a series of intrigues with the goal of firing Bank of Industry president Dale Walter, buying the silence of the bank tellers who had cashed his kickback checks, and, most surprisingly, spying on Agent Keller.

INVESTIGATING THE INVESTIGATOR

In late July, J. C. O'Neil, a private investigator working for Jack Barron and Associates, hired a second private investigator to get Keller's driver's license number and personal information from a sheriff who worked in the Sacramento forgery detail. Keller's highly sensitive file not only gave his address but also the license number of the car he drove and a mug shot, enough information to track the agent's whereabouts and alert townsfolk to his presence. O'Neil's achievement, it turns out, was a second try. Once before, someone in Barron's firm had tried to subcontract the job to a cutout with no ties to the agency. On that occasion, the

Department of Motor Vehicles had done what it was supposed to do: it withheld Keller's personal information to protect him from potential criminal reprisals or threats. The department also informed the FBI that someone was asking for Keller's information. O'Neil, who did not know that the FBI had been alerted the first time, made the mistake of using the same ploy with a different private investigator. The second try worked, but it also left a trail of evidence leading back to his firm.

On or about October 1, 1982, Keller's colleagues in the bureau tipped him off to the security breach and its source. When questioned by the FBI, O'Neil insisted that he did not tell the private eye he had hired who Keller was.[2] It did not matter whether or not he believed his reply; by putting O'Neil on notice, Keller had turned the tables on his would-be shadow. Now O'Neil's boss, John R. "Jack" Barron, a retired FBI supervisor, would have to cope with knowing that the agent had uncovered his firm's surveillance scheme.

Apparently, suspense got the best of Barron. Several months later, he telephoned Keller, nonchalantly addressing the agent as one professional to another and asking if he were the target of an obstruction of justice investigation. Keller answered that Barron was not, momentarily putting him at ease. What the agent said next, however, must have given Barron pause. Keller told him that his bungled surveillance had given the bureau enough evidence to make Barron a subject of the agent's "ongoing public corruption investigation."[3] That is, if Keller wanted to press the matter.

At this point, Keller asked Barron to name the person who had said that the agent wanted him for obstruction of justice. Barron, acting as if the situation were no big deal, identified Arch Fornier, former security director at the Industry Hills Exhibit-Conference Center. His answer did not satisfy Keller. He continued to question Barron until the private investigator offered what was essentially the verbal equivalent of a mock gesture of surrender: of course, he knew better than to interfere with an agency investigation. But Keller persisted, asking Barron to explain "his involvement with the City of Industry."[4]

Barron relented and began talking. He said that another former FBI agent had told him that Fornier needed someone to investigate the stealing going on at Industry Hills. According to Barron, Warner Hodgdon had already hired private auditors to find out why the facility was bleeding 300,000 dollars a month in losses.[5] In addition, Hodgdon had decided to hire Barron for that purpose. Now Keller asked Barron if he knew Jim Stafford. Barron said he did but tried to put his relationship with Jim above suspicion. He said that Hodgdon had introduced them, that they had subsequently met on a "social basis," that he "did not discuss his work at Industry Hills" with him, and that Jim "never paid him any money for anything."[6]

Although Keller's next question does not appear in his log, it clearly knocked Barron off balance. Suddenly, he was revealing that an attorney representing one of Jim's business partners had hired him to find out what he could about Keller's investigation. Barron quickly followed the revelation with a fumbling, solicitous, after-the-fact assertion: if the agent "was interested in talking to [Barron] about anything of concern to him concerning his involvement with the City of Industry, SA [Special Agent] Keller could have called him at any time and he would have offered an explanation to whatever it was that concerned or interested him." Keller, however, was not impressed. His log made it clear that "Barron did not volunteer anything about acquiring SA Keller's . . . driver's license" until he was forced to do so.[7]

Keller's entry signaled to his superiors that Barron could not be trusted and that Jim was committed to undermining the investigation. The agent's informants later confirmed those conclusions. One recounted a conversation in which Jim acknowledged telling Barron that the FBI was tapping his telephone. After sharing that tidbit, Jim remarked, "I have a guy investigating the investigator," a cocky reference to Barron.[8]

Confronting Jim's "Negative Influence"

At about the same time, Jim tried to retaliate against Dale Walter for breaking up his money-laundering mill, spreading the word that Walter was a lush and that he did a lousy job of investing the bank's money. Meanwhile, in March 1983, Walter again tried to reduce Jim's "negative influence" over the bank but without ratting him out to the police or to state banking authorities.[9] Walter had his reasons for avoiding the authorities. Showing them Jim's phony checks would have definitely stopped his meddling, but it would also have exposed Walter to a career-ending scandal. So the banker took a more cautious approach to saving his job and his reputation: he put together a group of directors to buy out Jim's most loyal allies on the bank's board.

Some of Walter's alleged supporters, however, told Jim about the plot. He answered by ordering King to immediately schedule a bank directors' meeting and to call a vote on Walter's dismissal. Jim did not invent a pretense for his decision. According to King, during one telephone call, Jim complained that "Dale Walter ain't gonna cash our checks. I think we ought to fire his ass. Why don't you and Eddie and I have a powwow?"[10]

King followed orders. In a certified letter dated April 6, 1983, he called the bank's board of directors to a special meeting in the Industry Hills laundry room. Set for April 13 at eleven o'clock in the morning, the meeting would be "for the sole and express purpose [of deciding] the status of Dale Walter, CEO, Bank of Industry."[11] But King canceled the meeting after Walter fired back a letter in which he threatened to notify state banking authorities of Jim's attempt to manipulate the board. After calling King's bluff, Walter then backed down from his threat. A few days later, King announced his decision to sell his stock in the bank and resign as board chairman, but not from his bank director post. King portrayed himself to Keller at that time as a man cracking under the emotional strain of being an FBI informant while pretending to maintain a friendship with Jim. But King's resignation only intensified the power struggle for the bank.

Walter worked to recruit the bank's next chairman from among the directors whom he believed were less beholden to Jim's influence. First, he asked Ike Keuning to run for the vacancy. When Keuning declined, he invited Donald H. Wheeler, Owen H. Lewis's business partner, to run. Wheeler accepted. When Jim heard that Wheeler would head Walter's buyout plan, he instructed his allies on the board to pick his friend and business partner Gary Bryce as their candidate, even though Bryce no longer owned shares in the bank.

Jim then turned to Ed Junior for support. But Roski's loyalties were divided, and Jim's request for help apparently put him under tremendous pressure. According to Walter, Roski explained his predicament to Walter, whom he had personally recruited for the position of bank president. A day before the April 19 vote, Roski seemed to tip his hand. He told Walter "he could support Wheeler" as an independent bank chairman. "However, true to form," Walter bitterly recounted, "Roski switched to Bryce . . . when the vote was taken." Jim's man had prevailed, although King and Wheeler had abstained from voting. Now Walter no longer had any illusions about who commanded more loyalty: "Roski simply cannot shake the hold Stafford has on him because of his business interests in the City of Industry."[12]

But Jim's power play did not stop Keller, who had already recruited a string of bank officials to help him trace the lineage of Jim's ill-gotten money. And Walter was finally ready to cooperate with the FBI investigation. The day after the vote, he gave up the name of the corporate bank account that Jim was using to channel his kickback checks. Walter remembered the name, the Michner Corporation, because he "had had a rubber stamp made for Stafford" to endorse the checks. Keller now had physical evidence.

Walter also told Keller what Jim had said when the bank president had asked what the Michner Corporation was: "You don't need to know."[13] But Walter still did not show Keller all of his cards, insisting that he did not know that he had been laundering kickback money until late in the game. Walter gave Keller a version of events that suppressed the ambiguities of a bank president who had enabled Jim's money laundering in its early stages and had signed off on a fraudulent loan to support his casino scheme. Apparently, Keller either believed Walter's version or reasoned that the president could help him more effectively if he continued to run the bank. The agent's questions let Walter paint himself as an unwitting victim who stood up to Jim. Yet in fact, Walter did not defy Jim until Jim's allies on the bank's board tried to depose him. Perhaps he did not change sides until he was sure that the FBI represented a more serious threat.

Whatever the motive, Walter's next decision triggered a rapid chain of events. He handed over evidence that pointed to Jim's use of the mail to defraud the city's redevelopment agencies, a classic violation of federal law that the U.S. attorney could use to indict Jim and his conspirators. Walter also notified the bank's directors that he would answer the FBI's questions. Bryce immediately resigned from his post as bank chairman. King and Mac McKeown, Jim's "staunchest" supporter on the board, followed suit and resigned from their bank director positions, clearing the way for Wheeler, Walter's choice, to fill Bryce's vacated post.[14]

Jim responded to these reversals with his first open expression of fear. Without a way to enforce discipline inside the bank, he raced to cover his tracks. His actions, which the FBI monitored, show that he believed that the bank tellers who had cashed his kickback checks—above all, Lucilla Rowlett—represented his biggest vulnerabilities. But Jim's methods of silencing his underlings could not match the state's ability to compel testimony and produce evidence. Agents in the FBI's New Orleans office had already traced Rowlett to her new home in Louisiana. The log of Keller's first interview with her on August 22, 1983, does not tell us exactly how he obtained her continuing cooperation: it does not identify her as a suspect or offer her immunity from prosecution. His tersely written entry merely states that, after being "interviewed at length" in Louisiana by another FBI agent, she had offered to tape-record her next telephone call with Jim.[15]

In his second interview of the day, Keller increased the pressure, telling Rowlett that she would be called to testify before a grand jury on November 9.[16] The FBI apparently had considerable evidence against her, enough to force her both to testify and to tape-record *all* of her future conversations with Jim.[17] The message was unstated but clear: Rowlett could only remain a friendly informant as long as she complied with the FBI's requests. Agents trained her to record the telephone calls they expected Jim to make, to carry a wire in her purse, and to ask certain provided questions. She did not have to wait long for Jim to make his next move.

READY TO TALK

On June 8, 1983, Jim's former wife, Jane Stafford, now living in Arizona, answered Agent Keller's telephone call. He had already eased her into talking to him, promising to protect her identity. Although he later noted in his log that Jane could offer "no direct evidence" of her husband's illegal pursuits, she still had plenty to say about the character of the man who ran the City of Industry.[18] She told Keller about Jim's alcoholism, his relentless pursuit of money, and his bitter envy of her wealth and her middle-class respectability. She told the agent about her ex-husband's verbal outbursts, about the ways in which he intimidated his family members.[19]

Winning her cooperation had not come easy. Jane had ignored Keller's repeated requests for a telephone interview. Not to be denied, he had tracked down her divorce attorney, who subsequently billed her for taking the agent's call. Changing tactics, Keller then persuaded her son Stephen to talk to his mother. He asked Stephen to assure Jane that she was not a subject of the investigation. No doubt, Stephen reminded his mother of what they had both suffered. No doubt, the memories of her year-old divorce were still fresh.

Whether she was motivated by guilt, expensive attorney's fees, or plain anger, Jane told her son on June 7 that she was ready to talk to Keller without the presence of her attorney. The agent called the next day from his office in the Westwood Federal Building and conducted the first of several telephone interviews with her. Five days later he recorded the interview in his log.

Keller had already conducted dozens of interviews with people who were linked to Jim. They had convinced him that Jim ran the city by cleverly exploiting his friendships and knowledge of the local culture and that the city, in turn, reflected Jim's twisted personality. Now he wanted to dig into Jim's mind, and give an account of it, so that the prosecutors could portray its perversity in court. Without a full confession, prosecutors would need to present his character and its motives, his state of mind when he committed his crimes, to a judge or a jury so that they might calculate the magnitude of his guilt and thus precisely calibrate a punishment for his body and what some believed to be his soul.[20]

So Keller needed Jane's help. Perhaps she could provide him with a dramatic anecdote or two. Perhaps she could bring the story to life by telling him what her marriage to Jim had been like. The agent did not need to worry about filtering out statements that might make Jim seem too sympathetic. All he needed to do was to make Jane feel safe enough to vent her bitterness. She would do the rest. And she did.

To hear Jane tell the story, she was the victim—the smart, respectable daughter of an Evanston, Illinois, surgeon who had lived in fear of Jim's violent temper for forty-one years. Her husband was a country boy, a son of a Louisiana farmer who had made it big as a grain dealer in El Monte. She met Jim at the University of Arizona. An agriculture major, he "was never a serious student" and dropped out after three years, choosing comfort over independence. After they married, Jim went to work at his father's mill in La Puente—what the locals called "old Mex-town." At this point in the interview, Jane's emotions began to tumble out, breaking her narrative flow. Jim was an "alcoholic," "[a] cruel and violent man toward her and her children and others who clashed with him."[21]

But Jane did more than paint a portrait of her ex-husband's character. She also helped Keller establish a crucial part of Jim's criminal motivation. "Mrs. Stafford stated her husband 'was always looking for money' as long as she had known him," Keller wrote in his log. "He was always looking for an angle to get money out of someone," including members of her immediate family. Jim had "respected her father very much" and had "always treated [Jane] and her children well" as long as money was not an issue. But everything changed after her prosperous father died in 1961 and Jim discovered that he couldn't control his wife's inheritance.[22]

Jane's father had left money for his daughter in a trust fund, arranging to have the bank pay her 1,000 dollars a month for the next twenty years. Jim was enraged. He had expected to get his hands on her father's estate and was "shocked and bitter," Jane said, "when this did not happen." She did not explain why, at this point, she had chosen to open a separate bank account but did acknowledge that her decision clearly marked a change of habit. She said she had "always turned over any money she had to her husband, like the 'old fashioned wife' that she was" or perhaps had been.[23]

Jane's decision to preserve her financial independence suggests that her relationship with Jim was already deteriorating. Perhaps her father knew that his daughter's marriage was unhappy, which might explain his effort to keep his money out of Jim's hands. Whatever the reasons for the arrangement, Jim retaliated. He forced Jane to live off her trust fund. If she needed more money, he told her, "she would have to ask him for it" because he controlled the family checkbook. Jane commented on Jim's stinginess with his family and his habit of "handing out money, jewelry, trips, jobs and gifts" to his friends and business associates. "Jim 'got brutal'" after her father's death, and "their marriage was never the same."[24]

For Keller, Jane's talk was both exhilarating and frustrating. But even though she gave him detail upon detail, he kept asking for more. The questions in his log are preoccupied with Jim's financial dealings, his control over city officials, his early political career. Most importantly, Keller wanted to know whether Jane could produce evidence of how Jim had corrupted local elected officials. At first, her answers revealed little about Jim's life outside the home. Her husband had only told her what he wanted her to know. She "was afraid to stand up to him," she confessed. He "had a violent temper and would beat her when he flew into one of his rages which came with heavy drinking."[25]

Jane's sudden turns and explosions of memory obeyed an emotional logic, not a neat chronology. She was reliving her struggle to survive Jim's alcoholism and protect her son. Eventually Keller recognized that she would be unable to answer his specific questions and changed his line of attack. Perhaps he could use her memories to create a character portrait that would persuade a judge or a jury of Jim's guilt. He gave up trying to control the interviews and let Jane keep talking.

She said that Jim had convinced himself that he was not an alcoholic because he did not begin drinking until after five in the afternoon, when he would come home from the mill and down eight beers in a row. He would then "begin picking on their son for no apparent reason . . . and verbal altercations would frequently lead to physical confrontations where the two would go at each other like combatants in a bar room brawl." She told Keller that, on one occasion, one of them had chipped her tooth when she tried to separate them. Jim shot back that "it was her own fault for getting [in the way]."[26]

According to Jane, Stephen was a skinny high school kid who did not stand "a chance against his father," "a powerfully built man." Their "fights would spill out into the hallways and rooms of the house leaving blood and torn clothing in their wake." Her inability to stop the fights so upset her that she would "go for a drive and not return until she thought [it was over]." Keller clearly identified with his informant's version of the story: "she literally cleaned blood from the walls and carpeting," he wrote, emphasizing the indignities she had suffered. Jane said Jim would "goad" his son into fighting "and then beat him unmercifully" when he struck back. She never understood Jim's animosity toward his son, saying that Jim did not give Stephen "a moment's peace after he became a teenager."[27]

But one can imagine how Jane's disdain for her husband and Jim's disappointment in his son might have awakened self-doubts that arose from his childhood traumas. His wife's financial independence and her narrative of family respectability must have reminded Jim of his own father's checkered past. Perhaps Jane's disapproving presence wordlessly recalled his father's humiliating exposure to public condemnation. Perhaps Jim tried to vindicate himself by acquiring wealth and power and by projecting his hunger into a generational quest. He may have heaped expectations onto his son because he wanted to shape him into the male heir that would have further cleansed his father's reputation. Stephen's defiance may have felt like confirmation of what Jim most despised about himself, those feelings of shame he tried to control by wrapping himself in his city and the unconditional love of his friends. Those feelings may also explain why Jim sought out surrogate sons, younger men who embodied the man he believed himself to be: to reassure himself of his worth despite Jane's disappointment in him.

But it was not as if Jim could not express a few concerns for his son. At the prompting of friends, and perhaps because he feared for Stephen's safety, Jim advised him to join the Navy after graduating from high school in 1966 rather than wait to be drafted into combat in Vietnam. Stephen obeyed and was assigned to an aircraft carrier. But Jane said that "Jim flew into a rage when" Stephen, home on a weekend leave, "tossed an empty oil can into a clean [garbage] barrel . . . while he was working on his car." In the ensuing altercation, Jim reached for "a long-handled shovel," which Stephen tore from his hands and brandished while yelling "that he was going to kill" his father.[28]

Stephen's ability to disarm his father did not earn him Jim's admiration. According to Jane, "Jim told him to get out" and swore that he would kill him "if he ever came back" home. But Stephen did not leave immediately. That evening, she said, Stephen asked his "father to drive him back to his ship," but Jim repeated his threat; so Stephen "got a friend to drive him." Now Jane understood that she would not be able to see

Stephen in Jim's presence again and that her relationship with Jim, despite years of marriage counseling, was beyond salvaging. She said that she was "so repulsed by her husband and distraught over the situation that she told [him]" to be out of the house before Stephen's next leave. But Jim left immediately to find his own apartment, where he stayed "until their next family reconciliation."[29]

They would attempt several more such reconciliations. Jim prolonged the torture by giving his son a job at the mill and bringing him to his meetings, believing he still could mold Stephen into an heir who deserved his wealth and power in the city. But Stephen lived on his own, expressed his opinions, disapproved of his father's methods, and tried to resist his father's overbearing demands. Inevitably, they would clash, and Stephen would storm out of the mill. At one point, he worked for a trucking firm, only to return to his old job soon after his marriage in 1973. That turbulent marriage disintegrated with Jane and Jim's.

Stephen's decision to take his mother's side in her 1979 divorce also forced him to quit his job at the mill for the last time. Before he left, father and son "agreed to stay out of each other's divorce proceedings." Two weeks later, however, Stephen walked into his father's office just as Jim was giving his wife more than 3,000 dollars in cash, the second of two payments totaling more than 10,000 dollars. Stephen also believed that his father had paid his wife's attorney's fees during their divorce and that he later sided with her in the custody battle that would deny Stephen visitation rights with his son.[30] Jim would have gone on to completely disown Stephen if Ed Junior had not stepped in to preserve the younger Stafford's right to inherit a half-interest in one of the civic center bank buildings. Jim had tried to give the building, which he co-owned with Roski, to Stephen's former wife.[31]

As soon as he had finished interviewing Jane, Keller knew that he had crossed a threshold. He had confirmed Jim's brutality toward his family, evidence that gave him the courage to continue his investigation at a time when his likelihood of success seemed uncertain. Although he did not admit as much in his log, Jane's story had inspired him to prove his theory of Jim's financial crimes. His interview with Jane, he later acknowledged, thus marked a turning point. "It goes to character, which was very important to me," he said. "It tells me he is a really bad guy. I like to know just how bad because it gives me a lot of pleasure to put him in jail."[32]

CHAPTER 14

PERFORMING
HIS WHITENESS

*Personality is a mirage maintained by conceit and custom, without
metaphysical foundation or visceral reality.*
          —Jorge Luis Borges, "The Nothingness of Personality"

Jim scheduled a September 13, 1983, meeting with Lucilla Rowlett and her
husband at the Howard Johnson's Motor Lodge in Leesville, Louisiana. In
the course of that meeting, he paid her the first of two 1,000-dollar bribes.
Rowlett tape-recorded the conversation with a voice-activated Nagra recorder that the FBI had put into her purse. The transcripts of this and
subsequent recordings would help the prosecution clinch its case against
Jim. They also showed his desperate bid to keep her loyalty. To do so, he
resorted to a personal cultural technology, the one he had inherited from
his father: he tried to behave like an authentic son of the south, an identity
performance he assumed that would score points with Rowlett.

Jim started his homecoming dinner with small talk intended to establish his Louisiana credentials. He offered to cover the dinner and drinks
and played the doting father, patiently quizzing Rowlett about what she
liked on the menu and then thoughtfully bringing her up to date on their
old friends at the bank. With feigned interest, Jim listened to Donald,
her husband (also known as Dwayne), talk about his plans to run several
hotdog stands. Then he tried to patronize Rowlett outright. Playing on her
pride, he acknowledged how much her corner of Louisiana had progressed
and how he would gladly give up all his wealth and possessions to live the
simple, worry-free life that she had wisely chosen for herself.[1]

Next, Jim tried to spin a funny story about a dear friend. According to him, Vincent Perez, who enjoyed a monopoly over the city's waste disposal and industrial recycling business (thanks to Jim), had an excellent ear for black speech. "Did you ever hear him get started on them?" Jim asked.

One digression deserved another. Rowlett, trying to show that she had not lost the thread of his story, knowingly declared, "He was in *Soap*." She blundered on. "Remember when he was in *Soap?*" mistakenly confusing Perez with Benson, the sardonic butler played by Robert Guillaume in the 1970s television satire.

"No, no," Jim interjected. "Vincent Perez. I'm talking about Vincent Perez. Don't you know Vincent Perez?" His exasperation began to show when he realized that Rowlett had failed to follow his story.

"No, I never knew him," she answered timidly. "I thought you were talking about the show on television."

"Oh no. No, no, no." We can imagine Jim at that moment trying to hide his disappointment with a smile but wondering how she could have treated him with such deference for so many those years without knowing all of his closest associates? Rowlett's error suggests that she might have been preoccupied with asking her scripted questions. But Jim did not see her inattention as suspicious and pressed on.

Perez had a talent for mimicking black speech, perhaps imitations of the *Amos 'n' Andy* locutions performed by white radio actors for audiences of his generation. Jim explained his admiration: he was impressed that a Spanish immigrant could master that accent and dialect. Perez's ferocious urge to ridicule black speech also amused him. Here, after all, was an outsider candid and honest enough to confirm what other whites were afraid to admit. Jim now believed he was doing Rowlett the same favor, repeating, with a wink and a nod, a white-supremacist narrative that any red-blooded southerner must naturally enjoy.

"You remember CORE, C-O-R-E?" Jim asked, referring to a major organization of the civil rights movement.

"Yeah," she answered.

"That was one of their first big pushes," he continued, showing surprising awareness of a movement for which he had little regard as well as a sense of relief at not having lost Rowlett's attention. Apparently, CORE had sent Jim an envelope "in the mail one day, you know, [and addressed it] something like, Dear Friend of CORE. Please send us anything you can afford, from a dollar on up. Do you hire any colored people? What's your name and address? Things like that." Here the tape recording becomes unintelligible until Jim says, "We filled the damn thing out and we put Vincent's name in there, see, signed his name and sent $20."

The Rowletts laughed appreciatively.

"If that guy ever had found out who did that he'd a killed us," Jim said. The Rowletts laughed again, giving him license to continue performing his white-man routine. Jim told them he was the son of a native son—that his father, C. C. Stafford, was from Tuscaloosa and that his grandfather was, "for all practical purposes," a slave-owning plantation owner who later dealt with sharecroppers.

"After the civil war," the grandfather's apocryphal story went, "all the colored people, hell, they wouldn't leave [the plantations]. Hell, that was their home." He did not need to tell Lucilla Rowlett how to interpret his anecdote. He expected her, as a real southerner, to know the moral of his story. The ex-slaves were too dependent on white kindness, too stupid, too feeble-minded, to run away and seize their freedom.[2]

Finally, after this last digression, Rowlett got down to business. She said that Keller had called to tell her that she would be called before a federal grand jury. The call had terrified her. She did not know how much Keller knew about Jim's check-cashing scheme. She was afraid to slip up. She cleverly asked Jim to coach her on what to say about the fake business accounts he had created. Over and over again, and with varying degrees of urgency, he repeated his advice: "Whatever they say, just tell them you don't remember."

Rowlett delivered her next line with conviction. She worried that Dale Walter, the Bank of Industry's president, would set her up to take the blame for the check laundering. But Jim reassured her, "Dale isn't going to do that and Dale isn't going to remember anything either."

"Okay," Rowlett answered meekly.

"Don't worry about that," Jim said.

"You have that covered," Rowlett said, inviting Jim to explain what the "that" in her sentence might be. He obliged her.

"With Roski," he added. He paused. "Roski will take care of [Dale Walter]." Federal prosecutors later interpreted this statement as "threatening" because it implied that Roski would neutralize the Walter problem. Jim left the exact nature of the solution to Rowlett's imagination.[3] Perhaps he would also ask Roski to "take care of" her in the same way. Jim wanted Rowlett to believe that he still had the pull to make people do things in the city, even people as wealthy and well connected as Roski was.

Jim's To-Do List

Lucilla Rowlett flew into Los Angeles International Airport with her husband, now going by Dwayne, on November 8, 1983, to testify before the federal grand jury. At 10:50 A.M., an FBI surveillance team spotted Jim Stafford in the Gate 66 boarding area waiting to greet them. The agents described Dwayne as a white male in his "early 40's, 5'9", 155 pounds, brown hair, wearing a white cowboy hat, white long sleeve shirt and brown leather vest." They described Lucilla as a "white woman, early 40's, 5'5", 130 pounds, dark hair, wearing a brown top coat and brown slacks."[4] Jim told the Rowletts that he had learned that she would be testifying, an idea she had planted when they had dined in Leesville.

After Lucilla excused herself to step into the restroom, Jim told Dwayne, "It would not look good for me to talk to Lucy because of what is going on. I need to talk to you in private. Since you're the husband, they can't do a damn thing to you."[5] Dwayne suggested that Jim rent a car and drive Lucilla to the New Otani Hotel, a few blocks away from the federal building in downtown Los Angeles where she was scheduled to testify the next day. Jim demurred. He persuaded the couple to drive back to the hotel with him in his gold 1977 Cadillac El Dorado. Lucilla sat in the front seat next to Jim. Despite her efforts to bring up the investigation, he stuck to the small talk.

The Rowletts checked in at the front desk and joined Jim ten minutes later in the Canary Room for lunch. The talk was casual and inconsequential until Lucilla went up to her room for a nap. Jim then walked with Dwayne into the Rendezvous Lounge next door for some private conversation. Jim asked for a piece of writing paper, and Dwayne fished out a small sheet from his pocket. But it wasn't large enough; Jim wanted him to go the hotel desk and ask for a bigger sheet. Dwayne came back with two sheets and prepared to take dictation. "It wouldn't look good for me to talk to Lucy so you impress on her the importance of these items I am going to tell you about." Jim then dictated the following list from a typewritten sheet he had brought with him:

1. Tell Lucy to keep her cool.
2. Those no goof [sic] son of a bitches are going to try to scare [the] hell out of her. Then they are going to get her on the stand and scare [the] hell out of her.
3. They'll tell her things like they have evidence on her and they will put her in jail if she doesn't cooperate.[6]

According to Dwayne, Jim said "something about his lawyer being a former United States Attorney" who had "told him what they would be doing with Lucy." He cited his attorney's credentials to make his witness tampering seem ordinary. Jim dictated more items from his list until he reached item 6: "They are going to ask her if I have ever given her any money. She is to tell them no." If the prosecuting attorney "asks her if we had a conversation in the car" on the way to the hotel, "tell them no." When the prosecutor confronts her with photocopies of checks she had cashed, "the best thing for her to do . . . is to say I don't remember [even] if she does remember." If they ask her if she challenged any of my checks, "her answer is to be no." He told Dwayne that the prosecuting team would offer Lucilla immunity from prosecution if she would agree to testify against Jim, but "they cannot give her immunity." He concluded with a point he had already made: "The best thing she can do . . . is to say I don't remember" or, if all else fails, "take the Fifth." In other words, Jim was asking Lucilla Rowlett to sacrifice herself for his benefit.[7]

The prosecution accelerated its case after transcribing Rowlett's tape-recorded conversations and hearing her grand jury testimony. Attorneys now had what they needed to bring Jim, his co-conspirators, and other witnesses before the grand jury. On December 12, 1983, Robert King signed a plea deal. He agreed to plead guilty to one felony count, answer all of the prosecution's questions, and pay restitution in exchange for a reduced sentence with no jail time and exemption from further criminal prosecution if his testimony proved to be useful.[8] In May 1984, three more of Jim's partners turned state's evidence. With the expectation, if not the promise, of lesser sentences, they gave assistant U.S. attorney Gary Feese the dates, names, and documents he needed to reconstruct his bid-rigging, contract-skimming, money-laundering, and loan-fraud conspiracies.[9]

Feese filed the first of three indictments on April 11, the day on which Jim turned himself in to federal authorities. He was released on a 1-million-dollar bond, which he posted by putting up one of his civic center office buildings as collateral.[10]

THE PATTERN REEMERGES

Press coverage quickly transformed Jim's story into California's biggest municipal corruption scandal of the 1980s. In the *Times,* in suburban newspapers such as the *San Gabriel Valley Tribune,* and occasionally in the *Herald Examiner,* Jim returned in his role as a rich grain dealer, rancher, and property owner, the same descriptors that had been affixed to

C. C. Stafford's name more than fifty years earlier. At the time, I was working as a reporter for the *Times*. Thanks to sources inside the FBI, fellow reporter Dan Morain and I had known for a few months that the indictments were coming, knowledge that had given us time to research and report on Jim's and the city's back story. We plotted a series of investigative articles, cultivating sources and insights that would help us contextualize the trial and put our newspaper's signature on the coverage.

Dan and I tried to ask the questions that *Herald Examiner* reporter Scot Paltrow had overlooked in his 1980 investigative series, and we thought we had succeeded. We uncovered the Southern Pacific's role in rescuing the nascent city from a crippling legal challenge, we revealed new conspiracies, and we updated the activities of the Industry Manufacturers Council in the state capitol and local politics.[11] Not surprisingly, the council had spent the hundreds of thousands of dollars that the city had allocated to it each year to promote connections between campaign contributors and their favorite legislators. For instance, from 1974 to 1984, state senator William Campbell, Industry's best friend in the legislature, received 61,002 dollars from the council's active members. Assemblyman William H. Lancaster, a Republican from Covina, pocketed 61,725 dollars during the same period. Since 1977, the council's members had given 42,152 dollars to the state assembly's Republican Political Action committee; and since 1974, they had donated 44,850 dollars to United for California, another pro-Republican committee. Even Democratic state senator Joseph Montoya had received members' contributions, pocketing 10,936 dollars after 1978, once he had stopped trying to regulate Industry's redevelopment agencies.[12]

Dan and I also managed another scoop: we uncovered some shadowy activities that suggested either illegal lobbying or the existence of an off-the-books political slush fund. By 1981, Mayrant Dorsey McKeown, a former Bank of Industry director who had backed Jim's failed bid to oust bank president Dale Walter, had become Industry's legislative consultant. McKeown, who had once been city manager of Artesia, ran his consulting operation through Municipal Research Analysts, a firm that gave the California Country Club as its official office address. The City of Industry had paid his firm "$9,500 a month—more than $430,000 since 1981—to provide 'legislative consulting services,'" but no city official could explain exactly what services he had performed. Although city manager Bob Baker said that McKeown's job consisted of "bird-dogging" bills that were affecting the city, he could not name any bills that McKeown was actually watching. Baker subsequently corrected his answer, telling us that McKeown had provided "written reports on the bills," but he declined to show his reports. Revising his answer again, Baker then said that McKeown had given "his reports by phone." But McKeown's social calendar suggests that he behaved more like a lobbyist than a bookish analyst. He organized luncheons in Sacramento for female legislators, a party for state senator John F. Foran (Democrat from San Francisco) at Industry Hills, and paid as much as 10,000 dollars to assemblywoman Sally Tanner (Democrat from El Monte) for her consulting services and procured thousands of dollars in contributions to Tanner from Industry Hills contractors. Although one might construe these activities as lobbying, McKeown had not registered with the state commission that regulated lobbyists.[13]

But our disclosures were incremental at best. The bulk of our coverage fueled the technology of exposure and shame—the criminal and fiscal consequences of the indictments. We did not know enough about the railroad's role in real estate development to fully reconstruct Industry's corporate genealogy or link the kickback scandal's underlying causes to the corporate privatization of the redevelopment system. Our assertions instead reinforced the confusion over the meaning of redevelopment. We correctly concluded that California's law was "made-to-order" for Industry yet still held to the notion that it had abused the federal redevelopment's "original concept."[14] We failed to explain that the Chandler-led elite of downtown Los Angeles property owners had re-purposed the state's law to subsidize corporate development on a massive scale before Industry opened its first redevelopment mill.

The indictments did, however, trigger unprecedented public discord in the Industry Manufacturers Council when it voted on April 22, 1984, to remove Robert King from its board. The action gave the council's executive director, Wilfred W. Steiner, a chance to announce that news of King's indictment "completely took us off our feet. I never suspected anything like this." His performance also allowed the council and, by extension, the city, to distance themselves from King.[15]

Then three of Jim's co-conspirators as well as another contractor pleaded guilty to helping Jim skim 750,000 dollars from Industry redevelopment contracts.[16] New evidence and testimony leveraged by these pleas helped the grand jury return a second indictment against Jim on August 16. It charged him with twenty counts of conspiracy and mail fraud connected to an additional 600,000 dollars in kickbacks from Industry Hills and related contracts.[17] Jim was now on the spot for defrauding Industry's redevelopment agencies of 1.35 million dollars.

He was also sick. Mounting legal pressure and decades of high living were taking their toll. In June, Jim's attorney, James Duff, reported that doctors had installed a pacemaker in his client's chest to correct an irregular heartbeat. Duff added that the doctors had also diagnosed Jim with "severe blockage of the arteries." Finally, in late August, the attorney told the *Times* that "Mr. Stafford could not stand the stress of a trial."

Edward Rafeedie, the federal judge who was presiding over the Industry corruption cases, ordered a medical hearing and issued a warning: "I'm very skeptical of medical disabilities that arrive on the eve of trial."[18] In light of prosecution statements and prior press coverage of Jim as a master deceiver, the judge's admonition appeared to be reasonable. Still, Rafeedie could not ignore the medical evidence, surely understanding that fear of prison time and loss of a fortune could stress the heart of the most committed megalomaniac. Duff meanwhile tried to persuade Jim to look beyond his fears and face the magnitude of the government's case against him. Fighting conviction was out of the question, but a full and sincere confession might win him some leniency. Jim was apparently ready to follow his advice.

First Reckoning

On September 9, 1984, Jim, with Duff at his side, sat down with Special Agent Keller and Prosecutor Feese. Duff offered a prelude to Jim's confession, describing his client as a "'broken man' who was prepared to admit to everything"—that is, everything that had been included in the plea deal that Duff had worked out with Feese. The prosecutor, who liked what he was hearing, let Keller take Jim's confession.[19]

Jim started by saying, "I owe the United States of America, and you, personally, an apology for my conduct in this matter. I am ashamed of myself for being so stupid and I'm sorry it happened."[20] These words must have struck Keller as odd at first and then, as time wore on, as frustrating. Given the strength of the evidence, he was fully expecting Jim to admit to every count in the indictment. Duff had assured him that Jim would also confess to his greed and to the prosecution's other accusations of gross moral failings. But Jim did neither. Instead, he played the role of the dumb and forgetful victim. Although he admitted to some crimes and acknowledged his minor participation in others, he repeatedly blamed his faulty memory for his failure to recall key details.

Duff became exasperated. When Keller's questions turned to the bribes, Duff had to remind Jim that the FBI had recorded him giving bribes to Rowlett and others. Yet Jim blundered on, insisting that Rowlett, like so many people who knew about his wealth, had had her hand out for a loan, not a bribe. Keller's patience was clearly strained, but Jim refused to acknowledge that he had violated any recognizable moral code. He simply admitted to being "stupid" as if he were apologizing for an embarrassing breach of etiquette. Worse, when laying out the chronology of his misdeeds, he claimed to have acted with lofty intentions, all because he loved what he still clearly thought of as "his" city. He blamed any mistakes on the bad company he had kept and filled his confession with so many memory lapses that it became essentially useless.[21]

Something was holding Jim back, freezing him. Perhaps he had succumbed to a sudden irrational hope of escaping punishment, of derailing Keller's efforts to portray him as the master conspirator. Avoiding conviction was out of the question; but reducing his punishment was another matter. He might succeed if he were willing to don a mask of ineptitude, but pursuing that option would require him to abandon the story upon which he had built his macho self-image. He would need to reject anything that painted him as the city's criminal overlord and instead feign ignorance and incompetence. If Jim had had a theological bent of mind, he might have imagined himself as a once-beneficent god who had lost interest in, or even knowledge of, his own creation.

Jim began his confession with an origin story, one that implicitly cast him as a farsighted city father. Years after the city's founding, he said, he and his colleagues realized they needed to do something about the landfill that overlooked city hall. They could not build their gem of a civic center at the foot of a small mountain filled with toxic chemicals and trash or let that valuable hill go to waste. The city also had to satisfy other needs if it expected to grow. It needed "restaurants, a hotel, and a recreational area to service the business community of the city." By happenstance, Jim said, the city chose to adopt his solutions for both problems.[22]

Because neither Jim nor the city's officials were engineers or architects, they needed professional technicians. Naturally, Jim got involved in hiring them (an unfortunate admission of his decision-making habits). He let National Engineering know that he thought Ron Rabin would be the best construction superintendent for the Industry Hills project. He liked Rabin's style and brashness. Jim told Keller that he asked Rabin to consider granting contracts to Industry's business owners, an acknowledgment that he not only knew the needs and wishes of the city's business owners but took it upon himself to reward those owners on the city's behalf. After all, wasn't showing a little gratitude for their years of selfless, often unpaid service to the city the right thing to do? Rabin's response, Jim wanted Keller to believe, completely surprised him. "There needs to be something in it for me too," Rabin reportedly answered. Jim said the reply made him suspicious.[23]

Keller was not impressed. Jim's claim of misunderstood loyalty read like a thinly disguised pitch for graft, a quid pro quo for unspecified favors that Jim had the power to grant. The city-elder role he emphasized in his confession confirmed what so many others had also said about him: that he had given himself the authority to intervene in the city's most sensitive affairs without bothering to hold public office. Sensing Keller's take on the matter, Jim quickly tried to cloud the insinuations he'd just made. "Rabin," he opined, "had probably been involved in the same kind of corrupt practices involving kickbacks on construction projects in New York . . . because he got right into it as though he were experienced in that sort of thing."[24] Blending bemused speculation with innuendo, he tried to dredge up the Big Apple's reputation for mob-dominated construction projects, a ploy that might have seemed plausible if Los Angeles had not also enjoyed a storied history of municipal corruption.

Jim next tried to play up his ignorance. He claimed to know "nothing" about the niceties of "bid rigging, change orders, or add-ons," implying that he had learned the technology of contract fraud from Rabin. Then he elaborated, telling the agent that he understood "nothing about the construction business and would not have known what to tell Rabin and the others as to how to go about rigging contracts." Jim blew his chances for sympathy, however, when he described Rabin as a "'New York Jew boy" who had led him astray. He had not bothered to consider that Prosecutor Feese might be Jewish. He simply blundered on, now trying to push the blame on King, whom he characterized as the truly greedy partner.[25]

Jim's blaming and confessions of ignorance made matters worse for himself. They demonstrated that he understood the charges and evidence that the government had collected against him but without making a credible show of contrition or revealing his reasons for committing his crimes. He did not, in other words, prepare his soul for courtroom display, thus preventing the court from knowing his motives at sentencing time. The prosecution would later characterize his silences as indicative of his utter contempt for the rule of law and his stubborn intention to continue running the City of Industry.

Jim's evasions did not postpone the September 11 court date on which he was scheduled to formally answer his indictment. Because of the plea bargain he had signed, the government had dropped two charges from the 1.35-million-dollar kickback case; the bargain also protected him from additional charges that might turn up during Keller's ongoing investigation. Because he had gotten his man, Feese was already describing the deal as a big success. "We have always believed that [Jim Stafford] was the one who had his fingers in everything that was happening [in Industry]," he told the *Times*.[26]

Jim, however, did not appear on the morning of his scheduled court appearance. Family members found him unconscious in his West Covina apartment, where he had apparently taken an overdose of sleeping pills. An ambulance rushed him to first one and then another local hospital, where they pumped out the contents of his stomach. Doctors found traces of Dalmane, a sedative. The West Covina police described the incident as a suicide attempt, and Keller later agreed: "The suicide attempt shows his sense of defeat better than any statement a person could make. It speaks for itself. He would have preferred to die than admit his crimes."[27] You might even say that Jim now refused to live with the identity Feese was busy crafting for him.

Guessing that calling attention to the overdose would not change the judge's verdict, Duff and Feese agreed not to take Jim's statement on the matter. They guessed correctly: on the next day, Judge Rafeedie asked "whether Stafford was 'sincerely trying to take his life, or if it was just a sham' to delay the case." [28] He scheduled a new sentencing date for November 29 "after receiving assurances from Stafford that his health would not be a problem." Meanwhile, Jim underwent what was vaguely described as "minor surgery" in the hospital while he recovered from the drug overdose.[29]

The psychiatric evaluation that Judge Rafeedie had ordered did confirm some of Duff's claims. Jim did have "a known history of heart disease." In addition to implanting a pacemaker in his chest in June to control his fibrillations, his doctors had prescribed "Digoxin and the diuretic Lasix." The surgery he underwent while recovering from his overdose consisted of an angioplasty procedure to unblock his arteries. Jim's medical history, however, did not alter Saul J. Faerstein's psychiatric evaluation. After conducting his interview, Dr. Faerstein concluded that Jim did understand the charges against him and the consequences of entering a guilty plea, which included putting himself at Rafeedie's mercy.[30]

On October 3, 1984, Jim formally reversed his not-guilty plea, pleading guilty to eighteen criminal charges, including fraud, obstruction of justice, and conspiracy. In light of Jim's cagey confession, his previous efforts to thwart Keller's investigation, and Keller's compelling biography, Feese submitted a memorandum recommending the stiffest possible sentence. He argued that Jim would continue to use his influence to abuse the city and its citizens if he were not severely punished, a reasonable conclusion, as far as it goes.[31] But the memorandum was freighted with unexamined assumptions and some historically significant assertions. For starters, Feese put Jim's greed, a well-understood moral fault rooted in the sin of avarice, into an explicitly political context. He also stressed Jim's greed for power, which could be described as avarice for the powers of the state.

Feese did not arrive at his conclusions alone. Their genealogical link to Paltrow's investigative articles became explicit when he attached the series to his memorandum.[32] Point by point, his references to Paltrow's series strengthened the existing bonds between the legal technology of the courts and the moral technology of the press. Feese's memorandum portrayed Jim as "the architect of a scheme to defraud" Industry's redevelopment agencies "of approximately $1,300,000 million." It held him "personally responsible for laundering most [of] the stolen money through several Southern California banks." It concluded that he had "corrupted at least six other persons who, before this case," did not have criminal records. It accused him of bribing "two witnesses to withhold information from the FBI." It argued that Jim's actions manifested "a pattern of conduct extending back to the formation of the City of Industry, a city treated by James Marty Stafford as his personal fiefdom."[33]

Feese again drew from Paltrow to recall how Jim, during the 1950s, had used his privileged position as a member of the Los Angeles County regional planning commission to influence the county's board of supervisors, with the help of "one or two other local land owners[,] to create the City of Industry." He noted that Jim went so far as to count the local sanitarium's mental and geriatric patients so as to satisfy the state's minimum residency requirements, a ploy that allowed him to carve out a city with "only about 630 residents and 150 voters." These anti-democratic exclusions, Feese maintained, gave Jim special powers: "From the beginning, Stafford has used his influence as the city's founding father to benefit himself and his friends." The prosecutor backed up his argument with a list of a dozen individuals "in positions of trust" whom Jim had ensnared in his net of business and personal relationships. He rounded out the list with the names of Edward P. Roski, Sr., and Edward P. Roski, Jr., owners and directors of Majestic Realty Company and Commerce Construction Company. Feese represented the pair as "close friends of Stafford," stressing Ed Junior's partnership with Jim "in a venture called S & R Investments," which, among other things, "owns the buildings housing the Bank of America and National Engineering Co."[34]

In his investigation, Keller had not overlooked the special treatment that the Roski firms had received from the city. His log, however, shows that he had not yet turned up anything for Feese to link Ed Junior to Jim's criminal enterprises. Defense attorney Duff went out of his way to stress in a separate legal filing that Jim's lie detector test (which had almost no legal weight) had cleared Roski of any involvement in his conspiracies.[35]

Still, Keller's evidence showed that a network of social and business relationships were binding him to Jim, that Ed Junior had cultivated his special access to the city by catering to Jim's emotional and financial needs. He had humored the old man by supporting his bank idea, by playing the enforcer in the bank's affairs, by listening to him, by drinking and dining with him, by taking and returning his telephone calls, by spending time and money with him in overseas gambling ventures—apparently by playing the part of the idealized son. Keller later reflected on Jim's troubled relationship with Stephen to explain his special link with Roski. According to the agent, Jim had convinced everyone in town "that Steve was a screwball," that he "didn't want to be like his father," that he "resisted him all the while he was growing up." Keller compared the situation to a father-son relationship in "a mafia family. If he had been a good son, he would have assumed the role of his father. . . . Roski was more like the son he didn't have."[36]

Ed, for his part, had given Jim plenty of reasons to prefer him to Stephen. Ed was a Marine who had bravely served in Vietnam. As a successful entrepreneur, he had given Jim an entree into investment deals he could not have swung on his own. Ed's success in Industry also ratified the excellence of Jim's vision for the city. Keller could not find illegality in their relationship, but he understood why Ed was so eager to please his benefactor. By keeping Jim happy, by including him in several real estate partnerships, Ed had secured Majestic's position as Industry's dominant developer.

To Feese, however, Jim's personal and business connections, including those with the Roskis, added up to more than good networking skills: they provided compelling proof of the ways in which Jim had "exerted his influence at all levels of government in the City of Industry. There is no door in the city that is closed to James Stafford, and few decisions on which his counsel is not sought." If anyone still had doubts about the prosecutor's debt to Paltrow, his next sentence dispelled them. He acknowledged that his investigation bore out "the fundamental allegations contained in [the *Examiner* series]."[37] But his concluding remarks suggested another nuance. Perhaps the influence Jim had used to execute his crimes went beyond simply defrauding the city of taxpayer dollars. "Though holding no office in the city or its redevelopment agencies, [Stafford] exercised control over the affairs of the city."[38] The words imply possession and tyrannical domination. They hint that Jim had had the temerity to stage a kind of personal coup to seize the political authority of the state.

Second Reckoning

On November 29, Feese elaborated on this theory of power when he stood before the sentencing judge to argue for Jim's incarceration. Before the session began, Jim, Duff, Feese, and Keller waited in front of the bench for Judge Rafeedie to take his seat. Keller, who would not have missed that day for the world, recalled later that Jim had tried to make small talk before delivering his formal statement. "I think that the judge is going to give me a break," said Jim. "He's an older guy [like myself] and he's bald." The remark baffled Keller. "What kind of ridiculous reasoning is that? It shows you where his head was," he said.[39]

Jim's formal statement was recorded and transcribed. "I don't think there are words that have ever been invented yet to describe the way that I feel and I will feel for as long as I live," he began in a strangely worded nod to the ineffable power of silence. He followed with an ambiguous assumption: "So rather than taking up the Court's time, I think that you can understand what I mean."[40]

Feese's response was passionate and compelling. He warned Judge Rafeedie against misreading Jim's last-minute, half-hearted attempts at contrition. He also brushed aside Duff's argument that, because Jim was a guilty but guileless tagalong, his probation should consist of community service and restriction to a halfway house. Feese reminded the court of the evidence, which showed how Jim had designed the bid-rigging and kickback schemes, how he had directed them as they had developed, and how he had pocketed most of the money he had skimmed. To illustrate Jim's premeditation, Feese pointed to the phony invoice, a veritable tutorial on bidding fraud, that Jim had drawn up for an accomplice on his own typewriter and reminded the judge of Jim's threats and bribes.[41]

Until this point, Feese's summation had relied on a character-driven narrative to frame Jim's criminal motives, implicitly ignoring the economic and technological powers that had created the founder and his kingdom. Now he dramatically declared, "What you have in front of you is, in my view, and in the view of the leadership of the United States Attorney's Office, . . . one of the . . . most significant public corruption cases to come before this Court in the history of the Central District of California." The leadership to which Feese referred was embodied in Stephen S. Trott, the central district's former U.S. attorney who had recently become U.S. assistant attorney general. "And [Trott] told me that in his twenty years he had never seen a situation where there was this kind of . . . public money . . . taken from public agents . . . to enrich those in power."[42]

In Feese's opinion, however, Jim's crimes went beyond old-fashioned money greed. He was "also motivated by the desire to wield power, by the desire to dominate, to manipulate, and to corrupt. And we believe that [if] Mr. Stafford is not put in jail for a lengthy period of time, that Mr. Stafford will not be deterred from his conduct." According to the prosecutor, the manner in which the city's officials had rallied to Jim's defense demonstrated how profoundly he had damaged the City of Industry. They not only showed no curiosity about the crimes committed against them and that undermined the city's integrity, but they also reacted to Keller's efforts to uncover the truth with open disdain. Their attitude was "why are you bothering us, there is nothing wrong here. It was as if the City of Industry had seceded from the United States, and that there was something outrageous or improper about the federal government examining the transactions, which were ultimately determined to be fraudulent."[43]

Feese found Jim's justification for his crimes even more galling. He had assured his co-conspirators that he was "only stealing government money; the government steals from us all of the time. It's our turn to get some of it back."[44] To Feese, Jim's contempt for the rule of law and the authority of the state was so crass, so absurd, that it did not merit a direct reply. But Feese, in brushing the remark aside, had passed up his chance to dissect the reasoning that inspired Jim's rant.

He could have recognized in Jim's defense of thievery the cynicism that wealth and privilege breed, that arrogant habit of power that insists on its right to make the truth that serves its purposes. He could have identified the voice of capital speaking through Jim when he matter-of-factly equated the federal government with a criminal enterprise and reduced its purposes to the quest for profit, not the sucker's dream of justice, equality, or community. He could have pointed out that Jim and his privatizing pals had demolished the defenses that prevented capital from overrunning a fortress of the state and consuming its citizens. He could have said more, but Rafeedie had heard enough. He told him that he was trying his patience, that he had better stick to the evidence and bring his argument home.

Feese complied, concluding with a utilitarian appeal. He warned that the precedent Jim's crimes had set could not be tolerated because they undermined respect for the rule of law. He reminded the judge that the

U.S. attorney's office already had its hands full rooting out public corruption that was then blossoming in the nearby single-use cities of Bell and Commerce. He concluded prophetically, "What these cases tell us is that the conventional wisdom about Southern California being a place where there is no official corruption . . . just is not true. . . . The government feels very strongly that the architects of these schemes must be made to pay, and if they're not made to pay, that there's no way to stop [such corruption]."[45] All Feese needed to do now was to name the vectors that had spread the contagion.

CHAPTER 15

BURYING THE BODY

Like in a lousy version of capitalist history, the priorities were ridiculously
clear: first the property, then the property owners, then their charges.
—Paco Ignacio Taibo II, *Pancho Villa: A Biographical Narrative*

The transcript of a September 17, 1984, telephone conversation between
Frank Wood and Roger Haines gives an early glimpse of how the City of
Industry was bracing itself for the legal onslaught it expected after Jim's
conviction. Haines, a contractor who had admitted to playing a minor role
in the bid-rigging conspiracy, had agreed to secure evidence against his
co-conspirators in hopes of receiving a reduced sentence. Wood, the general
contractor Jim had befriended in Carpinteria fourteen years earlier, had
been indicted for his role in the scheme. After trying several times to speak
to Wood ("FW" in the transcript), Haines (abbreviated as "RH") finally
persuaded him to return his telephone call. The FBI had already received a
court order allowing it to record the conversation.[1]

RH: Yeah, good morning Frank.
FW: How are you Roger?
RH: Good. Hey, Friday in the afternoon there pal, uh, I had to stop by
and see my lawyer before I came over, cause I, well, I'm kind of spooked
about this whole thing because I don't know what's going on. And, we
had a good conversation because, you know, Jim, called and he wanted
to meet me over there on the freeway with two other guys, never said
who they were and scared the hell out of . . . me, and I just want to
cover my bases, pal.
FW: You mean Jim?

RH: Yeah, a couple of weeks ago. He said he and two other people wanted to meet me on the Sixty freeway and Azusa Avenue, and I didn't know who the other two people were and I still don't. And before I came to see you I didn't know what's going on. . . .

FW: Well, I'd rather not talk about it over the phone Roger, but, uh, it's something pretty god damn serious. And, uh, but I, I, I tried, uh, it's just a warning, that's all, uh, it's uh, what could happen after all of this is over with.

RH: Well the thing is Frank, I don't know, you know, what your indictment reads and all. . . .

FW: I know that, I know that, but, uh, in, in your own indictment, I might as well tell you over the phone I guess, but in your own indictment, uh, it said something about uh, collusion, making up bids, and, uh, all of this sort of thing, well, uh, you know, the federal government can promise you all sorts of immunity. . . .

RH: Who?

FW: The federal government. . . .

RH:: Oh, oh, okay.

FW: Alright now, and I understand you're gonna change your plea.

RH: You understand that from who?

FW: Well, that's what, uh, my attorney was told.

RH: He hasn't talked to my attorney.

FW: Well, I'm real happy if you don't change your plea. But, uh, . . . I, uh, asked my attorney to call your attorney and uh, let him talk to your attorney about what I'm talking about, . . . and, uh, uh, if the line's being tapped or not, I, I really could care less now, but, if you change your plea to a guilty plea and they give you some kind of immunity, . . . but, if you, uh, should plead guilty to collusion, uh, rigging bids on those jobs, uh, after all this federal stuff is over, Graham Ritchie, the city attorney, is just sitting on the sidelines there waiting to slap a suit for triple damages [on you]. Now I got this [on] pretty straight dope. Now, now the only thing I'm, I'm saying is, ask your attorney if this is possible, and, uh, I know the in, the indictments there, you've got two, four million dollars worth of work, [let's say] six million, and if Ritchie, uh, does anything, it could go up to an $18 million suit. Now that's all I'm trying to tell you Roger. I don't want to, uh, scare you . . . regardless of what happens in the federal thing, you're not immune from a, a lawsuit from the City of Industry.[2]

Clearly, Wood was trying to scare his former colleague into agreeing not to testify against him. His swings between defeated resignation and stuttering upheaval, however, show that, even as he resisted persecutors such as Ritchie, he did their dirty work. The eavesdropping agents must have been gratified to hear that both Haines and Wood were trying to anticipate their physical pain and imagine their losses.

Several months earlier, in May, after the first indictments had been handed down, the City of Industry had intimated that it might take legal action, proclaiming itself to be the victim of financial fraud and vowing to recoup its losses and repair its reputation.[3] The legal technology through which the city planned to exact its punishment had a name: the Racketeering Influenced Corrupt Organizations Act, known to lawyers and law enforcement personnel as the RICO statute. Originally devised in the 1970s as a way to attack the Mafia's financial holdings, the federal act widened judges' latitude to freeze assets and assess treble financial damages against individual mobsters and their businesses. The RICO laws were specially designed for organized crime, and the feds could target Mafia businesses and rackets if those involved had received prior convictions or precedent felonies. By the 1980s, inventive attorneys, including the lawyers that Industry had hired, had come to believe that they could redirect RICO's powers against white-collar criminals if they could show that the crimes had met the statute's technical requirements. Industry's case was the statute's second known application on the west coast; and in their action, the city's lawyers would accuse the kickback conspirators of violating the anti-monopoly provisions of the Sherman Act and of breaking other codes for good measure.[4]

Wood and Haines therefore had every reason to worry. In the federal civil suit it filed in October 1984, the city demanded 33 million dollars in treble damages from Wood and the other defendants who were awaiting conviction for conspiring to skim 1.35 million dollars from city redevelopment projects.[5] Industry's case against Jim and the kickback conspirators argued that their scheme to defraud the city had started outside city hall and inside National Engineering, the private firm that had been charged with executing and coordinating Industry's redevelopment projects. It further argued that the city's elected and appointed officials were the conspiracy's unwitting victims, not its architects, an argument that underscored a hidden benefit of privatization. More importantly, the city pegged its legal reasoning to some, but not all, of the evidence admitted in the criminal case. The suit's most obvious omissions concerned its approach to Jim Stafford. While it had all the evidence it needed to portray the city founder as the architect of the conspiracy, it chose to represent him as an equal among scoundrels rather than the mastermind who ran city hall.

Regardless of the suit's legal merits, its silences served important functions. First, they deflected attention from Industry's responsibility for the conditions that had led to the scandal and gave the city room to portray Warner Hodgdon's National Engineering as the worst of the offenders. Tarnishing Hodgdon's reputation would come in handy later when the city needed reasons to cut its ties to National Engineering. Second, those silences allowed the city to downplay Jim's exaggerated image as Industry founder and criminal overlord, which, thanks to court rulings and newspaper stories, had taken on a life of its own. City lawyers knew that portraying the corruption to be a logical consequence of Industry's terrific concentration of wealth and power was no solution. If they wanted to prevent a more damaging round of investigations, they needed to turn attention away from city officials, including the mayor and the city's biggest developer, Majestic Realty, who had been mentioned in Keller's FD 302 reports. But because Industry's attorneys wanted to focus on showing that the conspirators had committed precedent felonies, as RICO required, their legal strategy did not require those chronicles.

All Roads Lead to City Hall

To defend themselves, the conspirators needed to show that the city's elected and appointed officials had turned a blind eye to Jim's affairs because they were too busy running their own scams from inside the city. At first, they held out hope. Agent Keller and Assistant U.S. Attorney Feese said they had turned over evidence to the district attorney's head of special investigation showing that city officials had violated the state's criminal and civil laws. According to the defendants' reasoning, Industry could not credibly present itself as a victim if a court had convicted its officials of raiding the city's purse for personal gain.

On September 13, 1984, Hodgdon resigned from National Engineering, a move that some of the RICO defendants saw as a good omen. The city had pushed him over the edge when it had asked him to post a 1.77-million-dollar bond to cover the "firm's potential liability for the $1.35 million [conspiracy]." He did not have the cash on hand to meet that demand.[6] A few weeks later, the city canceled its exclusive contract with National Engineering, eventually forcing him to declare bankruptcy. The city's action was not as draconian as it might seem to be; Hodgdon's former employees staffed the two new companies that were hired to pick up National Engineering's contracts. But Hodgdon's departure did clear the way for Ritchie, architect of the city's legal strategy, to fill his void and emerge as Jim's political heir.[7]

Meanwhile, certain Industry critics, seizing the opportunity raised by the kickback convictions and not trusting the district attorney to clean up city hall, took matters into their own hands. On October 12, two days before the city filed its suit, a few renegade business owners, including the owner of fruit-juice maker Kern Foods, filed their own suit against the city. The suit attempted to hold city officials accountable for permitting or participating in a scheme to defraud local taxpayers, but it would need to prove that these officials had knowingly broken the law.[8] The businessmen took heart when they learned that the RICO defendants were trying to compel the city to produce evidence showing the mayor's role in their conspiracy. Judging by the text of the critics' lawsuit, however, they did not know about and therefore did not request Keller's logs, thus denying themselves valuable evidence.[9]

The local press, for its part, was playing up the FBI's investigation of contractors who had received thousands of dollars to build "a massive concrete, brick and steel wall" around a home that Mayor John Ferrero and his sister Phyllis Tucker co-owned and where she resided.[10] At the same time, the city was paying Tucker a 26,716-dollar salary for serving as city treasurer and financial officer of two of its redevelopment agencies; and Jim Stafford was paying her to work as his private secretary and bookkeeper. State law required Tucker, as a public official, to report her private earnings and disclose her financial interests. But it did not make her spell out exactly how much Jim was paying her, only that the sum exceeded 10,000 dollars for the services she had performed for his milling businesses in 1984.[11] It is not hard to guess why Jim had kept Tucker on his payroll. In addition to contributing to his goal of keeping city business in the hands of family and friends, her presence gave him constant access to the city's most sensitive ledgers. He had a similar relationship with the bookkeeping firm Frazer and Torbet, which kept both Industry's and his own business books.

Keller took note of these connections. In the course of his investigations he began uncovering more financial information about Tucker and Ferrero. Haines, the contractor who had put up part of the wall around Tucker's house, said that Wood had paid him 32,000 dollars for doing the work, money that Keller traced back to Ron Rabin, National Engineering's construction coordinator at Industry Hills.[12] "The design of the wall at Tucker's residence," the *Times* noted, "is almost identical to the perimeter wall surrounding the more than 600-acre Industry Hills [facility]," then at the center of the bid-rigging and kickback scandal. Rabin also acknowledged paying between 10,000 and 15,000 dollars to an electrical contractor for rewiring the house, with the money coming from change orders billed to other city redevelopment projects. The contractors who did this work said that Rabin had told them that doing the job would keep them in the mayor's good graces. Moreover, Frank Wood had paid yet another contractor 6,067 dollars to install an electric gate on the same property, presumably billing the job as a cost overrun from another city project.[13]

Keller believed that both the wall's design and the admissions of Rabin and other contractors offered a clear evidentiary trail back to city hall. Ferrero and Tucker, however, declined to discuss these matters with the press. Their silence did not prevent Howard Matz, the attorney retained to represent the mayor, from stating in a RICO filing that "he believed from his client that said fence was paid for [with city money]."[14] Keller's investigation was also focusing on city councilman Patrick Perez's brother David, who had admitted, via his attorney, that he had billed the city for about 20,000 dollars' worth of work on the Ferrero-Tucker property. After Keller subpoenaed Zerep ("Perez" spelled backward) Management's financial records, David Perez admitted that he had installed cyclone fencing using Industry Hills leftovers and had laid a concrete footing for a new barn in the early 1980s but said that he had done so without his brother's knowledge.

Like the City of Industry Disposal Company, also owned by the Perez family, Zerep Management enjoyed an exclusive, no-bid contract with the city.[15] Haines, Rabin, and other players in Jim's conspiracy had tipped off Keller to the dealings of Zerep and other contractors, telling the agent that such firms had done thousands of dollars of work for the city, jobs that included remodeling the home of Jim's mistress and Industry Manufacturers Council staffer Janet Crowley with an expensive sound system, a remote-controlled gate and garage door, and other improvements. Typically, Wood found the contractors, while Rabin played paymaster, hiding the costs as Industry Hills project expenses.

Industry paid out city funds to hire attorneys to represent Ferrero and Tucker, although officials refused to talk to the press about the pair's home improvement projects. Crowley meanwhile insisted that she had paid for the improvements with inheritance money.[16] But there was more trouble ahead for Industry. Keller's probe was not limited to city contractors; it also reached into city government itself, when federal agents tried to ascertain whether city manager Bob Baker had surreptitiously taped conversations in his office à la Richard Nixon, another potential violation of state law.[17]

MORE GOOD OMENS

The hopes of Industry's critics rose again when a Los Angeles County grand jury committee announced in April 1985 that it had launched an investigation into the Industry Urban Development Agency, the city's largest redevelopment agency, citing the ongoing FBI and U.S. Attorney's Office joint investigation. "It's a very tight organization of family and relatives in the lead positions in the city," committee chair Robert Beckerman said. "We have to break into that and see what it looks like." Returning to a theme that had been highlighted in the *Times* coverage, he cited the city's more than 1-billion-dollar bond debt, a figure that included future interest to be paid on that debt and which at that time was the highest of any California city's, as another motive for the probe.[18]

On July 19, the accounting firm Deloitt, Haskins, and Sells released the grand jury's audit. According to that report, the city and its redevelopment agencies risked insolvency if they did not sell surplus land or issue new revenue bonds to deal with a growing bond-debt burden, which had hit 593 million dollars, not including interest, in fiscal year 1984.[19] The report went on to project a 45.7-million-dollar deficit for fiscal year 1986. Auditors claimed that the city had dug itself into debt by issuing new bonds to cover its Industry Hills operating costs, which exceeded revenues by as much as 6 million dollars a year. The report also said that the city lacked a staff large enough to manage its huge volume of redevelopment work, a deficiency that left its projects without leadership or direction. City staff, auditors noted, could not produce records for four of Industry's bond issues; and despite its high volume of bond work, the city spent "two to three times more money to issue its bonds than [did] comparable redevelopment agencies." The report also "criticized the city for failing to use competitive bids on engineering, professional," and other service contracts, a practice that allowed a few firms to monopolize city affairs. For example, Industry's reliance on accounting firm Frazer and Torbet was "questionable" because "the firm [was] in the position of auditing its own bookkeeping work." The report alleged that the city's lack of competitive bidding resulted in "contracts which appear to be unduly favorable to certain individuals and companies," citing the case of Mayor Ferrero, who leased six hundred acres of Industry Urban Development Agency land at no charge to his ranching business. "The question arises," said the auditors, "as to what consideration the [redevelopment agency] is receiving in return [for the mayor's services] or whether the right to use the land for grazing [free of charge] is a gift" and thus an unreported and therefore illegal campaign contribution.[20]

City attorney Graham Ritchie did his best to portray the report's criticisms as misguided or superfluous. He pointed out that Industry had already put some of its surplus property on the seller's block and planned to use money from that sale to pay off bond debt. Regarding the report's criticism of the city's no-bid contracting policy, he defiantly replied, "We will . . . seek competitive bids . . . when we need to, without much regard for their recommendations."[21] He explained that the city was complying with existing contract-city and home-rule laws, which authorized cities to forgo competitive bidding in specified situations. Moreover, he said, federal and local authorities had already investigated the mayor's land leases with the city and its agencies and had not challenged their legality. In other communications, the city also noted that it had recently cut its Industry Hills operating deficit in half, down to 3 million dollars a year.[22]

In his comments, Ritchie did eventually strike a more conciliatory note (no doubt for the benefit of bond investors), expressing assurances that the city had taken steps to reduce its bond costs when it had terminated its full-service "engineering, planning and bond consulting services" contract with National Engineering.[23] Addressing the city's lack of financial leadership, he acknowledged that National Engineering's departure had indeed left the city's financial affairs in disarray but said that newly contracted firms would soon rectify that problem, and at more reasonable rates.

Ritchie's replies, however, did not indicate just how deeply he had involved himself in resolving Industry's apparent financial crisis, although clearly the city attorney had taken advantage of Hodgdon's departure to expand his influence into the city's financial management. In August 1984, Ritchie recommended that the city award Hodgdon's financial services contract to Bancroft, O'Connor, Chilton, and Lavell (BOCL) without competitive bidding. His maneuver was successful, just as such maneuvers had always been successful in Industry. The handpicked redevelopment panels responsible for contracting decisions, often composed of retired ranchers, schoolteachers, and janitors, had a history of rubber stamping whatever the resident expert recommended. They rarely asked questions and almost never rejected proposals submitted for their approval. The proposal that Ritchie and BOCL made to the Industry Urban Development Agency was no exception. Of the agency's five directors, the two who returned telephone calls from the *Times* acknowledged that they had not fully understood the intricacies of the proposal they had voted for.[24] The panel approved BOCL's no-bid contract in January 1985, proof to some observers that the city had resumed business as usual. Ritchie had also proven that Industry's governmental apparatus did not need Jim's guiding presence to continue functioning.

And as Ritchie had promised, BOCL began issuing bonds for three times less than what Hodgdon had charged. The firm, along with its subsidiary municipal bond brokerage, agreed to a 0.5-percent fee for preparing new and refinanced bonds as opposed to Hodgdon's 2 percent. But city critics wondered why the city was still refusing to invite competitive bids. Ritchie argued that soliciting additional bids would waste time: BOCL had already mastered the city's bond-financing needs when it was hired to evaluate Industry's bond obligations in the wake of the kickback and bid-rigging scandal.[25]

Meanwhile, Stafford, King, and Rabin, three of the defendants in the city's RICO suit, requested that presiding judge Mariana Pfaelzer make Keller's FD 302s available to all the litigants and, as a consequence, to the public. Because the press had already reported on their misdeeds in detail, the defendants had much to gain from the publicity and little to lose. King and Rabin could present themselves as Jim's victims, claiming that he was the man who had run the city, planned the conspiracy, and pressured them to do wrong. Jim, for his part, could construct an unclean-hands legal argument that accused Industry officials of turning a blind eye to his dealings and engaging in their own schemes to defraud the city.

Jim's attorney went much further. He alleged that, because the city had been created and "operated for the private benefit [of] selected local property owners" and because its "decisions and activities [served] no real 'public interest,'" Jim's conspiracy could not have inflicted a public harm, especially since Industry's population was "minuscule" by design. In his attempt to squash the city's complaint, the attorney therefore acknowledged that the so-called public interests harmed by Jim's criminal schemes were really private ones.[26] The argument's reasoning might seem farfetched; after all, the city was justifying its case in the name of injured taxpayers. But the defense knew that it could complicate that justification by showing that Industry's redevelopment programs had deprived surrounding property owners of the benefit of many millions of dollars in property-tax revenues. Stafford, King, and Rabin therefore accused the city's unindicted officials of running schemes to defraud Industry of taxpayer dollars, asking the judge to accept into evidence press reports of city officials who had enjoyed home improvement work at city expense.

They assured her that they could substantiate these and other allegations if she would allowed Keller's 302s into the record and so embarrass the city into submission.[27]

The RICO defendants got what they wanted on February 2, 1987, when Judge Pfaelzer ordered the release of Keller's investigative log, a decision that triggered another round of arguments and bargaining. Industry's attorneys, who had opposed the release from the start, moved to halt the order's execution or at least to stipulate that the log be submitted under seal. They asserted, among other things, that the defendants' unclean-hands argument would not remove their liabilities under the Sherman Anti-trust Act and thus shield them from the city's RICO suit. The attorneys also argued that making the reports public could harm people "who may be rashly or unjustly derogated" and that the identities of Keller's interview subjects needed to be protected to avoid jeopardizing ongoing federal and local criminal probes of the city. This latter claim rested partly on the declarations of plaintiffs and defendants who had acknowledged that Keller had already handed over his log to someone in the Los Angeles County district attorney's office for follow-up prosecution of any violations of state law.[28]

Attorneys representing Jim, King, and Rabin countered that the information contained in the log could not be obtained in any other way, that the FBI had officially closed its investigation, and that the district attorney's interest investigating Industry's officials only bolstered the urgency of verifying their claims. The attorneys also argued that the benefits of full disclosure outweighed harm to personal privacy, and they expected the evidence of city corruption to validate their claims. They claimed moreover that the FBI had a perfectly workable policy for protecting the privacy of individuals who deserved that protection, and the defense promised to abide by those criteria.[29]

This last argument referred to the FBI's response to Judge Pfaelzer's February 2, 1987, release order. At that time, the FBI made it clear that the bureau saw very little in Keller's chronicle to withhold from the public. The special agent, Thomas E. Vornberger, who had reviewed the log's 1,782 pages and 411 documents noted that only one document required deletion because, in his words, releasing it "would be an unwarranted invasion of the personal privacy of individuals not parties to the litigation." Vornberger, chief of the FBI's Civil Discovery Review Unit I in Washington, D.C., deleted another sixteen documents on various statutory grounds, plus one more because it "would reveal the identity of an informant."[30]

This time, Judge Pfaelzer's ruling split the difference, thus deciding the log's literary fate. She would admit Keller's chronicle as evidence but only under seal. The final item in the order, entered by hand under the judge's stamped signature, stipulated that "these documents shall only be used by the parties, their counsel and people employed by their counsel to assist in this Litigation [and] for no other purpose."[31] By sealing the records, she had imposed a regimen of secrecy harsher than even the FBI's own strict standard. From a discursive standpoint, her order to include the log would have been a modest disappointment for the city, but admitting it "under seal" was far better than complete public disclosure. Industry, charged with representing the public interest, had succeeded in keeping the most authoritative account of Jim's saga of city- father-turned-criminal-master-mind out of the public arena. Stafford, King, and Rabin were also prepared to live with the deal, which gave them a way to hold the city accountable for the scandal and thereby neutralize the most onerous aspects of the RICO lawsuit.

It is not clear from the case file if Keller's log was the bargaining chip that brought both sides to the settlement table; they had, in fact, drawn up a tentative settlement months before. Still, the agreement's timing is suggestive. The defendants, not including Jim Stafford, agreed in November (about eight months after the judge had sealed the 302s) to settle with the city for 1.97 million dollars. Jim agreed to pay back an additional 2.5 million dollars, on top of the more than 1.3 million dollars he had already paid. According to this deal, Industry and its agencies recovered a total of 4.5 million dollars, or about 13 percent of the 33 million dollars in damages it was entitled to receive under the RICO statutes and less than half of the 10 million dollars that Keller believed that Jim and his colleagues had skimmed from the city's redevelopment projects.[32] Nonetheless, the settlement gave Industry more than enough room to defend its reputation. The city could point to the sum it had retrieved, despite the sizable attorneys' fees it had paid in order to retrieve the money. More importantly, it could claim that it did "not believe that the discovery process in this case uncovered any evidence which would have supported a finding [of the official wrongdoing] alleged in the complaint."[33] The conditional "believe" and "would have" phrasing in the passage did not sound very convincing, however. But weak language was a small price to pay for silencing Keller's investigative chronicle.

Assessing the suit's historical significance is another matter. Now one might argue that denying the public any knowledge of Industry's responsibility for the scandal had allowed the city to neutralize an enormous threat, second in magnitude only to the lawsuit that had threatened to derail its 1957 incorporation. The vehemence with which the city tried to exclude and later restrict public access to Keller's log underscores the significance of that threat. A functional argument is also possible. The log's exclusion from public discourse not only undermined voter efforts to hold Industry's officials legally accountable for crimes committed during their watch, but it also put a compelling tool out of voters' reach, one they could have used to examine and question the governmental technologies that had made the city so powerful.

Exclusion of the log also denied voter access to perhaps the most complete archive of the inner workings of Southern California's industrial development. Keller's 302s detailed how the city, with Jim working as the link between rentier and corporate capital, had hugely favored one developer, Majestic Realty, and two railroads in designing and executing its redevelopment plans. Ignorance of that history only adds to its damaging legacy. Without Keller's chronicle, the grand jury's audit merely nibbled at the edges of the city's sovereignty and the economic relationships its legal fortifications protected. Auditors could allege the misuse of taxpayer dollars, but they could say little about the laws that permitted the city to authorize those expenditures. Industry's strategic transportation assets, multiple tax-revenue streams, and reserves of valuable, undeveloped, industrially zoned land meant that the city's autonomy was only marginally vulnerable to fiscal assault.

In April 1986, a superior court judge dismissed the taxpayers' suit that local business owners had brought against Industry a month earlier, without having cited Keller's logs. In May 1987, the federal district court of appeals cut Jim's eight-year sentence in half, agreeing that his two charges of obstructing a criminal investigation should have been served concurrently. The pressure on Jim eased a bit more in January 1988, when federal authorities, citing his heart problems, released him from a federal correctional facility in Fort Worth, Texas, after having served less than three years of his sentence. Now seventy-one years old, he was confined to his West Covina home until becoming eligible for parole in May.[34]

Jim's incarceration, the settlement of Industry's RICO suit, and the judge's order to seal the investigative log should have ended the practical life of Keller's chronicle. Yet they did not, if we can believe the RICO records, which contain several declarations from complaining and defending attorneys who matter-of-factly confirm that the U.S. attorney's office had indeed delivered the 302s to the county district attorney's office.[35] Keller himself confirmed the handoff, an act suggesting that his words still might lead to the prosecution of Industry's political leaders and maybe even challenge the technology of the city's power.[36]

A Punishing Settlement

In March 1988, Los Angeles County district attorney Ira Reiner persuaded Graham Ritchie to accept a punishing civil settlement. One could not blame the newspaper readers who interpreted the deal as a continuation of the Industry Hills kickback scandal. After all, the charges that Reiner leveled against the Industry city attorney appeared to be cut from the same cloth.

Reiner's three-year conflict-of-interest investigation had focused on Ritchie's official role in two bond sales in two different cities and his private ties to the Century City firms that had prepared those bonds. The first sale had occurred in 1983 in Hawaiian Gardens, a new suburban city southeast of Los Angeles. BOCL, per Ritchie's recommendation, had prepared the bond but without disclosing that Ritchie's law firm had filed the brokerage's incorporation papers in 1983. His law firm's decision to represent BOCL would not subsequently have raised eyebrows if Ritchie had not "put up a $132,000 note as security for the firm to obtain a national license" and purchased 175 shares of its stock. Those legal and financial details suggested that Ritchie was involved in BOCL, perhaps even as architect of its formation, which would not have been a crime if he had not used his official positions to hustle work for the bond firm and consulting fees for himself. Ritchie allegedly crossed the criminal threshold when he "went before the City Council and recommended that Bancroft & O'Connor [BOCL's successor] be awarded the contract for underwriting and purchasing the $20 million bond issue." The city paid Ritchie, in his capacity as city attorney and redevelopment director, 87,000 dollars for his services in securing the financing for new construction in the city.[37]

The second alleged conflict occurred in August 1984 in the City of Industry, when Ritchie helped negotiate a "contract between the city and BOCL Securities," a corporate affiliate of Bancroft and O'Connor, "while he served as a private attorney for BOCL Securities in a different matter." The city paid him 75,000 dollars for his services in preparing an 87-million-dollar bond issue in which BOCL Securities acted as the city's financial consultant, also upon Ritchie's recommendation. His timing was impeccable: he made this pitch in the midst of the kickback convictions that had led to the departure of Warner Hodgdon, Industry's former bond dealer. Reiner later said that both Hawaiian Gardens and Industry had agreed to pay Ritchie handsomely if he could secure their bonds. "It is our position," Reiner said, "that, because of his financial interests in and professional relationship with the private bond firms, Ritchie was not in a position to give those cities unbiased legal advice."

The district attorney's evidence was strong enough to coax Ritchie into paying 300,000 dollars in fines, although he did not admit to any wrongdoing. The settlement also prevented him from ever providing legal services to any firm in which he had a financial interest and stipulated that cities must henceforth pay him either a salary or a flat hourly fee instead of hefty commissions charged for legal services.[38] Still, the settlement fell short of complete humiliation. Ritchie's attorney could minimize its significance, arguing that his client, harried by "28 months of scrutiny," had settled to avoid the aggravation and expense of proving his innocence.[39]

Keller, who thought Ritchie deserved what he got, was nonetheless disappointed. For him, the logical result of his investigation should have been the indictment of Mayor Ferrero and other city council members. The agent was frustrated by the district attorney's Special Investigations Division, which he believed was not moving on the evidence contained in his 302s. Keller maintains that he provided a copy of his chronicle to deputy district attorney Gilbert Garcetti, then head of the Special Investigations Unit; that he personally briefed both Garcetti and Monty Fligsten, one of the deputy district attorneys who investigated Ritchie; and that U.S. assistant attorney Gary Feese did the same with other members of the district attorney's office.[40]

Never doubting the quality of the evidence, Keller wondered why the district attorney's office had failed to follow through on a series of slam-dunk prosecutions. Why had it chosen to pursue a more speculative (though eventually fruitful) investigative line when it could have done both? But Fligsten, when I telephoned him in 2006, said he could not recall ever meeting Keller or receiving any documents from him while conducting the Ritchie investigation.[41] Likewise, in a response to an open-records request, Steve Cooley, who in 2006 had recently been elected district attorney of Los Angeles County, insisted that his office had no record of receiving Keller's 302s, despite declarations to the contrary in the Industry RICO case files.[42]

The silence separating these accounts remains a mystery. It is hard to imagine that the district attorney would not have enough evidence to indict Industry's political leadership. The quality and quantity of Keller's evidence therefore invites speculation. Perhaps someone in the district attorney's office considered Ritchie to be the most likely inheritor of Jim's power in the city. If so, a decision not to prosecute the mayor and other city officials could suggest that the district attorney's office saw them as less threatening than Ritchie. Or perhaps Reiner had decided, with whispered advice from other prominent county officials, that the county could not afford to prosecute Industry's leadership without exposing its governmental apparatus to new external assaults. For example, neighboring towns such as La Puente, which for decades had been deprived of industrial tax revenue, might have used the wholesale conviction of city officials as a basis for demanding that California's attorney general present to the legislature a case to decertify Industry's municipal charter. Simple parochialism or incompetence could also explain prosecutorial inaction. Reiner might have struck out at Ritchie to prove that he was not following the FBI's lead, a show of independence meant to make up for years of investigative passivity. Whatever the reasons, California criminal law gives county prosecutors the freedom to pursue some prosecutions and not others and to weigh some evidence and ignore the rest without having to explain those decisions to anyone. One result was clear, however: the life of Keller's 302s had fizzled to an anti-climactic end. The public had to endure another silence, one that proved the usefulness of the technologies of secrecy and further privatized a legal system already tilted in favor of those who could afford it.[43]

These results must have surely pleased Ed Roski, Jr., the richest and most influential member of Jim's inner circle, and a former target of Keller's investigation. He had survived unscathed; his role as Industry's chief developer, which Jim helped craft for him, had remained unchallenged. He could continue to leverage his accumulated knowledge, wealth, and influence to speed Majestic Realty's reach within and beyond Industry's boundaries. But first he had to take care of some unfinished business.

EPILOGUE

BECOMING HIS PAPER SON

Those who have a lot live enclosed in secure fortresses. . . . It's true, they're missing the moats filled with crocodiles and the majestic beauty of the castles, . . . but they've got the great raised bars, the high walls, the watchtowers, the armed guards.

—Eduardo Galeano, "To Be Like Them"

The 1988 settlement that the district attorney imposed on Graham Ritchie essentially erased his influence in the City of Industry. The city attorney had been one of the last obstacles preventing Ed Roski, Jr., from taking Jim's place in Industry. Now Ed made his move. He started making the big decisions in the city, started acting as if he had inherited Jim's power. Meanwhile, Industry underwent its own transformation.

Whether by accident or design, the metamorphosis started inauspiciously in April 1989, when Ed told city officials that he and his partners wanted to take up the city's earlier pledge to let them expand the hotel perched atop the Industry Hills Exhibit and Conference Center. The city turned them down, giving Ed and his partners a pretext to sue Industry in April 1991 for reneging on its promise.[1] Roski's partners followed with a second lawsuit against the city citing selected passages from the legal and journalistic narratives that had already been used against the city in the kickback case—without, however, including the story about Ed's reputation as Industry's favorite developer or mentioning Keller's investigative chronicle. The partners settled both suits in 1992 after the city agreed to buy back the hotel for 29 million dollars, which was 14 million dollars more than it had reportedly cost the Roski-Curci partnership to build.[2]

Next Ed took aim at Patrick Perez, the councilman who had led the opposition to his hotel expansion proposal. Roski's attorneys accused Perez, part owner of both the City of Industry Disposal Company and Zerep Management Company, of violating conflict-of-interest laws by serving on the council that was overseeing his firms. After Perez was forced to resign from the city council, Lawrence Mayo replaced him. Mayo, who was then seventy-seven years old, had worked for Jim's milling operation for fifty years and had previously served as a redevelopment board member.[3]

Meanwhile, Ed's real estate development empire was branching out. Ed had forged a partnership allowing him to sink 60 million dollars into the western-themed Silverton Hotel and Casino in Las Vegas.[4] He had also started several ventures with Philip Anschutz, the Denver billionaire who was busily merging the Union Pacific (which he then owned) and the Southern Pacific railroads. Anschutz's controversial 5.4-billion-dollar deal had now made him the largest shareholder of the Union Pacific, the nation's biggest railroad.[5]

To accomplish what President Teddy Roosevelt had undone almost a century before, Anschutz had lubricated the railroad merger with 673,584 dollars in campaign contributions to Republicans such as Senator Robert Dole of Kansas.[6] A few shareholders, however, had filed a lawsuit to halt it, predicting that follow-up cost cutting would trigger layoffs and encourage shoddy maintenance that would increase derailments, accident fatalities, gridlock, and service reductions along the Union Pacific's expanded network.[7]

MAPPING THE SCARS

The consequences of the railroad merger were particularly dire in Southern California.[8] In a 2003 incident, a runaway Union Pacific train "crashed into a City of Commerce neighborhood, destroying several homes and injuring a dozen people." In 2004, a derailment in nearby Whittier launched "three dozen cargo containers into backyards," damaging four homes. In 2005, there were three derailments: the first involved a chemical spill in one of Industry's few remaining residential clusters; the second and third took place in nearby Santa Fe Springs and Riverside. There were more Union Pacific derailments in San Bernardino County in 2006, one of them triggering a chlorine and chemical spill that required the evacuation of three hundred residents.[9]

In these and other cases, the Union Pacific derailments disproportionately hurt or endangered Latino residents, which is not surprising.

In Southern California, job proximity, lower housing, and transportation costs often pack working Latino families into the region's transportation corridors. But the human costs of these derailments did not interfere with Majestic Realty's business plan. Ed's company had already prepositioned factories, warehouses, and distribution centers throughout industrial Southern California as well as in strategic points beyond the Rocky Mountains, places where trains, trucks, and jets could haul in Asian goods from the ports of Los Angeles and Long Beach.[10] According to investigative reporter David Cogan, these on-the-ground developments had convinced Anschutz to reach out to Ed. Other partnerships followed, starting with the pair's joint purchase of the NHL's Los Angeles Kings, investments in the NBA's Los Angeles Lakers, and construction of the 350-million-dollar Staples Arena in downtown Los Angeles, which began in 1998 and was followed by talk of a second massive hotel, entertainment center, and housing project across the street.[11]

Meanwhile, the City of Industry decided in 2000 to lease the money-losing, 650-acre Industry Hills facility back to Majestic Realty. Ed and his partners agreed to pay 13.2 million dollars for a twenty-five-year lease, effectively ending the city's management of a facility that had "lost more than $16 million since 1995."[12] The city let Ed invest 32 million dollars in a makeover that boosted the hotel's capacity to 292 rooms and helped to erase the facility's sordid criminal past. The complex's new name, the Pacific Palms Conference Resort, looked westward, enticing new customers from across the Pacific with Asian-style decor, Chinese-language news-papers, Korean noodles, and iconic palm trees, a cliché of Hollywood glamour conveniently disconnected from Industry's recent past.[13]

For Industry, the makeover could not come soon enough. Dozens of *Fortune* 500 branch plants had skipped town after the kickback and bid-rigging convictions and the ensuing settlements. According to city records, by 2002, only 33 percent of Industry's more than 2,000 businesses had remained in manufacturing, compared to more than 70 percent (76 percent in one study) in the early 1970s.[14] City businesses now tilted toward warehousing, which included Wal-Mart–style retail variety, food-processing, and computer services. But these new employers, many attracted to Industry by global trade opportunities, paid less and offered fewer benefits than did the manufacturing jobs they were replacing.

According to a 1999 study, the nearly 300,000 jobs generated in Los Angeles County from 1993 to 1999 would have seemed impressive if the majority did not pay far less than the 40,000 to 60,000 dollars a year that a worker needed to support a nominally middle-income lifestyle. Most paid only 25,000 dollars annually, with only one in ten averaging 60,000 dollars a year.[15] A 2006 study confirmed that trend, showing a 41.4-percent drop in Los Angeles County manufacturing jobs from 1990 to 2005, compared to a 7.7-percent decrease for the rest of state during the same period.[16]

The San Gabriel Valley did not escape the slide. Between 2001 and 2004, its manufacturing sector, the valley's third-largest employer, lost 15,895 manufacturing jobs. In 2005, the valley had a total of 78,338 such jobs; it lost another 2,500 of them the next year. "Worse yet," reported the Los Angeles County Economic Development Corporation, a pro-business think tank, "these are well paying jobs, with an average wage of $39,959, versus an overall average for the Valley of $38,414." These figures put the valley significantly below the county's 45,112-dollar yearly average and far below the affluent west of Los Angeles 61,729-dollar average. The economic development corporation cited faster job growth in the lower-paying retail trade sector (which averaged 26,580 dollars a year in 2004) to explain why San Gabriel Valley wages ranked eighth in the county in 2005.[17]

The profound economic restructuring that was reducing Industry's manufacturing clientele coincided with new development opportunities, a maturing distribution technology, and a wave of deregulation. The rising volume of goods now produced overseas, mostly in China, meant that the Union Pacific, now bigger than ever, would realize its long-deferred dream of seeing Los Angeles take its place among the world's biggest trading cities, alongside Hong Kong, Shanghai, and Singapore.[18] The promised profits, however, would require activating another one of California's governmental technologies—an infinitely generative body of law known as a joint powers authority—to piece together a multi-agency organism capable of redesigning and refurbishing the county's rail grid.[19]

The resulting Alameda Corridor Transportation Authority, named after the boulevard that it paralleled, linked the ports of Long Beach and Los Angeles as well as key cities along the corridor's path as partners in a bid to sequester 2.4 billion dollars in federal, state, and local subsidies. Their plan was to build and own a transport system that would streamline rail service from the ports to the massive intermodal terminals east of downtown. Like previous forms of stealth government, the authority insulated itself from direct accountability to citizens by sharing its management with the two port authorities and with the Union Pacific and Burlington North Santa Fe railroads. Policymakers sold the twenty-mile-long project to residents by promising increased exports of U.S.-manufactured goods, improved air quality, and reduced freeway traffic. All of these promises later proved to have been exaggerated or plain wrong.[20]

Transforming the Union Pacific's line into a round-the-clock merchandise artery involved sinking part of it below street level to bypass traffic intersections, which did eliminate signal crossings and lower pollution levels from idling truck and train engines. Nonetheless, enhanced transportation efficiencies and the unstoppable surge of Asian trade eventually increased diesel-powered freight hauling, which negated any reductions in train and truck emissions. Moreover, the newly merged Union Pacific expected to gain more than better public relations from the project. Anschutz persuaded the authority to buy the railroad's harbor-to-downtown line (formerly owned by the SP) for 240 million dollars, a windfall that still left the Union Pacific with a second line that it could use to cash in on the containerized cargo that was being routed up the corridor to Las Vegas, Denver, and Omaha.[21]

The Alameda Corridor East, a 1-billion-dollar joint powers organism, was engineered to reduce emissions and increase freight volume on the rail line running southeast from downtown. The railroad merger that added what had been the Southern Pacific's trunk line through the San Gabriel Valley meant that the Union Pacific now controlled three of the four major lines handling cargo from the ports; it also had intermodal yards in the City of Industry as well as in Ontario, Upland, and West Colton in San Bernardino County.[22] The eastern corridor's improvements meant that about 1,500 cars delivered goods daily to its West Colton yard, which in turn meant more parts and merchandise for the warehouses and warehouse-like retailers stretching southeast from Industry to Ontario and Upland.[23]

SHELTERING NEW INEQUALITIES

Ed readied Majestic Realty for the tidal wave. The company's engineers and architects were prepared to design concrete rectangles for manufacturing or warehousing use, depending on the market.[24] Strategically located in the corridor's doorway, Industry represented the current status of warehousing in Los Angeles County, while cities such Ontario, located near the corridor's southern terminus in San Bernardino County, represented its future: in 2001, the city of Ontario had more than 16 million square feet of warehousing under construction, compared to the 8.6 million square feet then under construction in Los Angeles County. In 2000, manufacturers were estimating that cargo with a retail value of 166 billion dollars had moved through the corridor.[25]

The two Alameda corridor projects, whose construction costs eventually totaled more than 3.4 billion dollars, depended on the maturation of container transport. A rather simple mechanical technology, container shipping had first developed in 1956. Presorted cargo was loaded into truck trailers for ocean transit, thus giving shippers increased flexibility to coordinate ship, rail, and truck shipments into a seamless and responsive distribution network. As is often the case, however, an advance in mechanical technology cannot be fully exploited without a conceptual mapping of its uses and meanings. Therefore, a few decades passed before shippers realized that containerization not only reduced competition between rail- and truck-based distribution systems but could eliminate tens of thousands of high-paying union jobs, starting on the docks, which suffered a 75-percent decline in workforce by 1976.[26] Elimination of those jobs, coupled with the lower fuel costs of moving hundreds of containers via ship and train, resulted in major cost reductions and revived a rail industry that had not fully recovered from its trucking wars. "Container shipping thrives on volume," writes Marc Levinson, in his landmark study. "[The] more containers moving through a port or traveling on a ship or train, the lower the cost per box," an economy of scale that often trumps the costs of longer-distance transport. And intermodal flexibility wrought by containerization, Levison argues, produced a powerful domestic stimulus for globalization:

> In the 1970s and 1980s, when many U.S. industrial centers were dying, Los Angeles thrived as a factory location because it was home to the nation's busiest containerport, and Los Angeles thrived as a port because it was well located to handle import volume from Asia, not just California, but for the entire United States. The Pacific Rim became the world's workshop for consumer goods, in good part, because large ports for containers gave it some of the world's lowest shipping costs.[27]

Majestic's engineers and architects understood what containerization meant for Asian trade. Each node of the intermodal network needed warehousing and distribution facilities for storing, sorting, and moving goods. So they built more warehouses in Industry and San Bernardino and new warehouses in Las Vegas, Denver, Dallas, Houston, and Atlanta, from whence their operators distributed Asian-made goods to other warehouses and their retail variants, the big-box stores that were sprouting up east of the Rockies. Starting in Southern California, demographic growth in western and southeastern cities produced another globalizing synergy: ready-made markets that would finance distribution development east of the Sierras.

Trade specialists such as Wally Baker, senior vice president of economic and public policy consulting for the Los Angeles Development Corporation, recognized this trend. "Southern California," he said in a 2004 interview, "consumes half of what is going through the ports of Los Angeles and Long Beach. More than $70 billion of the $200 billion that comes through the ports of LA and Long Beach is consumed by Southern California. It's a huge thing, and is getting bigger every year." The size of the Los Angeles consumer market therefore favors the region's dominance in distribution and warehousing. "There are only nine other places in the world," Baker said, that "consume more than the [greater] LA [market]." Global trade "comes here because we are already consuming a ton of stuff" as retail and industrial consumers. There is also "a significant nexus between warehousing, manufacturing, assembly, and the selling of finished products. There is a huge demand for parts, which are assembled and repackaged here, and then sent out as a domestic product." The warehouses, which are part of the logistics chain, benefit from rail and freeway projects that increase freight tonnage and keep industrial vacancy rates "ultra-tight."[28]

The publicly funded corridor projects, one could argue, have therefore functioned as market subsidies for local warehouse owners, especially for Majestic, because of the sheer scale of its Los Angeles and San Bernardino county holdings, a structural advantage added to decades of redevelopment subsidies that the company has accrued in Industry and other Southern California cities. Not surprisingly, Baker identified Majestic as one of the biggest beneficiaries of the recent investments in the region's logistics infrastructure. "Of course," he said, "Roski's warehouses benefit from all the incoming and outgoing traffic on the Alameda Corridor East, and the freeways."[29]

According to a 2006 count, Majestic has built more than 73 million square feet of industrial and commercial space, making it the nation's biggest privately held industrial-commercial developer.[30] The core of its empire remains in Los Angeles County, where it has built more than 30.8 million square feet of space. The company has positioned itself to continue dominating the county's east-west transportation axis, snapping up enough land to plan another 10 million square feet of commercial development in an already land-scarce county.[31]

The synergies of global trade, combined with the Los Angeles consumer market's growing appetite, has also helped Majestic add Asian-owned computer and software firms to its client menu.[32] Its newer and older revenue streams and its insider positioning have converged to give the company a decisive advantage in the City of Industry. By early 2003,

Roski-controlled or -owned properties in Industry totaled more than 1,454 acres—19 percent of the city's total acreage—making Ed the biggest developer in the city. About 804 acres, or 55 percent of the real estate he owned in whole or in part, consisted of warehousing, light and heavy manufacturing, and undeveloped land; the remainder consisted of the 650-acre Pacific Palms Resort. Majestic owned more than 512 acres land of dedicated to warehousing and light industrial uses, an amount that may not seem impressive until we compare that acreage to the amount of land owned by the company's biggest competitors in the city. For example, Catellus Development Corporation, a 1994 Southern Pacific and Santa Fe railway spinoff later swallowed by ProLogis, was one of California's largest landowners and the world's biggest publicly traded warehousing and distribution conglomerate. Yet 2003 property records showed that Catellus owned only 16.25 acres of warehousing in Industry, while Majestic's two other biggest competitors together recorded only 36.63 acres, or less than 2 percent of Industry's 1,977 acres dedicated to warehousing and light manufacturing. Majestic, by contrast, owned 512 acres, or 26 percent, of Industry's warehousing and light manufacturing, more than nine times what its biggest competitors owned in that real estate market category. His firm's subsequent development of the raw acreage it owned in 2003, coupled with even larger acquisitions, undoubt-edly increased his share of Industry's warehousing and light industrial market. Industry served Ed the biggest of these slices when it approved Majestic's acquisition of the four-hundred-acre Grand Crossing Business Park. Ed struck a still bigger deal in 2005 when the city agreed to lease him another six hundred acres for sixty-five years to build a state-of-the-art stadium to lure a long-absent National Football League franchise back to the Los Angeles area. The latest development deal pushed his ownership or control of Industry holdings to 2,054 acres, or 27 percent of the city's 7,610 acres, ensuring his status as the city's reigning champion in development.[33]

But at the current mortgage meltdown demonstrates, a real estate parcel without financing is like farmland without water. Nothing illustrates that difference better than the city's effort to finance Majestic's stadium project. On January 20, 2009, the city's residents voted sixty to one to approve the sale of 500 million dollars in bonds to pay for infrastructure development in the city. From the start, the city's refusal to provide county residents with an analysis of the bond measure's fiscal impact slowed efforts to decode the measure's ultimate purpose. The city would only admit that the bond would be repaid with property-tax money and that an unspecified portion of that money would pay for Majestic's 800-million-dollar NFL stadium project. Some reporters speculate that Ed's cut of that money will be substantial, given the 829 million dollars of county property-tax money the city tried but failed to obtain from the state legislature when it formally announced the stadium project in April 2008. Other reporters hint that the bond measure resembles the 250-million-dollar bond package the city approved in 1978 to rescue its redevelopment projects from the strictures of Proposition 13. *Sacramento Bee* columnist Dan Walters says the city's intentions are not a mystery. In a column published a few days before the vote, Walters said that the city continues to lobby state legislators to persuade them to allow the city to add the stadium to one of its existing redevelopment projects.[34]

Extending the life of redevelopment in the city offers obvious attractions for Ed and the city. In addition to pairing a generous land lease with hefty financing, reviving redevelopment will allow Majestic to forgo the inconvenience of competitive bidding. Securing land, financing, and a bidding advantage would therefore give Ed a pass to that growing club of billionaire sports-franchise owners who build stadiums with public subsidies. The city, for its part, would circumvent California's tightened definition of *blight,* which now prevents the condemnation of farmland, and allow it to absorb six hundred acres of rolling pastures into its biggest redevelopment project area and continue diverting millions of property-tax dollars to projects that will otherwise soon expire. The city's fiscal fix, however, would spell continued pain for Los Angeles County government agencies that are desperate to see property-tax revenues return to their coffers as the current recession morphs into depression. And despite the predictable cheerleading of chamber of commerce types and sports fanatics who have never met a sports stadium or arena project they didn't like, the stadium's purported job-creating potential remains as elusive as ever, according to studies that have examined their unimpressive track records.[35]

The net of Majestic's development matrix, moreover, continues spreading beyond Industry's borders. A 2003 property survey showed that, in San Bernardino County, Majestic had also built and owned warehouses covering more than 655 acres—15 percent of all properties designated as warehouses in the county, most of them clustered around Ontario International Airport in the north. Together, these developments accounted for 22 percent of the 404 million dollars of assessed warehousing property in San Bernardino County at that time.[36] Cheaper property values and easy freeway, rail, and airfreight access explain why Majestic had surged into this region known as the Inland Empire. In 2001, the county had undertaken 16 million square feet of warehouse construction, compared to 8.6 million square feet in nearly built-out Los Angeles County.[37] Clearly, Majestic's tally of ownership and control painted more than a picture of market dominance. The scale and reach of the company's development network had redefined the entrepreneur's role in local development. By leveraging what it had learned and earned in Industry, Majestic had evolved from a local developer into a national facilitator of corporate globalization.

The effects of governmental technologies had also transformed the majority Latino and Asian cities and suburbs that surrounded Industry: La Puente, Baldwin Park, El Monte, West Covina, and Hacienda Heights.[38] Although Industry's agents represented the city as the region's necessary exception to the county's mixed-use tapestry, it actually illustrated the growing inequalities of Southern California's postindustrial order. Like the county's other wealthy cities, extremes of racial segregation and inequality, the highest in the nation, now surrounded it. Clearly, the city did not look like San Marino or Beverly Hills, those opulent enclaves so important to media constructs of the Los Angeles image; yet it resembled them in the ways that mattered most. All these cities shared technologies for sequestering and hoarding wealth. Industry's mansions just happened to take the form of factories, warehouses, and shopping malls.[39]

By the early 1990s, a small but growing number of scholars, journalists, and government reports began to examine the cost of Industry's unspoken covenant.[40] One series of studies confirmed that the city had indeed delivered jobs, more than 166 per hundred residents in 1994, generating a workforce that swells to as many as 80,000 people each day. In the same year, La Puente, the poor and majority-Latino neighbor carved from Industry's northern flank, ranked at the bottom of the county's class of job-growing cities that generated 1.2 to 18.7 jobs per hundred residents. La Puente had dropped to its lowly place during a period in which Industry's job-generating ratio grew by 12.3 percent or more.[41]

These studies suggested that Industry's jobs did not significantly improve the fortunes of the city's nearest neighbors. The data, when mapped, showed the growing inequalities that undermined the Latino and Asian households in the county's aging suburbs. In 1996, Industry's assessed property value per household matched or exceeded 548,753 dollars, putting it on par with the county's richest cities, while property values in La Puente, Industry's residential shadow, ranked second to lowest, at between 78,512 and 108,406 dollars per household. In the same year Industry's annual sales tax revenue reached or exceeded 87,467 dollars per household, bringing the city up to the level of the county's richest residential and industrial districts. La Puente's sales-tax base, by contrast, ranged between 9,832 and 14,469 dollars per household, evidence that the city was one of the county's poorest.[42]

Industry's other close neighbors faired only slightly better than La Puente. Their assessed property values and sales-tax revenue per household placed them in the middle and lower-middle wealth tier of cities in the county, a modest reward for having such a rich neighbor. When cities' revenue-generating power (via property and sales taxes) were factored using 1998 figures, Industry again stood out, garnering 1,335 dollars or more in revenue per household, while its San Gabriel Valley neighbors ranked at or near the bottom of the county's revenue earners. For example, in Hacienda Heights, Industry's southwestern neighbor, the tax-generating capacity per household was 262 dollars or less, dropping the municipality into the bottom tier of cities and unincorporated communities.[43] No doubt, income disparities in towns such as La Puente reflected the starkly racialized wage regime that divided Latinos, the county's new working-class majority, from other workers during this period. According to one study, the median Latino hourly wage in 1990 was $11.25, or 46.9 percent of the $19.92 that workers categorized as white were earning per hour. That wage divide widened in 2005 when the average Latino hourly wage came in at $11.25, or 50 percent of white workers' $22.50 hourly median.[44]

Contrary to prevailing media discourse, which blamed these disparities on the employment of illegal, mostly Mexican, workers, single-use enclaves such as Industry were serving as laboratories for the radical, post-Fordist reorganization of production. In their race to reduce cost and increase competitive flexibility, employers began in the 1970s to deconstruct and resignify commonly accepted meanings of industrial labor, representing unions, health insurance, pensions, job security, and high-wage, knowledge-based labor as competitive burdens and low-skilled, disposable immigrant workers as paragons of the American work ethic. Function paralleled discourse. Improvements in communications, travel, and distribution technologies such as containerization meant that more employers found their ideal workers abroad, in poor countries willing to bear the social and ecological cost of educating and supplying workers. Employers who could not globalize their factories inverted the logic of outsourcing, recruiting cheaper-priced immigrant workers to the newer, publicly subsidized, industrial suburbs.[45]

Today, the warehouse and big-box developments of Majestic and other builders aggravate these imbalances. They not only employ fewer people at lower wages than do the manufacturing jobs they replace, but the automation of warehouse technology, like the automation of the ports, also threatens to accentuate the contradiction between globalization's concentrated costs and its dispersed benefits. This is especially true for communities close to the Alameda corridors, the "trade losers" or "strugglers" that have seen incomes decline as service-sector jobs increase.[46]

The legacy of industrial development has also poisoned the physical environment of the La Puente Valley. Pollution of its once pristine aquifers began when waste from cattle ranches, dairies, feedlots, and septic tanks contaminated the valley upstream from the confluence of the San Jose and La Puente creeks. C. C. Stafford's mill supplied grain and feed to these ranchers, dairy farmers, and feedlot operators; he and his son also operated their own feedlots, whose nitrogen-rich runoff seeped through the valley's shallow clay beds. As the Southern Pacific's switching yards grew, the railroad's maintenance operations leached solvents and oils into the soil. The tool-and-die and aerospace industries that migrated to the area during and after World War II excreted yet more chemicals into the valley's groundwater. With the spread of new industrial cities such as Industry polluters found even more refuges, at least until these companies began to come under scrutiny in 1979, after the first signs of industrial groundwater pollution were discovered in Asuza, a neighboring San Gabriel Valley city.

As many as 48,000 firms have helped to pollute the resource that first fueled San Gabriel Valley sprawl: that huge supply of groundwater seasonally replenished by snowmelt from the San Gabriel Mountains, enough water to support 90 percent of the valley's more than 1.5 million residents. The most dangerous pollutants are volatile organic compounds—common industrial byproducts that degrade into human carcinogens—which are concentrated in five valley cities, including Industry. Year after year, the manufacturing firms in these cities have spewed, leaked, and dumped tons of hazardous chemicals into the air and water; the amount released by Industry, El Monte, and Azusa in 1987 has been estimated at 2.6 million pounds.[47] After the Environmental Protection Agency (EPA) declared in 1984 the aquifer under the 170-square-mile San Gabriel Valley to be the nation's largest Superfund cleanup site, "one-quarter of the valley's public water wells were shut down," and more than 50 million dollars were spent to assess the damage. Hundreds of millions more in public and private funds have been spent on filtering out the pollution.[48] In 1989, the EPA notified fifty of Industry's businesses that it had tentatively identified them as groundwater polluters.[49] Soon the agency raised that number to more than seventy businesses, which included Union Pacific rail and trucking operations acquired from Southern Pacific and a few Majestic-owned properties.[50]

Assessing responsibility has been slow because federal and state environmental scientists have had to trace specific chemical signatures to specific polluters. In some cases, the government has successfully forced offenders to pay for cleanup.[51] Yet such pressure has also given firms a pretext to skip town, moving their manufacturing jobs overseas where labor costs are lower and environmental regulation are lax.[52]

Meanwhile, Southern California's notoriously bad air quality worsened as Majestic and scores of other developers raced to cash in on the region's trade boom. More trade meant more ships, more trains, more big rigs belching diesel fumes, more port-to-warehouse and port-to-big-box traffic that released tiny particles of burnt and semi-burnt diesel fuel and ground truck tires into ultra-fine, noxious particles. A March 2000 landmark study by the South Coast Air Quality Management District (AQMD), the first of scores of studies, confirmed the bad news. Although the study reported recent successes in reducing ozone and other polluting gases, the fine particles that are a byproduct of diesel combustion had increased. By 1997, when AQMD had concluded the sampling phase of its study, diesel particulates (a once overlooked form of air pollution) accounted for a staggering 71 percent of the cancer-causing pollutants fouling the region's air. Not surprisingly, the study reported that the county's eastern industrial transportation corridor, where Industry and its clones are located, had some of the highest levels of particulate pollution.[53]

Since the release of its research, the AQMD and other researchers have reported new data suggesting a causal link between particulate pollution and the increasing incidence of brain cancer in the county's most affected communities. In an AQMD Foundation–funded study, a Cedars-Sinai team of neurosurgeons cited a more than 25-percent increase in brain cancers and other tumors among children and young people between 1973 and 1996. "Brain cancer is the most common cause of cancer death in young people," said Dr. Keith Black, study leader and director of the Cedars-Sinai Maxine Dunitz Neurosurgical Institute in Los Angeles, writing in October 2003. "Among the potentially toxic products of concern are the ultra-fine particles that come from diesel engines—particles that would likely be plentiful along freeways, in congested metropolitan areas, and in the immediate vicinity of diesel-burning vehicles."[54]

Death and Transfiguration

Even the text of Jim Stafford's death, one might argue, illustrates how Industry's technologies of power can be expressed on the seemingly molecular scale of personal relationships. On November 20, 2001, he succumbed at age eighty-five to stomach cancer in his home in Carpinteria, the Santa Barbara County beach resort where he had plotted his conspiracies. His death certificate gave Majestic's Industry mailing address and identified Ed Roski, Jr., as the "informant," a role typically performed by a close relative, who provides authorities with the deceased person's vital statistics.[55]

The awkward, forgiving words that Ed uttered at the memorial service he had organized for Jim reinforced the certificate's connotations. "Jim Stafford was a very, very good person," the local press quoted Ed as saying about a week before the service. "He got involved in a situation that any other time in his life he never would have. I felt very sorry for him."[56] Ed's ambiguous reference to Jim's crimes may have expressed emotional upheaval or been the kind of tactful comment that friends and family would have expected at such a time. But they ended on a pitiful note.

The *San Gabriel Valley Tribune*, to its credit, noted the irony of holding the memorial service in the redevelopment project that Jim had schemed to defraud as well as Ed's effort to erase that memory by giving the facility a new name. Yet at the service, in his last try at rescuing the man's public reputation, Ed noted that Jim had never given him any problems, an assertion that sounded rather lame, almost ungrateful, considering the rewards that his benefactor had lavished on him. Ed kept stacking one awkward sentiment onto the next: "[Jim] had a big heart and he was very helpful to a lot of individuals and in whole to the San Gabriel Valley."[57] Neither he nor Jim's other friends at the service volunteered a more candid appraisal of Jim's life or voiced any doubts about the scars he left on Southern California by encouraging a city's privatization.

The manner in which Ed settled Jim's affairs and administered his trust fund, however, said much more about which part of his legacy he most valued. About a month before his death, Jim had given Aida Serna, whom court papers later described as a "joint tenant," a 1-million-dollar cash gift and two cars, which included "his two-door Cadillac, valued at $31,970." After Jim died, Serna tried to pay her inheritance taxes and other expenses she had incurred from his gift using funds that had been deposited in two accounts (one containing 2.11 million dollars, the other 226,709 dollars), which she had previously opened with Jim at Santa Barbara Bank Trust. Her intention was to tidy up his affairs in Carpinteria with the leftover balance. But Roski's attorneys argued that the provisions of the trust superceded whatever banking arrangements Jim had agreed to before he died and that Serna's move violated the provisions of the trust. The settlement split the difference in Serna's favor. She got to keep her 960,000 dollars as compensation for unspecified services and was allowed to pay between 761,000 and 968,000 dollars in estate and other taxes from the joint accounts, with the balance going back to Jim's trust. For his part, Ed recouped Jim's leftover cash and reasserted his trusteeship of their jointly held real estate assets, the real prize in this dispute.[58]

Importantly, the text of Ed's devoted words and acts suggests a dual transformation. For all intents and purposes, he had become Jim's paper son, the consummation of a bond that had taken decades to achieve and that transcended conventional definitions of blood inheritance. After all, he had maintained control over the body of Jim's private estate and continued to win Industry's biggest development projects, a clear indication that he had also inherited his mentor's influence in the city.

Industry's continuing privatization teaches lessons that transcend the specifics of Jim and Ed's relationship. It now seems unavoidably plausible that one corporation, rather than a handful, may control this tiny micro-state with a strategically big role in global trade. The means of achieving that transformation, moreover, is by now a repeatable formula. For it is now entirely feasible for other corporations to create and nurture other cities to better harvest their hosts' governmental organs and indulge the incestuous possibilities that arise when one acquires the power to dominate a whole city's terrestrial domain. That nightmarish scenario also contains its cure. Decoding the privatized genomes of other micro-states holds out the possibility of a counter-technology for disrupting future privatizations and rooting out, like so many maggots, the market-driven truths that have brought our public institutions to the verge of collapse.

NOTES

INTRODUCTION

1. Steven P. Erie, *Beyond Chinatown: The Metropolitan Water District, Growth, and the Environment in Southern California* (Stanford, Calif.: Stanford University Press, 2006), 79–80.

2. Ibid., 11–12.

3. Vernon Shetley, "Incest and Capital in 'Chinatown,'" *Modern Language Notes* 114 (December 1999): 1098.

4. Michel Foucault, "Governmentality," in *The Foucault Effect: Studies in Governmentality, with Two Lectures by and an Interview with Michel Foucault*, ed. Graham Burcell, Colin Gordon, and Peter Miller (Chicago: University of Chicago Press, 1991), 102–3.

5. The echoes of Foucault's late work you hear are not accidental. I admit taking creative license with his work on the geology of knowledge, literary genealogy, discipline, and bio-power, which "Governmentality" tries to integrate. You may also hear echoes of Stuart Hall's critiques of media representation. I tried, via my self-induced susceptibilities, to suggest that we may understand more of these works than we realize, that we need them to make sense of our savage time.

6. Victor M. Valle and Alan Maltun, "Called to Account: Money Laundering at Bank Proved to Be Flaw in Stafford Scheme," *Los Angeles Times*, San Gabriel Valley ed., April 11, 1985, pp. 1, 7; Cecilia Rasmussen, "Community Profile: City of Industry," *Los Angeles Times*, November 29, 1995, p. B4.

7. San Gabriel Valley Economic Partnership, "San Gabriel Valley, Los Angeles County, California: 2006 Economic Overview and Forecast" (Los Angeles: Los Angeles County Economic Development Corporation, November 2006), 4.

8. Stephanie Chavez, "Los Angeles: Montebello Residents Sound Off about Trains," *Los Angeles Times*, January 11, 2004, p. B3; Ronald D. White, "Growing Problems Give Ports a Bad Reputation," *Los Angeles Times*, home ed., May 4, 2005, p. C1; South Coast Air Quality Management District, "Multiple Air Toxics Exposure Study (MATES II): Final Report" (Diamond Bar, Calif., March 2000, chap. 7, p. 1).

9. Ian Hart, ed., "Paying with Our Health: The Real Cost of Freight Transport in California" (Oakland, Calif.: Pacific Institute, November 2006), 28.

10. Dan Morain and Victor Valle, "City of Industry Founder Indicted in Kickback Case," *Los Angeles Times*, April 12, 1984, p. B14.

11. Charles L. Ponce de Leon, *Self-Exposure: Human-Interest Journalism and the Emergence of Celebrity in America, 1890–1940* (Chapel Hill: University of North Carolina Press, 2002), 22–24.

12. Ben Baeder, "City's Big Deal," *San Gabriel Valley Tribune*, accessed on July 3, 2008, from *http://www.sgvtribune.com/rds_search/ci_9733568?IADID=Search-www .sgvtribune.com-www.sgvtribune.com*.

CHAPTER 1 — HIS THEATER OF SHAME

1. "Complainant Masks Her Face: Book-keeper Formally Accuses Man," *Los Angeles Times*, March 29, 1929, p. A2.

2. Marc Wild, *Street Meeting: Multiethnic Neighborhoods in Early Twentieth-Century Los Angeles* (Berkeley: University of California Press, 2005), 38.

3. "Mystery Added to Kidnap Case: New Evidence Presented by Employer-Suspect," *Los Angeles Times*, Thursday, March 28, 1929, p. A2.

4. *People of the State of California v. Clayton C. Stafford*, case no. 278,394, Los Angeles Superior Court, May 15, 1929.

5. David Paul Nord, *Communities of Journalism: A History of American Newspapers and Their Readers* (Urbana: University of Illinois Press, 2001), 32–34.

6. Lisa M. Cuklanz, *Rape on Trial: How the Mass Media Construct Legal Reform and Social Change* (Philadelphia: University of Pennsylvania Press, 1996), 17–18.

7. Ibid.,19, 23–24.

8. "Riot at Fatty's Café Holds 5: Four Men and Woman Seized after Battle, 2 Face Serious Charges," *Los Angeles Evening Express*, May 21, 1929, p. 3.

9. David A. Yallop, *The Day the Laughter Stopped: The True Story of Fatty Arbuckle* (New York: St. Martin's, 1976), 279.

10. "Aimee Case Is Declared Dead," *Los Angeles Evening Express*, May 2, 1929, p. 2.

11. Jules Tygiel, *The Great Los Angeles Swindle: Oil, Stocks and Scandal during the Roaring Twenties* (New York: Oxford University Press, 1994), 248

12. Dennis McDougal, *Privileged Son: Otis Chandler and the Rise and Fall of the L.A. Times Dynasty*, (Cambridge, Mass.: Perseus, 2001), 98.

13. Yallop, *The Day the Laughter Stopped*, 279.

14. "Rich Altadenan up in Girl Case: Stafford, Accused by Girl in Attack Case, Beat Up Rev. Shuler," *Los Angeles Evening Express*, October 28, 1929, p. 7.

15. Mark Sumner Still, "'Fighting Bob' Shuler: Fundamentalist and Reformer" (Ph.D. diss., Claremont Graduate School, 1988), 145.

16. Ibid., 143.

17. "Rich Altadenan up in Girl Case," 7.

18. "Pastor's Foe Found Guilty, C. C. Stafford, El Monte Man, Fined $250 for Attack on Rev. Shuler after Conviction," *Los Angeles Times*, August 2, 1929, p. A1; "Battery Charge against Stafford," *El Monte Herald*, July 26, 1929, p. 1.

19. "Battery Charge against Stafford," 1.

20. "Shuler Battle Case Deferred: Drug Store Fight Set for Monday," *Los Angeles Times*, July 26, 1929, p. A1.

21. "Pleads for an Aroused Civic Consciousness: Pastor Denounces Those Who Frequent Suburban 'Hell Holes' and Drag Southland's Name in Dust," *Los Angeles Times*, December 27, 1920, p. B1.

22. Tygiel, *The Great Los Angeles Swindle*, 248

23. Matt Garcia, *A World of Its Own: Race, Labor, and Citrus in the Making of Greater Los Angeles, 1900–1970* (Chapel Hill: University of North Carolina Press, 2001), 91–92.

24. Carolyn Kitch, *The Girl on the Magazine Cover* (Chapel Hill: University of North Carolina Press, 2001), 60–61.

25. Robert Cushman, introduction, in *Mary Pickford Rediscovered: Rare Pictures of a Hollywood Legend*, by Kevin Brownlow (New York: Abrams; Academy of Motion Picture Arts and Sciences, 1999), 32; Eileen Whitfield, *Pickford: The Woman Who Made Hollywood* (Lexington: University Press of Kentucky, 1997), 94.

26. Whitfield, *Pickford*, 126.

27. Ibid., 126.

28. Ibid., 59–60.

29. Ibid., 128.

30. "Girl Attacked by Employer, Charge," *Los Angeles Record*, evening ed., March 25, 1929, p. 1.

31. "Girl to Accuse Stafford in Court," *Los Angeles Evening Herald*, October 30, 1929, p. A2.

32. "Stafford Case Girl on Stand, Miss Schade Gives Version of Asserted Attack, Luring to Lonely Cabin in Canyon Charged, Cross-examination Hints at Aims of Defense," *Los Angeles Times*, May 7, 1929, p. A17.

33. "Stafford Unable to Face Trial: Grain Dealer's Illness Delays Hearing on Charge of Statutory Rape," *Los Angeles Times*, September 20, 1929, p. A3.

34. "Defense in Stafford Case Open: Doctors Tell of Finding Bruises on Girl Accuser of El Monte Grain Dealer," *Los Angeles Times*, November 2, 1929, p. A16.

35. Ibid.

36. "Girl's Attack Story Stands: Cross-Examination Fails to Shake Testimony Given by Miss Schade," *Los Angeles Evening Express*, October 31, 1929, p. 3.

37. "Stafford Case Girl Testifies, Begin Presenting Evidence against Rich Man Accused in Attack," *Los Angeles Evening Express*, October 30, 1929, p. 4; Girl Accuser of Stafford Grilled," *Los Angeles Evening Herald*, October 30, 1929, p. A19.

38. "Girl Holds to Attack Story: Stafford's Accuser Ends Turn on Stand," *Los Angeles Times*, November 1, 1929, p. A16; "Girl's Parents to Tell Attack," *Los Angeles Record*, November 1, 1929, p. 1.

39. "Rich Altadenan up in Girl Case," 7.

40. "'Petting Party' Stafford Plea," Accused El Monte Broker Pleads Complaisance, Witnesses Tell of Actions of Girl Plaintiff, Embraces in Car Testified after Asserted Attack," *Los Angeles Times*, November 5, 1929, p. A12.

41. "C. C. Stafford Found Guilty; Grain Man Faces Term of One to Fifty Years," *Los Angeles Times*, November 10, 1929, p. A3; judgment book entry, *The People of the State of California, Plaintiff, v. Clayton C. Stafford, Defendant*, case no. 37,052, November 22, 1929.

42. "C. C. Stafford Found Guilty," A3.

43. *The People of the State of California, Plaintiff, v. Clayton C. Stafford, Defendant*, 3–4.

44. "Stafford Hurt in Jail Prank," *Los Angeles Times*, March 16, 1930, p. A12.

45. "Stafford Wins in Attack Case: El Monte Merchant Freed by Court," *Los Angeles Times*, November 20, 1930, p. 9.

46. Ibid.

CHAPTER 2 — A LEGACY OF DEBT, RAILS, AND NOOSES

1. "Death Notices," *Los Angeles Examiner*, March 2, 1942, sec. 1, p. 16.

2. McDougal, *Privileged Son*, 71; Roger Vincent, "At the End of the Line, a New Beginning for Historic Site," *Los Angeles Times*, November 5, 2002, p. C1.

3. Robert T. Lyans, "The Livestock Bulletin," *Los Angeles Times*, May 8, 1921, sec. 9, 15; "Landmark Goes at El Monte for New Structure" [local correspondence], January 11, 1925, p. E8; "El Monte Gets City Delivery of Mail" [local correspondence], October 4, 1925, p. 18; "Gains of Four Towns Recited: New Schools Highlight of Covina for Year," March 18, 1928, p. E3; "Will Feed Cattle," September 30, 1928, p. J4.

4. "Society: El Monte," *Los Angeles Times*, May 9, 1926, p. C1; "Society: El Monte," November 11, 1926, p. C7; "How Host and Hostesses of Season Entertain Their Guests: El Monte," February 2, 1927, p. C1.

5. "Al Smith Banquet Shrinks: Candidate on Democratic Ticket Orders Fifty Plates, but Soon Cuts down to Twenty-five, Then Only Eleven Diners Show Up," *Los Angeles Times*, August 24, 1928, p. A8.

6. "Abbey Changes to Stafford St.," *City of Industry News* 14 (October 1975): 1.

7. *Civic-Recreational-Industrial Authority v. James Marty Stafford*, case no. 84-7983, MRP, LA 194C-431-143-367, 9:1.

8. "'Nut Factory Blows Tooter': Puente Folk Complain That Whistle Sounds Like Fire Alarm," *Los Angeles Times*, May 2, 1928, p. A15.

9. "Abbey Changed to Stafford St.," 1.

10. Ibid.

11. Ibid.

12. "Stafford-Yorba Nuptials Celebrated," *City of Industry News* 7 (February 1973): 4.

13. "Abbey Changes to Stafford St.," 1.

14. Annual report of C. C. Stafford Milling and Warehouse Company, Inc., of Puente California, to the Railroad Commission of the State of California, for the year ending on December 31, 1937, p. 4.

15. Sandra Lee Snider, *Elias Jackson "Lucky" Baldwin: California Visionary* (Los Angeles: Stairwell Group, 1987), 58–60; grant deed, February 5, 1920, *Los Angeles County General Index of Grantors*, book 7,082, pp. 220–11.

16. *James O. Hamilton, et al., Plaintiff, v. James M. Stafford, et al., Defendant*, case no. 788,108, Los Angeles Superior Court, January 23, 1962; annual report of C. C. Stafford Milling and Warehouse Company, Puente, California, to the Railroad Commission of the State of California, for the year ending December 31, 1937, p. 2.

17. Annual report of C. C. Stafford Milling and Warehouse Company, 4.

18. "Abbey Changed to Stafford St.," 1.

19. "Abbey Changes to Stafford St.," 1.

20. Michel Foucault, "Nietzsche, Genealogy, History," in *Language, Counter-memory, Practice: Selected Essays and Interviews*, ed. Donald F. Bouchard (Ithaca, N.Y.: Cornell University Press, 1977), 146.

21. Michel Foucault, *The Order of Things: An Archaeology of the Human Sciences* (New York: Vintage, 1970), 200–201.

22. Marieke De Goede, *A Genealogy of Finance: Virtue, Fortune, and Faith* (Minneapolis: University of Minnesota Press, 2005), 26.

23. Ibid., 35–37.

24. Abstract of judgment, grantor C. C. Stafford, grantee Benjamin Tammler, February 2, 1928, *General Record of the County of Los Angeles*, book 8,026, p. 390, doc. 1,661; execution of judgment, March 17, 1928, *General Record of the County of Los Angeles*, book 7,856, p. 107, doc. 1,602; sheriff's certification of sale, April 28, 1928, *General Record of the County of Los Angeles*, book 7,731, p. 372, doc. 1,665.

25. *Civic-Recreational-Industrial Authority v. James Marty Stafford*, LA 194C-431-143, 9:2.

26. Trust deed, March 12, 1929, *General Record of the County of Los Angeles*, book 9,135, p. 51, doc. 641.

27. Ralph Selitzer, *The Dairy Industry in America* (New York: Dairy and Ice Cream Field; Books for Industry, 1976). 330.

28. Ibid., 335.

29. Abstract of judgment, May 5, 1931, *General Record of the County of Los*

Angeles, book 10,834, p. 365, doc. 1,212; grant deed, April 17, 1931, *General Record of the County of Los Angeles,* book 10,864, p. 14, doc. 982.

30. Articles of incorporation of Southwestern Feeding Yard, Inc., filed with State of California, Office of the Secretary of State, June 7, 1932, pp. 1–4; C. C. Stafford, itemized account, Southwestern Feeding Yards, Inc., January 1, 1938–March 2, 1942, p. 1, contained *In the Matter of the Estate of Clayton C. Stafford,* case no. 212-817, filed in Los Angeles County Superior Court, May 12, 1944.

31. Grant deed, December 7, 1933, *General Record of the County of Los Angeles,* book 12,436, p. 345, doc. 49; trust deed, July 31, 1935, *General Record of the County of Los Angeles,* book 13,471, p. 371, doc. 405.

32. Ronald W. Lopez, "The El Monte Berry Strike of 1933," *Aztlan* 1 (spring 1970): 101–4.

33. Luis Leobardo Arroyo, "Chicano Participation in Organized Labor: The CIO in Los Angeles, 1938–1950," *Aztlan* 6, no. 2 (1975): 277–86.

34. Annual report of C. C. Stafford Milling and Warehouse Company, 1–4.

35. "Puente Hay Dealer Charged with Assault," *Los Angeles Times,* March 8, 1938, p. A2; annual report of C. C. Stafford Milling and Warehouse Company, 4.

36. Abstract of judgment, October 5, 1938, *General Record of the County of Los Angeles,* book 16,036, p. 351, doc. 954; execution order, March 7, 1939, *General Record of the County of Los Angeles,* book 16,440, p. 273, doc. 853; sheriff's certificate of sale, May 17, 1939, *General Record of the County of Los Angeles,* book 16,608, p. 201, doc. 1,388.

37. Quitclaim deed, September 2, 1937, *General Record of the County of Los Angeles,* book 15,207, p. 197, doc. 1,270.

38. Richard Bigger and James D. Kitchen, *How the Cities Grew: A Century of Municipal Independence and Expansionism in Metropolitan Los Angeles* (Los Angeles: University of California, Bureau of Government Research, 1952), 8, 15, 84; James E. Vance, Jr., "Human Mobility and the Shaping of Cities," in *Our Changing Cities,* ed. John Fraser Hart (Baltimore: Johns Hopkins University Press, 1991), 78–80.

39. *In the Matter of the Estate of Clayton C. Stafford;* Stephen Stafford, personal interview conducted and tape-recorded by Allen Maltun, May 24, 1984; *Civic-Recreational-Industrial Authority v. James Marty Stafford,* LA 194C-143-367, 9:2.

40. Grant deed, January 24, 1940, *General Record of the County of Los Angeles,* book 17,173, p. 288, doc. 607.

41. Notice of action, July 2, 1941, *General Record of the County of Los Angeles,* book 18,574, p. 136, doc. 1,600; quitclaim deed, December 16, 1943, *General Record of the County of Los Angeles,* book 205,17, p. 167, doc. 491.

42. *Civic-Recreational-Industrial Authority v. James Marty Stafford,* LA 194C-143-367, 5:3.

43. The following city maps show a Southern Pacific rail spur running onto the mill's property: "Factors Affecting Development of the Civic-Financial Center," in

The General Plan of the City of Industry (City of Industry, Calif.: Industry Urban Development Agency, May 1971), 29; Zody's participation agreement, in "Industry Urban Development Agency Owner Participation Agreement," March 21, 1977, exhibit C.

44. "Grain Merchant and Two Others Victims of Traffic: Clayton C. Stafford Injured Fatally after Auto Stalls on Rails and Then Hits Truck," *Los Angeles Times*, March 1, 1942, sec. 2, p. 15.

45. C. C. Stafford's death certificate filed at the Los Angeles County Hall of Records, March 5, 1942; register entry signed by Coroner Frank A. Nanse and Deputy Coroner F. R. Monfort on March 5, 1942, County of Los Angeles, Department of Coroner, case no. 3,555, pp. 212–13.

46. Adrian Acevedo, M.D., a Kaiser Hospital emergency physician provided a written interpretation of C. C. Stafford's autopsy (email communication, September 16, 2005).

47. C. C. Stafford's death certificate, filed at the Los Angeles County Hall of Records, March 5, 1942; Los Angeles County coroner's register entry signed by Coroner Frank A. Nanse and Deputy Coroner F. R. Monfort, March 5, 1942, filed with the County of Los Angeles, Department of the Coroner, case no. 3,555, pp. 212–13; "Abbey Changes to Stafford St.," 1.

48. *Civic-Recreational-Industrial Authority v. James Marty Stafford*, LA 194C-143-367, 9:3.

49. New York Life insurance agent Marisha Chinsky wrote, "Unfortunately, we are not allowed to provide information about policyholders" (email communication, August 2, 2001).

50. Chattel mortgage, April 2, 1938, *General Record of the County of Los Angeles*, book 15,718, p. 106, doc. 672; chattel mortgage, August 18, 1938, *General Record of the County of Los Angeles*, book 15,970, p. 138, doc. 1,090; chattel mortgage, August 3, 1943, *General Record of the County of Los Angeles*, book 20,058, p. 190, doc. 1,097.

51. *In the Matter of the Estate of Clayton C. Stafford*, p. 3, schedule C.

52. Continuation of a lease agreement between C. C. Stafford and the Southern Pacific Company and its subsidiary the Pacific Electric Railway, May 16, 1924, *Los Angeles County General Property Record*, book 4,031, p. 149, doc. 1,591.

53. William Deverell, *Railroad Crossings: Californians and the Railroad, 1850–1910* (Berkeley: University of California Press, 1994), 130, 132.

54. Richard Saunders, Jr., *Merging Lines: American Railroads, 1900–1970* (DeKalb: Northern Illinois University Press, 2001), 15.

55. Roy Scott, *Railroad Development Programs in the Twentieth Century* (Ames: Iowa State University Press, 1985), 58.

56. Ibid., 4.

57. Ibid., 62.

58. Ibid., 4.

59. Ibid., 5–6.

60. Ibid., 13.

61. Deverell, *Railroad Crossings*, 145–46; Scott, *Railroad Development Programs*, 151.

62. E. O. Edwards, Geo[rge] T. Hanly, and John M. Davies, "Manufactures: Advantages of Los Angeles As a Manufacturing Point," *Los Angeles Times*, June 7, 1882, p. O3.

63. Quoted in Steven P. Erie, *Globalizing L.A.: Trade, Infrastructure, and Regional Development* (Stanford, Calif.: Stanford University Press, 2004), 45.

64. Garcia, *A World of Its Own*, 19.

65. John A. Nevins, "The Puente Area: A Study of Changing Agricultural Land Use," (M.S. thesis, University of California, Los Angeles, September 1951), fig. 24.

66. Ibid., p. 22.

67. Harry A. Gillis, Jr., and George R. Watts, *City of Industry: Its Economic Characteristics and Significance, 1957–1970*, project no. IS-4624 (South Pasadena: Stanford Research Institute, Southern California Laboratories, June 1964), 25; William F. King, *The San Gabriel Valley: Chronicles of an Abundant Land* (Windsor, Calif.: Alhambra Chamber of Commerce, 1990), 13.

68. "Events in El Monte: 1851–1937," [El Monte Historical Society and Museum] *Gazette*, n.d., p. 3.

69. Ibid., 26.

70. Ibid., 27.

71. Ibid., 33–34, 92.

72. Gilda L. Ochoa, *Becoming Neighbors in a Mexican American Community: Power, Conflict, and Solidarity* (Austin: University of Texas Press, 2004), 47–48.

73. King, *The San Gabriel Valley*, 11, 13, 18, 47; William F. King, "The Vintage Years: Our Valley before 1945" [white paper] (Walnut, Calif.: Mount San Antonio Community College Services, n.d.); *The Volume and Reference Works: Covering Bassett, City of Industry, La Habra, La Mirada, La Puente, Pico Rivera, Santa Fe Springs, Walnut, and Whittier* (Whittier, Calif.: Gallup, Martin, and Shepard, 1963), 2:21–24, 49, 56–59, 427–34, 467–78.

74. Ochoa, *Becoming Neighbors in a Mexican American Community*, 50–51; minutes of the board of trustees, El Monte Grammar School District, December 23, 1925; letters from the El Monte Grammar School District's superintendent Frank Wright to the board of trustees, February 22, 1927, and February 11, 1929; minutes of the board of trustees of the El Monte School District, May 10, 1938; "Bittersweet Memories: El Monte Museum Will Tell Local Mexican-American Community's Story—the Good Times and the Bad," *Los Angeles Times*, November 22, 2000, p. E2.

75. Lopez, "The El Monte Berry Strike of 1933," 103.

76. I obtained my copy of the El Monte Historical Museum's Gazette from the museum's reception desk in July 2005.

77. "'Monte Boys' Were Feared Vigilantes of Pioneer Days," [El Monte Historical Museum] *Gazette*, n.d., p. 1. Curator Donna Crippen said that the pamphlet's source materials come from the museum's *El Monte Herald* newspaper archive and that it is periodically reprinted (telephone interview, March 27, 2003; unless otherwise noted, all interviews were by the author).

78. Fred Love, El Monte History Museum docent and research librarian, telephone interview, July 3, 2001.

79. Ruby Gonzales and Steve Scauzillo, "Newspaper Stories Ran the Gamut," *San Gabriel Valley Tribune*, March 21, 2005, pp. 1–2.

80. Harold D. Carew, *History of Pasadena and the San Gabriel Valley: With Personal Sketches of Those Men and Women, Past and Present, Who Have Builded This "Glorious Empire within an Empire"* (Chicago: Clarke, 1930), 340.

81. Still, "'Fighting Bob' Shuler," 143.

82. "Monte Boys," 1.

83. "Landmark Goes at El Monte for New Structure" [local correspondence], *Los Angeles Times*, January 11, 1925, p. E8.

84. *Civic-Recreational-Industrial Authority v. James Marty Stafford*, LA 194C-431-143-367, 9:3.

CHAPTER 3 — IN THE SCHOOL OF POWER

1. *Civic-Recreational-Industrial Authority v. James Marty Stafford*, LA 194C-431-143-54, 12:1.

2. Ibid., LA 194C-431-143-62, 3:2.

3. Ibid., LA 194C-431-143-367, 9:4.

4. Rosie Ruiz, secretary of the Los Angeles County Regional Planning Commission, said that James M. Stafford served on the commission from 1954 through 1956 (email communication, July 28, 2003); "In the San Gabriel Valley Spotlight," *Los Angeles Times*, January 3, 1954, p. F8; Valdis Vilnis Pavlovskis, "The Economic and Fiscal Impact of the City of Industry on the Surrounding Communities" (M.A. thesis, California State Polytechnic University, 1973), 33.

5. Eric Avila, *Popular Culture in the Age of White Flight: Fear and Fantasy in Suburban Los Angeles* (Berkeley: University of California Press, 2004), 32–34, 40–41.

6. William Fulton, *The Reluctant Metropolis: The Politics of Urban Growth in Los Angeles* (Point Arena, Calif.: Solano, 1997), 14–15.

7. Roger W. Lotchin, *Fortress California, 1910–1961: From Warfare to Welfare* (Urbana: University of Illinois Press, 2002), 182.

8. Kenneth C. Burt, *The Search for a Civic Voice: California Latino Politics* (Claremont, Calif.: Regina, 2007), 18; Seth I. Colver, *The Historical Volume and Reference Works*, 2:108.

9. Edwards et al., "Manufactures," O3; Colver, *The Historical Volume and Reference Works*, 2:112.

10. Southern Pacific Railroad Company, "Sixty-First Annual Report Year Ended December 31, 1944" (San Francisco, 1944), 3; Southern Pacific Railroad Company, "Sixty-Second Annual Report Year Ended December 31, 1945" (San Francisco, 1945), 11; Southern Pacific Railroad Company, "Sixty-Fourth Annual Report Year Ended December 31, 1947" (San Francisco, 1947), 3.

11. Victor Valle, "Industry: Land Buyer Held a Key to Cityhood," *Los Angeles Times*, San Gabriel Valley ed., April 22, 1984, p. 1; Southern Pacific Railroad Company, "Sixty-Eighth Annual Report Year Ended December 31, 1951" (San Francisco, 1951), 1; Southern Pacific Railroad Company, "Sixty-Ninth Annual Report Year Ended December 31, 1952" (San Francisco, 1952), 14; Southern Pacific Transportation Company, CADD Bureau, "City of Industry Constructs Additional Tracks" [map], February 16, 1990, in the records of the Southern Pacific Railroad Company, Stanford University Libraries, M1010, RG-2, tube 237. The map shows the yard's planned expansion from eight to twenty-three siding lines.

12. Larry Mullaly and Bruce Petty, *The Southern Pacific in Los Angeles: 1873–1996* (San Marino, Calif.: Golden West Books; Los Angeles Railroad Heritage Foundation, 2002), 231; Gillis and Watts, *City of Industry*, 11, 25–26.

13. The words of Wilfred W. Steiner, former Southern Pacific land buyer, offer an insight into the rail giant's vision for the city: "A little about the Southern Pacific, departing from my prepared text. [Industry] was hand picked for its location with respect to the ports, with respect to transportation, with respect to the freeways, it's an ideal location for industry, and we've been tremendously successful" (testimony to the Foreign-Trade Zone Board, U.S. Department of Commerce, Washington, D.C., January 27, 1982). In his convoluted remark, Steiner clearly credits the railroad with the invention of Industry and betrays his habit of still seeing himself as a Southern Pacific employee.

14. Bill Boyarsky and Nancy Boyarsky, *Backroom Politics: How Your Local Politicians Work, Why Your Government Doesn't, and What You Can Do about It* (Los Angeles: Tarcher, 1974), 54.

15. Edward W. Soja. "Los Angeles, 1965–1992: From Crisis-Generated Restructuring to Restructuring-Generated Crisis," in *The City: Los Angeles and Urban Theory at the End of the Twentieth Century*, eds. Allen J. Scott and Edward W. Soja (Berkeley: University of California Press, 1996), 429–30.

16. J. Morgan Kousser, *Colorblind Injustice: Minority Voting Rights and the Undoing of the Second Reconstruction* (Chapel Hill: University of North Carolina Press, 1999), 72.

17. Ibid., 53–54.

18. Kenneth Hahn, telephone interview with *Los Angeles Times* reporter Dan Morain, February 2, 1984.

19. Harold H. Lutz, letter to the Los Angeles County Board of Supervisors, August 29, 1956, in the board's file on the incorporation of the City of Industry; Kenneth Hahn, interview with *Los Angeles Times* reporter Dan Morain, February 20, 1984.

20. Gary Miller, *Cities by Contract: The Politics of Municipal Incorporation* (Cambridge, Mass.: MIT Press, 1981), 48.

21. Los Angeles County Regional Planning Commission, *The East San Gabriel Valley: An Area Use Plan* (Los Angeles, April 2, 1956), 3.

22. Miller, *Cities by Contract*, 16.

23. "Lakewood: The City As New As Tomorrow, 1949–1959, Part 1 of 3 Parts," accessed on July 27, 2007, from http://www.lakewoodcity.org/civica/inc/display-blobpdf2.asp?BlobID=2162; John S. Todd [Lakewood city attorney], "A History of Lakewood, 1949–1954," accessed on July 27, 2007, from http://www.lakewoodcity.org/civica/inc/displayblobpdf2.asp?BlobID=2162.

24. Miller, *Cities by Contract*, 17.

25. Todd, "A History of Lakewood."

26. Miller, *Cities by Contract*, 12.

27. Todd, "A History of Lakewood."

28. Ibid.

29. Miller, *Cities by Contract*, 20–21.

30. Steven P. Erie, "Los Angeles As a Developmental City-State," in *From Chicago to L.A.: Making Sense of Urban Theory*, ed. Michael J. Dear (Thousand Oaks, Calif.: Sage, 2002), 136.

31. Robert O. Warren, *Government in Metropolitan Regions: A Reappraisal of Fractionated Political Organization* (Davis: University of California, Institute of Governmental Affairs, 1966), 112–14.

32. Dan Morain and Victor Valle, "City of Industry: It Has Clout Where It Counts—in the State Capitol," *Los Angeles Times*, April 5, 1984, p. A3.

33. Miller, *Cities by Contract*, 22–23.

34. Todd, "A History of Lakewood."

35. Miller, *Cities by Contract*, 31–32.

36. Todd, "A History of Lakewood."

37. Miller, *Cities by Contract*, 30–31.

38. Ibid., 33.

39. Ibid., 29–30.

CHAPTER 4 — GRADUATION DAY

1. *Civic-Recreational-Industrial Authority v. James Marty Stafford*, LA 194C-431-143-52, 2:1.

2. "Puente District Eyes Bright Future" [local correspondence], *Los Angeles Times*, May 23, 1954, p. F7.

3. *Civic-Recreational-Industrial Authority v. James Marty Stafford*, LA 194C-431-143-77, 3:3.

4. Deposition of Matthew Patritti, in *County of Los Angeles, City of Industry v. Consumers Holding Co.*, case no. 937,385, Superior Court of the State of California, July 1, 1969, pp. 29, 35.

5. Marianne Dissard, Amy Kitchener, Spike Marlin, Renee Nahum, Paul M. Neuman, and Dolores Petullo, eds., *City of Vernon: A Collection of Oral Histories* (City of Vernon, Calif., 1995), 7–9.

6. Ibid., 8.

7. Ibid., 7–9; Mike Davis, "Sunshine and the Open Shop," in *Metropolis in the Making: Los Angeles in the 1920s*, ed. Tom Sitton and William Deverell (Berkeley: University of California Press, 2001), 106–7.

8. Davis, "Sunshine and the Open Shop," 106.

9. Mike Davis, "The Empty Quarter" in *Sex, Death and God in L.A.*, ed. David Reid (New York: Pantheon, 1992), 58–59.

10. Charles John Hock, "City Limits: Municipal Boundary Formation and Class Segregation in Los Angeles Suburbs" (Ph.D. diss., University of California, Los Angeles, 1981), 209–10.

11. Robert S. Gorman [commission chair], introductory letter, in Los Angeles County Regional Planning Commission, *The East San Gabriel Valley*, 18; City of Industry, official history narrative, accessed on February 18, 2009, from *http://www.cityofindustry.org/picbase/picbase_dex.html*.

12. John R. Logan and Harvey L. Molotch, *Urban Fortunes: The Political Economy of Place* (Berkeley: University of California Press, 1987), 30–31.

13. Ibid., 29.

14. "Puente Files Cityhood Petition Second Time," *Los Angeles Times*, December 25, 1955, p. G1; Colver, *The Historical Volume and Reference Works*, 2:108; Pavlovskis, "The Economic and Fiscal Impact of the City of Industry," 15; Gillis and Watts, *City of Industry*, 27.

15. *People v. Herbert C. Legg*, grand jury indictment, case no. 175,786, Los Angeles Superior Court, October 6, 1955, pp. 1–10.

16. Pavlovskis, "The Economic and Fiscal Impact of the City of Industry," 30.

17. Miller, *Cities by Contract*, 50; Pavlovskis, "The Economic and Fiscal Impact of the City of Industry," 33–34.

18. Chester McIntosh, interview with *Los Angeles Times* reporter Dan Morain, February 2, 1984.

19. Miller, *Cities by Contract*, 48; Dan Morain and Victor Valle, "City of Industry Founder Indicted in Kickback Case," *Los Angeles Times*, April 12, 1984, p. A14; Pavlovskis, "The Economic and Fiscal Impact of the City of Industry," 33–34.

20. Boyarsky and Boyarsky, *Backroom Politics*, 58.

21. Los Angeles County Regional Planning Commission, *The East San Gabriel Valley*, 8.

22. *Civic-Recreational-Industrial Authority v. James Marty Stafford*, LA 194C-431-143-557, 12:1.

23. Gillis and Watts, *City of Industry*, 28; Scot J. Paltrow, "The City of Insiders: How the Rich Get Richer," *Los Angeles Herald Examiner*, June 25, 1980, p. A14.

24. General statement of information about the City of Industry's incorporation petition, filed with the Los Angeles County Board of Supervisors, June 11, 1956.

25. "New City of Industry's Boundaries Cause Delay: County Sets Hearing for Tuesday on Municipality with Only 100 Voters," *Los Angeles Times*, September 7, 1956, p. B6.

26. Edward J. Martin and Rodolfo D. Torres, *Savage State: Welfare Capitalism and Inequality* (Lanham, Md.: Rowman and Littlefield, 2004), 91.

27. Deverell, *Railroad Crossings*, 130, 132.

28. "Incorporation Code Revision to Be Sought," *Los Angeles Times*, October 19, 1956, p. A7; "Court Refuses to Halt City of Industry Vote," *Los Angeles Times*, November 30, 1956, p. B6.

29. "Writ Petitioned to Halt Industry City Election," *Los Angeles Times*, November 2, 1956, A28.

30. Hahn, interview with Morain, February 2, 1984; "City of Industry Protest Hearing Scheduled Nov. 23," *Los Angeles Times*, November 15, 1956, p. B11; Miller, *Cities by Contract*, 48; "Supervisors to Seek Laws on New Cities," *Los Angeles Times*, December 12, 1956, p. B12.

31. "Writ Petitioned to Halt Industry City Election," *Los Angeles Times*, November 2, 1956, p. 28.

32. "City of Industry Votes Today on Incorporation: Ballot to Settle Controversial Issue in Eastern San Gabriel Valley Area," *Los Angeles Times*, December 4, 1956, p. A9; "Industry City Status Snagged," *Los Angeles Times*, December 16, 1956, sec. 1, p. 1.

33. Miller, *Cities by Contract*, 23, 49.

34. Victor Valle, "Land Buyer Held a Key to Cityhood," *Los Angeles Times*, San Gabriel Valley ed., April 22, 1984, pp. 1, 7.

35. Ibid., 16.

36. "Industry City Status Snagged," *Los Angeles Times*, December 16, 1956, sec. 1, p. 1.

37. James F. Judge, telephone interview by *Los Angeles Times* reporter Dan Morain, February 7, 1984.

38. Valle, "Land Buyer Held a Key to Cityhood," 1, 7.

39. Option agreement, June 3, 1957, *General Record of the County of Los Angeles*, book 56,013, pp. 441–43, doc. 3,512; assignment of option, July 11, 1957, General Record of the County of Los Angeles, book 56,232, pp. 350–51, doc. 3,475.

40. Robert G. Beverly, telephone interview by *Los Angeles Times* reporter Dan Morain, February 7, 1984.

41. Valle, "Land Buyer Held a Key to Cityhood," 7.

42. Assignment of option, recorded July 11, 1957.

43. "Three Cities Incorporate," in *History of La Puente Valley, California: Reprints from the October, 6, 1960, 50th Anniversary Edition of the "La Puente Valley Journal" and Supplementary Articles, 1910–1960,* UCLA Special Collections, F868, L8H57, URLSCRA-B, p. 3.

44. Gillis and Watts, *City of Industry*, 45.

45. Darlene Hudson [Los Angeles County archivist], email communication, July 14, 2003.

46. "Herbert Legg, County Supervisor, Dies at 69," *Los Angeles Times*, March 28, 1958, p. A1; "Herbert C. Legg Funeral Monday," *Los Angeles Times*, March 29, 1958, p. A2; "Knight Defers Naming Legg Successor," *Los Angeles Times*, March 29, 1958, p. A2; "Supervisor Herbert C. Legg," *Los Angeles Times*, March 29, 1958, p. A4; and "Legg Hailed As Builder in Eulogy at Funeral," *Los Angeles Times*, April 1, 1958, p. C3.

47. Boyarsky and Boyarsky, *Backroom Politics*, 59, 63.

48. Ibid., 60; *Civic-Recreational-Industrial Authority v. James Marty Stafford*, LA 194C-431-143-170, 8:1.

49. Deposition of James M. Stafford, in *City of Industry v. Consumers Holding Co., et al.*, case no. 93,7385, Superior Court of the State of California, August 11, 1969, p. 95.

50. Pavlovskis, "The Economic and Fiscal Impact of the City of Industry," 37; deposition of James M. Stafford, case no. 937,385, pp. 97–98.

51. Pavlovskis, "The Economic and Fiscal Impact of the City of Industry," 110–13.

52. Miller, *Cities by Contract*, 50.

CHAPTER 5 — "WE DON'T LIKE THE DIRTY DEAL"

1. *Civic-Recreational-Industrial Authority v. James Marty Stafford*, LA 194C-431-143-365, 9:4–5.

2. Ibid., LA 194C-143-431-52, 2:2.

3. Paltrow, "The City of Insiders: How the Rich Get Richer," A10; "Grand Jury May Probe Land Deal: Industry Council to Seek Inquiry into Protestors Motives," *Los Angeles Times*, February 1, 1962, p. F1.

4. "Tycoon's Visit: Industry Plans Lunch for President of SP," *San Gabriel Valley Daily Tribune*, South Valley ed., January 5, 1962, p. 33.

5. "Rail President Tells Growth in Industry," *San Gabriel Valley Daily Tribune*, South Valley ed., January 10, 1962, p. 29.

6. Robert Gottlieb and Irene Wolt, *Thinking Big: The Story of the Los Angeles*

Times, Its Publishers, and Their Influence on Southern California (New York: Putnam, 1977), 527.

7. *Civic-Recreational-Industrial Authority v. James Marty Stafford*, LA 194C-143-431-52, 2:2; Paltrow, "The City of Insiders: How the Rich Get Richer," A10.

8. *James O. Hamilton, et al., v. James M. Stafford, et al.*, 7.

9. "City Leaders Named in Fraud Suit: Taxpayers Claim Price on Substation Land Is Too High," *Los Angeles Times*, San Gabriel Valley ed., January 26, 1962, p. A1; "Grand Jury May Probe Land Deal: Industry Council to Seek Inquiry into Protestors' Motives," *Los Angeles Times*, San Gabriel Valley ed., February 1, 1962, p. F1; "City of Industry Head Tells of Death Threat," *Los Angeles Times*, 2d ed., March 24, 1962, p. C7; "D.A. Given Report in Vote Quiz: Industry Attorney Says Registrar Has Jurisdiction," *Los Angeles Times*, April 26, 1962, p. H1.

10. "10 Industry Officials Face Fraud Charge: Plaintiffs Claim 'Deal' on Land," *San Gabriel Valley Tribune*, January 24, 1962, p. 1.

11. James O. Hamilton, letter to Judge Edward Rafeedie, November 20, 1984.

12. "City Leaders Named in Fraud Suit," A1; "Grand Jury May Probe Land Deal," A3.

13. "Industry's Manager Thrives in Arena of City Politics," *Los Angeles Times*, San Gabriel Valley ed., August 5, 1973, pp. 5, 7.

14. "Grand Jury May Probe Land Deal," F1; "City of Industry Head Tells of Death Threat," C7.

15. "Industry City Contract Will Be Discussed," *Los Angeles Times*, October 22, 1962, p. B2; "City Approves De-Annexation," *Los Angeles Times*, San Gabriel Valley ed., January 10, 1963, p. A1; Hamilton, letter to Rafeedie.

16. See sections stricken on April 18, 1962, from *James O. Hamilton, et al., v. James M. Stafford, et al.*, 1–25.

17. Paltrow, "The City of Insiders: How the Rich Get Richer," A10; "Legal Battle over Sheriff's Station Ended," *Los Angeles Times*, February 12, 1964, p. A2.

18. *Civic-Recreational-Industrial Authority v. James Marty Stafford*, LA 194C-143-431-52, 2:3; Hamilton, letter to Rafeedie; Scot J. Paltrow, "The City of Insiders: Landowners under the Officials' Thumbs," *Los Angeles Herald Examiner*, July 2, 1980, p. A11.

19. *Civic-Recreational-Industrial Authority v. James Marty Stafford*, LA 194C-431-143-880, 17:1.

20. Ibid., LA 194C-431-143-77, 3:3.

21. Ibid., LA 194C-431-143-50, 2:2.

22. Paltrow, "The City of Insiders: How the Rich Get Richer," A10.

23. *Civic-Recreational-Industrial Authority v. James Marty Stafford*, LA 194C-431-143-77, 3:6.

24. Ibid., LA 194C-431-143-29, 7:7; LA 194C-431-143-870, 17:3.

25. Helene Stapinski, *Five-Finger Discount: A Crooked Family History* (New York: Random House, 2001), 37.

26. *Civic Recreational-Industrial Authority v. James Marty Stafford*, LA 194C-431-143-239, 6:1; LA 194C-431-143-29, 7:2–3.

27. Scot J. Paltrow, "The City of Insiders: How the Mayor Farms City Land for Free," *Los Angeles Herald Examiner*, June 30, 1980, pp. C3, C10.

28. *Civic-Recreational-Industrial Authority v. James Marty Stafford*, LA 194C-431-143-87, 17:2.

29. Ibid., LA 194C-143-703, 15:4.

30. Gillis and Watt, *City of Industry*, iii.

31. Ibid., 10, 139; Bob Diebold, "Richest in Valley: City Spawns Factory Products, not People," *Los Angeles Times*, San Gabriel Valley ed., June 26, 1966, p. A6.

32. Gillis and Watt, *City of Industry*, 45; Miller, *Cities by Contract*, 50.

33. Gillis and Watt, *City of Industry*, 10, 49.

34. Ibid., 15.

35. Ibid., 2, 9.

36. *The General Plan of the City of Industry*, 40.

37. *Jane Chilcott Stafford and James M. Stafford*, case no. SED52447, December 26, 1975 p. 2, exhibits A–E and attachment A; *Civic-Recreational-Industrial Authority v. James Marty Stafford*, LA 194C-431-143-249, 7:11.

38. Richard Main, "Churchill Coach: City of Industry and Parliament Tangle," *Los Angeles Times*, August 31, 1965, p. B1.

39. "Briton's Plea Fails: Churchill's Funeral Coach on Way Here," *Los Angeles Times*, October 29, 1965, p. C17.

40. "City of Industry Sets Vote on Park, Exposition Center," *Los Angeles Times*, San Gabriel Valley ed., October 29, 1967, p. A6; "Voters Approve $8.5 Million Issue: Work on Industry's 500-Acre Park to Start This Summer," *Los Angeles Times*, January 18, 1968, p. A2.

41. Pavlovskis, "The Economic and Fiscal Impact of the City of Industry," 74.

42. Diebold, "Richest in Valley," A1, A6, A7.

43. Ibid., A6.

44. "Industry's Manager Thrives in Arena of City Politics," A7; Miller, *Cities by Contract*, 44—45; Paltrow, "The City of Insiders: How the Rich Get Richer," A10.

45. "Waste Firm Seeks to Block Lifting of Permit: Court Hearing Set Monday," *Los Angeles Times*, San Gabriel Valley ed., April 8, 1969, p. A4.

46. "Industry Has Half of Land for Park, Exposition Center," *Los Angeles Times*, San Gabriel Valley ed., August 11, 1968, p. A1.

47. Charles Elwell, "Dump's Fate Undecided during Stormy Hearing: Owners' Lawyer Charges Conspiracy by Industry City Council, Nearly Ejected," *Los Angeles Times*, San Gabriel Valley ed., March 30, 1969, p. 1; "Waste Firm Seeks to Block Lifting of Permit," 4; Peyton Canary "Legal Agreement Will Keep Dump Oper-

ating," *Los Angeles Times*, San Gabriel Valley ed., April 13, 1969, 1; *Industry Urban-Development Agency, a Body Politic, v. J. Marion Adsit, et al.*, case no. C203-051, Los Angeles Superior Court, February 8, 1985, pp. 3–4.

48. Ibid., 5.

49. *Civic-Recreational-Industrial Authority v. James Marty Stafford*, LA 194C-431-143-249, 7:11.

50. "An Ordinance of the City of Industry Regulating Industrial and Commercial Refuse Collection," ordinance no. 310, May 28, 1970, p. 11; Mayor John Ferrero, letter to all businesses in the City of Industry, June 29, 1970; Barry Siegel, "Can Anyone Take Trash? Guess Again," *Los Angeles Times*, August 24, 1976, D1, D7, D8; *Civic-Recreational-Industrial Authority v. James Marty Stafford*, LA 194C-431-143-142, 5:2.

51. *Civic-Recreational-Industrial Authority v. James Marty Stafford*, LA 194C-431-143-249, 7:11.

52. "City of Industry up in Arms," *Los Angeles Times*, August 24, 1970, p. C3; *Civic-Recreational-Industrial Authority v. James Marty Stafford*, LA 194C-431-143-142, 5:2.

53. "City of Industry up in Arms," C3; Siegel, "Can Anyone Take Trash?" D1, D7, D8; Scot J. Paltrow, "The City of Insiders: The Gardener's Golden Touch," *Los Angeles Herald Examiner*, June 29, 1980, A14.

54. Don Parson, *Making a Better World: Public Housing, the Red Scare, and the Direction of Modern Los Angeles* (Minneapolis: University of Minnesota Press, 2005), 17.

55. Ibid., 145–46.

56. Joseph E. Coomes, Jr., "Problem Solving through Redevelopment Agreements," paper presented at the conference "Making Better Use of Urban Space," sponsored by the Lincoln Institute of Land Policy, the University of Southern California Law Center, and the County of Los Angeles Department of Regional Planning, February 11–12, 1983; Scot J. Paltrow, "The Redevelopment of Industry," *Los Angeles Herald Examiner*, July 4, 1980, D4.

57. Miller, *Cities by Contract*, 52.

58. "Industry's Manager Thrives in Arena of City Politics," 5, 7; "Zoning Changes and a New Name—Cerritos," in *The Story of Cerritos*, accessed on January 28, 2009, from *http://www.ci.cerritos.ca.us/library/history/chapter7.html*.

59. Gottlieb and Wolt, *Thinking Big*, 484–86; City of Los Angeles, Community Redevelopment Agency, "Downtown Los Angeles: 1982" [brochure] (Los Angeles, 1982), 14, 18, 29; City of Los Angeles, Community Redevelopment Agency, "Bunker Hill Redevelopment Project, Biennial Report, 1993" (Los Angeles, 1993), 29.

60. "Industry's Manager Thrives in Arena of City Politics," 1, 5, 7.

61. Ibid.

62. Raul Homero Villa, *Barrio-Logos: Space and Place in Urban Chicano Literature and Culture* (Austin: University of Texas Press, 2000), 98.

63. Graham A. Ritchie, telephone interview, April 4, 1984.

64. *Civic-Recreational-Industrial Authority v. James Marty Stafford*, LA 194C-431-143-890, 17:16.

CHAPTER 6 — TRIANGULATING THE THRONE

1. Robert King, interviewed in the presence of his attorney, by special agents John F. Keller and James A. Rueb, in Whittier, California, September 8, 1983; Robert King, interview conducted and tape-recorded by *Los Angeles Times* reporter Victor Valle, October 22, 1984; Robert King, interview conducted and tape-recorded by *Los Angeles Times* reporter Alan Maltun, October 26, 1984.

2. *Civic-Recreational-Industrial Authority v. James Marty Stafford*, LA 194C-431-143-557, 12:2.

3. King, interview by Valle.

4. *Civic-Recreational-Industrial Authority v. James Marty Stafford*, LA 194C-431-143-557, 12:2.

5. King, interview by Valle.

6. *Civic Recreational-Industrial Authority v. James Marty Stafford*, LA 194C-431-143-44, 11:1.

7. Ibid., LA 194C-431-143-557, 12:3.

8. King, interview by Valle; *Civic-Recreational-Industrial Authority v. James Marty Stafford*, LA 194C-431-143-557, 12:3.

9. *Civic-Recreational-Industrial Authority v. James Marty Stafford*, LA 194C-431-143-557, 12:3.

10. King, interview by Valle.

11. King, interview by Maltun.

12. Ibid.

13. Scot J. Paltrow, "Where Did All the Money Go?" *Los Angeles Herald Examiner*, June 27, 1980, pp. C1–6; Victor Valle, "Indicted Industrialist Kicked Off Board: Rare Sign of Discord on Little-Known but Powerful Manufacturing Panel," *Los Angeles Times*, San Gabriel Valley ed., April 22, 1984, p. 7.

14. Valle, "Indicted Industrialist Kicked Off Board," 7.

15. *Civic-Recreational-Industrial Authority v. James Marty Stafford*, LA 194C-431-143-473, 11:2.

16. King, interview by Valle.

17. *Civic-Recreational-Industrial Authority v. James Marty Stafford*, LA 194C-431-143-44, 11:2.

18. Ibid., LA 194C-431-143-557, 12:3.

19. King, interview by Maltun.

20. Ibid.

21. Ibid.

22. Stan Wawer [special sections editor], " Life in Fast Lane Suits Him Just Fine," *San Gabriel Valley Tribune*, November 30, 2001, p. 1.

23. Edward P. Roski, Jr., "Roski's Remarks: In Memory of Edward P. Roski, Sr., October 9, 1916 to October 6, 2000," *Majestic Forum Newsletters* 12 (winter 2000), accessed on August 6, 2004, from *http://www.majesticrealty.com/news/nl_12/roskis_remarks.asp.*

24. *Civic-Recreational-Industrial Authority v. James Marty Stafford*, LA 194C-431-143-185, 6:1–2.

25. Figures obtained from a review of the City of Industry's city council minutes, 1971–75.

26. King, interview by Valle.

CHAPTER 7 — SOWING A FIELD, CLIMBING A TREE

1. *Civic-Recreational-Industrial Authority v. James Marty Stafford*, LA 194C-431-143-77, 3:2.

2. Ibid., LA 194C-143-77, 3:3; LA 194C-431-143-890, 17:1.

3. Southern Pacific Railroad Company, "Southern Pacific Company 1970 Annual Report" (San Francisco, December 31, 1970), 12; *Civic-Recreational-Industrial Authority v. James Marty Stafford*, LA 194C-431-143-250, 7:2.

4. Transaction appears in *Declaration of Sandra Lea Hobbs*, on page titled "Private Individuals to Roski or Alter Egos," March 1981.

5. *Civic-Recreational-Industrial Authority v. James Marty Stafford*, LA 194C-431-143-12, 4:1; LA 194C-431-143-890, 17:1.

6. Ibid., LA 194C-431-143-250, 7:10.

7. Scot J. Paltrow, "The City of Insiders: Million Dollar Bond Man," *Los Angeles Herald Examiner*, June 26, 1980, p. A14; "Warner W. Hodgdon Statement of Awards and Commendations," subsequently filed in *Civic-Recreational-Industrial Authority, et al., Plaintiffs, v. James Marty Stafford, et al., Defendants*, case no. 84-7983-MRP, U.S. District Court, Central District of California, October 16, 1984. The statement, which was compiled by Hodgdon's attorney, lists scores of plaques and awards given to him by youth groups, city councils, and political leaders.

8. Elizabeth Wheeler, "This Owner's Really in the Driver's Seat," *Los Angeles Times*, November 19, 1976, p. C3.

9. Craig Staats, "Warner Hodgdon: Controversial Millionaire," *San Bernardino Sun*, November 25, 1979, p. 6.

10. John Hall, "Racing's Santa," *Los Angeles Times*, June 6, 1980, p. C3.

11. "Warner W. Hodgdon Is in Jail," *San Bernardino Sun*, November 4, 1970, p. B1.

12. Paltrow, "The City of Insiders: Million Dollar Bond Man," A14; Joe Baker, "Man on the Go: Hodgdon Redevelopment Agency Boss, *San Bernardino Sun*, June

24, 1967, p. B5; Joe Baker, "Redevelopment Agency Chairman Hodgdon to Quit: Announces Multi-Million Bond Sale for Meadowbrook Project," *San Bernardino Sun*, December 18, 1968, pp. B1, B5; "Sale of Tax Bonds Elates Civic Leaders," *San Bernardino Sun*, December 18, 1968, pp. B1, B5; Joe Baker, "Hodgdon: Central City Corrective Action Needed," *San Bernardino Sun*, July 9, 1970, p. A6.

13. *Civic-Recreational-Industrial Authority v. James Marty Stafford*, LA 194C-431-143-12, 4:1.

14. Ibid., LA 194C-431-143-890, 17:1.

15. Ibid., 17:2–4.

16. Ibid., LA 194C-431-143-250, 7:8.

17. *The General Plan of the City of Industry*, 20–22, 29.

18. *Civic-Recreational-Industrial Authority v. James Marty Stafford*, LA 194C-431-143-7, 3:1–2, 4; LA 194C-431-143-67, 3:1; Paltrow, "The City of Insiders: Million Dollar Bond Man," A14.

19. Articles of incorporation of National Engineering Company, Inc., March 17, 1969, filed with the State of California, Office of the Secretary of State, p. 1.

20. *Civic-Recreational-Industrial Authority v. James Marty Stafford*, LA 194C-431-143-7, 3:1–2.

21. Ibid., LA 194C-431-143-67, 3:6–7.

22. Steiner acknowledged in a March 1, 1984 interview with *Los Angeles Times* reporter Victor Valle that National Engineering had hired him in a public relations capacity in 1972 soon after his retirement from the Southern Pacific's real estate division; *Civic-Recreational-Industrial Authority v. James Marty Stafford*, LA 194C-431-143-77, 3:1–3.

23. *Civic-Recreational-Industrial Authority v. James Marty Stafford*, LA 194C-431-143-7, 3:3.

24. Jack Birkinshaw, "Redevelopment Project Okd despite Protests: City of Industry Public Hearing Marked by Charges of 'Fraud' by Property Owners," *Los Angeles Times*, July 23, 1971, p. B6.

25. The claim that Industry was the first to use redevelopment law to acquire vacant farmland may have been premature. According to its own official history, the city of Cerritos began to redevelop 940 acres of dairy and pasture land a year before Industry founded the Industry Urban Development Agency (see "Zoning Changes and a New Name—Cerritos").

26. Industry Urban Development Agency, appendix 2, official statement on tax allocation and negotiable promissory notes, transportation-distribution-industrial redevelopment project no. 3 (1975), p. 12; Pavlovskis, "The Economic and Fiscal Impact of the City of Industry," 126.

27. Jack Birkinshaw, "Industry Sets Hearing on Renewal Proposal," *Los Angeles Times*, 2d ed., July 20, 1971, p. B6; Birkinshaw, "Redevelopment Project Okd despite Protests," 6; Rudy Villasenor, "Suit Filed to Block Industry Renewal Plan,"

Los Angeles Times, August 27, 1971, p. B7; Ann Frank, "School Boards to Meet on Redevelopment Suit," *Los Angeles Times,* September 18, 1971, p. B17; Ann Frank, "Schools to Get Taxes from Renewal Project," *Los Angeles Times*, San Gabriel Valley ed., November 17, 1971, p. 8.

28. Pavlovskis, "The Economic and Fiscal Impact of the City of Industry," 128–30.

29. Ochoa, *Becoming Neighbors in a Mexican American Community,* 62–63.

30. "Pact Bolsters City Hall Plans," *Los Angeles Times*, April 2, 1972, sec. 1, p. 8; Industry Hills Regional Public Park and Recreation Area, "Visitor Accommodations Center Air Rights Lease Agreement," (City of Industry, Calif., April 17, 1980), 1–2; Industry Urban Development Agency, "Reciprocal Easement Agreement for Area A and Basic Legal Documents" for civic-recreational-industrial redevelopment project no. 1 [Civic-Financial Center], April 23, 1975, pp. 1–2.

31. Grahame L. Jones, "Gentlemen's Agreement Asserted: Neighbor Cities Protest Industry's Mall," *Los Angeles Times*, San Gabriel Valley ed., February 6, 1972, p. 1; Mike Ward, "Funds at Issue: Schools Fear Renewal Plan for Industry," *Los Angeles Times*, San Gabriel Valley ed., June 18, 1972, pp. 1–2.

32. "Mayor Replies to Shopping Center Critics," *Los Angeles Times*, San Gabriel Valley ed., Feb. 13, 1972, p. 2.

33. Pavlovskis, "The Economic and Fiscal Impact of the City of Industry," 127.

34. "Redevelopment Project Postponed in Industry," *Los Angeles Times*, 2d ed., August 11, 1972, p. B6; acting city manager Graham A. Ritchie, letter to Howard R. Gilstrap, deputy county counsel, County of Los Angeles, August 1, 1972.

35. "Industry Keeps Council Seats in the Family," *Los Angeles Times*, 2d ed., December 5, 1972, p. B7.

36. *Industry Urban-Development Agency, a Body Politic, v. Rolena J. Harrison, Scella Harrison, Lewis E. Horst, et al.*, case no. 35,834, Los Angeles Superior Court, August 3, 1972, pp. 4–8; *Answer to Complaint in Eminent Domain* [parcels 421 and 422, 427 and 428], case no. 35,834, Los Angeles Superior Court, September 5, 1972, pp. 1–2; Mike Ward, "Industry's Renewal Project Disturbs Neighbors," *Los Angeles Times*, San Gabriel Valley ed., August 5, 1973, pp. 1, 4.

37. *Industry Urban-Development Agency, a Body Politic, v. Rolena J. Harrison, Scella Harrison, Lewis E. Horst, et al.*, 4–8; *Answer to Complaint in Eminent Domain*, 1–2 and first pretrial conference memo; Gruen Associates and National Engineering Company, Civic-Financial Center general street map and plan of development, prepared for Industry Urban Development Agency, July 28, 1972. The plan indicates the size (in square feet and acres) of lots owned by Stafford, Horst, and their wives. On a proposed Civic-Financial Center map appearing in *The General Plan of the City of Industry,* a superimposed text with an arrow pointing to the mill's property reads: "Structures on this site are incompatible with the proposed

Civic/Financial Center. Substandard, unsightly complex of old buildings should be cleaned up" (29).

38. Ward, "Industry's Renewal Project Disturbs Neighbors," 1, 4–5, 7.

39. *Industry Urban-Development Agency, a Body Politic, v. Rolena J. Harrison, Scella Harrison, Lewis E. Horst, et al.*, 4–8.

40. Ward, "Industry's Renewal Project Disturbs Neighbors," 4.

41. Ibid.

42. Industry Urban Development Agency, project no. 3, disposition agreement, exhibit G, "Plan of Development, Disposition and Implementation for the Pomona and 605 Freeway Interchange Redevelopment Area," November 25, 1975, p. 14.

43. Industry Urban Development Agency, project no. 3, disposition agreement, exhibit C, predisposition agreement for the Pomona and 605 freeway interchange redevelopment area, transportation-distribution-industrial redevelopment project no. 3, January 27, 1976, pp. 1–3; Scot J. Paltrow, "The City of Insiders: Industry's Multimillion Dollar Redevelopment Projects," *Los Angeles Herald Examiner*, July 3, 1980, p. A14; "City Will Pick Up Tab for Freeway Bridge: State Cannot Afford $6 Million for Needed Interchange Construction," *Los Angeles Times*, San Gabriel Valley, ed., January 18, 1981, p. 2.

44. Industry Urban Development Agency, appendix 2, official statement on tax allocation and negotiable promissory notes, transportation-distribution-industrial redevelopment project no. 3 (1975), p. 9.

45. Ibid., 28.

46. Ibid.

47. *Civic-Recreational-Industrial Authority v. James Marty Stafford*, LA 194C-431-143-67, 3:1–2.

48. Mike Ward, "Redevelopment Plans Sail Through Hearing: Industry Moves to Cover 80% of City In Expansion," *Los Angeles Times*, San Gabriel Valley ed., May 30, 1974, p. 2.

49. Ibid., 8.

50. *Civic-Recreational-Industrial Authority v. James Marty Stafford*, LA 194C-431-143-250, 7:12.

51. Ward, "Industry's Renewal Project Disturbs Neighbors," 1, 4; Paltrow, "The City of Insiders: Million Dollar Bond Man," A1, A14.

52. City of Industry, city council resolution no. 97, April 25, 1975; Industry Urban Development Agency, disposition agreement, civic-recreational-industrial redevelopment project no. 1, April 25, 1975; Ward, "Industry's Renewal Project Disturbs Neighbors," 4; Industry Urban Development Agency, "Reciprocal Easement Agreement for Area A and Basic Legal Documents," civic-recreational-industrial redevelopment project no. 1, April 23, 1975, pp. 1–2, 17.

53. *Civic-Recreational-Industrial Authority v. James Marty Stafford*, LA 194C-431-143-45, 10:6–7.

54. *Industry Urban-Development Agency, a Body Politic, v. James M. Stafford, Jane C. Stafford, Lewis E. Horst, et al., Complaint in Eminent Domain*, case no. C118,923, Los Angeles Superior Court, March 27, 1975.

55. Paltrow, "The City of Insiders: How the Rich Get Richer," A10.

56. *Civic-Recreational-Industrial Authority v. James Marty Stafford*, LA 194C-431-143-557, 12:4; "Abbey Changed to Stafford St.," 1.

57. "Abbey Changed to Stafford St.," 1.

58. *Civic-Recreational-Industrial Authority v. James Marty Stafford*, LA 194C-431-143-250, 7:12.

59. Ibid., LA 194C-431-143-67, 3:2.

60. The signed "Will of James M. Stafford," dated September 22, 1978, gives Stephen's birth date as September 1, 1949.

61. *Civic-Recreational-Industrial Authority v. James Marty Stafford*, LA 194C-431-143-249, 7:12.

62. Ibid., LA 194C-431-143-67, 3:2.

63. Ibid., LA 194C-431-143-249, 7:13.

64. Paltrow, "The City of Insiders: Million Dollar Bond Man," A14.

65. *Civic-Recreational-Industrial Authority v. James Marty Stafford*, LA 194C-431-143-890, 17:2.

66. State of California, Department of Corporations, "Notice of Issuance of Securities Pursuant to Subdivision (h) of Section 25102 of the California Corporations Code," December 28, 1976; *Civic-Recreational-Industrial Authority v. James Marty Stafford*, LA 194C-431-143-67, 3:2.

67. *Civic-Recreational-Industrial Authority v. James Marty Stafford*, LA 194C-431-143-12, 4:2–3.

68. "Restoration Planned for 3 Landmarks," *Los Angeles Times*, San Gabriel Valley ed., February 2, 1975, p. 1; Mike Ward, "City of Industry Ready to Sell $84 Million in Bonds: Monday Sale Will Retire Old Redevelopment Debt and Free Tax Revenues for Other Purposes," *Los Angeles Times*, San Gabriel Valley ed., June 15, 1975, p. 6.

69. Jan Garvin, "City Contracts Revised after Conflicts Arise," *San Gabriel Valley Tribune*, August 12, 1977, p. B1.

CHAPTER 8 — SCARING THE PESTS AWAY

1. Mary Barber, "Public Awareness of CRAs Put Them under Scrutiny," *Los Angeles Times*, May 13, 1976, p. 1.

2. Peter Schrag, *Paradise Lost: California's Experience, America's Future* (Berkeley: University of California Press, 2004), 133.

3. Mike Davis, *City of Quartz: Excavating the Future in Los Angeles* (New York: Verso, 1990), 181–82.

4. Ibid., 182; Schrag, *Paradise Lost*, 133; Fulton, *The Reluctant Metropolis*, 16.

5. Fulton, *The Reluctant Metropolis*, 17; Schrag, *Paradise Lost*, 135, 136.

6. Barber, "Public Awareness of CRA's Puts Them under Scrutiny," 1.

7. Miller, *Cities by Contract*, 53.

8. C. Edward Dilkes and Peter L. Wallin, "Redevelopment in California: Comments on the Need for Legislative Reform," self-published monograph presented to the California State Legislature, 1976.

9. Ibid., 1, 10.

10. Ibid., 11–12.

11. Ibid., 12–13.

12. Ibid., 14, 18.

13. "Amendment Exempts City of Industry: Redevelopment Controls Eyed," *San Gabriel Valley Tribune*, May 11, 1977, p. B1

14. California State Legislature, Senate Committee on Local Government, analysis of assembly bill 35, February 24, 1977, p. 1, 1st set, urgency clause; California State Legislature, Senate Committee on Local Government, "Legislation Passed in 1977 Affecting Redevelopment Agencies" (Sacramento, 1977), 1.

15. Morain and Valle, "City of Industry: It Has Clout Where It Counts," A36; California Legislature, Senate Committee on Local Government, "Legislation Passed in 1977 Affecting Redevelopment Agencies" (Sacramento, 1977); Ray Hebert, "Robbins Assailed on Renewal Bill," *Los Angeles Times*, September 2, 1976, pp. A1, A2.

16. Miller, *City by Contract*, 53; Morain and Valle, "City of Industry: It Has Clout Where It Counts," A36; Joseph B. Montoya, memorandum to all members of the California State Senate regarding assembly bill 35, California State Legislature, June 1977.

17. Eugene B. Jacobs, statement regarding assembly bill 35, presented to California State Assembly Conference Committee, August 24, 1977, pp. 3–4; Montoya, memorandum; *Assembly Final History, 1977–78* (Sacramento: California Legislature, 1978), 90.

18. Paltrow, "The Redevelopment of Industry," D4.

19. Jacobs, statement regarding assembly bill 35, 1–3.

20. Stephen Stafford, interview by Maltun.

21. Morain and Valle, "City of Industry: It Has Clout Where It Counts," 37; contribution totals obtained from Legi-Tech's data retrieval service in Sacramento and candidate contribution reports filed before February 1984 with the Office of the Los Angeles County Registrar-Recorder and cross-referenced with Industry Manufacturers Council membership directories, the names of Industry city officials, and known Stafford business associates.

22. Morain and Valle, "City of Industry: It Has Clout Where It Counts," 36.

23. Mike Ward, "Being Bought: Redevelopment in Industry among Most Ambitious," *Los Angeles Times*, San Gabriel Valley ed., February 22, 1976, sec. 1, pp. 1, 8.

24. "Railroads Form Joint Computer Hookup," *City of Industry News* 15 (April 1976): 1, 4.

25. "Bank of America Plans Open House," *City of Industry News* 15 (April 1976): 1; Industry Urban Development Agency, "Reciprocal Easement Agreement for Area A and Basic Legal Documents," civic-recreational-industrial redevelopment project no. 1, April 23, 1975, pp. 1–2.

26. Miller, *Cities by Contract*, 53.

27. "City Hall Dedication Ceremonies Held: City's 20th Anniversary Celebrated," *City of Industry News* 15 (July 1977): 1; "Victor Arenth Taken by Death," *City of Industry News* 15 (August 1977): 2; "City's 20-Year Growth Record Acclaimed: In Forefront of Industrial Expansion" and "Building Permits Near Record Mark," *City of Industry News* 15 (September 1977): 1; "Capacity Crowd Hears Reagan's Address: IMC Group of 400 Hears Ex-Governor," *City of Industry News* 15 (December 1977): 1–2.

28. *Industry Urban-Development Agency, a Body Politic, v. J. Marion Adsit, et al.*, 10; Paltrow, "The City of Insiders: How the Rich Get Richer," A10.

29. Frank C. Wood, letter to Judge Edward Rafeedie, in *United States of America, Plaintiff, v. Frank C. Wood, Defendant*, case no. CR 84-794, U.S. District Court, Central District of California, November 9, 1984, exhibit B.

30. Ibid.

31. Government's sentencing memorandum, in *United States of America, Plaintiff, v. Frank C. Wood, Defendant*, 2–4; *Civic-Recreational-Industrial Authority v. James Marty Stafford*, LA 194C-143-687, 14:1.

32. Mike Ward and Steve Simmons, "Bond Interest, New Taxes Hover over Industry," *Los Angeles Times*, San Gabriel Valley ed., June 18, 1978, sec. 1, pp. 1, 3; Miller, *Cities by Contract*, 53.

33. Ward and Simmons, "Bond Interest, New Taxes Hover over Industry," sec. 1, pp. 1, 3.

34. Dan Morain and Victor Valle, "City Isn't Shy about Going into Debt," *Los Angeles Times*, April 15, 1984, p. A3.

35. *Civic-Recreational-Industrial Authority v. James Marty Stafford*, LA 194C-431-143-576, 13:8–9; "Graham Ritchie Made City Attorney," *City of Industry News* 18 (April 1983): 1.

36. Valle, "Indicted Industrialist Kicked Off Board," J7.

37. *Civic-Recreational-Industrial Authority v. James Marty Stafford*, LA 194C-431-143-557, 12:5–6; LA 194C-431-143-559, 13:1.

38. Paltrow, "The City of Insiders: The Van de Kamp Connection," A1, A10; Valle "Indicted Industrialist Kicked Off Board," J7.

CHAPTER 9 — THE OTHER CHINATOWNS

1. Bill Dredge, "Grand Prix Set for Yearly Run: Drivers and Officials Pleased with Classic," *Los Angeles Times*, October 14, 1958, p. C1; Bill Dredge, "Facts and Figures on Grand Prix Events," *Los Angeles Times*, October 8, 1961, p. E1.

2. A computer-assisted search of the *Los Angeles Times* revealed that at least 285 articles, advertisements, and photos published between July 25, 1958, and October 5, 1966, were primarily concerned with the Times-Mirror Grand Prix; that is, they made a direct reference to the Riverside Grand Prix race in a photo caption, a news headline, or in the first two paragraphs of a news article, and the advertisements promoted particular aspects of the event (word string "Times-Mirror Grand Prix," *ProQuest* data archive, accessed on April 6, 2005, from *http://proquest.umi.com/pqdweb?RQT=403&TS=1112833111&clientId=17855*).

3. Wheeler, "This Owner's Really in the Driver's Seat," C8; Hall, "Racing's Santa," C3; Shav Glick, "Hodgdon's 1981 Purchase Set Track Record," *Los Angeles Times*, December 31, 1981, p. B7; "Motor Racing Vast Stock Car Empire of Warner Hodgdon Ends in Bankruptcy," *Los Angeles Times*, January 24, 1985, p. D10.

4. Articles of incorporation of the Campus Crusade for Christ, Inc., filed with the Secretary of State of California, August 25, 1953; U.S. Department of the Treasury, tax return of Campus Crusade for Christ International [tax-exempt organization], fiscal year July 1, 1980–June 30, 1981, form 990, part 6, item 72 [p. 4]and schedule 4; U.S. Department of the Treasury, tax return of Campus Crusade for Christ International [tax-exempt organization], fiscal year July 1, 1981–June 30, 1982, form 990, part 7, item 80 [p. 4] and schedule 12.

5. Russell Chandler, "Awakening: Aims to 'Saturate Country with Final Thrust,'" *Los Angeles Times*, July 25, 1976, p. C1; Marjorie Hyer, "Evangelist to Launch $1 Billion World Crusade," *Washington Post*, November 18, 1977, religion sec., p. 1.

6. Kenneth L. Woodward, "Politics from the Pulpit," *Newsweek*, September 6, 1976, pp. 49, 51.

7. David Halberstam, *The Powers That Be* (Urbana: University of Illinois Press, 2000), 114.

8. Gottlieb and Wolt, *Thinking Big*, 128.

9. Ibid., 130–31.

10. Ibid., 138; Steven P. Erie, Gregory Freeman, and Pascale Joassart-Marcelli, "W(h)ither Sprawl? Have Regional Water Policies Subsidized Suburban Development?" in *Up against the Sprawl: Public Policy and the Making of Southern California*, ed. Jennifer Wolch, Manuel Pastor, Jr., and Peter Dreier (Minneapolis: University of Minnesota Press, 2004), 47.

11. Gottlieb and Wolt, *Thinking Big*, 150.

12. McDougal, *Privileged Son*, 72–73; "Otis Chandler, 1927–2006," *Los Angeles Times*, February 28, 2006, p. A14.

13. McDougal, *Privileged Son*, 469.

14. Ibid., 115.

15. Ibid., 505.

16. Fulton, *The Reluctant Metropolis*, 111. Seven years earlier, Governor Brown had promised, "[The project] will provide an abundance of water for homes, farms, and factories. It will create billions of dollars in new wealth, making possible the continued expansion of industry, turning arid deserts into rich agricultural lands" (Edmund G. Brown, cover letter, in "State Water Project Inspection" (Sacramento: State of California, Department of Water Resources, April 22, 1966).

17. McDougal, *Privileged Son,* 477.

18. Nicolas C. Arguimbau, "The Los Angeles Times and the California Water Wars," *CBE Environmental Review* (May–June 1981): 9.

19. Robert Lindsey, "Oil, Water and Boom: Will They Mix?" *New York Times,* October 28, 1980, p. A16.

20. Joel Schwarz, *A Water Odyssey: The Story of the Metropolitan Water District of Southern California* (Los Angeles: Metropolitan Water District, 1991), viii.

21. George L. Baker, "Insatiable Thirst? South State Keeps Up Search for Water," *Sacramento Bee,* April 16, 1980, pp. A3, A14.

22. "Piedmont Nuptial Joins Miss Maurine Morrison and Preston B. Hotchkis," *Los Angeles Times,* December 28, 1951, p. C2; "Hotchkis Named by Eisenhower for U.N. Post," *Los Angeles Times,* January 16, 1954, p. A1; "By the Way . . . with Bill Henry," *Los Angeles Times,* January 25, 1954, p. B1; "Hotchkis Heads Brotherhood Week Activities," *Los Angeles Times,* January 29, 1954, p. B3; "Geneva to Test Russian Smile Hotchkis Says," *Los Angeles Times,* October 28, 1955, p. A16; "Proposition W Group Headed by Hotchkis," *Los Angeles Times,* April 22, 1956, p. A2; "Leaders Announced for Water Proposition OK: Southland Community, Business and Labor Figures to Work for Measure's Approval," *Los Angeles Times,* May 20, 1956, p. A36; Joan Martin, "Preston Hotchkis Will Wed Miss Morrison: Old California Families to Be Joined by December Wedding in Piedmont," *Los Angeles Times,* September 9, 1961, p. C3; "P. B. Hotchkis Elected to Bixby Ranch Post," *Los Angeles Times,* October 16, 1963, p. C10; "Chandler, Hotchkis on Federal City Council," *Los Angeles Times,* October 1, 1958, p. A5; Richard Bergholz, "Yorty Backers Miss Target—McGee Howls," *Los Angeles Times,* April 3, 1965, p. A3; "Two Will Lead Vote Campaign for Water Bonds," *Los Angeles Times,* November 30, 1965, p. A4; "Need for Water Bonds Explained" [letter to the editor], *Los Angeles Times,* December 18, 1965, p. C4; "2 Join Board of Goodwill," *Los Angeles Times,* January 11, 1966, p. A16; "Hotchkis Asks Public Support of Water Bond," *Los Angeles Times,* May 8, 1966, p. C7; "Mrs. Hotchkis Will Lead Fund Drive," *Los Angeles Times,* April 28, 1966, p. B8; "2 Appointed to Water Group," December 11, 1966, p. A4; "Hotchkis Will Lead World Affairs Council," *Los Angeles Times,* June 16, 1967, p. C16; "Most Cities in County Back Water Bonds," *Los Angeles Times,* April 10, 1968, p. C2; Preston B. Hotchkis, "Prop. 7 Vital for the Future," *Los Angeles Times,* February 14, 1970, p. B4;

Preston Hotchkis, "Prop. 7 Support" [letter to the editor], *Los Angeles Times,* April 8, 1970, p. B3; Preston Hotchkis, "Coastline Protection Bill Denounced As 'Power Grab,'" *Los Angeles Times,* November 27, 1971, p. B4.

23. Fulton, *The Reluctant Metropolis,* 108.

24. Mike Davis, *Ecology of Fear: Los Angeles and the Imagination of Disaster* (New York: Holt, 1998), 10–11; Robert Gottlieb, *A Life of Its Own: The Politics and Power of Water* (San Diego: Harcourt Brace Jovanovich, 1988), 5.

25. Erie et al., "W(h)ither Sprawl?" 46–48.

26. Fulton, *The Reluctant Metropolis,* 109.

27. L. E. Monroe, ed., "Report for the Fiscal Year: Twenty-Eighth Annual Report [July 1, 1965–June 30, 1966]" (Los Angeles: Metropolitan Water District, 1966), 79.

28. Bill Lundy, telephone interview, June 27, 1985; Monroe, "Report for the Fiscal Year," 81, 88.

29. S. M. Chavez, director, Right of Way and Land Division, memorandum to R. W. Balcerzak, Metropolitan Water District assistant general manager, about the Yorba Linda feeder 1605-09 series, September 2, 1987, pp. 1–2.

30. Engineering Science, Inc., cover letter, in "Technical Feasibility Report: Tonner Canyon Water Project" [prepared for the Pomona Valley Municipal Water District] (Arcadia, Calif., November 1972), 1–3; Engineering Science, Inc., "Summary Report for Northern and Southern Study Areas Supplemental Water Supply Project" [prepared for the Pomona Valley Municipal Water District] (Arcadia, Calif., October 1977), 1.

31. Pomona Valley Municipal Water District, "Approving Tax Statement to Be Mailed to Voters within Said District," resolution no. 8-75-186, August 19, 1975; Pomona Valley Municipal Water District, "Declaring the Results of the Special Election Held in Said District," resolution no. 11-75-189, November 4, 1975; Pomona Valley Municipal Water District, "Ordering, Calling, Providing for, and Giving Notice of a Special Election to Be Held in Said District on November 8, 1977, for the Purpose of Submitting to the Qualified Voters of Said District a Proposition of Incurring Bonded Indebtedness and Issuing Bonds of Said District," resolution no. 7-77-209, July 7, 1977; Pomona Valley Municipal Water District, "Declaring the Results of the Special Election Held in Said District," resolution no. 11-77-217, November 8, 1977.

32. Maurie Clark, "A Profile of Harold Arnold," *City of Industry News* 22 (September 1983): 4; Jerome T. Winstead, executive director of the Industry Urban Development Agency, letter to Victor M. Valle, reporter for the *Los Angeles Times,* November 9, 1984, including twenty-three pages that, according to Winstead, were excerpted from "the lease document that previously covered the Tres Hermanos property"; Chandis Securities Company, Josephine Scott Crocker, and William Keith Scott, "Application to Appropriate Unappropriated Water (with Appendix

Attached)," application no. 25,129, State Water Resources Control Board, Division of Water Rights, August 19, 1976; *Civic-Recreational-Industrial Authority v. James Marty Stafford*, LA 194C-143-857, 17:1.

33. Tres Hermanos partner William Keith Scott submitted the two-page development plan with map to Lewis J. Miller and Associates, real estate appraisers, during or before 1977.

34. Stan Kawa, general manager of the Pomona Valley Municipal Water District, letter with enclosed map to Wesley N. Taylor Company, August 18, 1977.

35. Willie Mae Sale, employee of Wesley N. Taylor Company, letter to Harold G. Arnold, transmitting "information on the area for the proposed dam for the Tres Hermanos, which you requested," August 19, 1977; *Civic-Recreational-Industrial Authority v. James Marty Stafford*, LA 194C-143-857, 17:1.

36. Harold Arnold filed a fictitious business name statement (a legal business name that does not include the business owner's name as required of for-profit businesses) for the City of Industry Security Company on May 18, 1975, listing the Tres Hermanos Ranch as his home address. According to the City of Industry's "Authorization for Payment of Bills," city check no. 78, dated November 4, 1975, "was made out to Arnold's [City of] Industry Security Co."; also see "Authorization for Payment of Bills" for 1976: January 22, February 13 and 26, March 11, April 8, May 13, June 10, July 8, Aug. 12, Sept. 10, Oct. 14, Nov. 11, and December 9; Paltrow, "The City of Industry: the Gardener's Golden Touch," A14.

37. Clark, "A Profile of Harold Arnold," 4; Paltrow, "The Gardener's Golden Touch," A14.

38. *Civic-Recreational-Industrial Authority v. James Marty Stafford*, LA 194C-143-857, 17:1–3.

39. Warner W. Hodgdon, letter to William Keith Scott, January 10, 1978; Warner W. Hodgdon, letter to attorney Richard S. Volpert of O'Melveny and Myers, January 10, 1978.

40. *Civic-Recreational-Industrial Authority v. James Marty Stafford*, LA 194C-431-143-890, 17:3–4.

41. Warner W. Hodgdon, letter to Industry city engineer John J. Radecki, Jr., January 25, 1978, pp. 3–4; Paltrow, "The City of Insiders: How the Rich Get Richer," A10.

42. Craig Staats, "City of Industry: Its Business Is Hodgdon's Business," *San Bernardino Sun*, November 25, 1979, p. 14; City of Industry, "A Resolution of the City Council of the City of Industry Authorizing Purchase of the "Tres Hermanos Ranch" and Authorizing Temporary Borrowing from the Bank of America in Connection Therewith," February 9, 1978; attorney Robert L. Toms of Caldwell and Toms, letter hand-delivered to attorney Richard Volpert of O'Melveny and Myers, January 27, 1978; attorney Richard Volpert of O'Melveny and Myers, letter

to Industry city attorney Graham A. Ritchie, sent "in accordance [to Ritchie's] request," February 10, 1978.

43. City of Industry, minutes of the city council meeting, January 30, 1978, pp. 1–2.

44. Industry city attorney Graham A. Ritchie, memo to the Industry city council concerning the "proposed acquisition of [a] site in San Bernardino County, California as a future site for water storage and reclamation," January 30, 1978, p. 2.

45. Craig Staats, "A Conversation with Warner Hodgdon: You've Got to Dig a Lot of Ditches to Get Ahead," *San Bernardino Sun*, November 25, 1979, pp. 16–17.

CHAPTER 10 — JIM'S BUSY PERIOD

1. *Civic-Recreational-Industrial Authority v. James Marty Stafford*, LA 194C-143-367, 9:8–9.

2. Ibid., 9:17.

3. Ibid., 9:13.

4. Ibid., 9:6.

5. James M. Stafford, will, September 29, 1978, pp. 1–21.

6. Ibid., 8.

7. Ibid.

8. Ibid., 13.

9. *Jane Chilcott Stafford and James M. Stafford*, case no. SED52,447, Superior Court of California, County of Los Angeles, December 26, 1979, exhibits A–E and attachment A.

10. Hobbs, declaration.

11. Ibid.; articles of merger, January 28, 1976, State of Utah, Office of the Secretary of State, and certificate of ownership and articles of merger, December 26, 1975, which combined the Union Land Company, the Kansas City Industrial Land Company, UPAC Construction Company, and the Las Vegas Land and Water Company (a Nevada corporation) into the Upland Industries Corporation, a subsidiary of Union Pacific Railroad.

12. Paltrow, "The City of Insiders: Million Dollar Bond Man," A14.

13. Industry Urban Development Agency, preliminary disposition and development agreement for the Gale Avenue commercial corridor, civic-recreational-industrial redevelopment project no. 1, June 14, 1978.

14. *Civic-Recreational-Industrial Authority v. James Marty Stafford*, LA 194C-143-8, 1:1.

15. Victor Valle, "Landowner Wins Round with City: But Industry Says It Will Appeal Court Ruling on Condemnation," *Los Angeles Times*, San Gabriel Valley ed., March 14, 1982, pp. 1, 2; Victor Valle, "Ruling on Landowner's Fight with City Delayed: Court Decision Would Affirm Challenge to Industry Condemnation

Power," *Los Angeles Times*, San Gabriel Valley ed., March 18, 1982, pp. 1, 13; Hobbs, declaration.

16. Photocopy of C. C. Stafford Milling and Warehouse Company, desk calendar entry, December 14, 1979; *Civic-Recreational-Industrial Authority v. James Marty Stafford*, LA 194C-143-250, 7:4.

17. Photocopy of C. C. Stafford Milling and Warehouse Company, desk calendar, 1979.

18. Mike Ward, "$18 Million Exhibit Center to Open in City of Industry: Two Days of Invitational Previews to Precede Public Viewing of Complex's Centerpiece on April 20," *Los Angeles Times*, San Gabriel Valley ed., April 5, 1979, pp. 1, 7.

19. Industry Hills Regional Public Park and Recreation Area, "Visitor Accommodation Center Air Rights Lease Agreement," 14–40 and enclosed "Project Description," 1–3.

20. City of Industry, city council approval of "Summary of Air Rights Lease" and "Summary of Operating Agreement," April 17, 1980; Paltrow, "The City of Insiders: The Gardener's Golden Touch," A14; Paltrow, "The City of Insiders: Industry's Multimillion Dollar Redevelopment Projects," A14.

21. Valle and Maltun, "Called to Account," 1, 7.

22. Dale E. Walter, letter "on behalf of the organizers of [the] Bank of Industry" to prospective shareholders that accompanied an "Application for Subscription for Common Stock" and stating that the offer would expire on February 27, 1981.

23. Stephen Stafford, interview by Maltun; King, interview by Valle.

24. David Scott, telephone interview by *Los Angeles Times* reporter Alan Maltun, before April 1985. Scott was deputy superintendent of the State of California's Department of Banking.

25. City of Industry, "An Ordinance of the City of Industry Amending Subsection A 3 of Section 17.12.020 of the Industry Municipal Code (Zoning)," ordinance no. 410, September 22, 1977, adopted on October 13, 1977; National Engineering Company, "The Preliminary Plan Report for the Redevelopment of Project Area No. 1, City of Industry, California" (City of Industry, Calif., October 28, 1971).

26. King, interview by Valle.

27. Scott, interview.

28. *Civic-Recreational-Industrial Authority v. James Marty Stafford*, LA 194C-143-328, 8:2.

29. Ibid., LA 194C-431-143-32, 8:1–2.

30. Ibid., 8:3–4.

31. Bank of Industry, "Notes to Consolidated Financial Statements," in "1981 Annual Shareholders Report of Financial Information" (City of Industry, Calif., 1981), 4.

32. Government's sentencing memorandum, in *United States of America, Plaintiff, v. James Marty Stafford, et al., Defendants*, case nos. CR84-359-ER, CR84-794-ER,

U.S. District Court, Central District of California, November 27, 1984, pp. 4–8; Bank of Industry, "Principal Occupation of Officers, Directors, and Organizers," in the bank's offering circular, January 9, 1981, pp. 3–5; *Santiago Corporation, a California Corporation, Plaintiff, v. the Industry Urban Development Agency et al.,* case no. 522,193, Superior Court of the State of California for the County of Los Angeles, November 13, 1984, p. 4; *Civic-Recreational-Industrial Authority v. James Marty Stafford,* LA 194C-431-143-318, 8:1–2; "Lewis Again to Head County Planning Body," *Los Angeles Times,* January 13, 1974, p. J44; Valle and Maltun, "Called to Account," 7.

33. *Civic-Recreational-Industrial Authority v. James Marty Stafford,* LA 194C-431-143-328, 8:2; LA 194C-431-143-32, 8:6; LA 194C-431-143-319, 8:3.

34. Ibid., LA 194C-431-143-32, 8:5.

35. Valle and Maltun, "Called to Account," 1.

36. Ibid.

37. *Civic-Recreational-Industrial Authority v. James Marty Stafford,* LA 194C-431-143-596, 13:1–2.

38. Ibid., New Orleans 194C-357, LA 194C-143-45, 11:1–2.

39. Ibid., New Orleans 194C-357, LA 194C-143-5, 12:2.

40. Lucilla Rowlett, telephone interview, March 19, 1985.

41. *Civic-Recreational-Industrial Authority v. James Marty Stafford,* New Orleans 194C-357, LA 194C-143-45, 11:4–5.

42. Ibid., New Orleans 194C-357, LA 194C-143-5, 12:2; New Orleans 194C-357, LA 194C-143-45, 11:4.

CHAPTER 11 — ASSEMBLING JIM'S PORTRAIT

1. Paltrow, "The City of Insiders: How the Rich Get Richer," A1.

2. Ibid.

3. Ibid., A10.

4. Paltrow, "The City of Insiders: The Redevelopment of Industry," A1, D4.

5. Paltrow, "The City of Insiders: How the Rich Get Richer," A10.

6. Paltrow, "The City of Insiders: How the Mayor Farms City Land for Free," A3, A10.

7. Paltrow, "The City of Insiders: How the Rich Get Richer," A1.

8. Paltrow, "The City of Insiders: The Van de Kamp Connection," A1, A10.

9. "Oh, What an Industrious City," *Los Angeles Herald Examiner,* July 4, 1980, A10.

10. Scot Paltrow, letter to Roy Ulrich, September 6, 1991, in which he writes: "The series touched off an FBI investigation, which led to the conviction of Stafford on charges of bid-rigging and witness tampering."

11. *Civic-Recreational-Industrial Authority v. James Marty Stafford,* LA 194C-431-143-880, 17:3.

12. Ibid., 17:4.

13. Ronald Kessler, *The Bureau: The Secret History of the FBI* (New York: St. Martin's, 2002), 20.

14. John F. Keller, résumé, October 10, 2002.

15. Kessler, *The Bureau*, 20.

16. Michele Foucault, "What Is An Author?" in *Language, Counter-memory, Practice: Selected Essays and Interviews by Michel Foucault*, ed. Donald F. Bouchard (Ithaca, N.Y.: Cornell University Press, 1980), 124.

17. Ibid., 130–31.

18. Valle and Maltun, "Called to Account," 1.

19. *Civic-Recreational-Industrial Authority v. James Marty Stafford*, LA 194C-431-143-32, 8:7; New Orleans 194C-357, LA 194C-143-45, 11:3.

20. Ibid., LA 194C-431-143-32, 8:7; LA 194C-431-143-328, 8:10; Valle and Maltun, "Called to Account," 7.

21. Valle and Maltun, "Called to Account," 7.

22. *Civic-Recreational-Industrial Authority v. James Marty Stafford*, LA 194C-431-143-32, 8:6.

23. Ibid.

24. Victor M. Valle and Rodolfo D. Torres, "Bank Job: Stafford Called on Roski in Bid to Control Local Lender," *L.A. Weekly*, November 13–19, 1998, p. 9.

25. Bank of Industry, "400,000 to 500,000 Shares No Par Common Stock" [circular], January 9, 1981, which names Donald R. Wheeler as the bank's chairman on page 14; Bank of Industry, annual report (City of Industry, Calif., 1982), which identifies Robert K. King as the bank's new chairman on page 17.

CHAPTER 12 — JIM'S HOT VEGAS TIP

1. *Civic-Recreational-Industrial Authority v. James Marty Stafford*, LA 194C-431-143-571, 13:1.

2. Victor Merina, "Lewis Expected to Retain Planning Post," *Los Angeles Times*, December 31, 1979, pp. B1, B3; Claire Spiegel, "Planning Agency Not Protecting Public Interest, Critics Charge," *Los Angeles Times*, July 9, 1979, pp. B1, B6; Bill Boyarsky, "Clash with Schabarum Perils a Supervisor Tradition," *Los Angeles Times*, January 2, 1980, pp. B1, B6; Victor Merina, "County Sets Probe of Lewis' Conduct," *Los Angeles Times*, January 3, 1980, pp. B1, B8; Victor Merina, "D.A. to Get Findings of Inquiry on Lewis," *Los Angeles Times*, January 22, 1980, pp. B1, B6; "Supervisors Schedule Hearing on Lewis: Will Allow Planning Commissioner to Respond to Charges," *Los Angeles Times*, January 23, 1980, p. B2; "County Planning Director, Target of Inquiry, Resigns," *Los Angeles Times*, January 24, 1980, pp. A1, A14; "Supervisors Will Ask D.A. to Pursue Lewis Inquiry," *Los Angeles Times*, January 25, 1980, p. B1.

3. Bill Farr, "D.A. Won't Charge Ex-Planning Aide. But Lewis Could Face State

Action in Conflict-of-Interest Allegation," *Los Angeles Times*, August 16, 1980, p. A32.

4. Michael J. Ybarra, *Washington Gone Crazy: Senator Pat McCarran and the Great American Communist Hunter* (Hanover, N.H.: Steerforth, 2004), 661.

5. Ibid., 672, 676, 683, 692.

6. Sally Denton and Roger Morris, *The Money and the Power: The Making of Las Vegas and Its Hold on America, 1947–2000* (New York: Knopf, 2001), 101–2, 107, 109, 114; Jerome E. Edwards, *Pat McCarran: Political Boss of Nevada* (Reno: University of Nevada Press, 1982), 149; Gilman M. Ostrander, *Nevada: The Great Rotten Borough, 1859–1964* (New York: Knopf, 1966), 217–18.

7. Dick Taylor and Pat Howell, *Las Vegas, City of Sin?* (San Antonio, Tex.: Naylor, 1963), 31; Rick Gotcher, "Cliff Jones Acquitted on Perjury Charges," *Las Vegas Review-Journal*, evening ed., June 15, 1972, pp. 1, 4; Maureen Reilly, "Cliff Jones Happy Man As Fed Jury Clears Him," *Las Vegas Sun*, final ed., June 14, 1972, pp. 1, 4; "Clifford Jones Sues State Bank," *Las Vegas Review-Journal*, January 1, 1975, sec. 3, p. 2; Bryn Armstrong, "Jones Aids Winnipeg Gaming Bid, *Las Vegas Sun*, June 10, 1976, sec. 1, p. 1; "Bankrupt Petition Filed," *Las Vegas Sun*, final ed., sec. 19, p. 1; Georgia Lewis, "Clifford A. Jones, Nevada Ambassador," *Las Vegas Review-Journal*, March 27, 1977, pp. 26–27; "Ex-Lt. Gov. Cliff Jones Marries Actress in D.C.," *Las Vegas Review-Journal*, April 16, 1979, p. A5; "Ex-Lt. Gov. Escapes Death in Shootout," *Las Vegas Sun*, September 20, 1979, p. 13; Phil Hevener and Scott A. Zamost, "Aggressive Young Lawyer Becomes Gamer," *Las Vegas Sun*, March 31, 1981, p. 31; Mary Manning, "Slovakian President Checks Out Gaming," *Las Vegas Sun*, August 14, 1995, p. 6A.

8. *Civic-Recreational-Industrial Authority v. James Marty Stafford*, LA 194C-431-143-571, 13:2; sentencing memorandum, in *United States of America, Plaintiff, v. Wesley R. Lind, Defendant*, case no. CR84-358-RJK, U.S. District Court for the Central District of California, September 27, 1984, p. 2.

9. Sentencing memorandum, in *United States of America, Plaintiff, v. Wesley R. Lind, Defendant*, 6.

10. Valle and Maltun, "Called to Account," 7; sentencing memorandum, in *United States of America, Plaintiff, v. Wesley R. Lind, Defendant*, pp. 2–6.

11. *Civic-Recreational-Industrial Authority v. James Marty Stafford*, LA 194C-431-143-557, 12:11.

12. Ibid.

13. Ibid., LA 194C-431-143-571, 13:3.

14. Ibid., 13:2.

15. Ibid., 13:4.

16. Ibid., LA 194C-431-143-5, 8:1–5; LA 194C-431-143-571, 13:2–3.

17. Ibid., LA 194C-431-143-571, 13:2–3, 6–7.

18. Ibid., 13:8–9; LA 194C-431-143-56, 13:3.

19. Ibid., LA 194C-431-143-56, 13:8–9.

20. Ibid., 13:3.

21. Ibid., LA 194C-431-143-479, 11:1–2.

22. Ibid., LA 194C-431-143-781, 15:2.

23. Ibid., 15:3–4; LA 194C-431-143-57, 13:3.

24. Ibid., 13:4.

25. Ibid., LA 194C-431-143-57, 2:2, 5, 7; LA 194C-431-143-56, 2:6; 194C-431-143-50, 2:2; 194C-431-143-47, 2:1.

26. Larry Stammer and Victor Valle, "Most Aliens Regain Jobs after Raids: Survey Contradicts INS Findings That Sweeps Succeeded," *Los Angeles Times*, August 1, 1982, pp. A1, A3, A24.

27. Victor Valle, "Couple Deported; Children Left on Own," *Los Angeles Times*, August 1, 1982, pp. A1, A27.

28. Victor M. Valle, "Business Losses Told in INS Raids: One Firm Says It'll Lose $125,000 a Week until Aliens Are Replaced," *Los Angeles Times*, San Gabriel Valley ed., April 29, 1982, pp. 1, 11.

CHAPTER 13 — A PUNISHING GAZE

1. *Civic-Recreational-Industrial Authority v. James Marty Stafford*, LA 194C-431-143-19, 1:27–29; LA 194C-431-143-142, 5:1–6.

2. Ibid., LA 194C-431-143-212, 6:1–2; LA 194C-431-143-213, 6:1–2.

3. Ibid., LA 194C-431-143-213, 6:1–2.

4. Ibid.

5. Ibid., 6:2; Mike Ward, "Exhibit Center Losing Money but Backers Predict Turnaround," *Los Angeles Times*, San Gabriel Valley ed., May 14, 1981, pp. 1, 6.

6. *Civic-Recreational-Industrial Authority v. James Marty Stafford*, LA 194C-431-143-385, 10:1–2.

7. Ibid., 10:2.

8. Ibid., LA 194C-431-143-576, 13:4; LA 194C-431-143-4, 10:3.

9. Valle and Maltun, "Called to Account," 1.

10. Ibid.

11. Ibid.

12. *Civic-Recreational-Industrial Authority v. James Marty Stafford*, LA 194C-431-143-387, 10:1.

13. Ibid.

14. Ibid., LA 194C-431-143-32, 8:11; LA 194C-431-143-328, 8: 9, 11.

15. Ibid., New Orleans 194C-357, LA 194C-143-457, 11:1.

16. Ibid., New Orleans 194C-357, LA 194C-143-459, 11:1.

17. Ibid., New Orleans 194C-357, LA 194C-143-520, 12:1.

18. Ibid., LA 194C-143-367, 9:1.

19. Ibid., 9:2–3.

20. Michel Foucault, *Discipline and Punish: The Birth of the Prison* (New York: Vintage, 1995), 18.

21. *Civic-Recreational-Industrial Authority v. James Marty Stafford*, LA 194C-143-367, 9:2, as well as reporter's transcript of proceedings, October 2 and November 29, 1984, p. 7.

22. Ibid., LA 194C-431-143-365, 9:3.

23. Ibid.

24. Ibid.

25. Ibid.

26. Ibid., 3:9.

27. Ibid., 3:10.

28. *Civic-Recreational-Industrial Authority v. James Marty Stafford*, LA 194C-431-143-890, 17:10.

29. Ibid.

30. Ibid., LA 194C-431-143-249, 7:19.

31. Ibid., 7:1, 11.

32. John F. Keller, interview, University of California, Santa Barbara, September 2003.

CHAPTER 14 — PERFORMING HIS WHITENESS

1. FBI transcript of James Stafford's September 13, 1983, meeting with Lucille Rowlett and Donald Rowlett at the Holiday Inn in Leesville, Louisiana (LA 194-143, pp. 1–14, submitted under separate cover in *United States of America, Plaintiff, v. James Marty Stafford, et al., Defendants*).

2. Ibid., 17–18.

3. *Civic-Recreational-Industrial Authority v. James Marty Stafford*, New Orleans 194C-357, Los Angeles 194C-143469, 11:2.

4. Ibid., LA 194C-431-143-542, 12:1.

5. Ibid., LA 194C-431-143-532, 12:1.

6. Ibid., 12:2.

7. Ibid., 12:2–3.

8. U.S. attorney Alexander H. Williams, III, copy of letter to Warren L. Etinger (Robert King's attorney), December 2, 1983, exhibit C in *United States of America, Plaintiff, v. James Marty Stafford, et al., Defendants*.

9. U.S. attorney Robert Bonner, copy of letter to Victor Kenton (C. Ronald Rabin's attorney), April 4, 1984, exhibit D in *United States of America, Plaintiff, v. James Marty Stafford, et al., Defendants*.

10. Morain and Valle, "City of Industry Founder Indicted in Kickback Case," A1, A3, A14; "The Region: Kickback Suspect Released," *Los Angeles Times*, April 13, 1984, p. A2.

11. City of Industry and the Industry Chamber of Commerce, "Agreement for

Advertising, Promotional and Community Relations Services," June 23, 1983, p. 3; City of Industry and the Industry Manufacturers Council, "Agreement for Advertising, Promotional and Community Relations Services," June 23, 1983, p. 3; Valle, "Indicted Industrialist Kicked Off Board," 3; Dan Morain and Victor Valle, "Owes More Than Any Other Municipality in State," *Los Angeles Times*, April 15, 1984, p. A7.

12. Industry Manufacturers Council, "The City of Industry Presents Ronald Reagan at a Luncheon, Wednesday, November 30, 1977, 12:00 Noon, California Country Club" [pamphlet]; Industry Manufacturers Council, "City of Industry Quarterly Luncheon Meetings—Previous Guest Speakers" [undated list]; Valle, "Indicted Industrialist Kicked Off Board," 1, 7.

13. Morain and Valle, "City of Industry: It Has Clout Where it Counts," A37.

14. Ibid., A36

15. Valle, "Indicted Industrialist Kicked Off Board," 1.

16. Edward J. Boyer, "3 in Kickback Scheme Plead Guilty to Fraud," *Los Angeles Times*, June 20, 1984, pp. B1, B3.

17. Valle, "Indicted Industrialist Kicked Off Board," 1.

18. William Overend, "City of Industry Founder Said to Have Heart Problem: Kickback Suspect Isn't up to Stress of Trial, Lawyer Claims," *Los Angeles Times*, August 28, 1984, p. A3.

19. *Civic-Recreational-Industrial Authority v. James Marty Stafford*, LA 194C-143-778,15:1.

20. Ibid.

21. Ibid., 15:72.

22. Ibid.

23. Ibid., 15:1–2.

24. Ibid.

25. Ibid., 15:3.

26. William Overend, "City of Industry Leader Pleads Guilty to Mail Fraud, Bribery," *Los Angeles Times*, October 3, 1984, p. B1.

27. Keller, interview.

28. "Sincerity of Suicide Bid Doubted," *Los Angeles Times*, late final ed., Sept. 12, 1984, p. A1.

29. Overend, "City of Industry Leader Pleads Guilty to Mail Fraud," 1.

30. Saul J. Faerstein, M.D., psychiatric evaluation of James Stafford, in *United States of America, Plaintiff, v. James Marty Stafford, et al., Defendants*, 3–4.

31. Government's sentencing memorandum, in ibid.

32. Ibid., exhibit 1 (which was Paltrow's *Herald Examiner* series).

33. Ibid., 3–4.

34. Ibid., 6–7.

35. *Civic-Recreational-Industrial Authority v. James Marty Stafford*, LA 194C-143-781, 15:7.

36. Keller, interview.

37. Government's sentencing memorandum, *United States of America, Plaintiff, v. James Marty Stafford, et al., Defendants*, 7.

38. Ibid., 4, 9.

39. Keller, interview.

40. Reporter's transcript of proceedings, *United States of America, Plaintiff, v. James Marty Stafford, et al., Defendants*, 61.

41. Ibid., 63–69.

42. Ibid., 62.

43. Ibid., 69.

44. Ibid., 64.

45. Ibid., 74.

CHAPTER 15 — BURYING THE BODY

1. *Civic-Recreational-Industrial Authority v. James Marty Stafford*, LA 194C-431-143-780, 15:1.

2. Ibid., 15:2–6.

3. Alan Maltun, "Possible Funds Loss to Be Investigated, *Los Angeles Times*, San Gabriel Valley ed., May 3, 1984, pp. 1, 10; Steve Tamaya, "Industry Agency to File Suit over Fraud," *San Gabriel Valley Tribune*, August 29, 1984, pp. B1, B2; "Industry: Board Confers to Recoup $," *Los Angeles Times*, San Gabriel Valley ed., August 30, 1984, p. 2.

4. Stephen M. Rosoff, Henry N. Ontell, and Robert H. Tillman, *Looting America: Greed, Corruption, Villains, and Victims* (Upper Saddle River, N.J.: Pearson Education, 2003), 257.

5. *Civic-Recreational-Industrial Authority, et. al., Plaintiffs, v. James Marty Stafford, National Engineering, et al., Defendants*, case no. CV84-7983, U.S. District Court of the Central District of California, October 16, 1984, pp. 1–91; William Overend, "City of Industry Sues 7 over Kickback Scandal," *Los Angeles Times*, October 17, 1984, p. A3.

6. Victor Valle, "Coordinator Quits Industry Project," *Los Angeles Times*, San Gabriel Valley ed., September 16, 1984, pp. 1, 7; Victor Valle, "Renewal Agency Director Resigns to Dispel Cloud," *Los Angeles Times*, San Gabriel Valley ed., January 17, 1985, pp. 1, 7.

7. Victor Valle, "Only Business Names Are Changed—People Are the Same: Industry Pulls out of Engineering Pact, Hires 2 New Firms," *Los Angeles Times*, San Gabriel Valley ed., October 25, 1984, pp. 1, 3.

8. *Industry Civic Planning Association, Inc., a California Non-profit Corporation; Kern Foods, Inc., et al., Plaintiffs, v., The Industry Urban Development Agency, a*

Community Development Corporation, et al., case no. C58,289, Superior Court of the State of California for the County of Los Angeles, October 12, 1984, pp. 1–59.

9. *Civic Recreational Industrial Authority, et al., Plaintiffs, v. James Marty Stafford, et al., Defendants. Jack R. Carpenter and Valley Planing Mill of Van Nuys, Inc., Counterclaimants, Cross-Complainants, and Third-Party Plaintiffs, v. Civic Recreational Industrial Authority, et al., Counter defendants, Cross-Defendants, John Ferraro, Phyllis Tucker, Graham Ritchie, Jerome Winstead, et al., Third-Party Defendants,* CV84-7983, August 30, 1985.

10. Bill Farr and Victor Valle, "FBI Probe Shifts to Mayor of Industry, Others," *Los Angeles Times,* December 5, 1984, pp. B2, B8.

11. Victor M. Valle, "Industry OKs Legal Counsel for Treasurer," *Los Angeles Times,* San Gabriel Valley ed., September 20, 1984, p. 4.

12. *Civic-Recreational-Industrial Authority v. James Marty Stafford,* LA 194C-431-143-703, 15:8.

13. Ibid., LA 194C-431-143-726, 15:1; LA 194C-431-143-703, 15:8; LA 194C-431-143-849, 16:1–3.

14. Farr and Valle, "FBI Probe Shifts to Mayor of Industry, Others," B8.

15. *Civic-Recreational-Industrial Authority v. James Marty Stafford,* LA 194C-431-143-8-842, 16:1–3.

16. Valle, "Industry OKs Legal Counsel for Treasurer," 4; Mark Adams, "FBI Investigates Home Improvements in Industry," *San Gabriel Valley Tribune,* October 8, 1984, pp. B1, B2; *Civic-Recreational-Industrial Authority v. James Marty Stafford,* LA 194C-431-143-859, 17:3.

17. Mark Adams, "FBI Ask about Hidden Recorder," *San Gabriel Valley Tribune,* September 6, 1984, pp. B1, B2; Farr and Valle, "FBI Probe Shifts to Mayor of Industry, Others," B8.

18. Victor Valle, "Grand Jury Probing Redevelopment Agencies," *Los Angeles Times,* San Gabriel Valley ed., April 4, 1985, p. 1; Victor Valle and Alan Maltun, "City of Industry Must Sell Land or Face Insolvency, Grand Jury Reports," *Los Angeles Times,* July 19, 1985, p. B1.

19. Valle and Maltun, "City of Industry Must Sell Land or Face Insolvency," B1.

20. Deloitte, Haskins, and Sells, Inc., "Fiscal and Management Review of the City of Industry Urban-Development Agency" [conducted at the request of the 1984–85 Los Angeles County Grand Jury], June 1985, pp. 1–22.

21. Valle and Maltun, "City of Industry Must Sell Land or Face Insolvency," B6.

22. City of Industry, "Positive Trend Established at Industry Hills" [news release], July 22, 1985.

23. Valle and Maltun, "City of Industry Must Sell Land or Face Insolvency," B6.

24. For example, Manuel Garcia, a redevelopment director who voted to approve the BOCL contract, seemed rather confused about the action he had taken when interviewed by Valle on or before January 11, 1985. First, he said that Ritchie "didn't

explain nothing" about the proposal. When pressed further, he said, "I don't know about. . . . That's was just our business. . . . I don't remember nothing about it."

25. Victor Valle and Alan Maltun, "Industry Bypasses Bids to Hire Bond Agency," *Los Angeles Times*, San Gabriel Valley ed., January 13, 1985, pp. 1, 8.

26. Stafford's memorandum of contentions of fact and law, *Civic-Recreational-Industrial Authority, et al., Plaintiffs, v. James Marty Stafford, et al., Defendants*, June 12, 1987, pp. 1–3.

27. Farr and Valle, "FBI Probe Shifts to Mayor of Industry, Others," pp. B2, B8; declaration of Victor B. Kenton, in *Civic-Recreational-Industrial Authority, et al., Plaintiffs, v. James Marty Stafford, et al., Defendants*, January 20, 1987, pp. 1–2.

28. Memorandum of points and authorities opposing a motion for a court order directed to FBI release of its reports to defendants, in *Civic-Recreational-Industrial Authority, et al., Plaintiffs, v. James Marty Stafford, et al., Defendants*, February 9, 1987, pp. 6–7.

29. Response to plaintiffs' motion for modification of discovery cutoff and continuance of pretrial conference and trial, in *Civic-Recreational-Industrial Authority, et al., Plaintiffs, v. James Marty Stafford, et al., Defendants*, January 26, 1987, pp. 1–15.

30. Thomas E. Vornberger, chief of Civil Discovery Review Unit I, sworn affidavit, in *Civic-Recreational-Industrial Authority, et al., Plaintiffs, v. James Marty Stafford, et al., Defendants*, February 24, 1987, pp. 1–3 and exhibit A, titled "Deletion Code"; Joseph R. Davis, assistant director and legal counsel, Federal Bureau of Investigation, letter to Victor B. Kenton, about *Civic-Recreational-Industrial Authority, et al., Plaintiffs, v. James Marty Stafford, et al., Defendants*, February 24, 1987.

31. Order directing the FBI to release records, *Civic-Recreational-Industrial Authority, et al., Plaintiffs, v. James Marty Stafford, et al., Defendants*, February 2, 1987, pp. 1–2.

32. Mike Ward, "Industry Takes $4.5 Million Settlement in Kickback Suit," *Los Angeles Times*, San Gabriel Valley ed., June 28, 1987, pp. BI, B5; "Metro Digest: Local News in Brief; Kickback Figure Paroled," *Los Angeles Times*, January 22, 1988, p. B2.

33. Settlement agreements and release, *Civic-Recreational-Industrial Authority, et al., Plaintiffs, v. James Marty Stafford, et al., Defendants*, October 28, 1987 and June 30, 1987; reply to memorandum of points and authorities in support of plaintiffs' motion for and order that finds the settlements to be in good faith, *Civic-Recreational-Industrial Authority, et al., Plaintiffs, v. James Marty Stafford, et al., Defendants*, November 9, 1987, p. 2.

34. *United States of America, Plaintiff-Appellee, v. James Marty Stafford, Defendant-Appellant*, case no. 86-5268, U.S. Court of Appeals for the Ninth Circuit, 831 F.2d 1479; 1987 U.S. App. LEXIS 14,764, July 12, 2006, pp. 1–9; "Metro Digest: Local News in Brief; Kickback Figure Paroled," B2.

35. Memorandum of points and authorities, 7.

36. Declaration of Victor B. Kenton in support of motion to release FBI records, *Civic-Recreational-Industrial Authority, et al., Plaintiffs, v. James Marty Stafford, et al., Defendants,* December 8, 1986, p. 2; response to plaintiffs' motion for modification of discovery cutoff, 2.

37. Mark Arax and Victor Valle, "Lawyer to Pay $300,000 to Settle Interest Conflict Suit," *Los Angeles Times,* March 9, 1988, pp. B1, B3.

38. *People of the State of California, Plaintiff, v. Graham A. Ritchie, Defendant,* case no. C679,079, Los Angeles Superior Court, March 8, 1988.

39. Arax and Valle, "Lawyer to Pay $300,000 to Settle Interest Conflict Suit," B1, B3.

40. Declaration of Victor B. Kenton in support of motion to release FBI records, 2; response to plaintiffs' motion for modification of discovery cutoff, 2; memorandum of points and authorities, 7.

41. Monte Fligsten, telephone interview, September 11, 2006.

42. District Attorney Steven Cooley's September 9, 2006, letter to Victor Valle states: "Our search has yielded no files or documents that relate to an investigation of city of Industry officials by the District Attorney's office contemporaneous with or subsequent to the Graham Ritchie civil settlement, or that contain any documents referred to this office by FBI Agent Keller." Keller, however, insisted in email replies received on September 8 and 11, 2006, that the U.S. attorney's memorandum referring to his 302s would reveal the name of the county prosecutor to whom the package had been addressed.

43. Ted Gup, *Nation of Secrets: The Threat to Democracy and the American Way of Life* (New York: Doubleday, 2007), 218–19.

EPILOGUE

1. *Industry Hills Visitor Accommodation Center, a California General Partnership, v. City of Industry, Civic-Recreational-Industrial Authority,* case no. C757-925, Superior Court of California, County of Los Angeles, April 1991.

2. *Edward Page Roski, Sr., et al., Plaintiffs, v. John Ferrero, et al., Defendants,* case no. KC669, Superior Court of California, County of Los Angeles, April 24, 1991; "Suit against City Officials Alleges Financial Conflict," *Los Angeles Times,* June 8, 1990, p. B3; Irene Chang, "Suit Claims Tax Funds Misused," *Los Angeles Times,* San Gabriel Valley ed., June 10, 1990, p. 2; judgment pursuant to stipulation and stipulation for entry of judgment, *Industry Hills Visitor Accommodation Center, a General Partnership, v. City of Industry, Civic-Recreational-Authority,* August 21, 1991.

3. Robert Moran, "Mayo Joins Council after Perez Resigns," *Los Angeles Times,* San Gabriel Valley ed., January 30, 1992, p. 1.

4. "Boomtown Inc. Signs Agreement to Build New Hotel Casino in Las Vegas," *PR Newswire*, March 15, 1993.

5. Glenn F. Bunting, "Special Report: A Denver Billionaire's Invisible Hand," *Los Angeles Times*, Orange County final ed., July 23, 2006, p. A31.

6. David Barnes, "CSX, Union Pacific among Top Donors to Dole's Campaign," *Virginian-Pilot*, September 13, 1996, p. D6; "Closeup: What They Want from Washington," accessed on December 21, 2006, from http://www.opensecrets.org/include/formattoprint.asp?Page=/alerts/v2/ALRTV2N26.asp, which explains that "all figures represent data available for the 1996 election cycle from the FEC as of July 2, 1996. Totals include PAC contributions, individual contributions ($200+ from company executives, and 'soft' money donations from firms and their affiliates. Totals reflect contributions to federal candidates and national party committees"; Maury Klein, *Union Pacific*, vol. 2, *1894–1969* (Minneapolis: University of Minnesota Press, 2006), 175.

7. *Robert Bassman on behalf of himself and all others similarly situated, Plaintiff, v. Union Pacific Corporation, Richard K. Davidson, Philip F. Anschutz and Joseph E. O'Connor, Jr., Defendants*, case No. 3-97CV2819-G, U.S. District Court for the Northern District of Texas, Dallas Division, November 18, 1997, pp. 1–21; Ed Quillen, "Tracking a Merger: Monopoly Derails Service, Economy," *Denver Post*, 2d ed., November 30, 1997, p. G1.

8. Walt Bogdanich, Jenny Nordberg, Tom Torok, and Eric Koli, "Death on the Tracks: How Railroads Sidestep Blame," *New York Times*, July 11, 2004, p. A1; Walt Bogdanich and Jenny Nordberg, "For Railroads and the Safety Overseer, Close Ties," *New York Times*, November 7, 2006, p. A1; Jenny Nordberg and Walt Bogdanich, "Regulators Plan to Step Up Union Pacific Safety Checks," *New York Times*, November 17, 2004, p. A1; Walt Bogdanich, "Unions Ask Agency to Oppose Union Pacific on Inspections," *New York Times*, December 2, 2004, p. A35; Walt Bogdanich and Jenny Nordberg, "Head of Railroad Administration, Facing Two Inquiries, Is Quitting in Two Weeks," *New York Times*, December 18, 2004, p. A16.

9. Cara Mia DiMassa and David Pierson, "Los Angeles: Freight Train Jumps Tracks," *Los Angeles Times*, October 17, 2004, p. B1; Caitlin Liu and Doug Smith, "Near the Rails, on the Edge: Southland Residents Near Train Tracks Live with Noise, Dirt, and Danger," *Los Angeles Times*, April 6, 2005, p. A1; Wendy Thermos, "21 Freight-Train Cars Derail," *Los Angeles Times*, March 9, 2005, p. B3; Lance Pugmire and Monte Morin, "300 Evacuate in Another Derailment," *Los Angeles Times*, April 5, 2006, p. B1; Susannah Rosenblatt, "Derailment Aftermath Is Tough on Residents: After Monday's Accident in San Bernardino, People Are Still Kept from Their Homes While the Mess Is Untangled and Poisons Contained," *Los Angeles Times*, April 6, 2006, p. B9.

10. David Cogan, "Power Player: Ed Roski Jr. Owns a Piece of the Kings and the Lakers," *L.A. Weekly*, November 12, 1998, p. 24; Dorothy Pomerantz, "City of

Greed: The Secret behind the Wealth of Las Vegas' Newest Mogul Is Found in the Murky History of a Smelly Little California City called Industry," *Forbes*, October 2, 2000, pp. 98–102.

11. Jim Newton, "Staples Owners Propose Huge New Project," *Los Angeles Times*, May 4, 2000, pp. A1, A34–35.

12. Dereck Andrade, "Industry Hotel Deal Working: City Expected to Give Approval to Resort Lease," *San Gabriel Valley Tribune*, March 22, 2000, p. B1.

13. Joe Florkowski, "Resorting to New Measures," *San Gabriel Valley Tribune*, June 4, 2005, p. C1; Roger Vincent, "Pacific Palms Conference Resort," *Los Angeles Times*, September 30, 2005, p. C2.

14. Don Jergler, "Different Visions for Industry," *San Gabriel Valley Tribune*, business sec., July 31, 2002, p. 12; Pavlovskis, "The Economic and Fiscal Impact of the City of Industry," 82–83. The Industry Manufacturers Council's 1984 report "General Information on Industry, California" put the total number of the city's manufacturing employment at 45,000, or 82.7 percent, in 1980 (15).

15. Don Lee, "L.A. County Jobs Surge since '93, but Not Wages," *Los Angeles Times*, July 26, 1999, p. A1.

16. Alissa Anderson Garcia, David Carroll, and Jean Ross, "Left Behind: Workers and Their Families in a Changing Los Angeles," rev. ed. (Sacramento: California Budget Project, September 26, 2006), 5.

17. Los Angeles County Economic Development Corporation, "San Gabriel Valley, Los Angeles County, California: 2006 Economic Overview and Forecast" [prepared for the San Gabriel Valley Economic Partnership], November 2006, p. 5.

18. Evelyn Iritani, "Business Surges at L.A. Ports," *Los Angeles Times*, January 22, 1997, p. D2.

19. California Governmental Code, sec. 6,500, first enacted in 1949, combined several previous statutes and has since been revised several times. It permits cities to form hybrid agencies from their existing governmental repertoire or to join other governmental agencies to form hybrid bodies with the authority to issue bonds and incur debt for the purpose of combining "their powers and resources to work on their common problems." See Trish Cypher and Colin Grinnell, "Governments Working Together: A Citizen's Guide to Joint Powers Agreements" (Sacramento: California State Senate, Local Government Committee, August 2007), 3, 10.

20. James F. Peltz, "Union Pacific Still Struggling with Congestion: The Rail Operator Has Added Locomotives and Workers," *Los Angeles Times*, January 10, 2005, p. C1; Deborah Schoch, "Panel Backs Plan to Curb Pollution at Port," March 4, 2005, p. B3; Ronald D. White, "Retailers See Trouble on Ports' Horizon: Despite Smooth Sailing in the U.S. Now, Firms Brace for a Logjam As Trade Pushes Capacity," July 24, 2006, p. C1.

21. Bunting, "Special Report: A Denver Billionaire's Invisible Hand," A31.

22. "Alameda Corridor—East Project San Gabriel Valley" [map], accessed on January 30, 2009, from *http://www.theaceproject.org/photo/intermodel1.jpg*.

23. Mark Davis, director of regional public affairs, Union Pacific Railroad, email communication, November 3, 2006; Ronald D. White, "Railroads Back on Track? They're Posting Record Profits and Expanding Their Operations, but Rising Rates and Delays Irritate Some Customers," *Los Angeles Times*, February 21, 2006, p. C1; David Lustig, "Railroads Invest in Extra Capacity to Move Asian Import Windfall," *Railway Gazette International* 162 (August 2006): 453–57; Bill Mongelluzzo, "Rail Volume Surges in L.A.," *Traffic World*, August 2, 2006, p. 1; Bill Mongelluzzo, "Rail's Win Truckers Loss," *Traffic World*, August 7, 2006, p. 1.

24. Manuel Pastor, Jr., "Times Board of Advisors, Insight," *Los Angeles Times*, December 8, 1996, p. D4.

25. Bob Howard, "Commercial Real Estate: Warehouse Project Is Latest in Inland Empire," *Los Angeles Times*, April 10, 2001, p. C8; Los Angeles Economic Development Corporation and Orange North American Trade Rail Access Corridor (OnTrac) Joint Powers Authority, "OnTrac Impact Study: National Economic Significance of Rail Capacity and Homeland Security on the Alameda Corridor East," September 11, 2003, p. 4.

26. Marc Levison, *The Box: How the Shipping Container Made the World Smaller and the World Economy Bigger* (Princeton, N.J.: Princeton University Press, 2006), 274.

27. Ibid., 269.

28. Wally Baker, telephone interview, April 12, 2004.

29. Ibid.

30. "Majestic Realty Co. Chairman and CEO Edward P. Roski Jr. Elected to National Geographic Board of Trustees," *Daily Business News*, March 5, 2007, p.1.

31. "Largest Commercial Real Estate Developers in Los Angeles County, Ranked by Commercial Square Footage Developed and Completed," *Los Angeles Business Journal*, January 19, 2004, accessed on January 30, 2009, from *http://www.legacy partners.com/pdfs/com/bol/lacd_labj_011904.pdf*.

32. "Demand Grows for Southern Calif. Warehouses," *Real Estate Alert*, February 7, 2001, p. 1; Jergler, "Different Visions for Industry."

33. Brad Berton, "Majestic Realty to Launch Business Park in Industry," *Los Angeles Times*, June 26, 2001, p. C7; Ben Baeder, "City's Big Deal," *San Gabriel Valley Tribune*, accessed on July 3, 2008, from http://www.sgvtribune.com/rds_search/ci_9733568?IADID=Search-www.sgvtribune.com-www.sgvtribune.com.

34. Patrick McGreevy, "Subsidy to Lure NFL Is Blocked," *Los Angeles Times*, April 17, 2008, p. B1; David Haldane, "NFL Bid Passed to Handful of Voters in Town," *Los Angeles Business Journal*, accessed on January 5, 2009, from *http://www.labusinessjournal.com/article.asp?aID=56733668.41616.1726465.635229*.

823176.161&aID2=132796; Dan Walters, "Redevelopment Scheme Floated Again" *Sacramento Bee*, January 6, 2009, p. 3A; Cara Mia DiMassa, "Industry OKs Sale of Bonds with an Eye on NFL Stadium," *Los Angeles Times*, January 20, 2009, accessed on January 21, 2009, from *http://latimes.com/news/local/la-me-industry21-2009jan21,0,3332004.story.*

35. Sarah Wilhelm, "Public Funding of Sports Stadiums," in *Policy In-Depth* (Salt Lake City: University of Utah, Center for Public Policy and Administration, April 30, 2008), 1; Mark S. Rosentraub, *Major League Losers: The Real Cost of Sports and Who's Paying for It* (New York: Basic Books, 1997), 17; Raymond Keating, "We Wuz Robbed! The Subsidized Stadium Scam," *Policy Review* (March–April 1997): 57.

36. We conducted this research between November 2002 and May 2003 at the University of California, Santa Barbara, using data downloaded from Win2data, a national real estate database classified by land use, square footage, county, zip code, and other factors. (First American Real Estate Solutions, which owns and operates Win2data, updates its data every six months, which can result in a filing lag, depending on the date on which a transaction is officially recorded in a county archive.) Our search quantified and mapped all Los Angeles and San Bernardino County real estate that was, at the time of study, controlled or owned in full or in part by Edward P. Roski, Jr., and his various alter egos. After adjusting the data, we generated statistics by focusing on two fields: land value (in U.S. dollars) and lot size (in acres). Redundant fields were erased. To show that data were not acquired from Win2data but from the developer's own representations, we separately noted property that had been recently acquired by Majestic Realty Corporation.

37. Howard, "Commercial Real Estate," C8; Rodney Tanaka, "Growth Swells Industry: Value of New Projects 4 Times That of Previous Year," *San Gabriel Valley Tribune*, June 25, 2001, p. B1.

38. The 2000 U.S. census reports an 83.1-percent Latino population in La Puente, a 72.4-percent Latino population in El Monte, and a 71-percent Latino population in Baldwin Park. It also reports a combined 67.7-percent Latino (45.7 percent alone) and Asian (22 percent alone) population in West Covina and a combined 74.3-percent Latino (38.3 percent alone) and Asian (36.1 percent alone) population in Hacienda Heights.

39. Mary Williams Walsh, "Latinos' Net Worth Shrinking despite Boom Times," *Los Angeles Times*, March 25, 2000, p. A16; Marla Dickerson, "State's Poverty Profile Changes Economics: In Contrast to the U.S., Nearly Half of Impoverished Children in California Live in a Two-Parent Household," *Los Angeles Times*, August 26, 2002, p. A1; Scott Martelle and Erin Chan, "Income Drop in '90s Cut a Broad Swath, Data Show," *Los Angeles Times*, August 27, 2002, p. B1.

40. A 1998 report by the California State Assembly's Select Committee on the California Middle Class on income inequality showed that, in 1996, 41 percent of

residents in Los Angeles County lived in households with annual incomes below 20,000 dollars, and fully two-thirds lived in households with annual incomes below 40,000 dollars. In 1996, only 26 percent lived in middle-income households earning between 40,000 and 100,000 dollars; but 8 percent earned more than 100,000 dollars, a figure that shows the dramatic expansion at the top of the county's income pyramid.

41. Myron Orfield and Thomas Luce, *California Metropatterns: A Regional Agenda for Community and Stability in California* (Minneapolis: Metropolitan Area Research Corporation, April 2002), 20–21.

42. Ibid.

43. Ibid., 12.

44. Garcia et al., "Left Behind," 15.

45. Victor M. Valle and Rodolfo D. Torres, *Latino Metropolis* (Minneapolis: University of Minnesota Press, 2000), 16–17, 26–27.

46. Gregory F. Treverton, "Making the Most of Southern California's Global Engagement" (Los Angeles: Pacific Council on International Policy, June 2001), 3.

47. Berkeley Hudson, "Rain Clouds Had a Silver Lining," *Los Angeles Times*, San Gabriel Valley ed., February 20, 1992, p. J1; Maura Dolan, "L.A. County Firms Blamed for 40% of Toxic Emissions," *Los Angeles Times*, April 21, 1989, p. B1.

48. Frank Clifford, "Superfund Well Cleanup Drains Money, Confidence," *Los Angeles Times*, March 19, 1994, p. A1; Richard Simon, "House OKS $85 Million to Clean Up Tainted Water," *Los Angeles Times*, March 29, 2000, p. B1; Richard Winton, "8 Firms to Clean Drinking Water Pollution: Agreement Comes More Than 20 Years after Chemicals Were Found in San Gabriel Valley Supply," *Los Angeles Times*, January 29, 2002, p. B1; Ralph Vartabedian, "San Gabriel Valley a Hotbed of TCE Contamination," *Los Angeles Times*, March 30, 2006, p. A10; Arin Gencer, "State Funds Sought for San Gabriel Valley Basin Cleanup," *Los Angeles Times*, June 5, 2006, p. B4.

49. Mike Ward, "EPA to Contact Possible Water Contaminators," *Los Angeles Times*, San Gabriel Valley ed., September 10, 1989, p. 1.

50. "EPA Proposes Plan to Address Ground-Water Contamination at Puente Valley Operable Unit," in *San Gabriel Valley Superfund Site Operable Unit Proposed Plan* (San Francisco: U.S. Environmental Protection Agency, Region 9, January 1998), 1.

51. David W. Myers, "Firm Held Liable for Permanent Land Damage," *Los Angeles Times*, January 13, 1994, p. D2.

52. Lee Romney, "Leaving Town Is Becoming Big Business," *Los Angeles Times*, San Gabriel Valley ed., February 14, 1993, p. 1.

53. Deborah Schoch, "Ships Are Single Largest Polluter of Air at Port of L.A., Study Finds," *Los Angeles Times*, July 8, 2004, p. B3; South Coast Air Quality Management District, "Multiple Air Toxics Exposure Study (MATES II): Final Report,"

March 2000, chap. 7, p. 1; Frank Clifford, "Study Correlates Smog to Heart, Lung Ailments," *Los Angeles Times*, home ed., November 20, 1997, pp. A1, A2.

54. South Coast Air Quality Management District, "Possible Brain Cancer–Air Pollution Link to Be Studied, by Internationally Renowned Neurosurgeon and ACMD Foundation" [news release], October 1, 2003, accessed on July 27, 2007, from http://www.aqmd.gov/news1/2003/braincancerstudypr.html. For those interested in the latest scientific studies assessing impacts of particulate pollution, I recommend a visit to "Trade, Health, and Environment Impact Project: A Collaborative of Community and University Partners," funded by the California Endowment, at http://hydra.usc.edu/scehsc/web/index.html.

55. Certificate of death, State of California, Santa Barbara County Vital Records, November 21, 2001.

56. Cogan, "Power Player," *L.A. Weekly*, 1–6.

57. Rodney Tanaka, "Industry Founder James Stafford Dies," *San Gabriel Valley Tribune*, November 29, 2001, p. A3.

58. Objections to application for an order determining whether a proposed petition constitutes a trust contest, *In the Matter of the James M. Stafford Trust*, case no. BP73,043, Superior Court of the State of California, County of Los Angeles, July 19, 2002, pp. 1–11; settlement agreement and release, *In the Matter of the James M. Stafford Trust*, Oct. 11, 2002, pp. 1–5 and exhibit A.

INDEX

ABOUT THE AUTHOR

Victor Valle is a professor in the ethnic studies department at California State Polytechnic University. An investigative reporter formerly with the *Los Angeles Times,* he is the coauthor of *Latino Metropolis and Recipe of Memory: Five Generations of Mexican Cuisine,* as well as several other books, articles, and literary collections.